ANIMATION:
ART & INDUSTRY

ANIMATION: ART & INDUSTRY

**Edited by
Maureen Furniss**

British Library Cataloguing in Publication Data

Animation: Art & Industry

A catalogue entry for this book is available from the British Library

ISBN: 9780 86196 680 6 (Paperback)

Cover: Visual development sketch by Jules Engel, courtesy of the artist.

Published by
John Libbey Publishing Ltd, 3 Leicester Road, New Barnet, Herts EN5 5EW,
United Kingdom   e-mail: libbeyj@asianet.co.th; web site: www.johnlibbey.com

Direct orders (UK and Europe):
direct.orders@marston.co.uk

Distributed in North America by **Indiana University Press**, 601 North Morton St, Bloomington,
IN 47404, USA. www.iupress.indiana.edu

Distributed in Australasia by **Elsevier Australia**, Elsevier Australia, Tower 1, 475 Victoria Ave,
Chatswood NSW 2067, Australia. www.elsevier.com.au

Printed in Malaysia by Vivar Printing Sdn. Bhd., 48000 Rawang,
Selangor Darul Ehsan

Contents

ANIMATION IN AMERICA

Introduction

Maureen Furniss

The concept of animation – bringing objects to life – has fascinated humankind since its earliest days. Throughout the years, animated movement has been employed in religious, scientific, educational, and entertainment contexts to explain everything from the spirit world to the mechanics of mundane objects. Some of the most recognizable icons of modern culture have emerged from animated productions, and some of our greatest works of art have been created using multiple frames that have brought still images to life.

This book focuses primarily on animation as entertainment and art, with an emphasis on work created for television and theatrical release. It surveys major artists working throughout history in various national contexts. While it touches on digitally created work, the main concern is with classical animation of the 20th century: pioneers, trendsetters, and critically acclaimed individuals and works within the field. It contains writing and interviews by influential historians and practitioners, including both reprints of significant essays (some of them updated) and previously unpublished writing. Topics covered range from aesthetics to business concerns, such as the role of merchandising and censorship in shaping the content of animation.

Essays are historical, as well as theoretical, reflecting the spectrum of writing on animation that began appearing in the 1980s. While examples of critical writing produced prior to this decade do exist, one finds that the real blossoming of animation studies literature occurs at the end of the 20th century, in part reflecting the growth of animated imagery in society. Animation has become ubiquitous, flowing from many sources: the Internet, cable television programming (for example, on Nickelodeon, the Disney Channel, Comedy Central, and especially Cartoon Network), television advertising, training materials, gaming, scientific applications, theatrical features, and more.

The first half of the book presents essays that overview animation history, aesthetics and theory in a global context. The volume begins with an essay by Cecile Starr, an important pioneer in the realm of fine art animation. Not only did she contribute a seminal book in the field, *Experimental Animation* (co-authored with Robert Russett), but she distributed and advocated the work of a number of international artists who otherwise might not have been 'discovered' by the larger animation community. In her essay, she argues that animation is deserving of more respect within the art community, and hopes for the day when animated productions will be as common within museums as paintings and other forms of expression.

It is not difficult to regard the detailed, ornate works of German animator Lotte Reiniger as art. In his essay, William Moritz focuses on the tradition of paper cutting, which Reiniger employed to make figures for her silhouette films – including one of the first feature-length productions ever produced, *The Adventures of Prince Achmed*, which was completed in 1926. Moritz suggests that Reiniger's work can be considered in feminist terms, explaining how her aesthetic developed around the scissor craft learned by many German women at the time.

Even one of the most commercially successful figures in animation history – Mickey Mouse – began its life with ties to the fine art world. Esther Leslie's essay focuses on the inception of Disney's most famous creation, describing the relationship between early animation practice and the larger realm of international art production. Leslie explains how Mickey Mouse's image slipped from the realm of the avant-garde, as it caught the attention of cultural critics during the early 1930s, to the tamer, more commercial domain it still occupies today.

Norman McLaren, who is best known for heading the animation unit at the National Film Board of Canada, created many celebrated animated productions employing a wide range of techniques. McLaren's animation was substantially motivated by his social consciousness, as Terence Dobson's essay suggests: his travels to China and India for UNESCO had a great impact on him. This essay also explains how his work in other countries may have shielded him from political problems of his time – specifically, blacklisting within North America due to associations with the communist party.

American animation dominated world production throughout most of the 20th century, just as US-produced live-action media did. However, its power has not been absolute. Japanese animation is now popular worldwide, and its impact on the aesthetics of animation production have been felt globally. The growth of home entertainment media fueled distribution of work that was once the domain of a tightly knit fan culture that valued and explored the visual and narrative devices specific to anime. Patrick Drazen's essay on conventions and clichés in Japanese animation opens the issues of cultural context and identity for discussion outside the scope of anime as well.

Helen McCarthy's essay on Hayao Miyazaki, the best-known Japanese animation director worldwide, expands along these lines, explaining how a variety of factors have influenced the themes and content of the artist's work. McCarthy focuses on one of his most popular films, *My Neighbor Totoro* (1988). This work reflects the filmmaker's concern with such issues as the environment, the spirit world, the realities of children, and the aesthetics of traditional Japanese arts. It is also probably the best known of Miyazaki's films, having been widely distributed outside Japan.

Nick Park is yet another director to challenge the dominance of Hollywood production. This British stop-motion animator established his reputation with such works as *Creature Comforts* (1989) and a series of three "Wallace & Gromit" films, especially *The Wrong Trousers* (1993). His first feature-length production, *Chicken Run* (2000), was a phenomenal box office success. Marion Quigley's essay on Park examines the ways in which this film can be seen as both global and local in its sensibilities, at once appealing to a worldwide audience and addressing particular notions of 'Britishness'. She sets this investigation into the wider framework of international media production, noting examples of other works that cross and blur boundaries.

Reflexivity, or the tendency to look back on oneself, is a common attribute of animated production. Terry Lindvall and Matthew Melton explore this quality within the scope of postmodern aesthetics, tracing it back to the early years of animation and following it through to recent examples. They also explore the relationship between the animated work and its viewer, or 'reader', explaining how productions reference their creators through various processes of self-figuration. Closing the essay is discussion of numerous examples of reflexive cartoons, which reveal elements of the animation production process in their narratives.

Understanding the relationship between the viewer and the viewed is also a key consideration when it comes to censorship, as we try to understand the effects media have on their audiences. Jørgen Stensland examines this subject in respect to electronic games, looking at various rating systems in different national contexts and discussing primary areas of concern: principally, sexual content and violence. He also presents research on the ways in which children use and are affected by these media.

The second half of the book focuses on the development of the American animation industry. It begins with essays on pioneers Winsor McCay and Margaret (M.J.) Winkler. John Canemaker focuses on McCay, whose work represents highpoints in the development of animation art, particularly during the early silent era. Characters from his *Little Nemo* (1911) and *Gertie the Dinosaur* (1914) are icons of the American animation industry. In his essay, Canemaker discusses McCay's formative years, including his background in print comics, and then examines his animated films.

While McCay represented an artistic vision for early cinema, Margaret Winkler was much more commercial in her concerns. Winkler distributed the early work of Walt Disney – his "Alice Comedies" series – as well as the immensely successful "Felix the Cat" and "Out of the Inkwell" series, produced by Pat Sullivan and Max Fleischer, respectively. Although her tenure as an independent businessperson was relatively short-lived (she got married to Charles Mintz and he largely took over operations), her accomplishments are noteworthy. Her career reflects the opportunities open to women in a field that was not yet solidified as an industry – as Kaufman suggests, at perhaps no other time in cinema history were women able to command as much power, relatively speaking, as they did during the silent era, through the late 1920s.

It was about that time when the animation industry developed into a studio system. Disney, Warner Bros., and eventually UPA were among the best known. Disney made a name for itself with its "Alice Comedies" of the silent era, as well as the "Mickey Mouse" and "Silly Symphony" series films of the late 1920s and beyond. It solidified its place in history during the late 1930s and early 1940s by releasing the first animated feature produced in America, *Snow White and the Seven Dwarfs* (1937), and the noteworthy but commercially disappointing *Fantasia* (1940); other classics, such as *Dumbo* (1941) and *Bambi* (1942) also came out at this time. As Bill Mikulak demonstrates in his essay about Disney and the art world, the company's alignment with various art institutions was a great business decision. It also provides yet another example of how animation often has slipped between the registers of elite and popular culture.

Disney was not the only studio gaining popularity during the 1930s. Leon Schlesinger's studio, which made animation for distribution by Warner Bros., flourished at this time as well, creating "Looney Tunes" and "Merry Melodies" short films featuring a host of now famous characters, such as Bugs Bunny and Daffy Duck. Although several notable directors emerged from the studio, among the best known is Chuck Jones. Jones helped perpetuate his fame through a variety of activities, including opening his own business, lecturing across the world, writing books, and granting numerous interviews for publication. The John Lewell interview included here was conducted in 1982; in it, Jones describes his perceptions of the art of cinema, the relationship between animation and the live-action Hollywood film industry, and his feelings about the work of other artists in the field.

This kind of interview format typified much of early writing on animation history, featuring personal, often anecdotal accounts of how things were in years past.

The 1940s brought the advent of World War II, which thrust animators and studios into 'active duty' of sorts, creating animation for wartime documentaries, instructional films, and works of entertainment. Charles Solomon's essay on Disney's wartime production describes the situation, in which the military literally moved onto the back lot and set up shop. The studio's production turned to a variety of military functions, and Disney himself was sent to Latin America on a 'Good Neighbor' tour meant to enhance relations between the United States and various countries seen as susceptible to the influence of enemy nations. Solomon also discusses Latin American themed films that resulted from this trip, such as the feature *The Three Caballeros* (1944).

Another WWII-related development was the formation of the influential United Productions of America studio, generally known as UPA. The studio embraced modern art aesthetics and stylized limited animation techniques that paved the way for television production developing during the 1950s. In his essay, Jules Engel describes his recollections of the studio and its sensibilities. Works such as *Gerald McBoing Boing* (1951), *Rooty-Toot-Toot* (1952), and *Madeline* (1952) continue to influence the style of animation today.

After WWII ended in 1946, the United States experienced a period of economic prosperity that was much welcomed after the Great Depression of the previous decade. For many, the 1950s were a period of opportunity. However, the 1950s also brought a great deal of uncertainty – for example, in respect to the 'Cold War' that resulted from the development of atomic bombs in the United States, Russia and China. In the U.S., government committees (such as the House Un-American Activities Committee, or HUAC) were formed to investigate the background of many people, including a number of individuals in the film industry. Karl Cohen's essay documents these turbulent events, beginning with strikes (primarily during the early 1940s) and continuing through committee hearings and testimony, as well as the aftermath of blacklisting. These purges were not limited to the United States; Cohen also discusses investigations taking place in Canada.

Michael Frierson grounds his discussion of Art Clokey and the "Gumby" series within the context of early television production. Gumby is a beloved icon, and an important milestone in the history of stop-motion animation, as one of the first widely popular, commercial uses of the clay technique in the United States. Frierson discusses Clokey's creative process, including diverse inspirations for his work: these include the experimental filmmaker Slavko Vorkapich and especially the filmmaker's spiritual practices.

No discussion of American television would be complete without consideration of the Hanna-Barbera studios, responsible for such series as "The Flintstones" and "Scooby-Doo". An essay written by studio head William Hanna with Tom Ito focuses mainly on another of Hanna-Barbera's famous series, "The Jetsons".

Hanna explains how he and his partner, Jo Barbera, tackled the day to day realities of television series: a faster production schedule and a lower budget than they were allowed while creating their award-winning short films at MGM. Hanna-Barbera often has been derided for its role in perpetuating limited animation, which many have felt led to the downfall of animation during the 1960s and 1970s – Hanna addresses this perception from a practical point of view, explaining that they could either get out of the business altogether or play by what he felt were its rules.

The 1960s and 1970s saw a rise in college programs aimed at teaching animation as an art. George Griffin was among the individuals who took such courses, eventually founding his own studio in New York, where he continues to work today. Besides creating personal films, Griffin has been an advocate for animation art, publishing essays and artwork that he feels demonstrates the potential of animated imagery. The essay published here was written a number of years ago, and it expresses strong youthful feelings; among other things, he takes on the notion that animation is mostly suited for young audiences, describing how his own work breaks that mould.

On the horizon of the 1980s were new technologies that would bring further changes to the field. When the American Film Institute held two ground-breaking conferences funded by the veteran animation figure Walter Lantz, the panel speakers included a relative newcomer to the digital scene: John Lasseter, who had created a series of critically acclaimed short films at Pixar. In this interview, he focuses on the significance of storytelling in his work. Lasseter went on to direct *Toy Story* (1995), which paved the way for future development of computer-generated 3D features, among many other accomplishments.

As animation studies has matured as a discipline, writers have embraced a number of concerns in keeping with the larger context of media studies literature. Among them are issues of representation and industrial histories. These perspectives are represented here in writing by Sean Griffin and Linda Simensky. Griffin focuses on the Disney feature *Aladdin*, discussing such issues as sexual identity (particularly in terms of gay themed content), the portrayal of women, and racial stereotyping – in this case, related to Arab characters.

Simensky looks at merchandising strategies behind the Warner Bros. Studio Stores. She describes the way in which the stores positioned themselves in relation to competition (notably, the Disney Stores) and shows how planners targeted adult shoppers representing a wide range of consumers, from casual buyers to hardcore collectors. In a conclusion to the essay, which she added as an update, Simensky looks back at the closing of these stores, the result of corporate decision-making following mergers and an increasingly conservative approach to product design, as well as market saturation.

While animation studies as a discipline is relatively young, already a broad scope of analysis has been developed. The essays included in this anthology constitute a representative sample of the subjects being explored and the methodologies being employed. I saw this project as a terrific opportunity to share my perceptions with individuals in many contexts, from general readers to college students enrolled in animation programs and media scholars from other fields. I hope it encourages readers to investigate further – particularly in terms of seeking out the original sources of these essays, some of which have been edited for inclusion here. My apologies if the book seems a bit tilted toward essays first published in *Animation Journal*, which I edit and publish. Over the seventeen years since it was founded, I've had the good fortune to print many interesting works by great writers – just a few of them have been republished here.

I would like to thank the many contributors to this anthology who embraced the project, and often have supported my work in the past as well. Thanks also to my publisher, John Libbey, who stuck with it through the years. I'd like to dedicate my work on this anthology to William Moritz and Jules Engel, who were friends and mentors to many, including me. 🍎

Global Perspectives

1

Fine Art Animation

Cecile Starr [1987]

Fine art animation is the new name of an art that began early in this century, when Furturists, Dadaists and other modern artists were eyeing the motion picture as the medium that could add movement to their paintings and graphic designs. Not long after Winsor McCay made his first animated cartoon, based on his comic strip *Little Nemo* in 1911, Leopold Survage created sequences of abstract paintings (in Paris) which he called Colored Rhythms, and patented what he considered to be a new art form. Failing to persuade the Gaumont Company to film his work in their primitive new color system, Survage abandoned his invention and spent the rest of his long life as a Cubist painter.

Later, in postwar Berlin, while Max Fleischer was making his first Koko the Clown cartoons in the U.S., three abstract artists named Walter Ruttmann, Hans Richter and Viking Eggeling created their history-making films, *Opus I, Rhythm 21* and *Diagonal Symphony* respectively, thus crossing what Survage had called "the glistening bridge" from still to moving art. Eggeling died soon after his film was completed; Richter and Ruttmann worked in animation for only a few years, then abandoned it for live-action experimental and documentary films. "Pure cinema",

as the first abstract animated films were sometimes called, won the respect of other artists but was still almost unknown to the general public.

Despite this unpromising start, major careers were established in the new art form in the 1920s and '30s by Oskar Fischinger, Len Lye, Norman McLaren, Alexander Alexeieff and Claire Parker in Europe, and by Mary Ellen Bute in the United States. They worked on 35mm film, usually sponsored by advertisers or government agencies, and generally they remained outsiders in the world of art, as well as in the world of film. Today there are hundreds of independent artist-animators in this country alone, working in various graphic techniques, in direct animation and collage, in computer and video technologies. What they all have in common, and what distinguishes them from their colleagues in entertainment and advertising, is that they work on their own, or with a small team, rarely seeking or finding popular success. But they are stubborn, patient and inventive, and they know that art is indeed long.

University film schools and art colleges helped create today's large and productive generation of young animation artists, by offering opportunities to learn the manual skills and providing access to new, complex and costly equipment. They also opened the door to women for the first time in the history of American animation, which has led to refreshing new styles and subjects, often reflecting a decidedly feminine point of view. Recent films by female animators include Maureen Selwood's *The Rug*, selectively colored line drawings, based on an Edna O'Brien short story about an Irish countrywoman's life of disappointments; Joanna Priestley's *Voices*, humorous self-portraits about fear and uneasiness; Amy Kravitz's *River Lethe*, near-abstract graphite drawings and rubbings on paper, evoking life beyond consciousness.

Other distinctive animation films I've seen recently are Stan Brakhage's *Garden of Earthly Delights*, a collage of flowers and grasses placed between pieces of splicing tape, creating a visual parable of the struggle of plants to exist; Dwinell Grant's *Dream Fantasies*, abstract hand-painted animation with live-action photography of two female nudes, with an electronic score by the artist; Ed Emshwiller's *Sunstone*, a fantasy landscape that turns into three-dimensional abstractions through various film and video manipulations. Brakhage, Grant and Emshwiller all began working in animation decades ago and can be considered "old masters".

Films by relative newcomers include Robert Ascher's *Cycle*, frame-by-frame abstract hand-painting on film, with a vocal rendering of an Australian Aborigine myth; Flip Johnson's *The Roar From Within*, a personal, psychological horror film, painted on paper in dark watercolors; Steven Subotnick's *Music Room*, geometric computer-generated abstractions, completed as a student's first film; Reynold Weidenaar's *Night Flame Ritual*, live-camera images digitized and processed in a computer, on the dynamics of ritual.

These films, which run from two to twenty-three minutes long, touch upon literature, psychology, nature, anthropology, and, of course, painting and graphic arts. Each film reflects the unique vision and skills of a single artist, in concept and form, in style and substance. Together they represent the new art which the French poet Guilluame Apollinaire said, back in 1914, had to come. Now it is here, but yet to find a place for itself in the world of film or the world of art.

There are signs of increasing recognition for animation as a fine art in some recent and ongoing undertakings. The American Film Institute gives animation its own special category in the annual Maya Deren avant-garde film awards. The first two winners of the $5,000 bonuses were Sally Cruikshank and Robert Breer; and it is interesting to note that winners in other categories (Ed Emshwiller, Stan Brakhage) also use animation and related techniques in their films.

It is also encouraging that new technologies now offer direct access to the films of animation artists. Already films by Oskar Fischinger, Harry Smith, and John and Faith Hubley have been released on video-cassettes, along with the partly animated classic *Ballet mécanique* by Fernand Léger and Dudley Murphy. Videodiscs of work by Fischinger, McLaren, Alexeieff and Parker, John Whitney, Charles and Ray Eames and other artists are scheduled for release later this year. Accessibility of this kind can only broaden the film tastes of the public, especially those segments that already respond strongly to the other arts.

With the decline of government grants to artists and art institutions, fine art animators have been seeking and finding recognition for their talents in commercial animation – TV spot advertisements, feature film credits, music videos. Their work may help to change the image of popular animation, as well as help to open doors for their own personal animation as well. Animation may also win recognition through hybridization with other arts. Kathy Rose's animation-and-dance performances, Anita Thacher's sculpture-and-film installations, and Suzan Pitt's animation decor for opera help focus public attention on animation as art, rather than animation as entertainment or sales device.

Full recognition for fine art animation is coming, I am convinced, but it might come sooner if some of us helped it along. We might urge our museums and independent showcases to screen at least one appropriate short film with every feature. This policy would reward filmmakers of all kinds (including animators), expand film curators' outlooks, and introduce audiences to the riches of the many short film genres. Large corporations could be invited to finance short film projects and new creative means of presenting them in public places. Public television stations could be asked to honor the short films they show by calling them by some more respectful name than "fillers".

Festivals and other competitions could provide separate categories for fine art animation, and grants could be given for different kinds of programming of short films for television and film showcases. Film magazines could include regular picture-spread (frames and movie-strips) of animated films, the essence of which rarely can be described in words.

Sooner or later a major museum will present a retrospective exhibition of films and related drawings, paintings and sculpture by the great pioneers of fine art animation. (Such an exhibition was shown in Europe some years back, but not in the United States.) A comprehensive collection of fine art animation on 16mm film could be purchased for as little as $5,000 or $10,000. Museums could use such a collection to familiarize their patrons with a dazzling array of films that are fine art in themselves – rather than show didactic (and frequently dull) films about painters and paintings. (One needn't interfere with the other, as they are entirely different in their functions.)

I can remember my first visits to the Museum of Modern Art in New York City some decades ago, when a small handful of people, gawking and perplexed, could be found staring at the Museum's handful of bewildering Picassos. In contrast, on a recent visit to that enlarged, jam-packed museum, I heard a loud voice call out excitedly to his companions: "Hey look, a whole room of Picassos!" It seems inevitable to me that some day, in some elegant new hi-tech museum, someone will holler out in recognition and affection: "Hey look, a whole room of Fischingers!" – or Len Lyes – or any of the great artist-animators of our century. They are the undiscovered treasures of our time. 🍏

Starr, Cecile. "Fine Art Animation". *The Art of the Animated Image: An Anthology*. Ed. Charles Solomon. Los Angeles: The American Film Institute, 1987. 67–71.

2

Some Critical Perspectives on Lotte Reiniger

William Moritz [1996]

Lotte Reiniger was born in Berlin on 2 June 1899. As a child, she developed a facility with cutting paper silhouette figures, which had become a folk-art form among German women. As a teenager, she decided to pursue a career as an actress, and enrolled in Max Reinhardt's Drama School. She began to volunteer as an extra for stage performances and movie productions, and during the long waits between scenes and takes, she would cut silhouette portraits of the stars, which she could sell to help pay her tuition. The great actor-director Paul Wegener noticed not only the quality of the silhouettes she made, but also her incredible dexterity in cutting: holding the scissors nearly still in her right hand and moving the paper deftly in swift gestures that uncannily formulated a complex profile.

Wegener hired her to do silhouette titles for his 1916 feature, *Rübezahls Hochzeit* (Rumpelstilskin's Wedding), and for his 1918 *Der Rattenfänger von Hammeln* (Pied Piper of Hammeln) she made not only titles but also animated rat models (since the real animals refused to follow the piper). Through Wegener she met Hans Cürlis and Carl Koch of the Institute for Cultural Research, which produced educational films. They helped her make her first independent animation film, *Das Ornament des verliebten Herzens* (Ornament of the Loving Heart), in the fall of 1919. On the basis of the success of this film, she got commercial work with Julius Pinschewer's advertising film agency, including an exquisite "reverse" silhouette film, *Das Geheimnis der Marquise* (The Marquise's Secret), in which the elegant white figures of eighteenth-century nobility (urging you to use Nivea skin cream!) seem like cameo or Wedgwood images. These advertising films helped fund four more animated shorts: *Amor und das standhafte Liebespaar* (Cupid and The Steadfast Lovers, which combined silhouettes with a live actor) in 1920, Hans Christian Andersen's *Der fliegende Koffer* (The Flying Suitcase) and *Der Stern von Bethlehem* (The Star of Bethlehem) in 1921, and *Aschenputtel* (Cinderella) in 1922.

The success of these shorts convinced the banker Louis Hagen to finance the production of a feature-length animated film, *Die Abenteuer des Prinzen Achmed* (The Adventures of Prince Ahmed), based on stories from *The Thousand and One Nights*. Production on this feature took three years, 1923 to 1926, with a staff of six: Reiniger; Carl Koch (now her husband); the experimental animators Walter Ruttmann and Berthold Bartosch, who did "special effects;" Walter Türck, who manipulated a second level of glass for animation of backgrounds, etc.; and Alexander Kardan, who kept track of the exposure sheets, storyboard and such technical details. The young theater composer Wolfgang Zeller wrote an elaborate symphonic score for the film, which launched him on a long career as a film composer.

The great success of *Prince Ahmed* encouraged Reiniger to make a second feature, *Doktor Dolittle* (based on Hugh Lofting's book[1]), which premiered in December 1928 with Paul Dessau conducting a musical score that included music by himself, Kurt Weill, Paul Hindemith and Igor Stravinsky.

At Prince Ahmed's French premiere in July 1926, Carl and Lotte met Jean Renoir and became life-long friends, which involved their collaboration on Renoir's features, *La Marseillaise*, *The Grand Illusion* and *Tosca*. Renoir also appeared as a actor in a 1930 live-action feature Lotte co-directed, *Die Jagd nach dem Glück* (The Pursuit of Happiness), which also starred Berthold Bartosch in a love story set in the milieu of a carnival shadow-puppet theater. This feature, no less than *Dr. Dolittle* and *Prince Ahmed*, fell victim to the new fad for talking pictures: shot as a silent film, *Pursuit of Happiness* was converted into a sound film using the voices of professional actors, but the lip-synch was far from perfect, and though critics praised Reiniger's script, direction and animation,[2] the film could not compete with the sharp, elaborate UFA musical *Love Waltzes*, with Lilian Harvey, or the impressive Conrad Veidt war film, *The Last Company*, which opened in the weeks preceding Reiniger's feature.

Reiniger returned to making her silhouette shorts, of which she completed

some thirteen before the war, and after the war, living in England, she made some twenty-three more, half in color, most of which were shown on British and American television. In 1970, after the death of her husband, she wrote a definitive book, *Shadow Theatres and Shadow Films*.[3] She also made additional advertising films, several documentary films, live shadow-theater performances, and gave various workshops before her death on 19 June 1981.

Such a distinguished biography – and a filmography of more than seventy items – begs the question of why Lotte Reiniger remains rather undervalued. Despite the occasional nod to her as having made one feature-length animation film before Walt Disney (when indeed she made two), most critics today still tacitly assume that silhouettes constitute a secondary or inferior form of animation, so that Disney's cartoon *Snow White* counts as a real first animation feature.

As with most other animation pioneers, one key factor in Reiniger's neglect must be the unavailability of good quality prints. When Reiniger fled to England in the 1930s, her original negatives remained in Germany, and most were dispersed or lost at the end of the war. While many of her films are available in England, not all of these represent an excellent reproduction of Reiniger's original art: some have virtually lost their backgrounds through repeated duping from available prints, others are coupled with modern soundtracks (which cause the animation to move a third faster at "sound speed") that banalize the narrative with kitsch music and redundant voice-over. Only a few Reiniger films are available for rental in the U.S., none in superb editions except the National Film Board of Canada's *Aucassin and Nicolette*, which is hardly Reiniger's best work – not that it is a bad film, by any means, but the convoluted medieval adventure story, with its battles, escapes and disguises, does not lend itself easily to imaginative touches (though Lotte manages a few, such as the rats cavorting on the prison bed before the humans arrive), and the realism of the tale (which might as well have been done by live actors) tends to raise a "realism" question about the silhouettes in relation to the multi-color backgrounds.

The early critics of Reiniger's work recognized the special power of the pure black-and-white silhouette: Béla Balász in his essay "The Power of Scissors" noted that any literary text seemed hardly competitive with the imaginative quality of the silhouette.[4] Rudolf Arnheim, in his review of the *Doctor Dolittle* feature, went so far as to claim that all children's films should be made in the silhouette technique, because the imagination of a child can make a monster more frightening, an exploit more daring and extravagant, a maiden more beautiful (or more personally human in their own image) than the literal representations in puppet or cartoon, which automatically limit and impoverish the visionary, fantastic mental imagery of the viewer.[5] When Lotte Reiniger began to use multi-color backgrounds (and in some cases figures) due to the demands of television in the mid-1950s, her films also entered the terrain of the "cartoon" film which gives more information than necessary for imagination – but while perhaps they can not match the brilliance of the early Reiniger films, they are still superior to many other conventional animations.

The genre of silhouette films also constitutes for Reiniger a kind of feminist validation of a women's folk art form. Although silhouette cutting had enjoyed a general vogue in the era before photography and lithography allowed easier forms of recording and reproducing portraits, after the middle of the nineteenth century it came to be practiced more and more by women who were not allowed access to other art training but who learned scissor-craft as part of their household duties.[6] So Martin Knapp's 1914 *German Shadow and Silhouette Pictures from Three Centuries*[7] shows a preponderance of women artists in the 1900s: Maria Lahrs, Elisabeth Wolff-Zimmermann, Charlotte Jancke-Sachs, Greta von Hörner, Dora Brandenburg-Polster, Lotte Nicklaß, Gertrud Stamm- Hagemann, Cornelia Zeller, Magda Koll, Johanna Beckmann, Lisbeth Müller, Hildegard von Bayer, and Hertha von Gumppenberg – to whom could be added Lore Bierling, a Munich silhouette artist who also made animation films according to the German edition of Lutz's *Animated Cartoons*, which contains four elegant illustrations from her "many" silhouette films (though I have never met anyone who had seen one).[8]

Looking at the 300 plates in Martin Knapp's book, we can discern some of the aesthetic challenges of this genre. In Emma Eggel's "Kriemhild viewing Siegfried's Corpse" (an illustration for the *Niebelungenlied* from the 1880s), the complexity of the hall in which the hero lies obviously demonstrates a bravura intricacy of cutting in decorative elements that might not be necessary for the narrative aspect of the image: pencil-thin curving lines vaulting the ceiling, a pine-tree with hundreds of needles outside one wall, and seven niches with tiny but fully-detailed holy pictures in them – these aside from the perspective of tiles and the main figures, of which Kriemhild is caught rushing in, strands of her hair fluttering behind her. Eggel's "The Holy Grail" confirms this with the complicated bowed leading of arched stained-glass windows, and a delicate balance of thirteen swirling angels in flight. Dora Brandenburg-Polster's 1911 "Battle", in a more modern, expressionist style, still meets a challenge for intricacy and dynamics, with ten foot-soldiers encircling a man on horseback with no less than 20 spears menacing the steed who rears and twists, its whirling mane and tail contrasting to the jagged trajectories of the spears. Maria Lahrs' similarly expressionist 1910 "Fishermen at Königsberg" delights in capturing the abstract rippled reflections in the water. Whether in light, open compositions such as Cornelia Zeller's "Storm" and "Dragon-Kites" with the sky as a blank matrix for jagged and twining lines, or in the dark, thick "Pierrot's Death" of Lotte Nicklaß with its textured stage curtains, tutu, ruffs and flowing black robes, the silhouette artist strives to infuse the stiff, frozen image with a balance of pattern and positive/negative space, with implied energetic dynamics, and with an "impossible" sense of intricacy and fluidity that defies our assumptions about scissors and paper.

Lotte Reiniger, when taking this tradition into the animated film, needed not only to fulfill these expectations but also to devise a time-based dynamic that choreographed and balanced these elements as they developed within scenes, made transitions, and expressed something about the various characters and narrative twists. The opening sequences of *The Adventures of Prince Ahmed* demonstrate that she succeeded brilliantly.[9]

The first appearance of the evil Sorcerer shows him unfold in medium close-up, his eyes rolling, his fingers articulating like spider legs; the light void that surrounds him at first yields to his conjuring, filling with polymorphous oozes of organic forms (created by Walter Ruttmann with Oskar Fischinger's wax-slicing machine) that finally resolve into the magic horse. The Caliph's birthday festival opens with elaborate architecture along a horizon line from which appear diagonal lines of multi-national courtiers bearing gifts; the diagonal composition remains constant for these characters each time they are seen. In details such as Dinarzade's lacy curtains and veil, the Caliph's palanquin and the mane of the magic horse (as well as the architecture of the Caliph's palace) we see the impossible intricacy. In the arrest of the Sorcerer (similar in design to Dora Brandenberg-Polster's "Battle") the irregular trajectories of the guards' spears encircling their victim depicts the dynamic tension of the moment. Prince Ahmed's flight into the stratosphere is supported by multiple layers of soft clouds and hundreds of stars moving in perspective. The palace of Peri Banu, with its carved jali screens, lacy curtains and pierced lanterns again astonish with their impossible intricacy. And Peri Banu's bath in the forest pool (with reflections of the palm trees, and rippling reflections of Peri Banu herself, as well as her servants and a doe – recalling Maria Lahrs' "Fishermen") provides an ecstatic moment of bravura animation magic. These sensitive and spectacular effects continue throughout the film – the gorgeous sinuous layers of the Chinese mountain landscape, for example, or the exquisite miniature image of Ahmed inside the Sorcerer's conjuring hair-ball (like the holy niches in Eggel's "Kriemhild").

While Reiniger definitely designed and directed her films, and to her belongs the full artistic credit for their successes, another mark of her genius lies in her choice of experimental animators like Walter Ruttmann and Berthold Bartosch to work for her. On one hand Ruttmann's soft, sensuous paintings on glass and his jagged expressionistic lightning and his exciting pulsating effects in the climactic duel between the Sorcerer and the "Ogress", and Bartosch's dizzying multiplane starscapes and hypnotic waves in Peri Banu's waters all add just the right complementary virtuosity and variety to Reiniger's cutout figures and backgrounds. On the other hand, Reiniger's support of these film artists helped them to develop and continue their own work, for Ruttmann produced his abstract films *Opus 3* and *Opus 4* under Reiniger's aegis, and the experience Bartosch culled from *Prince Ahmed* and *Dr. Dolittle* made possible the refined layering and luminous effects in his own subsequent masterpiece *The Idea*.

In a famous conversation at the animation stand,[10] Walter Ruttmann asked Reiniger:

> "Lotte, why are you making a fairy tale film like this?"
>
> "I don't know either", she replied.
>
> "What has it got to do with the year 1923?" he pursued.
>
> "Nothing at all. And why should it? I'm here, living in the year 1923, and I have the chance to make this film, so naturally I'm going to do it. That's all it has to do with the year 1923."
>
> "That doesn't seem right to me", he insisted.

But despite his socialist principles, Ruttmann continued to work on *Prince Ahmed*, because 1923 was a bitter year of the German inflation, when a loaf of bread cost thousands of marks.

This anecdote has been interpreted to suggest that (a) Reiniger's films are just children's films with no broader significance, and (b) Reiniger herself had no political conscience. Neither of these assumptions is true. Not only did she surround herself with communists and socialists (including Ruttmann, Bartosch, Carl Koch, the Institute for Cultural Research, Paul Dessau, Kurt Weill and Lotte Lenya, Bertolt Brecht, Jean Renoir) but believed enough in those humanitarian ideals that she could not stay in Nazi Germany and emigrated at great personal danger and discomfort – not able to get a permanent visa to another country, she spent several years traveling back and forth between France and England on visitor's passes. Although her artform, silhouette animation, lent itself to children's films and fantasy works, she thought consciously of a socialist responsibility to infuse these films (which would be seen by young, impressionable minds) with constructive and thought-provoking ideas. In Renoir's *La Marseillaise*, Reiniger's shadow puppets do not appear as the "ombres chinoises" of the idle aristocracy, but rather as a political theater of the revolutionaries, presenting a satirical parable "King and Nation". *Das gestohlene Herz* (The Stolen Heart, 1934) presents a similar anti-Nazi parable: an ogre who wants to control everything, own everything, steal everything others find meaningful, especially since this means violation of privacy, hoarding and joy in others' misery; the musical instruments rebel, refuse to be silenced, trap the ogre in his own web, fly home to their lovers, watchmen, chamber players and women at their sewing. I, personally, have always imagined that there was something of the advanced socialist tolerance for birth control and abortion rights (suppressed by the Nazis) in the satirical literalness of the mad proliferation of little Papagenos and Papagenas at the end of Reiniger's 1935 *Papageno*.

In the 1920s equal rights for women and homosexuals formed part of the agenda for socialists, and Reiniger also treated those issues with good consciousness. The kind, resourceful and powerful African magician in *Prince Ahmed* (somewhat inaptly called an "Ogress" in the new English-language titles) represents a traditional priestess of the old goddess religions, who uses her healing powers for good, as opposed to the evil male Sorcerer who exploits people with magic tricks for his own benefit. The good and capable woman wins out over the sleazy male trickster.

In Reiniger's *Carmen* (1933), we see another kind of feminist re-interpretation: her Carmen is inventive and self-sufficient, while the "macho" José keeps being tripped up by his own vanity, quite literally when he enters with his nose in the air and stumbles over his own sword. The smoking Carmen (freedom for women to smoke was then a feminist issue as well) aggressively seduces him, steals his clothes while he sleeps, and resourcefully pawns them to buy herself a new outfit. His mad attempts to stab her all fail. The similarly vain toreador blithely knocks her down as he passes, but Carmen gets revenge by outshining him in the bull ring: bravely feeding the bull a rose from her mouth and converting the blood-sport back into its ancient Cretan-goddess religious ritual by somersaulting over the bull's horns and dancing with him.

The little-seen *Der scheintote Chinese* (Seemingly-Dead Chinaman) was originally animated as an episode for *Prince Ahmed* but was omitted from the feature not only to reduce the running time (which some distributors feared might be too long for children's attention span) but also because men were nervous about the homosexual content. Reiniger had read the essay by Sir Richard Burton, English translator of *The Thousand and One Nights*, about "The Sotadic Zone" and how important homosexual relationships were in the world of *Prince Ahmed*. She also knew Kurt Hiller, who was not only a key member of the Socialist party but also of Magnus Hirschfeld's homosexual liberation movement in Berlin. "Of course, I knew lots of homosexual men and women from the film and theater world in Berlin, and saw how they suffered from stigmatization", she told me. "By contrast, I was fascinated by how natural love between members of the same sex was depicted in the *Arabian Nights*, so I thought, let's be casual and honest and truthful about it. In movies like *Different from the Others*, poor Reinhold Schünzel and Conrad Veidt had to grovel and suffer; I suspect that when the Emperor kisses Ping Pong, that must have been the first happy kiss between two men in the cinema – and I wanted it to happen quite calmly in the middle of *Prince Ahmed* so children – some who would be homosexual and some who would not – could see it as a natural occurrence, and not be shocked or ashamed."[11]

Lotte Reiniger did not talk much about her ideas, or the meanings of her films, partly perhaps because, like many emigrants from Nazi Germany, she suffered not only a dislocation of language (which made it difficult to express things precisely or correctly), but also a spiritual displacement – the terrible task of always trying to (always having to) explain how things were before the Nazis, how things were during their reign of terror, how things were afterwards. But she was confident that what she really had to say was contained in her films, so it is imperative for us to revive them, study them and show them more often. Perhaps, if the original negatives were destroyed, the quality and details of backgrounds should be reconstructed by computer enhancement, with the original music and written texts also restored. But until then, Reiniger's films, even in their present condition, remain one of the chief treasures of animation. 🍎

Notes

1. Hugh Lofting, *The Story of Doctor Dolittle* (New York: Frederkick Stokes, 1920).

2. The collected reviews reprinted in *Lotte Reiniger: Eine Dokumentation* (Berlin: Deutsche Kinemathek, 1969), 59–63.

3. Lotte Reiniger, *Shadow Theatres and Shadow Films* (New York: Watson-Guptill, 1970).

4. Béla Balász, "Die Gewalt der Schere", *Der Geist des Film* (Halle, 1930), 122–123.

5. Rudolf Arnheim, "Lotte Reinigers Schattenfilm", *Die Weltbühne* 52 (24 December 1928): 961.

6. Joseph and Yehudit Shadur, *Jewish Papercuts: A History and Guide* (Berkeley: Judah L. Magnes Museum, 1994).

7. Martin Knapp, *Deutsche Schatten- und Scherenbilder aus drei Jahrhunderten* (Dachau: Der Gelbe Verlag, 1914).

8. Konrad Wolter, *Der gezeichnete Film* (Halle: W. Knapp, 1927), 109, 197, 210, 212.

9. A scene-by-scene description of *Prince Achmed* with frame enlargements for each scene was published in Alfio Bastiancich's excellent *Lotte Reiniger* (Turin: Centro Internazionale per il Cinema di Animazione, 1982), 12–70. A German picture book with 32 full-page plates from *Prince Achmed*, originally published in 1926, and re-published in 1972 [Lotte Reiniger, *Die Abenteuer des Prinzen Achmed* (Tübingen: Ernst Wasmuth, 1972)], shows how much detail has been lost from the backgrounds in many scenes.

10. Recorded in Alfred Happ's "Die Mozart Schnitte Lotte Reinigers", *Mozart, die großen Opern in Scherenschnitten von Lotte Reiniger* (Tübingen: Heliopolis, 1988), 320.

11. Interview with Lotte Reiniger, London, 1970. *Anders als die Andern* (Different from the Others), a 1919 feature by Richard Oswald, contained an appearance by Magnus Hirschfeld pleading for tolerance and equal rights for homosexuals; see *Richard Oswald, Regisseur und Produzent* (Munich: Text + Kritik, 1990), 25–35. Information also appears in James Steakley, *The Homosexual Emancipation Movement in Germany* (New York: Arno, 1975) (English-language), and *Eldorado: Homosexuelle Frauen und Männer in Berlin 1850–1950* (Berlin: Berlin Museum, 1994).

Moritz, William. "Some Critical Perspectives on Lotte Reiniger". *Animation Journal* 5:1 (Fall 1996). 40–51. This paper was delivered at the Fourth Annual Society for Animation Studies Conference, Sunday, 25 October 1992, California Institute of the Arts. ©1996 William Moritz

3

it's mickey mouse

Esther Leslie [2002]

After the studio which was distributing the Disney cartoons appropriated the Oswald character, Walt Disney created Mortimer Mouse, and then changed the mouse's name to Mickey. Animated by Ub Iwerks in less than two weeks, Mickey Mouse's first role was motivated by Charles Lindbergh's transatlantic flight. *Plane Crazy* (1928) mustered all the lunacy of technological modernity. This was graphically represented by the plane as it circled and swooped, and also in the cartoon's look, in the multiple changes of angles of vision, and the speed of movement of things and the fast pace of actions. The audience twists and turns with the plane or with the line of vision that follows the plane. The whole image surface is animated. It is not one single activity that we follow, but a dispersed scene – it cannot all be taken in at one viewing. And the whole world is alive. A church spire crumples itself up to avoid the passing plane. Bodies elongate and detach parts at will. Substance mutates. Reality, objects, are always working to solve problems, efficiently. So, Mickey is able to yank a fan-tail from a turkey to place on his new airplane. Human relations are brutal too. Minnie has to be terrified into kissing Mickey. Then came *The Gallopin Gaucho* (1928), with Mickey

Mouse in a Douglas Fairbanks pastiche, but distributors showed little interest. The first film to get a release, *Steamboat Willie* (1928), would have to present a special selling point. *Steamboat Willie*, which premiered in November 1928 in the New York cinema Colony Theatre, was an exercise in strange literalism: a goat eats a musical score and then its tail is cranked to produce music, which appears on the screen as notes floating through the air. And when the cow is fed hay it immediately assumes the size and shape of the bale it is fed. A ratty Mickey Mouse was made of a rubber-hose-type torso, which did not snap back into place when stretched, but dangled for as long as was necessary for the gag. The special selling point of the first successful cartoon film with Mickey Mouse – the thing that hooked the crowds – was its sound.

The Disney team was not the first to use sound. Through the 1920s the Fleischer brothers experimented with soundtracks for *Song Car-Tunes*. Paul Terry, producer of more than two hundred silent *Aesop s Fables* for Amadée Van Beuren, made a synchronized sound film called *Dinnertime* in the summer of 1928. When Disney's third film was underway, *The Jazz Singer* was being talked about in Hollywood and elsewhere. But it was obvious to many that animation had a particular affinity to sound and music. Music and film both move through time, but in cartooning, with its frame-by-frame fully controllable structure, the links between sound and image could be drawn so tightly that a symbiosis, a perfect rhythmic synchronization, could occur. Music was often visualised in the silent animations, in countless scenes of misbehaviour in the dance halls, or more inventively, as in *Alice the Firefighter* (1926) when a rag piano player uses musical notes to climb up to a hotel window. *Steamboat Willie* presented the tensions between brutish Peg-Leg Pete, Minnie Mouse and Mickey Mouse. Many of the gags involved sound - the cow whose mouth is pried open, so her teeth may be played as a xylophone, for example. A 'bar sheet' was used for *Steamboat Willie*. This was a chart for each musical action or phrase – every toot and whistle and melody – linking it to a description of the screen action it was to accompany. The camera operator's exposure sheet was prepared before the animators set to work. Everything was precisely charted to allow synchronization. This system, in its more evolved form, came to be known as 'Mickey Mousing'. This sonic universe accepts no differences among sounds, no hierarchies of tone. All noises take their place on the soundtrack and get their turn. A violin phrase is no better than a cracking walnut or a squelching kitten body. The art lies in the arrangement of materials, from wherever they stem. Simultaneously, in Vienna, twelve-tone analysed the issue of democracy in sound. Kurt Schwitters knew of the democracy of materials too and put its principles into practice in his Merz collages. His was an art of the ragpicker and it knew no hierarchies of stuff, for, as Hans Richter relates in his autobiography, Schwitters

had a habit of foraging in rubbish bins for scraps to use in his collages. One memorable ripe cheese paper rescued from a bin stunk out an entire first class hotel in Switzerland.[1] Leger imported the ragpicking technique to America, telling Richter one day that he painted American landscapes: 'Americans throw everything away into the landscape, and I paint it'.[2] But Disney and the Fleischers and Sullivan and the others were already doing this, re-imaging the landscape, bringing the abject back to life, giving it all voice, from the tin cans to the torn cats to the rednecks.

Disney was sure that sound could be used even more effectively in his cartoons and so he set about devising his Silly Symphonies series. The gags were milder. The point was the synchronicity of sound and image. The cartoons were more slowly paced than the slapstick knockabouts. Here the music really did seem to be antecedent. *The Skeleton Dance* (1929) was the first Silly Symphony. Ub Iwerks drew it and Carl W. Stalling composed the music. It opened with two huge disc-eyes, and crashing music. The view draws back to reveal an owl. There is the sound of caterwauling in the graveyard and it sounds like a curious music. All the movements are synchronized with sound and music. Stretchy and squashy skeletons dance in formation. One skeleton borrows the bones of another's legs to play him as a ribcage xylophone. A cat's tail is played as a cello. Everything is in movement all the time. *The Skeleton Dance* was perhaps the most successful of all the Silly Symphonies. Jean Prevost, in a 1938 article from *Vendredi* entitled 'Walt Disney, the man who never had a childhood', noted that it had been made without worrying about audience reactions. Yet public and critics alike were charmed. Dorothy Richardson had praised Felix in the modernist film journal *Close Up* in August 1928, and *transition,* the house journal of the modernist avant-garde, went *so* far as to print a still from *Steamboat Willie.* In a special programme on 10 November 1929, the rather dandyish London Film Society, under the direction of Ivor Montagu, and before an audience that included Eisenstein, John Grierson and Aldous Huxley, showed Jean Epstein's *The Fall of the House of Usher,* Grierson's *Drifters* and Eisenstein's *Battleship Potemkin* together with Disney's *The Barn Dance*?[3] Eric Walter White, in a study of silhouette animations by Lotte Reiniger, put out by Leonard and Virginia Woolf's Hogarth Press in 1931, defended animation as 'pure cinema':

> At the present moment the cartoon film is by no means confined to the United States. Countless imitations of Mickey Mouse have sprung up in France and Germany; and Russia (as might be expected) has turned out a series of modernised *Aesop s Fables,* in which the human roles are played by machines and the moral emphasises the necessity for collectivist as opposed to individual action. It is not improbable that in the near future musicians will be found writing scores for short trick film operas; a pair of collaborators like Bert Brecht and Kurt Weill, who produced *Der Plug der Lindberghs* for radio performance in 1929, are certainly capable of inspiring such a musical trick film, in which they could remedy all the unfortunate errors made by Pabst in the screen adaptation of their *Threepenny Opera.* However that may be, the trick film in its original form remains one of the purest manifestations of cinema, and there is no doubt that a century hence (if the films have not perished by then) the best work of Walt Disney and Lotte Reiniger will be looked upon as primitives in the same way as the present generation looks on the paintings of Simone Martini and Sassetta or the music of Byrd and Monteverdi.

White explained Disney's speciality:

> The important discovery made by Walt Disney in his cartoon films concerns the unexpected relations that exist between visual and aural phenomena. For instance, when a stream of bubbles appears on the screen, Mickey will almost certainly prick them with a pin, and as they explode they will play a tune in which the frequency of the wave-vibration of each note will be inversely proportional to the size of the bubbles. Other purely visual discoveries are the spectacular entry made by the plaice in the opening submarine scene of *Frolicking Fish,* where the plaice, having swung in from the side, reaches the centre of the screen, turns round and reveals the fact that it is as thin as a lath, and the solo dance of the frog in the Silly Symphony, *Spring.* This particular frog is dancing by the bank of a stream, and at first his shadow dances with him in obedience to the physical laws of light. But suddenly the frog and his reflection part company: as the frog dances to the right, his shadow dances to the left, and *vice versa.* This piece of optical nonsense is as purely cinematic as the Oceana Roll in the *Gold Rush;* and many other instances (often more vulgar) can be found in Walt Disney's work.[4]

This was not just children's stuff, and certainly not sugar-sweet. Whether they were for adults or children was indeterminate. They were simply for anarchists of any age. Cartoons, for all their slapstick playing, seemed to appeal to intellect and imagination. Critics noticed that those made prior to 1928 were primarily concerned with ideas. Robert Feild, who spent time at the Disney studios in the late 1930s and wrote the first 'serious' study, *The Art of Walt Disney* (1942), understood the cerebral nature of animation. Film, he notes, has the ability to overcome the limitations of time and space to which we are normally subjected. The imagination of the audience can be appealed to in such a way that it is freed from the restrictions of the physical world.[5] 'What is Mickey anyway but an abstract idea in the process of becoming?'[6] Philosophy and animation unearth each other.

Lack of speech, but presence of noise, facilitated the cartoons' success on the international market. By 1930 Disney's mouse was an international phenomenon. Mickey Mouse conquered Germany in 1930. In January of that year the first Mickey Mouse film seen was *The Barn Dance*. In February five more films were shown, including *The Skeleton Dance.* Disney was conquering Europe. The actions portrayed in these early Disney films were irrational and physics-defying, sometimes violent and raucous, but only one ran into problems with the censors: *Barnyard Battle*, a farmyard knockabout based on the World War of 1914–18, where the Hun are German cats, defeated ignominiously by the French Mickey-style mice. National pride was at stake: the film's German censors justified their decision to ban the film by arguing that it besmirched German honour. With a world market to sell on, Walt Disney Enterprises had been established in 1929. It was a licensing agency. Felix the Cat was the first animated character to become a successful toy, and Little Nemo, Krazy Kat, Mutt and Jeff, The Katzenjammer Kids and others had all appeared. There were plenty of Disney character effigies and images, from various unlicensed sources – some more, some less similar to their on-screen counterparts. Such markets were open for expansion, and studios saw opportunities

for tie-in products, from Hollywood fan magazines and fashion lines to games and toys. In 1929 the rights to use Mickey on school writing tablets were sold to a company in New York. In February 1930, Walt Disney agreed to a contract with the George Borgfeldt Company for the international licensing, production and distribution of Mickey Mouse merchandise. Borgfeldt made Mickey Mouse toys that tumbled and squeaked. He made Mickey Mouse sparklers and spinning tops – and often from the cheapest materials of celluloid and tin.[7] Mickey Mouse's popularity in the years of depression convinced Disney that more revenue needed to be generated through character merchandising, and Herman Kamen was employed to consolidate and expand sales – in-house – through merchandise tie-ins, cinema decorations, badges, posters, masks, balloons. It might have been the merchandising, and a toy market to exploit, that compelled Mickey Mouse to become cuter, more toy-like, but also a vehicle for good behaviour – at the Saturday afternoon Mickey Mouse Clubs, children learnt how to cross the street, wash behind their ears and respect their elders. Children were formed into conformist adults.

In any case Mickey Mouse changed. He became a person, rather than a rat, by the time that *Plow Boy* appeared in 1929. He adopted white gloves in 1930. In 1931, in *The Mouse Hunt,* Mickey Mouse turned into the unsophisticated boy, and he went around with his dog. He was supposed to be an average boy of no particular age, fun loving, clean living in a small town. Freddy Moore introduced a new plastic style of drawing to the Disney studios as the 1930s drew to a close, and so Mickey Mouse became cuter, softer, rounder, of flesh and blood. Moore gave the face more character and definition, and his pliable body had a constant volume. His pear-shaped body could be better 'squashed and stretched', though never too traumatically; this allowed for a world of cause and effect matched by psychological validity.[8] Now his eyes had irises and pupils, which meant that they looked more realistic, more human and could effect a greater range of expression; perhaps it might be imagined that Mickey Mouse was also in possession of a soul. By now animators had worked out ways of endowing a character with apparent weight, ending staccato, jerky and unanchored movements. Weight and weightlessness had begun to preoccupy Disney's animators, though it had not been at issue for Cohl, in his world of hot-air balloons and vaporization. Where once gravity-defying tricks were the essence of cartooning, a realist injunction was now invading the look. But could all that embodiment and all that personality keep the wolf from the door? The Disney studio was in financial crisis in 1934. The headline of the *New York Telegraph* reported in late 1933 that Disney's three little pigs were scoffing all the profits. In March 1934 the *New York Herald Tribune* declared: 'Mickey Mouse as actor a dud at making money'. Still, by then, Disney had other ideas – feature films, human beings – in mind, and animation already had a history, if, at points, an unrespectable one. 🍎

Notes

1. See *Hans Richter by Hans Richter*, edited by Cleve Gray, Thames & Hudson, London 1971, p. 187. Richter uses the word 'ragpicker' to describe Schwitters, p. 152.

2. Ibid., p. 155.

3. See Don Macpherson, ed., *Traditions of Independence: British Cinema in the Thirties*, BFI, London 1980, p. 101.

4. Eric Walter White, *Walking Shadows: An Essay on Lotte Reiniger s Silhouette Films*, Hogarth Press, London 1931, p. 30.

5. See Robert Feild, *The Art of walt Disney*, Collins, London and Glasgow 1944, p. 14.

6. Ibid., p. 2n.

7. See Robert Heide and John Gilman, *Disneyana: Classic Collectibles 1928–1958*, Hyperion, New York 1991, p. 39.

8. See Michael Barrier, *Hollywood Cartoons: American Animation in the Golden Age*, Oxford University Press, Oxford 1999, pp. 89–90.

Leslie, Esther. "it's mickey mouse". In *Hollywood Flatlands*. London: Verso, 2002. 25–32.

4

Norman McLaren: His UNESCO Work in Asia

Terence Dobson [2000]

Norman McLaren twice spent lengthy periods in Asia working for UNESCO (United Nations Educational, Scientific and Cultural Organization). His task was to teach a selection of local artists how to make visual aids suitable for use in fundamental education for the general community. In August 1949, he went to Peh pei in western China, where he stayed until April 1950. Later, from November 1952 to May 1953, he worked in India, first in Delhi and then in Mysore.

The circumstances leading to and surrounding his work in Asia reveal McLaren's analytical and sympathetic approach to his work in terms of both filmmaking and teaching. This paper overviews McLaren's experiences in Asia and pursues developments which arose from his time there.

Before Asia: The Early years at the NFB

By 1949, when he left for China, Norman McLaren had been working at the National Film Board of Canada (NFB) for eight years. At the invitation of John Grierson, the NFB's founder and first Commissioner, McLaren had joined the organization two years after its 1939 beginning.[1] The young McLaren was a committed pacifist who had fled Britain just before the outbreak of the Second World War for the sanctuary of New York. When Grierson approached him, he was reluctant to go to Canada, which at that time, 1941, already was fighting in the War. McLaren did not want to be engaged in making hard-sell war-propaganda films. However, Grierson wanted McLaren's work as a contrast to the NFB's worthy yet somewhat heavy programs of informative and pointed documentaries. Grierson wanted "... a little lightness and fantasy".[2] He assured McLaren, "Come and do what you want"[3] and "... you will see that you can make cinema as you understand it".[4] Grierson was true to his word. The titles of McLaren's early films at the NFB are indicative of their whimsical, playful content: *Hen Hop* (1942), *Fiddle-de-dee* (1947), and *Begone Dull Care* (1949) are obvious examples.[5]

These and other films caused McLaren's reputation to spread. He was approached by UNESCO to conduct a pioneering experiment in visual education for "backward areas"[6] in China. John Grierson's term as NFB Commissioner had finished in 1945 and it was Arthur Irwin, who had subsequently been appointed Commissioner, who oversaw McLaren's China leave proposal. The background to this is intriguing.

In the communist-hunting aftermath of Canada's great Gouzenko Spy Scandal of 1945, the NFB was one of the various sections of the public service that was suspected of harboring communist cells. Indeed, there was a tenuous attempt to implicate Grierson himself by way of his secretary's alleged connections. In early 1950, the Royal Canadian Mounted Police (RCMP) presented Irwin with a list of 36 names of people who were 'security' risks. Decisive action was expected of him.[7]

McLaren's background made it extremely probable that his name was on the list. As a student in Scotland he had joined the Scottish Communist Party and remained a member until he left the UK in 1939. In his final year in Glasgow, where he attended the School of Art, he made a strident, uncompromising, anti-war, anti-capitalist film with Helen Biggar (*Hell UnLtd.*, 1936). Then, after his shift to London and the GPO Film Unit, he teamed with Ivor Montagu to act as cameraman for the latter's film *Defense of Madrid* (1936), one of the few films to depict the Spanish Civil War from the Republican view.

However, at the NFB, apart from his 'poster' films of the war years,[8] McLaren's subsequent film output had been devoid of social comment. As if his growing preoccupation with abstract films were not enough, in January 1947 McLaren issued a political disclaimer in a *Liberty* magazine interview:

> Once, I took a lively interest in politics and in the world around me. I saw a lot of things were going wrong and wanted to do something about them. I joined a radical party in Scotland, participated in study groups, and was fair set to become a reforming young zealot. Then, as time passed, my passion for creative work grew to a point where it usurped my active political interests. Now, I feel I can be of more value making an artistic rather than a political contribution to society. Is that bad?[9]

Given McLaren's impeccable reputation for integrity,[10] the sentiments he expresses in the interview can be accepted. However, what is less certain is whether or not his disclaimer was prompted by the anti-Communist atmosphere of the time and reflects an attempt to remove himself and the NFB from culpability. Despite this, a person with McLaren's obvious political sympathies, who had been selecting staff for the newly established Animation Department at the NFB, was unlikely to be above suspicion in those paranoid years. Commissioner Irwin, who had been appointed to restore public confidence in the NFB, would have been aware of McLaren's vulnerability. He supported McLaren's plans to take leave for a year to work for UNESCO in China. It was while McLaren was in China that Irwin received the RCMP's list of thirty-six names. Not only was McLaren out of the way, he was working for an internationally prestigious organization (UNESCO) and, moreover, was invited by and working in the territory of a government that was not only anti-Communist but was engaged in fighting a civil war against a communist enemy.[11] Had McLaren's name been on that list, to sack someone of his growing artistic reputation, especially while working indirectly for Nationalist China, would have invited public ridicule. McLaren was not sacked. In fact Irwin did not fire thirty-three of the thirty-six on the list.

McLaren had left for China easy in the knowledge that the Animation

Department at the NFB which, as has been mentioned, he had established and of which he was head until 1945, would continue without him. The nature of his proposed work in China was also something which McLaren keenly anticipated for ironically it awoke that which had been professionally dormant – his social conscience. He wrote enthusiastically to his mother about the planned project:

> I am going to teach a group of Chinese artists how to make animated films, so that they can start making them themselves in order to help educate the people in the backward villages there, who [can't] read or write, and who need films made to teach them how to have a *healthy* village. Films of vaccination, [hygiene], and all matters about health... . I shall be working with a Mr. Hubbard, an educationist from [UNESCO], and the project we are working on is called the CHINESE AUDIO-VISUAL PROJECT. What we do with it is supposed to act as a model for all other member-nations in [UNESCO] who want to do something about education in their backward areas.[12]

The "Healthy Village Project" in China

Once he got to China, McLaren found he was able to undertake the socially-useful work he anticipated. His part of the UNESCO "Healthy Village Project" had two objectives. Naturally enough, the first was to carry out the piece of educational work at hand. The second objective was "... to place the experience of the Chinese Project at the disposal of educators elsewhere",[13] so a meticulous record of the project, augmented by photographs and diagrams, was prepared by McLaren and published by UNESCO in 1951.

Although McLaren was an expert in film,[14] he did not begin the Project with

film-making. Of the five main categories into which he divided the Project, only the last deals with film. However, the other four non-film topics – static posters and wallsheets, picture books, mobile posters, and film slides and filmstrips – display a progression from purely static work towards movie-making.

The first section, dealing with static posters and wallsheets, moves from simple, single-image posters to those using the comic-strip method of a series of images to tell a story. The second section's title, picture books, is self-explanatory. Large books (the larger sizes incorporating portable easels to display them) were made in which each page or sheet related to its adjacent ones. Thus, by using pictures in a series, these sections of the Project imply change and movement.

In the third phase of the Project, McLaren incorporated actual movement into the static material either through mobile-posters or through the use of scroll-boxes. Mobile posters were ordinary posters which had holes cut into them and, behind the poster, a rotatable disc revealed part or parts of itself through the various apertures. McLaren discarded other methods of revealing hidden parts that used levers and shutters of sliding elements because they were more prone to develop frictional or mechanical trouble. The moving-wheel posters, however, gave him plenty of scope for variation. He devised single-wheel posters and multi-wheel posters; posters with single holes (these holes varied from poster to poster in size and shape); and multi-apertured posters with a similar range of sizes and shapes.

The means of turning the wheels also was thoroughly explored. McLaren looked at pegs and also notches before adopting finger-holes operated through a finger-slot on the front so that the amount of movement of the disc could be controlled by the artist. During field trials, it was discovered that for about fifteen per cent of the time, even with the use of indicating arrows, users would turn the wheels in the wrong direction, thus delivering the story in the reverse order. To avoid this potentially disastrous misreading of the story, McLaren devised a simple ratchet system that prevented the wheel from being wound backwards.

The scroll-box also was subject to modification and development. The initial idea was to use the traditional Chinese scroll to display a series of related images, but it was found that it was slightly cumbersome to wind and unwind by hand. McLaren explained his modification and its rationale: "... we thought it better to house [the scroll], thus making the winding arrangement easy, protecting the scrolls, and framing the visible part of the picture. We therefore mounted the two rollers in a shallow wooden box, and fitted each roller with a small [winding] handle that protruded from the box".[15] A rectangular viewing aperture was cut into the face of the flat box between the two rolls. However, this form of scroll-box had a serious flaw.

Since the sequence of visual information flows in one direction, an operator would be needed because the casual onlooker, after looking at one wind-through, would leave the scroll at its end. The next person would be unlikely to rewind the scroll before the subsequent viewing, which then would be of a reversed order. Not being able to afford an always-attentive scroll operator, McLaren and his team devised several solutions. The first and most obvious solution was to make the scroll into a single continuous loop and to add a mechanism that allowed winding in only one direction. This solution had a major disadvantage: the scroll would be very short. McLaren solved this problem by building a box with many rollers, around which a longer loop-scroll could snake its way backwards and forwards.

The increased mechanical complexity and the associated probable increase in mechanical failure caused McLaren to opt for a further solution which was elegantly simple: building the box with a viewing aperture on both sides and painting a continuation of the story on the other side of the scroll. On winding to the end of the first side of the scroll, there would be a title reading, "Turn the box round so the other side is facing you, and continue winding". At the end of the second side of the scroll, a second title would read, "To begin the story again, turn the box round and start winding". Arrows under each aperture would indicate the direction of winding. To prevent people watching both sides at once (in this situation viewers of the other side would see the sequences wound in the incorrect reverse order), the scroll-box would have to be placed on a table backed by a wall. Otherwise, as McLaren puts it, "... the viewing system is almost foolproof and self-operating".[16]

McLaren's wide range of possible solutions to the scroll-box problems, and his assessment of them, attest to his characteristic inventiveness and thoroughness. The motive for the large effort in producing effective moving-posters and scroll-boxes is contained in the three assumptions which underlay the use and development of the moving-poster and the scroll-box. Firstly, McLaren believed that "... a visual aid is more effective if it reveals its information in a specific sequence, rather than all at once (as do ordinary posters ...)".[17] He also believed that effectiveness would be enhanced if the visual aid incorporated movement or change. Finally, some action or participation on the part of the observer was held to improve the work's efficacy.[18] These assumptions are evidence of McLaren's constant awareness of the purpose or function of each section of work. That they show his high regard for the filmic quality of movement is also pertinent.

The fourth category of work undertaken in "The Healthy Village Project" covers film slides and filmstrips. These visual aids gave McLaren the chance to explore techniques and equipment used in drawing directly on both clear and black film stock. The techniques used included drawing or painting with ink or paint; removing black emulsion, ink or paint by scratching or scraping; combining these two basic methods; and making use of both sides of the film. Even an in-fill with ink into scratches made in clear film was explored. These techniques were identical to those used in directly-drawn animation. The equipment used included specially-made sloping bench-tops which had slots for carrying the film-strips. These benches also could be used later in the animation section of the Project. Thus, the exploration of the techniques and equipment used in the this category of work had not only intrinsic value, they also prepared McLaren's students for using similar techniques and equipment in film animation and so contributed to that culminating section of the project. Although filmstrips and slides are normally regarded as static media, McLaren, not surprisingly, saw a way to introduce movement.[19] A quick flick from one projected image to the next image, which is identical except in one small

way, would provide the illusion of an image that was steady, except for one small moving part. Two filmstrips were produced that included the flick-frame idea (*Good Habit Song* made by student Hsu, and *Dreadful Smallpox* made by student Ma), but McLaren felt there were more conditions and possibilities to explore. For example, what would be the optimum amount of movement? What is the largest proportional area the moving part could be before the illusion breaks down and two successive but entirely different images are perceived?

In the fifth and final category of the Project, McLaren examined the uses and possibilities of film animation itself, in what should have been the culmination of his efforts in China. Unfortunately, the film animation stage of the "Healthy Village Project" was not reached until October/November, by which time the damp and cold of winter had set in. McLaren observed:

> ... the atmosphere was excessively humid and very cold; satisfactory house and room heating was not usual and difficult to arrange for; the linear images in India ink drawn by the artists on the film took such a long time to dry that, in the process, the ink in any image would distribute itself unevenly along the line, forming puddles here and shallow patches there; especially as the film was on a slanting bench (for easier drawing) the ink would flow downwards and form blobs at the bottom of each image and shallow patches at the top.[20]

Although some films were made by directly drawing on the film, McLaren felt it prudent to concentrate on what he called the 'paper method', which was a simplification of cel animation. Instead of drawing on transparent cels, McLaren's method involved drawing on small sheets of paper (about A6 size , i.e.; 10.5 x 14.8

cm or 4.1 x 5.8 inches). This was a much cheaper use of materials. The smaller size also saved drawing time and increased the boldness and simplicity of line which McLaren believed was advantageous in fundamental education. The boldness was further enhanced by the new pens McLaren took with him for the Project. The *Flo-Master Fountnbrush* [sic] was an early form of felt pen which not only produced bold lines, but also employed ink which dried almost instantly, thereby eliminating the need for inconvenient drying racks. McLaren realized the possibility that this pen could solve the problems of non-drying ink used in the directly-drawn film animation; unfortunately, the *Flo-Master* ink produced only a faint line when used on celluloid.[21]

Despite being slower to execute, the paper method had several inherent advantages for the Project over the direct method of animation. Because it involved photographing drawn images onto 35mm film, it was a simple process to re-photograph various drawings; thus, a 'hold' could easily be executed. Similarly, if a sequence of drawings was re-photographed a number of times, a 'cycle' of movement could be repeated. Reverse motion could be achieved by photographing a sequence in reverse order. It also was possible to save labor by using clear celluloid on which the static parts of a sequence were depicted. The celluloid image could then be used as an overlay on different paper drawings that depicted movement in the sequence.[22]

Unfortunately, the shooting of the drawings was held up and McLaren and the artists working on the Project endured further frustration. McLaren's own words convey the difficulties:

> ... the Sept camera has been tied up with the shooting and printing of the project's filmstrips; the voltage of the electricity supply for doing this fluctuated so much that an exposure averaging 10 seconds for each frame was necessary (the number of seconds for each frame being varied to compensate for the voltage at the particular moment of shooting). This meant that the material was turned out very slowly. A further factor was the lack of a competent or adequately trained person, until the first of October, to take charge of the shooting and processing. Since that date [the new assistant] has had his hands full improving the equipment [and] keeping up with the filmstrip work ... Only in December did we get around to building a camera-stand suitable for shooting animation.[23]

The animated film section of the project was not the culmination McLaren would have wished. Only six films were shot (four were made using the paper method, one by the direct method, and the sixth used both methods). The processing of the films caused further complications. The original intention was to have the processing of directly-drawn films, as well as the shooting, developing and printing of the paper films, done in Nanking, Shanghai or Hong Kong; however, China's civil war prevented that. Such were the problems McLaren encountered in movie-making that he expressed strong doubts as to the suitability of the medium in such remote areas:

> Compared with the foregoing four categories of audio-visual aids, movie production and screening involves a great deal more technical complication, time and expense; so much so that from our experience here in West China it is appropriate to ask whether it is advisable to consider its use at all in certain areas where facilities are lacking. Its great asset of movement can easily be found in many older, traditional and technically less cumbersome media.

Our project did not have the time or staff to try putting these older techniques to use, but we have seen performances of semi-didactic political songs, dances, mimes and plays put on by school students and clubs in celebration of the New Regime which made it quite apparent that that these media could be harnessed for the teaching of health ideas. In a country where there seems a wealth of talent for acting, singing and the like, and a great dearth of motion picture photographic, developing, printing and projection apparatus and stable electricity supply, it seems only sensible to discard the idea of movie production in favour of more intimate and technically simple substitutes.[24]

In a sense, these were difficult words for McLaren to write. He had gone to China holding the belief that movies, with their element of movement, could play a significant role in fundamental education and, moreover, that his extremely cheap method of movie-making would be well-suited to the conditions he was likely to encounter. That he was able to see and acknowledge the profound limitations of the medium in such circumstances show that McLaren maintained a clear view of the over-riding aim of such projects, which was to help educate poor people in remote and difficult areas. Living with poor people in such places provided a daily reminder of the objective. It also reinvigorated McLaren's social and political conscience.

In western China, McLaren observed economic conditions hauntingly similar to those he found in Spain fourteen years earlier. His horror at what he saw in China is revealed in a 1949 extract from his diary:

The farmers are all dreadfully in debt, and are forced to borrow money from the landowners and richer folk at interest rates of about 50 per cent and that is not a typing error for 5, I really mean FIFTY. The landowners take practically all the crops from the farmers, and generally exploit the farmers shockingly by all sorts of practices. When the harvest is in, he will come round to the farmers' houses and expect to be given a great feast in his honor at each house (this, after arranging to take away most of the fruits of the farmer's labor as interest on the money he has lent the farmer.). This puts the farmer further in debt, and so the vicious cycle goes on.

The Nationalist government enacted new laws to do away with [this], but the influence of the landowners has corrupted the law courts, and so the legal decisions are all still in the landlord's and moneylender's favor, even tho [their practices] are against the law. The whole situation is filthy and degenerate and evil; and there is no wonder the communists are eagerly welcomed with their program of land redistribution and [abolition] of usury.[25]

This statement certainly contrasts with the political abstinence expressed in the Canadian *Liberty* interview which, it will be recalled, McLaren gave in January 1947. There is some irony in the fact that it was within the anti-Communist regime, where the former radical would be expected to be safe, that McLaren's political attention was re-aroused. There is further irony in the fact that the communist advance soon encompassed Peh pei while McLaren was working there.[26]

McLaren saw out his term in China under the communists. He was impressed. A sober contrast between the successive Chinese regimes was depicted in an article he published in *McLean s* magazine on his return to Canada. In it he said, "There's much enthusiasm by the country folk for the new regime, for the old government was so evil, corrupt and full of graft; the old authorities lived lavishly and luxuriously, while most of the farming folk are near starvation; the new authorities live very humbly, and are very strict and puritan."[27]

Return to the West

Apart from the *McLean s* article, and despite his feeling "very socially aware" and wanting to do a "serious piece",[28] McLaren's return to the West did not produce any immediate effect of his experience in China. After China, McLaren was immersed in the challenge of making two animated stereoscopic 3D films for the upcoming 1951 Festival of Britain. Raymond Spottiswoode, one of Grierson's important early recruits to the NFB, had subsequently returned to Britain and invited his former colleague at the NFB to produce the films: *Now is the Time* and *Around is Around* (both 1950–1951) were the results.

In the meantime, the NFB had come into some money from a strange source. The Canadian Government's top-secret Psychological Warfare Committee had been in existence since the war's end and, with the intensification of the Cold War between the Western democracies and the communist bloc, it took on the responsibility of fostering propaganda films which were to promote the virtues of the democratic system. An administrative program, Freedom Speaks, was set up within the NFB and $250,000 was provided by the Psychological Warfare Committee for making such films. One didactic propagandist film, *Germany, Key to Europe* (1953), directed by Ronald Dick, was made using part of these funds. Having thus assuaged the government critics with this film, Commissioner Irwin spent the rest of this money on "... fairly non-political subjects".[29]

McLaren was oblivious to all this

and, after completing the 3D films, he returned to the NFB in Canada where he then got together with Grant Munro to explore a fresh animation technique, which he termed pixillation. Based upon the same principal used in animating lifeless objects, the pixillation technique could endow animated people with fantastic means of movement, including sliding, gliding and even flying. The film McLaren and Munro started on was about highway safety.

Irwin, however, was curious to know what McLaren was up to. The Commissioner was excited by the pixillation technique and suggested that McLaren consider a new theme, an international one, for which there were funds. Although he did not tell McLaren, Irwin was of course referring to the Freedom Speaks money. A few days later, on seeing the Highway test rushes, McLaren saw two figures "... exchanging supernaturally violent fisticuffs".[30] McLaren recalled, "Immediately, I said to myself 'I've got it'. And my ideas took shape from there[:] Two men, friends to begin with, but whose relationship gets steadily worse until they end up fighting. The idea of the flower [over which the men fight] came shortly after that as well."[31] Thus the germ for his film *Neighbours* (1952) was created.

McLaren was passionate about the topic and *Neighbours* became the vehicle whereby he expressed his re-aroused feelings on war. In a 1977 interview, he explained, "My sympathies were divided at that time. I felt myself to be as close to the Chinese people as I felt proud of my status as a Canadian. I decided to make a really strong film about anti-militarism and against war."[32]

The paradox is that *Neighbours* – McLaren's statement concerning the futility, horror and destruction of an incremental antagonism – was funded by money which was intended to be used to show the superiority of one antagonist (the West) over the other (communism). Had McLaren known of this paradox, it would have amused him greatly and would have added to his satisfaction at *Neighbours'* success.

The success of *Neighbours* was remarkable. The stylization of movement, imagery and sound (a synthetic score was created) helped to remove the film from a specific context. Indeed, the film is a parable and assumes a universality of application. Such an obvious anti-war, anti-violence statement expressed in *Neighbours* was a brave one to make in the 1950s North America of McCarthyism and the Korean War. In that context, the film takes on the mantle of a political statement. In 1953, the film won an Oscar, which McLaren saw as a political gesture by Hollywood against the rages of McCarthyism, which was then sweeping the United States. In any case, the Oscar stimulated even greater demand for the film, whose distribution success has been long-lasting.[33] Throughout the years, *Neighbours* has been considered the film that most reflects McLaren's personal perspective on human relations.

The Influence of India

McLaren returned to Asia in May 1952, this time going to India for a year. He began in his usual thorough manner. The work he planned in India not only included the posters, picture-books, filmstrips and animated films from his previous UNESCO experience. Following the recommendations of his own UNESCO report on China, this time he envisaged making greater use of local art forms and talent; his list of work included puppet shows (using traditional Indian methods of rod-puppets, transparent-parchment shadow puppets, and glove puppets), songs, games, dances and dramatic plays with actors, as well as live-action films.[34] His topic list also was much wider-ranging. It included literacy, the telling of Indian epics, improved agricultural methods, health and hygiene, civic rights and duties, occupational methods of city workers, trade unionism, and motherhood.

Realizing that not all techniques or topics could be tackled, McLaren envisaged that the talents, needs and interests of the trainees would help determine the areas of specialty.[35] However, the selection of the projects' staff and trainees caused McLaren difficulties and misgivings. Nepotism and cronyism were aspects of the culture that he found frustrating. The appalling and massive poverty he saw also affected him and he became despairing of the attempts, both Indian and non-Indian, to alleviate it.[36] McLaren even became disenchanted with his own contribution: "I have come to feel certain that this Fundamental Education is no more than giving aspirin for an abscessed tooth. In the long run perhaps a bad thing."[37]

Nonetheless, the effects of McLaren's work in both China and India continued to find expression in his work. For example, *A Chairy Tale* (1957), which was made with Claude Jutra as co-director and with the help of Evelyn Lambart, is a parable of the exploited. Using a manipulated form of live-action, the film shows the increasingly energetic evasions of a chair which refuses to be sat upon. The Indian caste system, the plight of Chinese villagers and personal as well as social subjugation, are each implicated in the theme of *A Chairy Tale*.[38]

Indian music also had made a deep impression on McLaren: the music of *A Chairy Tale* is one obvious manifestation. McLaren invited sitar player Ravi Shankar to provide music for the film, augmenting its international appeal (with the cultural neutrality of the plain backdrop, chair and clothing). The structure of Indian music interested McLaren, who noted that "... [In Indian music] you get one germ in the raga, and that germ is developed and developed and developed. And it builds all the time ... it's just a constant build."[39] In another discussion of Hindi musical structure, he elaborates, "... it slowly keeps building up by a series of progressively more intricate and more rapid variations, until a high speed climax terminates the work".[40] This accumulative structure mirrors the form of some of McLaren's earlier films, such as *Dots* (1940), as well as later works such as the two "Lines" films (1960, 1961) and their off-shoot, *Mosaic* (1965).

As for the general consequences of his visit to India, McLaren's optimism – despite his frustration before the enormity of the social and economic problems there – remained undimmed. However, as his reservations on the effectiveness of the Fundamental Education programs imply, he came to see his contribution to society as being within the NFB and that is precisely where he spent the further 31 years of his professional life.

Conclusion

Through those 31 years, McLaren's film output oscillated between abstract films and those that displayed social concerns. The socially-oriented films continued to depict conflict, although the concern of the later films such as *Pas de deux* (1969) and *Narcissus* (1981) shifts towards an inner-conflict. As well, McLaren wanted his films to be understood internationally and so he eliminated, reduced or avoided culturally or nationally specific aspects of film.[41] Early in his career, he identified movement as film's most important element; national, regional and cultural reductionism helped to further distill his films.

McLaren's concern for the positive and international effect of his work is clearly displayed in the following anecdote: "A few years ago, ... I found our title department making the title for *Neighbours* in several different African languages. It turned out they wanted to show the film to a number of warring tribes with the hope of convincing them of the futility of war. That's the kind of recognition I most appreciate."[42]

Of all his fifty or so films, *Neighbours* was the film that gave McLaren most satisfaction and it was the one which he most wished to save for posterity.[43] McLaren believed that any art which carried the quality of "... a consciousness of the human intelligence, of the human spirit, that man is a social creature" was necessarily superior to non-referential or abstract art.[44] This point was further underscored by the criteria to be used for McGill University's Norman McLaren Award and by the words Norman spoke when he accepted the inaugural award in April 1986. The award was to be "presented annually to the student whose work demonstrates similar social concerns to those of Norman McLaren".[45] And in his acceptance speech McLaren said, "I had a lasting social conscience and feeling about the humanity around me and I have felt very frustrated, often, at never being able to do much about it in my films ...".[46] In part, modesty probably accounts for McLaren's apparent disregard for his socially-conscious films, such as *A Chairy Tale* and *Neighbours*.

Clearly, McLaren felt a strong desire to assist fellow humanity and to make a difference, preferably a practical one, in people's lives. His UNESCO projects in Asia reflect this desire. McLaren's work was judged successful in that he established a prototype for other projects.[47] More importantly, he demonstrated a flexibility and willingness to adapt to and make use of the local community's attitudes and resources. In terms of his own work, McLaren's experiences in Asia re-awoke his long-dormant social and political concerns, thereby inspiring some of his major filmic statements. 🍎

Notes

1. The career paths of McLaren and Grierson crossed on a number of important occasions. For an account of these occasions and their implications see: Terence Dobson, "McLaren and Grierson: Intersections", *Screening the Past* November 1999.
   URL: http://www.latrobe.edu.au/www/screeningthepast/index.html

2. Norman McLaren, recollections in Gavin Millar, *The Eye Hears, the Ear Sees*, NFB/BBC Film, 1970.

3. McLaren, in Millar, *The Eye Hears*.

4. McLaren, in Guy Glover, *McLaren* (Montreal: NFB, 1980), 10.

5. As the obligation to make films with war-time messages ceased, and as his commitment to accepting films commissioned from elsewhere in the NFB diminished (e.g. the series of films he did which were centered on French Canadian folk songs), McLaren's immediate post-war output became more clearly abstract, culminating in *Begone Dull Care*. This astonishing film, which he and assistant Evelyn Lambart did in association with the jazz pianist Oscar Peterson, achieves an energetic fusion of Peterson's jazz with painting directly on the film.

6. McLaren, letter to his mother, 1 May 1949: 2. Grierson Archives, University of Stirling, GAA: 31:63.

7. Gary Evans, *In the National Interest: A Chronicle of the National Film Board of Canada, 1949–1989*, unpublished manuscript (1990), 23–24, 26–27, subsequently published by University of Toronto Press, Toronto, in 1991.

8. 'Poster' films is how Grierson described McLaren's work of the war years, which contained messages (for War Bonds, for example) at the very end. It should be remembered that the poster film messages were in line with the government's then war-efforts (albeit the non-violent aspects) and supportive of Canada.

9. Norman McLaren as quoted in Gerald Hawkins, 'Liberty Profile: Norman McLaren', *Liberty* 18 (January 1947).

10. Various colleagues of McLaren have each independently attested to his integrity. Rene Jodoin, personal interview, 5 November 1990; Colin Low, personal interview, 9 November 1990; Robert Verrall, personal interview, 14 November 1990.

11. McLaren's time in China coincided with the final stages of the civil war, which was between communist and anti-communist forces.

12. Norman McLaren, letter to his mother, 1 May 1949: 2.

13. Norman McLaren, "Preface", *The Healthy Village: An Experiment in Visual Education in Western China*, Monographs in Fundamental Education 5, Art Department Report (Paris: UNESCO, 1951).

14. In June, just before he had left for China, he submitted his report to UNESCO: Norman McLaren, *How to Make Movies Without a Camera* (Paris: UNESCO, 1949).

15. McLaren, *The Healthy Village*, 49.

16. McLaren, *The Healthy Village*, 50.

17. McLaren, *The Healthy Village*, 49.

18. McLaren, *The Healthy Village*, 49.

19. McLaren, *The Healthy Village*, 80–82.

20. McLaren, *The Healthy Village*, 84.

21. McLaren, *The Healthy Village*, 92.

22. These labor-saving methods, deriving from Disney-type production methods, are described and acknowledged by McLaren, *The Healthy Village*, 88–92.

23. McLaren, *The Healthy Village*, 94.

24. McLaren, *The Healthy Village*, 83.

25. Norman McLaren, Diary, 24 October 1949: 3–4. Grierson Archives, University of Stirling, GAA: 31: 63.

26. McLaren's account of the liberation of the town by the Communists reveals his appreciation of the absurd as well as the peaceful transformation to communist rule of this bit of China. As the communist's Red Army advanced, the anti-Communist Nationalist forces had evacuated the area. Left to their own devices, the town's civilian authorities decided to give the Red Army a rapturous, banner-strewn welcome. At the correct time, the streets were lined not only with bunting but also crowds of excited school children. Instead of the anticipated triumphant battalions of Red Army troops, the town's liberators drove by in only one solitary truck. Norman McLaren, "I Saw the Chinese Reds Take Over", *McLeans* (15 October 1950), 73–75.

27. McLaren, "I Saw the Chinese Reds Take Over", 76.

28. Evans, 53.

29. Evans, 47.

30. Evans, 54.

31. Norman McLaren as quoted in "Interview", *Norman McLaren: Exhibition and Films* (Edinburgh: Scottish Arts Council, 1977), 28.

32. McLaren, "Interview", 28.

33. In the NFB's complete film-booking figures up to 1987, *Neighbours* comes out as the NFB's most popular film ever, with 108,000 bookings at home and abroad. Evans, 71.

34. Norman McLaren, Statement Delhi, 23 November 1952: p. 1. Grierson Archives University of Stirling, GAA: 31: 78.

35. McLaren, Statement Delhi 1.

36. Norman McLaren, Statement Delhi 1, and letter to Jack and Joan (McLaren), 18 December 1952, Grierson Archives, University of Stirling, GAA: 31: 86.

37. McLaren, Statement Delhi 1.

38. McLaren, in "Interview" 72, mentioned the film was also a reaction to being sat upon by friends.

39. McLaren as quoted in Donald McWilliams and Susan Huycke, *Creative Process: Norman McLaren*, dir. Donald McWilliams, NFB, 1991, script 14.

40. McLaren as quoted in Donald McWilliams, *Creative Process*, proposal July 1985 35, NFB Archives 10.

41. These are detailed in: Terence Dobson, "Norman McLaren and Internationalism", paper delivered at the 9th Australian and New Zealand History and Film Conference, Brisbane, November 1998.

42. McLaren as quoted in Susan Carson, "Bore People? Fat Chance, Norman McLaren", *Toronto Telegram Weekend Magazine*, 30 March 1974: 20–21.

43. McLaren in Maynard Collins, *Norman McLaren* (Ottawa: Canadian Film Institute, 1976) 69, and in *Creative Process: Norman McLaren*, script 28.

44. Norman McLaren as quoted in *Creative Process*, proposal 35.

45. *Creative Process* dir. Donald McWilliams, 1st Assembly, (film) 1989.

46. McLaren speaking in *Creative Process* 1st Assembly, (film).

47. *Creative Process*, script 28.

Dobson, Terence. "Norman McLaren: His UNESCO Work in Asia", *Animation Journal* 8:2 (Spring 2000). 4–17. ©2000 Terence Dobson

5

Conventions versus Clichés

Patrick Drazen [2003]

Anime is supposed to make the audience feel something. This chapter looks at why fans feel what they feel: visual, auditory, and social conventions from Japanese daily life embedded in anime.

Every once in a while anime discussion groups on the Web get choked with run-downs of the "clichés" of anime. It may not be the most overworked word in discussions of the topic, but it is certainly the most misunderstood. Before we proceed any further, we need to understand why.

Art does not exist in a vacuum; its time and place determine the aesthetics the work can get away with. And for art to be considered acceptable by its audience (and this is true whether talking high or pop art), it has to be recognizable as art. How? By embodying the rules pertaining to that work in that time and place.

Let's not kid ourselves: art is defined by its rules. Only in recent decades, with the likes of seemingly random artists like Jackson Pollock, has art without rules even been a concept, much less a possibility. Pop culture, to be popular, avoids the avant-garde, which by definition sets out to break the rules, to lead rather than follow, and to upset the bourgeoisie at every turn. Changes in culture are usually incremental rather than wholesale; rules are amended rather than abandoned.

We tend to forget this, since history changes our perspective. Beethoven was an innovator, writing Romantic music while the Classical school was still in vogue. However, he developed Romanticism by modifying Classicism, not by throwing it out altogether. Only a few avant-gardists have gone for the sweeping change, and their names are seldom remembered. Few remember Harry Partch, the composer who decided that the "well-tempered" scale of the Western musical tradition was no longer interesting – he redivided the octave and, because most musical instruments couldn't adjust, invented his own. ...

The point of this digression is to recognize that the word "convention" has positive connotations and the word "cliché" has negative connotations, but not everyone who uses the words understands why. A gesture, a plot-point, a speech, or a bit of business – these are not necessarily clichés simply because they are used a lot. In some circumstances, these often-used devices still have the power to thrill and amuse and move an audience.

Attending the Conventions

Take one of the most popular ballads of nineteenth-century America: "Home Sweet Home". In and of itself, the song is, to a modern audience, corny and saccharine, and playing it while looking at a character's home could be considered trite and unimaginative. Yet that same song, in a scratchy turn-of- the-century gramophone recording, is played near the end of *Hotaru no Haka (Grave of the Fireflies)* as the camera surveys for the last time the swampy home of the two dead children. The moment is definitely not a cliché, crowded as it is with so many messages to the audience, not the least of which is: They would never have been driven to this place were it not for American bombing and adult indifference.

Therefore, and let's keep the distinction clear:

A *convention* is an acceptable device that is intrinsically part of the narrative or character design, and which, although old, can still be used in fresh ways.

A *cliché* takes the place of creativity. Clichés are used by lazy and untalented artists to finish off a work, rather than finding fresh uses for the conventions that inform the work at its best.

An example: in any given swordfight, from *Ruroni Kenshin* and *Utena* all the way back through live-action samurai epics to Dr. Tezuka's gender-bender swashbuckler *Princess Knight*, there is a standardized bit of choreography. The opponents start separated by some distance. They run full-tilt at each other, pass by each other in such a way that you can't tell if anyone was even hit, and then stand dead still in a dramatic pause. It takes another second or two to reveal the damage.

When used creatively, or sincerely (meaning with a complete reliance on the validity of this device as a part of telling the story, without tongue in cheek, and without looking for a quick expedient to meet a deadline), this does not become a cliché. Look at the first duel in the first episode of *Utena* (1997). Saionji tries to slice a flower from Utena's coat with a mystical saber. Utena showed up for the duel armed only with a wooden practice sword. In spite of the mismatch, you know who will win. However, the action is nonetheless exciting. Another example: this choreography is also used in the 1988 film *Akira*, except that motorcycles replace the swords in a high-speed game of chicken. The convention only becomes a cliché through overuse or when used by the numbers.

At the end of Rumiko Takahashi's *Maison Ikkoku* (1988), Yusaku Godai finally marries his beautiful widowed landlady, Kyoko Otonashi. If that were the sum total of the story, it would be a cliché: a predictable ending that was just sitting in the wings, waiting for its cue to come onstage. However, in the manga form of the story, Takahashi stretched the courtship over seven years, and the reader (and viewer of the anime series) saw it end in an amazing inversion of stereotyped gender roles: Kyoko continues to be the building manager, while her husband works in the otherwise completely feminine world of day-care.

The Sound of Anime

Maison Ikkoku is one of the more interesting anime series in its use of conventional symbols and cues; the shorthand, as it were, of Japanese cartoons. These things communicate to an audience in the know, and baffle those who don't know. For example, an exterior shot of the boarding house often has a weird horn sounding in the background. A Japanese audience recognizes not only what it is (the horn traditionally blown by a tofu-maker at close of business) but when it is (late afternoon) and where it is (the Nakano neighborhood of Tokyo, where Takahashi lived as a college student and the location of the building that inspired the series).[1] But the viewer never sees the tofu-maker; we just hear the horn. Through sheer repetition, a Western viewer may only pick up the fact that the scene with a horn takes place in the afternoon.

Another example of the creative use of a sonic convention is in the entire *Evangelion* series, begun in 1995.

Many of the outdoor scenes, including establishing shots of Misato's apartment building, take place with the droning of insects in the background. In fact, it is the sound of cicadas, noisy little insects that assert themselves in Japan every summer. However, they are exclusively summer insects. Evangelion features their buzzing week after week, month after month. To someone who was only used to hearing them for a short time each year, this is profoundly discomforting. In the plot, this reflects the changed climate of Japan after the Second Impact, when the Earth shifted on its axis and Japan's climate became permanently tropical. The constant hum of cicadas is a reminder to the viewer (at least, the viewer who knows cicadas) that this is a world in which something has gone horribly wrong.

Listing all the elements of anime shorthand and their meanings would take a separate volume, but there are a few broad conventions that absolutely must be understood at the beginning. Many of these conventions began in manga and carry over to anime.

Inside the Lines

Perhaps the most distinctive convention is the tendency, in moments of action or high emotion, for the background to vanish entirely. Instead, we see broad sweeping lines suggesting speed or power. This device focuses our attention on the character, but also cues us that the character is engaged in a major struggle or effort. Examples abound; it is a rare anime that does not have such a scene.

This character focus is linked in part to a storytelling element of both anime and manga: the preference for long story-arcs. This kind of storytelling not only allows for elaborate plot development, but for character development as well. In anime, the latter is usually the more important. People who watch anime expect to see characters grow and change and react to stress. The reactions can be subtle or raving, but in any event the focus is on the character. When the background vanishes, that focus becomes literal.

Loose Lips

The second example of an anime convention is the apparent lack of naturalness in the movement of a speaking character's mouth. For those who were raised solely on Disney theatrical animation (as opposed to their recent made-for-television animated series), the staccato up-and-down mouth movements of anime characters is fake-looking.

You are left feeling even more uneasy when, watching a subtitled anime and hearing the original Japanese dialogue, you realize that the mouth movements still don't precisely match the spoken words. What kind of shoddy workmanship is this?

It's not shoddiness. It's not even universal, since some studios are more conscientious than others about matching lip movements to spoken words. There are, in any case, several reasons why this might be so.

It s just different over there. Hiroki Hayashi has directed one of the most popular of all anime, *Tenchi Muyo*, as well as *Bubblegum Crisis* 2040.[2] He also worked as an artist on the American series *Thundercats.* As he pointed out recently:

> In an American series the dialogue is written and then recorded first and the pictures are done to go along with it. This is different in Japanese [sic], where pictures are done first and then the voices are recorded afterwards ... . Generally we only use three pictures [of mouth movements] for when the character is talking, as opposed to in the American series, in which we had to do eight.[3]

Earlier media. Before television and mass distribution of magazines, one classic type of Japanese storyteller was the *kami-shibai* man. He would set up an easel with a series of drawings that he used as illustrations for his stories, supplying the various voices and sound effects himself.[4] In that case, in the unmoving mouths of Bunraku puppets, and in Noh theater, in which the protagonists usually wear masks, Japan has a history of giving the audience mouths that move without speaking or speech from a mouth that doesn't move.

Western examples. Most Western television animation actually has the same problem. Yogi Bear's mouth movements are not much more precise than Speed Racer's. Indicting the entire medium because of this convention is petty at best.

Eastern preference. Here again, we find a priority on the emotional life of the character, with less concern as to whether the cartoon is technically perfect. Anime voice actress and pop singer Megumi

Hayashibara tells in her autobiography (published in manga format) of classes she took to prepare for voice work. "The most important thing for a voice actor is not to try and match the voice [to the mouth movements], but to get as close as possible to the way the character feels."[5] In any event, the erratic lip-synching is fairly easy to get used to, and does not take away from the enjoyment of watching anime.

Do Blondes Have More Fun?

Another convention to note traces back to the early twentieth century. During the Meiji period (1868–1912), Japan ended two centuries of isolation from the rest of the world by discarding many of its traditional ways. Anything modern was automatically "in", and anything Western was by definition modern. So newspaper comic strips began in Japan by copying Western characters, and animation followed suit decades later. The result was a string of characters that looked "white" or had "blonde" hair, even if they were ethnically Japanese. It has literally taken decades before the recent crop of manga artists, born after World War II, began to draw Asians that look Asian. In the meantime, a character like Sailor Moon can be understood by Japanese viewers to *be* Japanese, her blonde hair notwithstanding.

Get Real

A fourth convention is connected to the third, and goes back to the 1960s, when artistic styles in manga began expanding beyond the cartoony look of the postwar years. Manga fans who grew up to be the next generation of artists began to choose either to keep to the older style in emulation of Dr. Tezuka, Reiji Matsumoto, Shotaro Ishinomori, Ryoko

Ikeda and other major names, or to surpass them and work in a more realistic style. This "realistic" style actually ranged from caricature to hyperrealism and everything in between. The new style even rated its own name – *gekiga* (drama pictures) – to distinguish it from manga. The bottom line is that anime shows the same range, from the highly detailed to the blatantly cartoony. In recent years, a trend has arisen to take realistic, even serious, characters, and submit them to caricature as "little kid" versions of themselves. These are sometimes called SD (for "super-deformed") or CB (which means either "child body" or *chibi* – "shorty", "runt"). These letters in a title usually mean comedy ahead.

Body Talk

Other manga/anime conventions are more culturally specific to Japan. These include:

- Scratching the back of the head when embarrassed
- The appearance of a giant drop of sweat (not to be mistaken for a teardrop) or the apparent outline of a large X on a character's temple in times of stress
- Blood gushing from the nose when sexually aroused
- A large bubble of phlegm coming from a character's nose denoting that the character is asleep.
- Extending a fist with the pinky finger stretched straight out is a gesture (usually by a male) to indicate that the speaker or the subject of the sentence "got lucky".[6]

All of these conventional gestures cue the audience not only as to what is happening (or about to happen), but also how to feel about it, by invoking similar situations in previous anime. Far from being "spoilers" about the plot, they are in their own way reassuring.

There is a still shot during the opening credits of *Princess Nine*, a 1999 series about a girls baseball team challenging their male counterparts, that demonstrates this quite nicely. The series is built around Ryo Kawasaki, a fifteen-year-old pitching phenomenon who apparently inherited her fiery left-handed style from her father, who was also a professional-class pitcher (and who was killed in a traffic accident when Ryo was five). The scene shows Ryo's face, caked with dirt and streaked with tears, under the stadium lights – but they are tears of joy, as she looks toward Heaven. Anyone who's seen any sports manga or anime at all knows what's happening: the battle is over, the hard-fought victory is won, and she is communing with her father in Heaven.

If handled casually or cynically, this scene would not carry half the power it does. Instead, it's a cue to the audience that, despite the hurdles Ryo has to face, both athletically and personally, right will prevail.[7] It's a reassurance that the audience needs to hear more and more, ironically enough, as it gets older and has to cope with the complexities of Japanese society. 🍎

Notes

1. See Toren Smith, "Princess of the Manga", *Amazing Heroes* 165 (15 May 1989): 23

2. This is the 1999 made-for-television series, revisiting the OAV series of the 1980s directed by Katsuhito Akiyama.

3. From an interview with Geoffrey Tebbetts, *Animerica* 7, no. 8: 15, 33.

4. Frederik L. Schodt, *Manga! Manga!: The World of Japanese Comics* (Tokyo: Kodansha International, 1983), 62.

5. http://www.nnanime.com/ megumi-toon/mgbko22.html

6. An illustration of this gesture is an episode of the manga *Maison Ikkoku*. Due to a misunderstanding, Godai has checked out of the boarding house; by the time that error is cleared up, another one pops up and Kyoko refuses to rent his old room back to him. His search for someplace to stay takes him to the apartment of his college friend Sakamoto. Godai knocks on the door; he hears some running and thumping inside the apartment. The door opens a crack to show Sakamoto's face and his hand with outstretched pinky. The message is clear: "I've got a girl in here and we're a little busy right now ... " It would be awkward to have to say that in so many words, and an embarrassment to the girl. With a gesture, the meaning is communicated wordlessly.

7. The personal arena alone can get quite complicated; a mere romantic triangle is rather simple geometry these days. In *Princess Nine*, for example, Ryo soon finds herself having to choose between the Boy Next Door and the Baseball Phenom at the high school that has recruited her; the Baseball Phenom, meanwhile, is being set up in the media to be the beau of the school's Tennis Phenom ... and so it goes.

Drazen, Patrick. "Conventions versus Clichés". *Anime Explosion! The What? Why? & Wow! of Japanese Animation.* Berkeley, CA: Stone Bridge Press, 2003. 16–27. Edited

6

My Neighbor Totoro

Helen McCarthy [1999]

Not so very long ago, two little girls and their father moved into a beautiful old house in the Japanese countryside. With their mother ill in the hospital and their father busy at work, Mei and her big sister Satsuki soon find themselves in a world of wonders, where cuddly creatures called Totoros can soar on spinning tops above the world, tiny seeds can turn into huge trees, and buses shaped like cats bound across the countryside completely unseen by grownups. Nature and imagination work their magic for Mei and Satsuki when they most need help and comfort, showing them how powerful and how precious the beautiful world around us is.

Origins

As with the projects that were to become *Castle in the Sky* and *Princess Mononoke,* the idea that was to grow into *My Neighbor Totoro* was first pitched to Tokuma [Shoten] in the early 1980s but was rejected. However, Miyazaki places the origins of the story long before then. He said in an interview in *Animerica* magazine that, *"Totoro* is where my consciousness begins", and told his friend, the famous novelist and cultural historian Ryutaro Shiba, that the central figure of Totoro

was a figment of his imagination, inspired by his childish imaginings of fearsome creatures living in the forest.[1]

It was a struggle to get the green light on the project in 1987. Producer Toshio Suzuki says that when he first showed the sketches for the character of Totoro to the finance and distribution executives, the men in suits didn't think the furry giant could take off, literally or figuratively. He thinks this is because Totoro's appeal doesn't wake until you see him in motion, animated on the screen.[2] (Ryutaro Shiba agreed with him, telling Miyazaki that he had been struck by the way the big Totoro's belly ripples as he sleeps, just like a living creature's.)[3] Suzuki, an expert at surmounting obstacles, came up with a unique pitch. He proposed that the film should form a double bill with a production for publisher Shinchosa. If a film were made of their book *Grave of the Fireflies,* a novel of childhood suffering by a survivor of the fire-bombings in World War II, school classes would be taken to see it because of its historical content, and that same audience would then stay on to see another movie on the double bill. Shinchosa wanted to break into movies and was not too worried about losing money to do so; this was an ideal opportunity for them. *Grave of the Fireflies* would be directed for the screen by Miyazaki's colleague Isao Takahata.

It was far from an ideal pairing; *Grave* is a dark, demanding piece aimed at somewhat older viewers, and Suzuki was worried about the impact each film would have on the other's intended audience. There was also the problem that animation based on Japanese contemporary experience wasn't exactly big box-office at the time. Distributors simply didn't believe there was an audience for a story about two little girls and a monster in modern Japan. [4] And the pairing meant that two feature films had to be completed at the same time. Studio Ghibli was breaking new ground in a number of directions. Suzuki simply hoped for the best.

As it turned out, things went better than he could have dreamed. At first, *My Neighbor Totoro* performed respectably but not superbly at the box office. A little merchandise was generated, but there was no hint of the tidal wave to come. In 1990 Studio Ghibli yielded to persistent requests to license a range of cuddly toys based on the film, opening the floodgates for a massive merchandising success. Profits from subsidiary rights on *Totoro* alone soon reached a level where they could sustain the studio year in and year out. [5] In America fans began to wonder when the film would reach the States, since it was so obviously a perfect vehicle for the merchandise-obsessed U.S. market, but Studio Ghibli was in no mood to repeat the experience of *Warriors of the Wind*. It took until 1993 for rights to be licensed to 50th Street Films for American theatrical release – and Fox Lorber for video – and the deal was done by Tokuma, not Ghibli. Even then, there were no merchandise rights attached,

though Suzuki told me that this was more owing to American concerns than Japanese. Apparently, U.S. companies wanted to edit out two sequences – the bathtub sequence and the early scene where the two girls amuse themselves by jumping around on the tatami mats in the old house – because they felt these sequences were unlikely to be understood by American audiences. Still smarting from what they and their Western audience perceived as the butchery *of Nausicaa of the Valley of the Winds,* Studio Ghibli insisted that no cuts be made. Obviously, no sensible company was going to put large amounts of money into merchandising a film it thought its audience would find culturally alienating.

As American video sales began their climb past the half-million mark and the promotional offer of a cuddly blue Totoro toy was massively oversubscribed, the mistake became just as obvious. Roger Ebert gave the film a rave review in the *Siskel and Ebert at the Movies* syndicated show; Gene Siskel took longer to be won over, finally capitulating after seeing the film in the company of children. In America as in Japan, the initial press wasn't uniformly ecstatic – some found the movie's pace too slow and its simplicity too boring – but a number of big guns like the *New York Times* came out in favor. The movie's potential to cross the line from cult favorite to Western children's hit was beyond question. By 1996, when the Disney-Tokuma deal was made public, the question on fans' lips was, How long before the Mouse finally teams up with Totoro? It's a question that still has to be answered.

The Fox dub of *My Neighbor Totoro* was not, in fact, commissioned specifically for the U.S. video market. Tokuma had previously commissioned a dub from Carl Macek of Streamline Pictures for showing on trans-Pacific flights of Japan Airlines. The translated script had been submitted for Miyazaki's personal approval and amendment prior to recording, and it was this dub that was released by Fox.[6] The dub also had an airing in the U.K. prior to its U.S. release, when the movie was shown at the Barbican Cinema in London in the summer of 1991 as part of the Japan Festival, a nationwide program of events celebrating every aspect of Japanese culture.

It took exactly a year to complete *My Neighbor Totoro,* starting in April 1987. Miyazaki knew that he wanted to make a warm film, something that stood apart from the confrontational kids-against-adults stories of so many Japanese animated works, a film that would not fill a young audience's minds with conflict and struggle.[7] Yet, when he had to get the story down on paper, his mind went blank. A social visit to a colleague shortly before production was due to start saved the day. Miyazaki often mentions books or articles that he saw by chance that later proved to be potent sources of inspiration. It had happened on *Castle in the Sky,* and it happened again when he picked up his colleague's copy of the *Mainichi Graph* supplement entitled *Japan Forty Years Ago.*[8] He decided to return to the pastoral innocence of a country childhood before the advent of television and before the expansion of Tokyo had consumed so much of the rural landscape, sometime around the end of the 1950s. 9

This, of course, was the time in which he grew up. A war baby, he entered his teens in the mid-1950s, lived in the area around Tokyo, and could clearly remember the kind of landscape he was describing. But there was an even more personal link between his life and his movie, since his mother had been hospitalized or bedridden with spinal tuberculosis for most of his childhood. We are never explicitly told the nature of Mother's illness in the movie version of *My Neighbor Totoro* (though in Miyazaki's novelization of the movie, the illness is explicitly named as tuberculosis), but the Shichikokuyama Hospital in which she is being treated was a real-life center of excellence for the treatment of tuberculosis at the time, and little Mei is around the same age as the young Hayao was when his mother first became ill. At the time, tuberculosis could and often did kill. For all its sunny optimism, the movie expresses the dread of loss that a very young child cannot articulate, from the heart of one who remembers its power.

The setting also had resonance for the grown-up Miyazaki, who lives in Tokorozawa City in Saitama Prefecture where the movie is set. It's now a bedroom suburb of Tokyo, but at the time the story took place it was a farming community set in the Sayama Hills. Parts of the region still have remnants of woodland, and Miyazaki has given and continues to give support to an organization dedicated to the preservation of the remaining ancient forests. They have raised funds to buy the forested land they call Totoro's Forest, and Miyazaki has donated artwork to be used for fundraising as well as a substantial cash gift to the cause of forest preservation. (Some visitors to the forest are said to be extremely disappointed that they don't see any Totoros, but all have an opportunity to appreciate the natural beauty around them.)

Once he started work, the ideas flowed fast. Early on in the writing process, the story revolved around one red-haired six-year-old girl, but as time went on Miyazaki changed the cast to feature two sisters ages four and ten. The small sister kept the auburn ponytails of her precursor, and Tokuma has since caused some confusion for fans by using early preproduction drawings of the first character to publicize the completed movie in which she does not appear. In June 1987, talking to Hong Kong magazine *A-Club,* Miyazaki said that the production was "already a quarter done" and described the Totoros and the Catbus in some detail. He referred to Totoros as "nature spirits" of the same kind as those familiar in Japanese religion, but despite the film's setting at a time when traditional values still held firm, and despite the elements of Japan's religious culture used on screen, he was adamant that "this movie has nothing to do with that or any other religion".[10] And although determined not to create conflict between children and adults in this work, he was equally determined that the movie should be set in a child's world. Only children can see Totoros and their fellow spirits, and children and spirits can understand each other without the need for words.

Miyazaki says he makes movies primarily for entertainment, and doesn't try to give his audience any particular message. Yet in *My Neighbor Totoro,* it seems to me that he is making a statement. The title tells us that humans and the rest of nature are neighbors; we should strive to be good ones, or the relationship between us will break down. Look, Miyazaki seems to say, at this beautiful country. This was ours not so long ago. Japan is very beautiful and the world is very beautiful, but we can't take it for granted. Be careful.

Art and Technique

The dominant image of the movie is the largest Totoro, called O-Totoro (King Totoro) in Japanese and Big Totoro in the existing U.S. release. There are elements of a number of creatures of nature and folklore in its makeup. It is related to the tanuki, the Japanese raccoon, with its playful spirit and magical powers. There are also links to the owl – its round eyes, its arrow-marked chest, and its hooting song, which was rescored by composer Jo Hisaishi onto the film soundtrack, played on the ocarina. The cat, long credited with shape-shifting ability in Japanese legend, lent some genes to the Totoros and their companion the Catbus. Lewis Carroll, creator of *Alice in Wonderland,* threw some elements into the mix for both – the ability to vanish at will and the huge, infectious grin. Many adult Totoro lovers also find that Big Totoro's comforting bulk and warm, uncritical nature bring back delightful memories of their favorite childhood teddy bear.

With *My Neighbor Totoro,* more than with any other of his works, Miyazaki is his own strongest influence. Reaching back into his youthful memories, he accessed both the most painful and the most joyous portions of childhood. He also paid homage to some of his favorite scenes from children's literature. Little Mei's fall down the tunnel in the camphor tree into Totoro's nest is another homage to Lewis Carroll. The two rides in the Catbus strongly reminded me of C. S. Lewis's description of Susan and Lucy's ride through Narnia on Aslan's back in *The Lion, the Witch and the Wardrobe.* I can never see the sisters swaying happily on the fur-covered seats with the rhythm of the Catbus's twelve-legged stride without thinking of Lewis's passionate evocation of rough fur and soft footfalls padding through the blossoming glory of summer woods. Yet the magic that suffuses Narnia is different, more a subversion of nature than a celebration of it. Mei and Satsuki are not a pair of princesses riding on the back of Christ in a neo-Dionysian post-sacrificial celebration; they are a pair of ordinary children on a bus ride to see their mother and go home again. Miyazaki's magic does not need to take us into a hidden kingdom to show us wonders.

Lewis placed religion at the heart of his created universe; *My Neighbor Totoro*'s plot deliberately sidelines religion in favor of nature. Because it's set in Japan, the trappings of rural religious tradition are clearly visible, but as far as the plot is concerned, they're decorative, not functional. Miyazaki uses religious iconography to send one clear signal, which will be lost on most American audiences: when Mei is lost, she sits at the feet of a row of statues. They are dedicated to a traditional Japanese deity who protects children, and this sends a subliminal message to the audience that she will be safe. Elsewhere in the movie are roadside shrines to which the characters pay the respect that good manners and tradition demand. There are statues of foxes and protective deities, Shinto shrine gates, and ritual cords of rice straw and paper streamers around the trunk of the camphor tree, but none of this affects Totoro and the Catbus or the daily life of the forest creatures. Religion is a human construct and has nothing to do with nature. Nature spirits live outside it, creatures of simple goodwill who mean no harm.

The forest in which the movie takes place is firmly set in the real world, even though its world has now vanished. But like the movie's story it also has other, less tangible roots. It is an allegory of pastoral perfection, the longing for which goes all the way back to classical Greece and Rome when sophisticated writers and poets yearned for the peace and simplicity of rural life, and praised the simple virtues though their practice had been abandoned by most wealthy urbanites. Chinese literati were saying much the same thing long before the birth of Christ. That yearning has echoed through the literary ages in both Eastern and Western traditions.

American scholar Harold Bloom described *As You Like It* as the sweetest-tempered of Shakespeare's plays and its heroines as fortunate in living in an idyllic forest world in which "no authentic harm" could come to them.[11] Totoro's forest is just such a place of peace and simplicity, and from that peace and simplicity the movie derives its sweetness of temper. The forest is perfectly poised at the point in history in which a small community can live comfortably and safely amid its wonders but still marvel at them and show no desire to dominate them or wipe them out. One could describe it as the balance point between *Princess Mononoke* and *Nausicaa,* before population pressure causes domestic exploitation to tip into wholesale destruction.

Though nature and its spirits can express themselves in hurricanes and howling winds, the struggle and spite of human society are unknown to them, and the natural cycle of life and death is essentially a cycle of goodwill. No harm will come to our two heroines in the forest's sunlit glades and mysterious shadows. They may be afraid sometimes when they glimpse the power and majesty around them, but it is the scale of the power itself they fear. They know instinctively that nature has no malice.

Like Satsuki's and Mei's childhood, the delicate balance of forest and farmland cannot last. The adult in the audience knows that in a few more years Tokyo will swamp the small fields and quiet lanes, while the child in the adult is glad that Miyazaki has kept them alive and beautiful, giving us, whatever happens to our world, the key to the door into summer.

Commentary

My Neighbor Totoro possesses one of the strongest critical commendations in film history: it was among the relatively few Japanese films on director Akira Kurosawa's list of his hundred best movies of all time, along with such world classics as *Gloria* and *My Darling Clementine*. Kurosawa[12] said he was very moved by the film, and particularly loved the Catbus, but he also lamented that all the talents he wanted to see in the movie industry had gone into animation. There are, it is true, not enough fine directors of film, but there are even fewer fine directors of animation. Anyone who can make a movie as honest, beautiful, and benign as *My Neighbor Totoro* must be cherished, because movies like this are very, very rare. In animation, though, they're even rarer. Miyazaki is one of the few contemporary makers of animation who truly respects his audience, his material, and his medium.

My Neighbor Totoro exhibits a level of attention to detail that is exceptional even in the Ghibli canon. I've watched the movie many times, and every time 1 find my attention caught by fleeting moments of perfection. Most recently, 1 was struck by a two-second shot in the opening sequence of the little family's arrival at their new home. We cut from a wide view of flooded rice paddies being tended and scenes of the day-to-day activity of a fanning community to a close-up view of water gleaming as it runs quietly over a stone in a little stream. That tiny image shows a level of technical mastery that commands respect – the convincing naturalistic animation of water is a difficult task, and one at which Ghibli excels. More importantly, it sets up a link between the particular and the general, between the little natural stream and the ordered work of the farmers, between beauty and utility. And most important of all, it makes you catch your breath at its simple, perfect loveliness.

There are many such naturalistic images to marvel at. In the sequence in which the girls meet their neighbor Totoro at the bus stop, a golden brown toad is allowed to take its own time in progressing across the frame, and grounds that marvelous encounter with a huge final belch, its gaping mouth echoing Totoro's own smile. As a long afternoon fades, a snail crawls up a grass stem, perfect against the golden light. Mei bends over the garden pool and is enchanted, like us, by the irrepressible wriggle of tadpoles through the water. In Nanny's garden, a basket of vegetables put into the stream to cool is hauled out glistening, making our mouths water in anticipation of the ripe meat of the tomatoes and the crispness of the cucumbers. And which artist painstakingly practiced scratching a message on a corn husk, to be able to render it so perfectly in the last hospital scene? The everyday magic of life is depicted with a depth of love and respect that cannot help but touch the most determined urbanite.

The other magic, the mystery of nature and its legendary manifestations, is linked with this through a series of images that, by accepting the presence of the supernatural as part of the natural, make us accept it on the level of a child. Seeing as the young protagonists see is a vital step toward entering Totoro's world, and Miyazaki uses the contrast between darkness and light effectively to blur the boundaries between the real and the mysterious, the predictable and the uncertain. When the light floods in to the darkened attic upstairs, we can see the little bits of darkness fleeing into the corners, and share the girls' fascination with the dust bunnies. Darkness under our control is fascinating, even charming. When Satsuki steps outside the back door at night to get some more fuel for the boiler that's heating the bathwater, the wind rushes wildly across the grass, and for a few moments the familiar landscape is transformed into something strange and menacing. Its shape shifts out of the natural and toward the formless, and its colors are subdued and changed by the darkness so that instead of grass and sky and solid ground we might be surrounded by deep water or the swirling nothingness of a nightmare. Darkness all around us, out of control, can be scary. Kazuo Oga's wonderful backgrounds are as effective at conveying abstraction as hyper-realism.

Jo Hisaishi's score is a work of magic. Taking elements as disparate as playground songs and orchestral chorales, he has created a perfect counterpoint to the film's visual splendors. There is much playfulness – the Catbus theme is an eight-bar boogie-woogie any jazzman could pick up on and relish, and the opening theme is infuriatingly infectious. I can testify to this: returning from a visit to Studio Ghibli, I was crossing a road in Shinjuku in the evening rush hour when a boy of about seven and his sister, perhaps a couple of years older, passed me going the other way. As we drew level, the boy sang out the first few lines of the Totoro opening theme loud and clear.

Hisaishi's score also demonstrates that he understands the power of silence, a much neglected element in contemporary Western cinema. The whole soundtrack is well planned in this regard. The relationship of natural background sounds, such as wind and the chirping of crickets, dialogue, and music, is perfectly balanced to enhance the imagery. Just as places and objects can be changed by darkness, so can sound. Is that an owl hooting, or a spirit playing its clay pipe in the treetops? Is that rustling in the attic a squirrel, or a ghost, or something really horrid – like a rat? The fun of making sound, the pleasure it gives to small children, is emphasized. When Totoro roars, the sound waves bend trees and shake rocks; no wonder Mei wants to roar too, to join in the fun of creating such an impressive noise. When Totoro leaps joyously into the air at the bus stop, his face split in a grin of anticipation, we are partly – but only partly – prepared for the wonderful shock of the cannonade of falling water onto his borrowed umbrella. We experience that glorious noise as gleefully as children, thanks to the careful balance of low-key night sounds and silence throughout the preceding scene.

The relationships within the movie work to emphasize the theme of goodwill and neighborliness. The family depicted in My Neighbor Totoro is one of the sanest and sunniest on film. Professor Kusakabe is a good husband and father: loving, supportive, perhaps a little absent-minded, but a wonderful companion and a rock-solid source of support in times of trouble. His wife is a woman of good sense and good temper, and although she is away from her family her influence is obvious. This was the first time that

Miyazaki had portrayed an ordinary, happy family, and it is a charming portrait. The strength that sustains the girls' happy childhood is obvious, and the stress of their mother's illness, a threat that Satsuki recognizes with dread and Mei is only dimly aware of, is the one real shadow over the film's joyous world.

The two scenes that originally worried American distributors are integral to the film, though for a Western audience one may be problematic. In every culture in the world, children love to run around empty houses and make noise, so although Americans may not realize that jumping up and down on handmade, traditional tatami mats can seem shocking to the Japanese, they will understand the excitement and energy expressed in that scene. The bathtub sequence, in which father and his daughters share a traditional Japanese family bath, may raise worries for some but could provide a valuable point for discussion with children about appropriate and inappropriate actions and relationships, about setting their own limits with adults, and about deciding what is and is not right for them. I will only add that it is a sad culture that can see nothing in a father's loving relationship with his children but the potential for abuse.

Satsuki is a fascinating character. Miyazaki was to approach the problems of the transition into adult life in more detail in *Kiki s Delivery Service;* in Satsuki, he gives us a delightful portrait of a child not yet ready to start moving into the adult world, but with some of its responsibilities forced on her by circumstance. Unlike Sheeta in *Castle in the Sky,* she is not alone in the world or pressured into adult difficulties and decisions, but she has begun to realize that such things do happen. When Satsuki

hangs back a little as Mei leaps into her mother's arms, or hesitates before accepting Totoro's unspoken invitation to fly with him, she is expressing our own fears that leaving childhood behind means leaving spontaneity and unconditional delight as the province of the young. Her mother's love and Nanny's wisdom show her that there are pleasures ahead, as well as duties and responsibilities; but it is Totoro who tells her, and us, that flinging caution to the winds and flying off on a spinning top can be fun at any age.

Mei, on the other hand, is the natural child, almost a spirit herself in her blithe disregard for the world's tedious detail. She is still at the age when her own wants, needs, and reactions can legitimately form the center of her universe without turning her into a monster. In the same way that Mei imitates Satsuki, hoping for her sister's experience to rub off, the small Totoro imitates his giant brother, holding a leaf umbrella aloft, piping on a little ocarina. The cycle of life continues through young and old. Mei, Satsuki, Mother, and Nanny form a composite image of the development of female warmth, strength, and grace, adding a human rhythm to the natural cycle of growth and fertility around them.

All the sophistication and intelligence that Miyazaki and his team bring to *My Neighbor Totoro* is devoted to the most difficult task for any artist: to create a work that appears as simple and natural as breathing. A doctor or scientist understands the complex mechanisms of physical and chemical exchange that keep the human organism's lungs at work; a child only knows that it breathes in and out and can float dandelion seeds and feathers on its breath. To draw in their young audience, and to enable the rest of us to enter Totoro's rich and complex world in the spirit of childhood, the director and his staff have made a world that works – down to the smallest detail. We don't think of it as art; we accept it as life.

In comparison to the complexity of the visual world and the density of the relationships, the plot appears as slight as a dandelion seed, but this slightness is heroically deceptive. Mei and Satsuki are on a quest as compelling as any fantasy hero's journey; they are seeking the magic in their everyday world. The treasure they win will be the ability to find that magic, whatever circumstance or experience may hide it. The sequence of seemingly unconnected incidents subtly escalates the level of the quest – from Mei's accidental discovery of Totoro's world through his casually stepping into their world to catch a bus; his showing them the miracle of life; and Satsuki's fears of life being taken away, first from her beloved mother and then from her little sister. At the moment of resolution, when Satsuki has found Mei and the two have seen for themselves that Mother is safe, the power of love pierces the blinds on adult eyes that keep us from seeing magic. Just for a moment, Mother thinks she can see her children smiling at her from the trees outside her hospital window. Few heroes achieve such triumph.

The pace that seems slow to those fixated on fast cuts and fast action is dictated both by nature and by childhood. Time is cunningly telescoped; days are elided through devices like Satsuki's writing to Mother at night, Mother reading the letter in the next cut, then back to Father putting up the mosquito nets to protect them from bites while they sleep. Time used to vanish like that when we were children. Events were mysterious – it seemed as if the seeds we buried would never sprout, then, suddenly, as if by magic, there were plants in the once-bare soil. Miyazaki has the supreme courage to let the movie grow at a pace that suits its purpose, and trusts his audience to walk with it.

My Neighbor Totoro is both my favorite Miyazaki work and my favorite film. Its apparent simplicity masks a depth of wisdom and grace found in few works for any medium. It is accessible to even the youngest child, yet it respects the intelligence of the most literate and cultivated adult.

If you don't believe me, take your children to see it. They'll convince you. It worked for Gene Siskel.🍎

McCarthy, Helen. "My Neighbor Totoro". *Hayao Miyazaki: Master of Japanese Animation*. Berkeley, CA: Stone Bridge Press, 1999. 116–123, 132–138.

7

Glocalisation vs. Globalization: The Work of Nick Park and Peter Lord

Marian Quigley [2002]

The concept of 'globalization' is generally perceived as a phenomenon involving cultural homogenization, whereby one societal or regional culture (notably America) dominates all others.[1] However, a number of media theorists have argued that the processes of globalization also include heterogenizing aspects; in other words, local elements are not only retained but also arise in response to global characteristics. Related to this argument is the term "glocalisation" (or "global localization") utilized in Japanese business to represent "a global outlook adapted to local conditions."[2] Media theorist Roland Robertson argues that glocalisation is a more useful term than globalization in describing "the simultaneity and the inter-penetration of what are conventionally called the global and the local, or – in more general vein – the universal and the particular."[3] This paper proposes that the production, exportation and reception of Nick Park and Peter Lord's clay animations – particularly *Chicken Run* (2000) – exemplify the processes of glocalisation.

The Concept of Glocalisation

'Hollywood' films are seen to be produced for global consumption and popularly received, despite cultural differences amongst their audiences.[4] In contrast, local cinema is regarded as being more responsive to its society or culture – and therefore, less likely to be internationally popular. According to this view, the wide distribution and acceptance of 'Hollywood' product is likely, over time, to result in "greater global cultural homogenisation or 'Americanization'".[5] In 1969, Guback claimed that "Successful exportation ... implies getting other people to 'like' the product, and this often leads to homogenization, blurring the differences which are the sharp edges of distinct cultures. With film, this growing similarity ... is taking a leap onto an international plateau where local idioms are erased or played down in favour of broader ones."[6] ...

More recently, however, a number of media theorists have taken issue with this so-called media 'imperialism'. Denis McQuail – while conceding the 'imprecise' nature of the notion of cultural identity – asserts that, in Europe, the development of globalized media culture involves the retention of culturally unique features as well as the addition of shared cultural elements. Media-cultural 'invasion', he argues, can be resisted or can result in a new cultural hybrid.[7]

Robertson claims that the term 'globalization' tends to inculcate the binary opposition of the global and the local, and in doing so, misrepresents the complexity of the communication processes involved. He believes that the local can more properly be seen as "an aspect of globalisation". Citing the example of global television, particularly CNN, he claims that so-called globalization has involved both the consolidation of the nation-state and at the same time, the development – mainly through mediasation – of a 'borderless world'. Moreover, what is termed 'local' is in fact largely constructed on a global basis.

As Robertson explains, an "'international' TV enterprise like CNN produces and reproduces a particular pattern of relations between localities, a pattern which depends on a kind of recipe of locality. This standardization renders meaningful the very *idea* of locality, but at the same time diminishes the notion that localities are 'things in themselves'."[8] Therefore Robertson proposes that 'glocalisation' is a more useful term.

The idea of glocalisation in its business sense is closely related to what in some contexts is called ... 'micro-marketing': the tailoring and advertising of goods and services on a global or near-global basis to increasingly differentiated local and particular markets. Almost needless to say, in the world of capitalistic production for increasingly global markets the adaptation to local and other particular conditions is not simply a case of business responses to pre-existing global variety – to civilisational, regional, societal, ethnic, gendered and still other sets of consumers, as if such variety or heterogeneity existed simply 'in itself'. To a considerable extent, micro marketing – or, in the more comprehensive phrase, glocalisation – involves the *construction* of increasingly differentiated consumers ... To put it very simply, diversity sells. On the other hand, from the consumer's point of view it is an important basis of cultural capital formation.[9]

Furthermore, as Tom O'Regan points out, both the equation of Hollywood with America and indeed, the concept of 'Hollywood' itself are slippery issues. He writes, "Hollywood is ... a collection of tendencies and filmmaking strategies which are being constantly renovated and transformed ... Simultaneously, Hollywood is a national film industry; an international film financing, production and distribution facility; and a name for globally popular English-language cinema."[10] The 'Hollywood' film is not necessarily made in Los Angeles – or the United States – and even when it is, it may be financed and produced by foreign investors. Nonetheless, O'Regan concludes, 'Hollywood' largely comprises the US film industry that, while heavily reliant upon the domestic market, distributes North American popular product internationally.

O'Regan argues that Hollywood's global success is due to its diversity of output, which negotiates rather than eradicates socio-cultural cleavages in the international market; for example, some Hollywood films, such as *Green Card* (1990), attract greater audiences overseas than in the US. At the same time, he contends that competition from

Hollywood "may have *increased* rather than *reduced* the diversity of cinema and television"[11] by leading to the adaptation of Hollywood strategies by some local producers – such as Australia's "Mad Max" series (1979, 1981, 1985) and *Beneath Clouds* (2002), described by one critic as "[transcending] its own cultural specificity whilst actually specifying it"[12] – and by the adoption of 'product differentiation strategies' by others.[13] Such product differentiation includes the development of new or hybridized TV formats or genres. Australian examples include limited series such as the 'reality TV' program "Big Brother" and the weekly youth-oriented comedy/news hybrid "The Panel".

In addition, as Robertson asserts, the major producers of 'global culture', such as 'Hollywood', adapt their products to local markets by, for instance, utilizing a multinational cast of actors and a number of local settings in order to attract a global audience. Recent examples include the growing number of Australian actors cast in leading roles, such as Nicole Kidman in *The Others* (2001) and Russell Crowe in *A Beautiful Mind* (2001), and the New Zealand location of *Lord of the Rings* (2002). These products are then subject to differentiated interpretations by their various producers and audiences. Moreover, global 'mass culture' contains elements of non-Western genres, values and ideas and there is a considerably large movement of cultural products from the 'periphery' to the 'center'.[14] Examples include Japanese anime, which has grown from a marginalized cult form to an "established facet of American popular culture",[15] and Australian animator Yoram Gross's "Dot" series (loosely based on the Australian children's book classic *Dot and the Kangaroo*) that, though

aimed at an international market, arguably retains 'local' cultural identity.

Aardman and Glocalised Production

David Sproxton and Peter Lord established Aardman Animations in Bristol, England in 1972. In 1985, internationally acclaimed animator Nick Park joined the studio. Altogether, Aardman's distinctively 'English' work has been nominated for American Oscars seven times and their internationally acclaimed 'Wallace and Gromit' films (1989, 1993, 1995) have won three.[16] In what has been described as "an unprecedented launch for a British film" in the US, *Chicken Run* was released in more than 3,000 cinemas in America[17] and became the third highest grossing film ever in the US with total box office takings of over 115 million dollars.[18]

Aardman made its name in industry from 1984 through advertising (for example, the award winning British 'Heat Electric' campaign based on Park's 1990 film *Creature Comforts*). From a small company priding itself on a distinctively 'handmade' look, Aardman has grown to employ approximately 300 staff. Its development over the last twenty years has resulted in the formation of an animation community within the city of Bristol, one of a number of small centers outside London concentrating on productions such as television series and individual short films.[19] Aardman's success reflects a larger trend in the development of innovative animation in Britain, aided by the significant growth in college animation courses as well as funding from advertising agencies and television channels such as the BBC and Channel 4.

The films of Peter Lord and Nick

Park contain both localized and globalized elements that flow from each other, clearly exemplifying the processes of glocalisation in terms of both industrial practices and content. Notably, the films are produced in an animation studio outside of Hollywood – and even peripheral to England's cultural center, London. However, the success of Aardman's early works has led to an alliance with the powerful American studio Dreamworks and global exportation.[20] While Aardman adopted 'Hollywood' generic conventions and production practices in *Chicken Run,* the studio has strenuously avoided the "smooth, perfect and showy" style[21] characterized by Disney and Dreamworks animations and has retained its aesthetically distinctive style and model animation technique along with a recognisably 'British' humor, settings, characters and dialogue.

Although Hollywood has provided influence, inspiration, audiences and more recently, finance for Aardman films, the latter nonetheless retain a cultural and aesthetic distinctiveness that has no doubt contributed to their national and international success. The quintessentially 'English' characters and rituals of the Wallace and Gromit films draw on director Nick Park's childhood experiences (his father's tool shed, drinking tea) and evoke a more innocent age populated with simple people and problems.[22] One reviewer of *The Wrong Trousers* remarked, "There's a calmness and precision to the tone and humour here that marks its creator as British. Indeed, it is the very quietness of this film – in which your attention is drawn to the sound of the scrape of a knife spreading jam on a piece of toast – that makes such a blessed contrast to much American

animation."[23] It seems, therefore, that while the notion of cultural distinctiveness is (increasingly) nebulous – and while it may be constructed and/or reinforced by the media itself – it is apparently recognizable.

Nick Park's work has been a major contributing factor in Aardman's commercial success. Park produced the internationally successful Wallace and Gromit films and, although, for the first time, he and co-director Peter Lord forfeited the hands-on animation to a large team in Aardman's first animated feature, *Chicken Run,* they retained creative control.[24] The film retains recognizable characteristics of Park's earlier work, including his characters' trademark 'coat hanger' mouths.[25] Sibley claims that Park's "strong cinematic awareness" has been a major contributing factor to the success of his films.[26] Other likely factors include American's long-standing familiarity with British cultural exports (like America, Britain has itself been a significant exporter of television programs for a number of years); the similarities as well as the differences between American and British cultures; and Aardman's high production values and diversity of styles.[27]

The international co-production of *Chicken Run* reflects the fact that in Britain, major animation projects are difficult to finance.[28] At the same time, however, America's domination of global media has lessened during the last three decades and it, too, has become more dependent on international partnerships.[29] In recent years, European animation companies have opened offices in the United States and European producers, like their American counterparts (particularly Disney), have become involved with merchandising and promotion. An example from Germany is

EM-Entertainment's 'Tabaluga' cartoon character, which led to an international co-produced series and associated product marketing.[30] The success of the Wallace and Gromit series is strongly linked with the international marketing of associated products that, unlike the bulk of Disney merchandise – and in a strategy unusual for animation licensing programs – are aimed at the less crowded adult market and sold through "upscale retailers such as gift shops and department stores rather than through mass merchants".[31] Apart from videos, products include boxer shorts, 'knit kits', *Close Shave* razors and their own brand of Wensleydale cheese. Though Aardman's licensing is fairly extensive (it now makes about the same amount from licensed product as it does from making animated commercials), it determines its own marketing strategies and until recently, Nick Park personally oversaw the manufacture of its products.[32]

Park and Lord had previously avoided making a feature-length film because they believed it too difficult to mass-produce their work while retaining their distinctive clay animation style.[33] Throughout the years, one can see resistance to any form of production that removes the artists from their materials. In 1997, Lord was asked whether he would consider scanning his clay models and animating them within a computer. He replied,

> ... there is something about working with the materials. There is a fundamental difference between working with your hands and your arms and your fingertips, and working on the keyboard ... You grab the puppet with two hands, and you feel the whole thing move, you feel the twist of the chest away from the hips, the roll of the shoulders ... The camera has to move

right, the light has to be right, the actor has to do the right thing – make-up, costume, everything has to be right. Just for one moment in time. That's the way we work. I believe that the humanity in what we're doing, the process, all comes through in the final film.[34]

In the making of *Chicken Run*, the necessities of mass production impacted on Park and Lord's clay technique only to the extent that silicon forms replaced plasticine for the bodies of the 387 model chickens.[35] Computer technology also was utilized for editing purposes and in order to help visualize and plan film sequences.[36] As Lord explains, computer technology

> hasn't actually changed the heart of [the animation method] for us at all, except now you can record what you do on computer as you go along... . It's made life much easier but in [*Chicken Run*] the heart and soul is definitely done the traditional way: handmade manipulations.
>
> But there are things in there – the elemental things like fire, water, and gravy – that you can't do nicely in stop-framing ... they were done in CGI. At the end of the film, we spent several months retouching and repairing in a digital form at a computer film company in London, because all the chickens were supported on huge steel rigs, which we had to make disappear.[37]

When they undertook production of *Chicken Run*, Lord and Park were determined that the company remain independent and in Bristol. As Lord explained, "our big kick is independence ... Not that I think the studios want to crush us at all ... it's just that we've got different agendas. For example, the film will be extremely English in sensibility."[38] Consequently, Aardman rejected offers from Disney,[39] Warner Bros. and Fox studios, instead forming a partnership with Dream Works SKG and the French company Pathé.[40]

Despite its 'English sensibility', *Chicken Run* features a number of recognizable 'Hollywood' generic conventions. Among them is a hallmark of American animated features, the musical song and dance routine, though used more sparingly than in most US works. The setting of the film is Northern England and, for the most part, the Yorkshire idiom is retained. In fact, an edition of the *Los Angeles Times* included a glossary of Yorkshire slang used in the film.[41] Though Ginger is an English character, she and the 'leading man', Rocky, are modeled on the American Hollywood celebrity duo of Katherine Hepburn and Spencer Tracey.[42] Rocky is American but his voice is provided by the American-born, Australian-raised actor Mel Gibson. Gibson's career, too, makes an interesting study in the ambiguity of cultural boundaries, given the hybrid nature of his upbringing as well as his career. As a film performer, Gibson's voice bears no trace of accent and to the general public he would be recognized as a 'Hollywood' star, while Australian audiences, aware of his upbringing and his early career roles in Australian films,[43] are more likely to claim him as their own.

An examination of *Chicken Run* reveals an array of American and English references. Its dark-edged humour and the sense of the absurdity of human life recall the comedies of the British Ealing studios.[44] The film also makes allusions to both British and American war films of the post-WWII era, such as *The Great Escape* (1963) and *Stalag 17* (1952), and it includes a stock RAF veteran, Fowler, typical of British films of the period. *Chicken Run* playfully draws on the British wartime cultural experience of wealthy American GIs seducing British women.[45] It also makes a number of allusions to American 'imperialism', suggesting a modern day Marxist fable in which the (local) worker-chickens are (literally) "in danger of being devoured by [global] capitalism's avaricious corporate machine".[46]

The film, like the chickens, seems, at least on this occasion, to have overcome the threat posed by 'imperialism' and technology. Just as the found-object-created aeroplane enables the chickens' escape from death by technology (Mrs. Tweedy's pie machine), Park and Lord's dedication to their traditional clay animation technique enables their maintenance of artistic freedom. The success of the Aardman studio – and, in particular, the animated films of Nick Park and Peter Lord – reveals that the processes of glocalisation involve the generation of wider audiences for previously marginalized and/or localized media forms and that association of local and global media cultures may enable the growth rather than the destruction of diversity. Aardman Animations exemplify the contemporary media-cultural phenomenon that posits the global in the local and the local in the global.❦

Notes

1. There are many texts devoted to 'globalisation' and its effects, including Wiseman, referenced in endnote 7. For an online example, see: G.J. Robinson, "Information Highways and Democratic Participation", www.undp.org/info21/bg/robinson.htm.
2. Roland Robertson writes, "The idea of 'glocalisation' seems to have originated in the specific context of talk about globalisation, in Japanese business methods in the late 1980s; although by now it has

become quite a common marketing perspective". Roland Robertson, "Globalisation or glocalisation?", *Journal of International Communication* 1:1 (1994), 33.

3. Robertson, 38.

4. These may include films produced in other parts of North America for domestic and international mass audiences.

5. Tom O'Regan, "Too Popular By Far: On Hollywood's International Popularity", *Continuum* 5:2 (1992), 303–304.

6. Guback, quoted in O'Regan, 303.

7. Denis McQuail, *McQuail's Mass Communication Theory*, 4th edn (London: Sage, 2000): 237. In a similar vein, John Wiseman states: "Paradoxically, the globalisation of culture has also given rise to heightened localised resistance and the remixing of cultural flows and identities often referred to as 'hybridisation'". *Global Nation? Australia and the Politics of Globalisation* (Cambridge UP: 1998): 16–17. National variations of the American soap opera genre can be seen to exemplify this process. Australian programs such as *Neighbours* focus on everyday middle class life in the suburbs and are aimed at the teenage market. British soaps such as "Coronation Street" and "Eastenders" often have centered on working class life and are characterized by a more gritty realism. In comparison, American soaps such as "Days of Our Lives" and "The Bold and the Beautiful" tend to be much more melodramatic.

8. Robertson, 38–48

9. Robertson, 36–37.

10. O'Regan, 305.

11. O'Regan, 307.

12. Renay Walker, "Blood on the Tracks", *Metro* 133 (2002), 13.

13. O'Regan, 307.

14. Roland Robertson, 46.

15. Fred Patten, "Anime in the United States", in John A. Lent, ed., *Animation in Asia and the Pacific* (Eastleigh, UK: John Libbey, 2001), 66.

16. *Business Wire* (6 July 2000)

17. http://www.telegraph.co.uk (4 July 2000).

18. http://www.aardman.com

19. This community includes companies such as A for Animation, Bolex Brothers, Cod Steaks, and Elm Road Productions. John Southall, "Aspects of Contemporary Animation in Great Britain: Organization and Production", *Animation Journal* 1:1 (Fall 1992), 48–49. The company was founded following the BBC purchase of Sproxton and Lord's short 2D film featuring a Superman character, called Aardman. After experimenting with various media, they began making clay animation, inspired by a combination of Terry Gilliam's work on *Monty Python's Flying Circus* (1969–1974) and Ray Harryhausen's skeleton figures in *Jason and the Argonauts* (1963). The flexibility of plasticine added to the fact that it was a medium used by few other studios, provided the basis of its appeal to the animators and the television executives and advertising agencies that commissioned their work.

20. Nick Park came up with the idea of a film about chickens. He and Peter Lord, Michael Rose (Aardman's executive producer) and Jake Eberts (Allied Films executive producer) flew to Los Angeles to discuss the idea with Dreamworks staff. http://www.aardman.com.

21. Claire Sutherland, "Cheep Thrills", *Herald-Sun* (7 December 2000), Hit15.

22. *Wallace and Gromit go to Hollywood: The Story of Aardman Animation* (Iambic Productions, 2000). I am indebted to Chris Kuan (and the Aardboard, www.aardman.com) who provided me with copies of this documentary, along with *The Making of Chicken Run* and the Wallace and Gromit films.

23. Reviewer, *Entertainment Weekly*, quoted in Sibley, 169.

24. The animation units of the directors Park and Lord each employed 7 key animators working with 3–4 animators, 2–4 assistant animators and 5 trainee animators, as well as a mass of 'cross-team players'. Sibley, 167.

25. Giannalberto Bendazzi, *Cartoons: One Hundred Years of Cinema Animation* (John Libbey, 1994; Bloomington: Indiana University Press), 278.

26. Sibley, 10.

27. Kathy Desalvo, "Tea time: Brit doodlers alter Yank taste in toons. Cream anyone?", *Shoot* (26 June 1998). Aardman allows for a number of individual styles of animation under its company umbrella,

including the children's subject "Morph", the adult series "Conversation Pieces" and the Internet animated series "Angry Kid".

28. Southall, 30.

29. McQuail, 232; Stuart Cunningham and Elizabeth Jacka, *Australian Television and International Mediascapes* (Cambridge, MA: Cambridge UP, 1996), 25–26.

30. Maureen Furniss, *Art in Motion: Animation Aesthetics* (Sydney: John Libbey, 1998), 223.

31. Karen Raugust, "Wallace and Gromit Spur Worldwide Licensing Activity", *Animation World Magazine* 2:11 (Feb 1998)

32. Raugust.

33. One of the most arduous forms of cinematography, stop-frame animation using clay or plasticine requires the resculpting of the moving parts of 3D figures and filming frame by frame.

34. Lord, quoted in Wendy Jackson, "An Interview with Aardman's Peter Lord", *Animation World Magazine* 2:2 (May 1997).

35. At the rate of 24 frames per second, for the eighty-minute feature *Chicken Run* this meant approximately 100,000 individual frames. One day's shooting generally produced, at most, about ten seconds of footage. Although the large body parts were made from silicon over underlying metal armatures, the chickens' plasticine heads and wings had to be continually replaced. Moreover, the need for meticulous lip-synching meant that their beaks had to be replaced for every syllable – requiring the creation of approximately twenty different mouths for the character Rocky.

36. Rather than constructing a cardboard mock up, for example, computer graphics were used to calculate the dimensions of a set and to plan camera angles. Computers also enable the enhancement of the film's visual appearance. An example is the chicken catapult sequence in which the support for the 'flying' chicken was digitally removed. Sibley, 160.

37. In Jeffrey Wachs, "Fire, Water, and Gravy: the Secrets of *Chicken Run*", http://www.reel.com (2001).

38. Lord, quoted in Jackson.

39. The only other two feature-length model animation films made in recent years have both been Disney productions: *The Nightmare Before Christmas* (1993) and *James and the Giant Peach* (1996). Sibley, 14.

40. Dreamworks SKG was formed by Steven Spielberg, David Geffen and Jeffrey Katzenberg.

41. Nigel Reynolds and Boyd Farrow, "22m chicken out to conquer US for Gromit's creator", hyperlink "http://www.telegraph.co.uk" (16 June 2000).

42. John Anderson, "Chicken Run", *Film Comment* (July 2000).

43. These include *Summer City* (1979), *Tim* (1979), *Gallipoli* (1981), *The Year of Living Dangerously* (1982) and the *Mad Max* films cited earlier.

44. David Stratton, "Chick flick as escapist fare", *Weekend Australian* (9–10 December 2000), Review, 22; Andrew Osmond, "Stop Motion City: Visible and Invisible Production in Bristol", *Animation World Magazine* 3.11 (February 1999); S.F. Said, "Chicken Coup", *Sunday Age* (7 December 2000), Today, 1+3. The Ealing comedies include *Kind Hearts and Coronets* (1949), *The Lavender Hill Mob* (1951), *The Man in the White Suit* (1951), and *The Ladykillers* (1955).

45. Wachs.

46. Tom Ryan, "A prison escape drama with plenty of pluck", *Sunday Age* (10 December 2000), Review, 8.

Quigley, Marian. "Glocalisation vs. Globalization: The Work of Nick Park and Peter Lord". *Animation Journal* 10 (2002). 85–94. ©2002 Marian Quigley

8

Toward a Postmodern Animated Discourse: Bakhtin, Intertextuality and the Cartoon Carnival

Terry Lindvall & Matthew Melton [1994]

n *Rabelais and His World*, Mikhail Bakhtin celebrates the universal, ambivalent, and grotesque "carnival comedy" of the sixteenth century. He complains that Voltaire and Enlightenment wit lacked the full-bodied comedy of the Medieval marketplace.[1] While enlightenment laughter is primarily mocking and satiric – subverting the folly of the hierarchy in its feasts of fools, asses, and administrators – medieval comedy affirms, renews, and revitalizes the old, bringing forth new birth, life, hope, and laughter. It simultaneously takes apart and puts together the Body of Humanity and the Christian Church. By deconstructing and then reconstructing, carnival laughter simultaneously derided and delighted in the social and cultural apparatus of its era.

Medieval laughter reduces the mysteries of social and religious existence by playing with their forms without denying them. The highest stands with the lowest; the vulgar gives the pre-eminent meaning. The clown sits on the throne.

Nonsense rules sense's domain. Humor is intertwined with the humility and humanity of all those who came from the dust (or *humus*, the root of humanity, humility and humor) and would return unto it.

A frequently overlooked contemporary (or postmodern) form sharing the playful dynamism of the carnival spirit is the self-reflexive animated cartoon, particularly that of the comic genre ("animation" as a form extends beyond the realm of the "cartoon", which is defined in this paper as "comic animation"). Like medieval comedy, the cartoon mocks itself, romping with its audience. It re-creates (makes again) and recreates (enjoys) its own being. In ways that will be shown, Bakhtin's notion of carnival provides an inspired model for analysis of comic genres like the animated cartoon, genres often overshadowed by more "significant" cinemas. Whereas the clown once ruled, or misruled, in medieval comedy, it is now the turn of the animator to show his motley.

Theoretical Heritage

The casual way in which animation and the cartoon have been treated by film theorists is due in part to the self-deprecating humor of the cartoon itself. Like the Postmodernism of Jean-Francois Lyotard, the cartoon is a playful art. Without pretensions, it teases both those who neglect it and those who take it too seriously. Vladimir Propp's discovery of a basic morphology in the Russian fairy tale should encourage us not to despise the little, common, vulgar things of this world.[2] But when modernist Siegfried Kracauer separated animated cartoons from true photographic film, he essentially banished them from his theory, warning that in certain cartoons of Disney, a "false devotion to the cinematic approach inexorably stifles the draftsman's imagination."[3]

Jean Mitry treated animation with little more attention, though he did praise the assimilation of image and sound in Alexander Alexeieff and Claire Parker's noncomic pinscreen animation, *Night on Bald Mountain* (1933). It offered, he claimed, "a succession of imprecise, ghostly, hallucinatory forms, that Moussorgsky's work seems to call up from the underworld, animating with a glorious, life-giving breath".[4] This "inspired" view of animation was echoed by Erwin Panofsky, who said the "very virtue of the animated cartoon is to animate; that is to say, endow lifeless things with life, or living things with a different kind of life. It effects a metamorphosis."[5]

One of the most significant treatments of animated film is Dana Polan's "A Brechtian Cinema? Towards a Politics of Self-Reflexive Film." Polan suggests that a Hollywood cartoon like *Duck Amuck* (1953) embodies a consciously apolitical self-reflexivity. It is a playfully disengaged art form wholly concerned with "the nature of animation technique itself."[6] Postmodern sensibilities are stylistically realized in this artform with the fusion of high and low art, the tinkering with hybrid forms, the tones of irony and parody, the incredulity toward metanarratives, and the principle of double coding, all of which frolic merrily in the realm of the intertextual. The self-reflexive cartoon is a cultural practice operating as one of Lyotard's language games where rules and players are in constant flux. It comically renders transparent the workings of the text, providing a Brechtian distance from the work and upending the dominant classical narrative style to revitalize traditional pleasure in the act of viewing.

The animated film mediates between two competing epistemological methods, between what Paul Ricoeur designates in hermeneutics as "synthetic" and "analytic".[7] C.S. Lewis expresses it as the difference between "looking along" and "looking at," corresponding respectively to the French verbs *connaître* and *savoir*.[8] The first is a knowledge by acquaintance; the latter a knowledge by description. One might define them as a hermeneutics of faith and a hermeneutics of suspicion – both being necessary for a full knowledge of the object.

As the cartoon reflects upon its own construction and its relationship to the context out of which it has been created, it deconstructs the imposed reality of cinematic discourse. The cartoon, in Polan's terms, "explicitly signals its cartoon-ness" and an awareness of its means and motives of production.[9]

Self-reflexive Cartoons

Animated films demonstrate self-reflexivity in three general and overlapping ways. First, they comment on filmmaking and the film industry and by unveiling the raw materials and methods of the filmmaking process, cartoons reveal their own textuality. Second, animated films possess the ability to function as discourse, speaking directly to their audiences. Third, animated films reflect their relationships to their creators. The animators themselves enter their cartoons and become deconstructive agents of their own artifice. Animated film is a form in which the auteur is not only dominant, but able to speak directly to her or his audience. As Steve Schneider notes, "animation is probably the ultimate auteurist cinema".[10]

The irony of filmmaking as the subject of film draws attention to the craft, the business, and the visions behind such enterprises. The writer/director is able to explore his or her work and question it, its techniques, and its values. These films are not mere exercises in vain speculation, but serve as excursions into the fundamental nature and purposes of film.

Many cartoons have demonstrated this ability to reflect upon their own nature as drawn, celluloid products (see end of essay for examples). This self-consciousness about textuality exhibits itself in several ways: by (1) exposing and dismantling the filmmaking process; (2) alluding to other texts and contexts beyond itself, thus grounding itself in reality; or (3) addressing the plastic nature and raw material of celluloid and the frame itself.

The dynamic cartoon text extends into other texts, the filmmaking processes, the Hollywood industry (e.g. the interdependence of cartoon to the studio system is evidenced by the Fleischer cartoons utilizing and dismantling Paramount's musical scores), and the raw material of film itself. The cartoon also unveils the classical cinematic disguise of being a self-contained, closed structure by becoming open to the experience of the reader as well. By acknowledging familiar topoi, issues, and personalities, these cartoons begin to establish a common ground for communication with their readers.

Discursive Cartoons: Text and Reader

How does a text invite a relation with its reader? What kind of reading(s) does a discursive cartoon demand? Can cartoons call to the reader, as Ricoeur argues, as a person calls? Or in Bakhtian fashion, can we find dialogism, the "necessary relation of any utterance to other utterance" in a cartoonic complex of signs?

Many cartoons, particularly those of Disney, are narratives constructed in the classical cinema mode, the *histoire*. But some cartoons have a playfully perverse tendency to disrupt the normal codes of a hermetic narrative. Other cartoons, placed under the rubric of comedy, follow the disruptive strand and fit very neatly into Steve Seidman's generic category of "comedian comedy".[11]

Comedian comedy comes from vaudeville and burlesque where the on-stage or on-screen character addresses the audience directly. We see this when Bugs Bunny speaks directly into the camera at the conclusion of *Duck Amuck*: "Quite a little stinker, ain't I?" This is discourse, animated dialogue between the polyphonic text and the reader.

Even as Barthes called for a playful science of signs and imaginative pleasure to replace "theological" science, a proper reading of the cartoon text should evoke anarchic pleasure. This translates as a reception of the text itself, a surrender to the posture a film demands of the reader. C.S. Lewis distinguished "receiving" a work of art from "using" it, as in forcing psychoanalytical or Marxist paradigms on a textual structure that recommends its own hermeneutic. Lewis's crucial objection to "using" an aesthetic text was that, as readers, we "are so busy doing things with the work that we give it too little chance to work on us. Thus increasingly *we meet only ourselves.*"[12] We contemplate, but do not enjoy; or as Ricoeur would put it, we place priority on structure over interpretation.

A film text offers a network of discourses. This calls for responsibility on the part of the reader, who is always tempted to force the text onto his or her Procrustean bed of analysis. By interacting with the voice of the author, the reader may discover the *sensus plenoir* of the text. This "fuller meaning" emerges only after proper exegesis, in which the reader listens to the text in light of its historical, linguistic, and ideological/theological contexts.

Cartoons, however, do not need the consistency or internal logic of a realist film. New codes can emerge when a reader encounters the unpredictable articulations of the cartoon. The super-textual can break into the text at any moment. It may even be planted as an integral part of the text, derailing it from the inside to transform the narrative into discourse, into dialogue with the reader.

Tex Avery's slow but supernaturally speedy dog, Droopy, engages in regular dialogues with his audience. In the beginning of *Dumb Hounded* (1943), Droopy introduces the cartoon by announcing: "Hello all you happy people.

You know what? I'm the hero." Later, when he breaks "character" by barking back to another dog, he explains to us humans, looking directly and plainly into the camera: "Dog talk". This Tex Avery trademark also appears in a similar scene in *Northwest Hounded Police* (1946), where Droopy deadpans: "Monotonous, isn't it?" Droopy's ironic detachment, what Mast calls "katastasis", addresses the spectator with wry commentary, as though confiding to us the contrived nature of the cartoon. "I surprise him like this all through the picture", Droopy explains in his funereal voice.

The Brechtian style of address subverts the self-contained universe of the conventional narrative, bringing the enunciator down from the screen, as in Woody Allen's *The Purple Rose of Cairo*. The character becomes a more objective cultural identity. This may not hold for Bob Hope or Woody Allen, who have actual personalities beyond the dramatic persona. But there is no possibility of bumping into Porky Pig, no matter how many bars or sties we frequent.

When the text acknowledges the presence of a generalized reader, it procures from the audience the plausibility of existence. It is imbued with life – *animated* – much as Tinker Bell came alive when Peter Pan persuaded the children to clap. Daffy Duck speaks to his spectators, appealing to their good sense. Bugs is like the dapper French comedian Max Linder, who, as Andre Bazin noted, plays "directly to the audience, winks at them, and calls on them to witness his embarrassment, and does not shrink from asides".[13] Bugs Bunny's discursive behavior enables the spectator to attribute more actuality to him than to either Popeye or even Donald Duck.

Woody Allen talking to us is

unremarkable. But for Bugs and his ilk, the word and image become the miracle of new creation. He who has no being, whose presence in film is a veritable absence, now exists in a phenomenological encounter. We listen to him as he weaves his witty spells. He gets us to laugh, to join in his conspiracy. He gets us to believe in him and surrender to his magic, or at least to appreciate his magical creators.

Chuck Jones's unparalleled classic, *Duck Amuck*, involves the reader in one of the most discursive and hilarious self-reflexive texts. Leonard Maltin cites Louis Black on the levels of interpretation offered the spectator in *Duck Amuck*: "The cartoon stands as an almost clinical study of deconstruction of a text, in the way it presents a whole at the beginning and then dismembers every facet of the cartoon, only to put them together at the end".[14]

In the film, Daffy Duck not only performs for us, but begs, cajoles, and berates his spectators, and, more significantly, his spectating Creator. The film draws attention to the art of making cartoons, to the mysteries of production, and to the dependent nature of the cartoon character. Maltin observed that when "Daffy yells for a close-up, the camera moves in so far that the screen is filled with Daffy's bloodshot eyes".[15] Daffy, as a cartoon Job, is stuck in a seemingly arbitrary and nonsensical universe. After the setting changes arbitrarily from old MacDonald's farm to an Arctic setting with igloo, Daffy asks: "Would it be too much to ask if we could make up our minds? Hmmm?" When all the backgrounds are erased, Daffy grits his beak and declares: "Buster, it may come as a complete surprise to you to find that this is an animated cartoon and in animated cartoons they have scenery". He

appeals to the normal grammar of cartoon syntax to recover some regularity for this world gone askew.

At the mercy of an unseen and whimsical power, Daffy seeks to adapt to the chaotic changes in his environment and the bizarre metamorphoses of his own image. "Who is responsible for this?" he screams. "I demand that you show yourself! Who are you?" A mysterious and sovereign creator whose malevolent whimsy makes sport with him frustrates him at every turn. Finally, the camera pulls back to show the unseen artist as Bugs Bunny. "He is his own auteur", wrote Richard Corliss, "the cartoon director's alter-ego. He knows what's going to happen, in the next frame or three scenes away, and he knows how to control it."[16]

Daffy's appeals for us to help him uncover the source of his troubles go unheeded as the spectator himself or herself is at the mercy of the dynamic comedy. The final unveiling of Bugs Bunny as the tormenting "stinker" behind the whole mess elicits one last laugh, but also leads to an awareness of the supernatural or supercelluloid Artist, who does exist and seems to "play" with the creatures. The joke expands and culminates as one realizes that the impish and sadistic rabbit exists only as the imaginative expression of another – albeit genuine – cartoon draftsman. In the chaotic world of the simulacra one finds not a referent, but an author.

Transcendent Toons: Text and Author

If the cartoon is discourse, who is the discourse-maker? For Barthes, "the birth of the reader must be at the cost of the death of the Author".[17] In the discursive cartoon this is not so. To have discourse, one must have communicating subjects, one of whom is the author, or *auteur*. This revived and reformed "auteurist" approach must distinguish between the independent animator and the studio-driven, mass-produced cartoon. Yet, even in the latter, the voices of many authors whisper through the Studio Babel. The consciousness of the reader (his/her birth) occurs in encountering the author(s) in the words and images of the created text. The reader is neither a passive consumer of unyielding ideologies nor an independent constructor of brave new worlds, but one who seeks a meeting of minds in the text.

Cartoon authorship may involve a screwy coterie of animators on Termite Terrace or just one auteur like the incomparable Norman McLaren, but the cartoon is a genre, like the avant-garde film, that highlights the name below the title; the authors leave their signatures or thumbprints on their work. G.K. Chesterton observed that "as God made a pigmy-image of Himself and called it Man, so man made a pigmy-image of creation and called it art".[18] Men and women, as *imago Dei*, imitate their Creator, becoming what J.R.R. Tolkien called "sub-creators".[19] Their cartoons carry what Peter Berger has called "signals of transcendence," clues and hints to a reality beyond their two-dimensional existence.

Signals of transcendence occur most clearly when the author personally enters the text, like Woody Allen's Mr. Kugelmass, a bored character who lusts after the ideal women of literature and goes to live and love in books like *Madame Bovary* (students reading this work would ask their teachers: "Who is this character on page 100? A bald Jew is kissing Madame Bovary?").[20] The entrance of the otherworldly creator into the world of his or her creation is a sort of incarnation, or incartoonation, and occurs in both live-action alloys and full animation. The intrusion of an outer reality, even as small as the cartoonist's hand or drawing tools, transforms the cartoon world. The presence of the maker endows the inanimate with a magical ontological concreteness; that is, it somehow makes the imaginary cartoon character, Felix or Dinky or Bugs, more real.

Crafton makes this point in relation to the silent animated film, arguing that self-figuration, the "tendency of the filmmaker to interject himself into his film ... can take several forms; it can be direct or indirect, and more or less camouflaged." Early on, animators interjected themselves audaciously into their work, but later the practice took on a subtler, cleverer, almost hierophanous quality. The animator, Crafton notes, not only bestowed a mythological status on his or her role, but imaged the artist as "a demigod, a purveyor of life itself".[21]

The grand incarnation of animator into animation can be found in Otto Messmer's Felix the Cat. Felix, Crafton avers, is "an index of a real personality ... .":

> One realizes that the personality is that of the creator. With Felix, the quest for self-figuration reaches its end. Messmer no longer feels obliged to physically enter the image (although in *Comicalities* he did briefly toy with the "hand of the artist" convention.) Instead, he enters the film through total identification with the character.[22]

Felix follows the generic signs of self-figuration associated with animator-artist Emile Cohl's clown, the character being an "incoherent" theophany of the incoherent artist.[23]

Examples of self-figuration can,

however, be found in many different contexts. The opening title sequence signaling the inauguration of the 1986 Hamilton International Animation Festival transforms the festival's character logo, a Canadian owl, into a known (in the sense of *connaître* rather than *savoir*) personality. A golden egg bounces onto and on the screen. It first hatches into a fluffy, downy, Disneyfied white baby owl. Suddenly a pencil appears and erases the figure in the egg shell and draws another. This time a wild, raucous, punk version of the owl appears. Immediately, the pencil rushes in, erases, and gives birth to the genuine representative of the festival to the cheers of the audience. This clever introduction worked to make one aware (and appreciative) of the artistry behind the film. We become cognizant of the labors and frustrations of the artists in conceiving and giving birth to this familiar feathered character.

L invité (1984), by Guy Jacques, poignantly reveals both the lonely, tedious work of the animator and the curious personal relationship between the artist and his work. A clay animator shapes, frames, moves, and shoots a life-size clay human character one click of the camera at a time, slowly filming a sequence in which his character-man walks into the animator's home. Through stop-motion, the animator brings his inanimate guest into his life, including himself in each shot, so that it appears that they sit, sup, and chat together. After his devoted labors are completed, he projects the film – which shows host and guest eating, drinking, and communing. The solitary artist has not only brought his lifeless sculpture to life, but has labored to give birth to friendship and fellowship. A step toward transcendence occurs, in the "communion" between a work of art and the viewer/reader. In *L invité*, the author of the cartoon within the cartoon is the primary reader, drawn out of himself to experience a transcendent moment of communion through art. The audience of secondary readers become sympathetic communicants with this lonely old animator, identifying with him and his art. We also become the suffering animator who creates a world and incarnates himself into it.

The union of creator and creature in a single story contrasts with the rebellion of other creatures in Messmer's *Trials of a Movie Cartoonist* (1916). Crafton says the "first half of this film shows the trials and tribulations of a movie cartoonist at work. The figures that he draws become rebellious and refuse to act as he wants them to, so he has a terrible time to make them do his bidding. They answer back and say that he has no right to make slaves of them even if he is their creator."[24]

"If you want to make a good cartoon, you have to be in one first", one of the characters in Kathy Rose's *Pencil Bookings* (1978) tells the artist. Rose has directed a dreamy and fluid cartoon in which she appears in two cartoon forms: in her own rotoscoped cartoon incarnation and in the redrawn image of her cartoon characters. The film begins with her sitting at her drawing table and her tiny cast of bubbling characters emerging from a bottle complaining about their voices. One whines that its voice is too squeaky. Others chime in: "I don't like my voice either". "We don't want to be in your film." The characters incessantly give advice to their creator, often ordering her where and when to insert a "nice cycle".

Eventually Rose reproves them: "I can't make a film if everyone here is fighting." She makes a brief exit, and when she is gone, the characters decide to remake their own world. "Hello, I'm Kathy's pencil", one says and joins the others to "make our own film just like Kathy". Exhilarated by freedom from Kathy's control, they reconstruct their universe with a goofier, cartoonier image of their maker. They want to make their distorted image of Kathy talk like they do. However, no one will participate unless they can have their own way, so they float without direction or order until communication with their creator is re-established and life begins anew. Through identification with her doodled characters as a doodle herself, Kathy is able to communicate with them and gain their obedience. The author recognizes how her text can take on a life of its own and add to the original text. John Canemaker praised Rose's ability to draw us into this original, fascinating world, and make "us believe in its special reality ... . In one breathtaking scene Ms. Rose 'becomes' one of her characters ... Later, Ms. Rose oozes and bleeds her cartoon cast from her body, as strong a visual statement of an artist's identification with her art as you're liable to find in animation."[25]

Rose and her fellow artists are in the same tradition as those who, at some time in their careers, sought to represent themselves in their work. Painters like Dürer, Rembrandt, Van Gogh, and Norman Rockwell handed down a habit of famous self-portraits mirroring their own variegated souls. They signed their work with an image rather than a signature. For artists like Camus, "art detached from its creator is unthinkable".[26]

If any genre can subvert recent materialist theory that banishes the personal voice in the film's relation to its audience, it is the animated cartoon. Of particular relevance are those discursive works from outside the studio system, and the Warner Bros. material. Their work and that of a diverse body of independent and irrepressible animators can be submitted as evidence of personal speaking in the artistic process. Chuck Jones, Tex Avery, Friz Freleng, Bob Clampett, *et al.*, merely addressed their films to themselves, aiming to entertain themselves. These animators were both authors and readers. Jones confessed that they didn't design their pictures for kids or adults: "My cartoons", he says, "weren't made for children. They were made for me."[27]

Independent animators like Kathy Rose are also true auteurs, incarnating themselves, or at least their voices, into texts. Their sovereignty over all aspects of production allows them to claim the camera as Astruc's *stylo*. Carolyn Leaf acknowledges, "I like to control everything within my frame ... I like to make things move. It is like making them alive."[28] Eliot Noyes, Jr., also testifies to the appeal of personal authorship, of creating animation "the way a painter would use paints and a canvas. The reason I am in animation is that it is a form of self-expression; what I want to get across is mostly a very personal view of the world."[29]

The personal attention of the author may lead to her or his involvement in the cartoon, leaving traces (and even faces) of the self as playful signals of transcendence. Hints of a supernatural cosmos, of a world outside the celluloid, are laid about like nets to catch the reader unawares and draw attention beyond the text to the author and his/her world. The artists whisper the answers to the questions of who framed and drew Roger Rabbit or Daffy Duck.

One of the most exhilarating moments for my graduate students was when we placed Mike Jittlov's pixilated *Wizard of Speed and Time* (1980) on the Steenbeck to ascertain whether we were "seeing" something subliminal tucked away in the frame. His secret signatures were unveiled clearly in the frame-by-frame analysis. In his frames, Jittlov spelled his name out in lights, hid messages against the Hollywood industry, and even listed his home phone number on a clapboard, inviting any detective who discovered this message to call him. We immediately dialed the number and had a live, direct line back to a very live and friendly author. Attending to the dynamic force of the textual discourse and probing into its secrets led us to a dialogue beyond the text.

Conclusions

With its potentially heuristic and pragmatic values, the animated film serves as a site for exploring certain aspects of postmodernism, particularly the realms of double-coding, intertextuality, and carnival comedy. Its use of pastiche and parody, of extended quotation, and of multiple perspectives – of heteroglossia within one small discourse – situate it as prime property for postmodern analysis.

The mere cartoon offers a vital sample for lively discourse and for the discovery of the carnival spirit in cinema. As a pervasive source of pleasure and consumption, it merits critical attention as ideological product. As a phenomenological text, it invites consideration of a "theological" encounter, a meeting with the quiddity of the text and even with the author of the text.

Reflexive cartoons are also blatantly disruptive of Jean Baudrillard's diabolical seduction of images. Strategically, images seem to refer to "the real world, real objects, and to reproduce something which is logically and chronologically anterior to themselves".[30] Cartoons do not even pretend to have a referent. In fact, they function as referents for a legion of simulacra that have become consumer products: those large, cuddly products that walk around theme parks and malls, selling their stuff and seducing innocents into a reading of reality that is only cartoon illusion.

The cartoons presented here are exemplary of the intertextual practice of alluding to, plagiarizing, absorbing, imitating, quoting, and playing with ironic self-reflexive references to the entire cinematic apparatus, from its plastic raw material to its spectatorship. But certain of these cartoons extend beyond their textuality. They are transcended by authorship and signs of a super-celluloid existence. As postmodern texts, they may eschew and even mock classic narrative paradigms, but they do affirm personal narrators.

Animated films are the deconstructing agents that have Subjects who created them; they do have authors. And it is the company of authors who communicate not only with themselves, but with spectators who play along with them in their intertextual games.

Addendum:
Reflexivity in Animation

Reflexive cartoons – those that revealed something about the art of animation and filmmaking in their narratives – appeared early in film history and have continued to be produced throughout the years. This portion of the essay is devoted to a discussion of but a few of these works.

Early in the century, reflexivity was

already becoming characteristic of the animated film. In the live-action/animation, *Little Nemo* (1911), American cartoonist Winsor McCay bets comedian John Bunny and company that he can make his sketches move, and proceeds to show the long and sometimes frustrating process of bringing Little Nemo and his cartoon characters to life. The secrets of the enchanted drawings were revealed within the text itself, demythologizing the mysteries of the esoteric art. Other filmmakers of the period, including John Stuart Blackton and Max Fleischer, also invaded the illusory worlds they had made with their own presence; see, for example, Blackton's *The Enchanted Drawing* (1900) or the Fleischer "Out of the Inkwell" series of films.

Other animated films show a live-action character who plays the part of "an animator" interacting with animated characters; these narratives often seem to comment on the profession of animation itself. In Hy Gage's *Kartoono* (ca. 1922), an animator creates a creature that seeks his creator's destruction. The starving artist, Kartoono, practices his lightning sketches on an easel, drawing a hungry dragon that eats his meat and drinks his beer. The artist talks to his creation and confesses: "I'm Busted, Starving, Got Cold Feets. Now to get Busy. No Work, No Eats!" – as if Gage was crying his own woes about the poverty that his chosen profession has brought to him. Unfortunately, the giant winged dragon drawn by the miserable artist shows no empathy and chases Kartoono throughout the cartoon. Ultimately, an intertitle asks: "What's This, Kartoono, Stumped Again? No, Just Watch My Trusty Fountain Pen." At this point, the cartoon artist draws an escape vehicle and bombs the monster. The triumph over the beast is followed by a hand signing the name of Hy Gage and then, in lightning sketch fashion, drawing a caricature of the real animator out of the signature. As if such a graphic representation were insufficient evidence for the artist's work, Kartoono ends with a live-action shot of Gage tipping his straw hat to his audience.

Jack King's *A Cartoonist s Nightmare* (Warner Bros., 1935), clearly draws a portrait of what animators feel about their craft – as early scenes show a bunch of crazies leaving an asylum. In the film, a wife pulls her husband away from his magnificent obsession, but he resists, claiming: "I gotta finish tonight". Falling asleep at his drawing board, one of his wicked characters pulls the sleeping cartoonist into the cartoon – much like actors in the Joe Dante episode of *Twilight Zone: The Movie*, being caught and incarcerated in a cartoon television program. The hairy monster drags him down the corridors through the gag department, the story and music departments, down to the dungeons of "cartoon villains" such as Spike the Spider. Each is assigned a number: #130 for Dirty Dan and #20 for Battling Barney. These wayward characters, creations fallen from his own imagination, sing to him: "It's our turn. Now you are in our clutches! We are creations from your pen, it's in your hands we lie; you always manage to have us sin, now by your own hand you die." These characters seem to prefigure Jessica Rabbit (from *Roger Rabbit*, 1988), who confides to Eddie Valiant that she really isn't bad; she is "just drawn that way".

Two animated films from the silent era unveil the art of filmmaking in narratives about filmmakers – with added commentary on the scandal of adultery.

Revenge of the Kinematograph Cameraman (1912) is a satirical puppet film using waxed insects, made by Russian entomologist Wladislaw Starewicz (*aka* Ladislas Starevich). In the film, a businessbug from the country, Mr. Zhukov (a beetle), leaves his bugwife and goes to the city where he succumbs to the lusty temptation of a Dragon-fly cabaret dancer. A jilted suitor, the grasshopper, who happens to be a cameraman, bicycles around and films the bad beetle and his paramour from behind bushes and through the keyhole of a hotel bedroom door.

The completed film is then shown at an outdoor cinema that Mr. Zhukov and his wife are unsuspectingly attending. Mrs. Zhukov sees the sin of her husband on the big screen and, enraged, demolishes both her husband and the screen. The film within the film exposes the hypocritical behaviors of the bugs and insinuates a parallel within the real film community. It portrays an insect's drudgery of filmmaking, loading and transporting equipment, and setting up and shooting – but, finally, the exhilaration of exhibiting one's work. Its function is shown to be the confrontation of the spectator with hidden and expressed desire. All the insects attending the premiere become neighborhood voyeurs, sharing in the spy work of the grasshopper cameraman. The consciousness of the spectator in recognizing or projecting one's life onto the screen is played out in all its irony as the beetle's lovemaking scene has been recorded, even as one of Kracauer's "found stories", wherein the spectator catches nature in the act.[31]

Catching "nature in *the* act" is also an implicit theme of American Otto Messmer's *Flim Flam Films* (1927). After Felix the Cat buys a movie camera, he turns it over to his mischievous kids. They use the camera to capture their dad's dalliance with a bathing beauty, getting Felix in loads of trouble with his infuriated spouse. The power of the camera in this Jazz Age cartoon is its ability to reconstruct such events as feline infidelity, but Felix's cartoon also shows problems inherent in the filmmaking process, such as improper framing, disjointed camera angles, and inverted images.

Another film in which animated characters both make and watch cartoons is American Tony Sarg's impressive silhouette animation of 1922, *The Original Movie*. In the film, Sarg explores the entire process of filmmaking from the perspective of a stone-age filmmaker. A screenwriter hires Stonehenge Film Co. to produce his film. They cast the parts and shoot his script of "Who's the Goat?" using a monkey camera operator hanging from a dinosaur's neck for a primitive crane shot. Censors arrive to cut up Mr. A. Flintpebble's film. The final product is a very short film that its writer cannot recognize. The intertitles announce Sarg's cynical moral: "It's a wise scenario – that knows its own author after it gets in the movies".

Various American studios also produced films with reflexive elements. From the Van Beuren studio in 1931 came the clever, frenetic *Making em Move* (*aka In a Cartoon Studio*), a film about the madcap lunacy of animators and the creative anarchy that reigns in a cartoon studio. This unusually delightful exception to the run-of-the-mill Aesop Fables series sneaks a cartoon character (and us) into the secret recesses of a cartoon studio. Ominous signs along the corridor leading to the inner sanctum demand

"SILENCE". Dozens of cartoon artists are diligently drawing in what appears to be a Taylorized, capitalistic animation factory. A typical menagerie of cartoon animals form a busy musical band to keep the peon animators from rebelling or forming a union. The enslaved but happy animators create flipbooks of a hootchy-kootchy dancer, which are then shot by a camera on a tripod, and the little band is placed on the film to produce the sound track. Finally, the film premieres with the titles announcing: "A Movie Cartoon Today – Fables Animals Presents 'Little Nell'." The sawmill melodrama is acted out by stick figures (twice or thrice removed from the real). The actors bow and, when the villain appears, the crowd hisses and boos. The villain responds with bronx cheers for which the audience punches in the screen.

From Warner Bros. came *You Ought To Be In Pictures* (Friz Freleng, 1940), wherein Porky Pig meets with Leon Schleschinger to discuss his contract. In another short, *Porky s Preview* (Tex Avery, 1941), Porky Pig produces his own cartoon. Holding a special screening for animal friends, Porky revels in his crude, stick-figure scrawls, which Leonard Maltin points out bear a remarkable resemblance to the later UPA animation. Porky brags that it wasn't hard because, "shucks, I'm an artist". Avery's text is a gentle piece of self-mockery and irony on the "low art" of animated cartoons. All these cartoons are affectionate footnotes to the magic of film and television, simultaneously debunking that magic by dismantling the cinematic apparatus.

Throughout film history, cartoons have commonly quoted and referred to other cartoons and cinematic texts. *Who Framed Roger Rabbit* (1988), for example, cascades with animated allusions, inside references and jokes, such as the ubiquitous ACME or Daffy Duck complaining in his customarily irascible fashion that he can't understand the squawking of Donald Duck. But the practice of intertextual footnoting originated much earlier. Even Walt Disney in his sketchy *Puss n Boots* (1922) advertised not only the Newman Kingville Theater, as it was supposed to do, but also a Rudolph Valentino character, who would, it was promised, "throw the bull in six parts".

Some cartoons are endowed with a sense of consciousness that humorously connects them to points of art and culture outside themselves. Dozens of cartoons have paid tribute to Hollywood, its stars, and its films. For example, caricatures of famous film luminaries are spotlighted in Disney's *Mickey s Gala Premiere* (1933), in which Greta Garbo embraces a giggling Mickey Mouse, and *Hollywood Steps Out* (Tex Avery, 1941), in which Clark Gable is recognized by his oversized elephantine ears. Such cartoons were peppered with playfully coded references to the cultural texts of Hollywood. The same pattern is evident in the "Flip the Frog" short, *Movie Mad* (1931), from Ub Iwerks, and in Warner Bros.'s *Coo-Coo Nut Grove* (Friz Freleng, 1936). Donald Crafton notes the irony of the Pat Sullivan/Otto Messmer production of *Felix in Hollywood* (1923) that ends "with Cecil B. DeMille handing Felix one of those long term contracts just when Sullivan and Winkler were haggling over renewal ...".[32] Stanley Cavell points out that the "lows of culture" generally do burlesque "the conditions of high art, [as] the highs often need decanting, and the lows are often deeper and more joyful".[33] The lowly cartoon is a most apt vehicle for cracking the pretensions of the dominant cinema.

Caricature has functioned as a point of contrast with the real world, parodying the Hollywood Star System. Scores of back-handed tributes played with the dominant characteristics and circulating gossip of key actors and actresses. Mae West rumbles her way into Disney's 1935 parody *Who Killed Cock Robin?* Katharine Hepburn made frequent cartoon cameos; in Disney's *Mother Goose Goes Hollywood* (1938), she is a forlorn Little Bo Peep, while her distinctive voice pervades Warner Bros.'s *Hamateur Night* (Tex Avery, 1939). Many other star parodies came from Warner Bros. as well. For example, Humphrey Bogart and sizzling Lauren "BeCool" Bacall, whistling like a construction worker, are featured in the studio's *Bacall to Arms* (Bob Clampett, 1946). Gregory Peck cuts his steak with a Spellbound-like knife in the studio's *Slick Hair* (Friz Freleng, 1947). Inside jokes on Bing Crosby and his obsession with horse racing decorate many cartoons, such as Warner Bros.'s *Hollywood Daffy* (Friz Freleng, 1946), in which Daffy also disguises himself as Duck versions of Charlie Chaplin, Billy Durante, and even the Oscar statuette.

In fact, the list of quotation films from Warner Bros. is very long. To name but a few: *Bosko s Picture Show* (Hugh Harman, 1933), *Hollywood Capers* (Jack King, 1935), *Porky and Gabby* (Ub Iwerks, 1937), *The Film Fan* (Bob Clampett, 1939), *A Star is Hatched* (Friz Freleng, 1938), *Porky s 5 & 10* (Ben Hardaway and Cal Dalton, 1938), *Porky s Movie Mystery* (Bob Clampett, 1939) *What s Cookin Doc?* (Bob Clampett, 1944), and *Bunny and Claude* (Robert McKimson, 1968). *Daffy Duck in Hollywood* (Tex Avery, 1938) mocked the studio world of Wonder Pictures, where the motto was "If We Make It, It's a Wonder!" In *Stage Door Cartoon* (Friz

Freleng, 1944), Bugs Bunny and Yosemite Sam watch a black and white cartoon, "One 'o them thar B.B. cartoonies!" A film clip of Errol Flynn as Robin Hood punctuates the finale of *Rabbit Hood* (Chuck Jones, 1949). After cutting away to Flynn, a skeptical Bugs Bunny looks into the camera and mutters, "Naw, that's silly. It couldn't be him;" the episode cleverly inverts the concepts of reality and illusion by allowing the cartoon to pass judgment on the live-action film, even denying its plausibility. A parodic apotheosis occurs in *Hollywood Canine Canteen* (Robert McKimson, 1946), in which all the actors and actresses are dogs.

In the Academy Award winning UPA cartoon *When Magoo Flew* (Pete Burness, 1955), old Mr. Magoo boards a plane that he mistakes for the Rialto Theater. He watches real life policemen chase a crook on the plane and thinks he is watching a "realistic 3-D" movie. His only complaint when he deplanes is that there was no cartoon; he asks, "You don't happen to show cartoons of that funny little near-sighted man, do you?"

Of all genres, cartoons seem particularly suited to deconstructing the film medium itself. Films like Robert Swarthe's *Kick Me* (1975) dabble with the limits of the frame. Swarthe's cameraless animation begins by announcing: "Ladies and Gentlemen, this animated film is made of tiny little pictures drawn on Motion Picture film." The protagonist, a stick figure, falls outside the frames on a strip of celluloid. Trying to get back, he is chased by a large black spider from frame to frame. Just as he is to be caught, he is rescued *deus ex machina*, by what appears to be the burning of the film. However, the burning becomes a new pursuer. In a brief segment in *Allegro Non Troppo* (1976), Bruno Bozzetto's grand parody of

Disney's *Fantasia* (1940), a little fellow also discovers the transitory, flammable nature of film. As the paper on which he was drawn burns him into oblivion, he bravely waves farewell.

The nature of the film medium is also foregrounded in Wolfgang Urchs's *Contraste* (1964), in which a rumpled housewife decides to modernize her home. She trades in traditional furniture for abstract, fashionable objects: a classic piano for a new technological music machine, Renaissance paintings for contemporary art works. Finally, she exchanges her pipe-smoking, traditional husband for a Picasso-like lover, who immediately seeks to find himself a more-up-to-date mate. Realizing she has discarded what was truly valuable to her, she stops the cartoon by stepping out of the frame to the sprocket holes and begins to reverse the flow of time. By speeding the frames in reverse, the hausfrau is able to restore her life to the beginning of the film, bringing back all her drab furniture and retrieving her original dull, but faithful, husband.

Another well-known example of reflexive film is the 1985 Grand Prize winner at the Hiroshima Animation Festival, Osamu Tezuka's hilarious *Broken Down Film*. In this delightful homage to American Westerns, with gags borrowed from Keaton and other silent comedians, the cartoon becomes a projectionist's nightmare, with two countdown leaders, inverted title cards, shifting frame lines, scratches drawn on the film, and animated hairs apparently stuck in the gate. In Tezuka's film, humor arises out of the breaking of spectator expectations and the frame-play breaks the illusion of watching a film. *Broken Down Film* disrupts the set of shared codes for even an animated film, deconstructing the conventional grammar and reworking the codes into a fresh perspective on the nature of film itself. ✆

Notes

1. Mikhail M. Bakhtin, *Rabelais and His World*, trans. Helene Iswolsky (Cambridge, MA: MIT, 1965). Comic ambivalence can be defined as a perpetual dynamic relationship between opposites such as life and death; the grotesque involves the "funny monster" wherein horror has been infused with comedy; and the universal demands that the comedy laugh at everyone and everything, including itself and its forms. Such playfulness in light of the terrible is a characteristic of postmodernism. Susan Ohmer suggests that *Who Framed Roger Rabbit* might be considered the first postmodernist cartoon, "for the way it appropriates narrative and visual elements from other sources and juxtaposes them to create new relationships with the past". Susan Ohmer, "*Who Framed Roger Rabbit*: The Presence of the Past", *Storytelling in Animation*, ed. John Canemaker (Los Angeles: AFI, 1988): 102. This paper, however, argues that such practice occurred since the genesis of the animated film.

2. Vladimir Propp, *Morphology of the Folktale*, trans. Laurence Scott (Austin, Texas: U Texas P, 1968).

3. Siegfried Kracauer, *Theory of Film* (New York: Oxford UP, 1960), 90.

4. Jean Mitry, *Le Cinema experimental* (Paris: Editions Seghers, 1974), 204.

5. Erwin Panofsky, "Style and Medium in the Motion Pictures", *Film Theory and Criticism*, ed. Gerald Mast and Marshall Cohen (New York: Oxford UP, 1979), 252.

6. Dana Polan, "A Brechtian Cinema? Towards a Politics of Self-Reflexive Film", *Movies and Methods*, Vol II, ed. Bill Nichols (Los Angeles: UC Press, 1985): 667. In contrast to the self-referential quality of the Hollywood musical (insightfully demonstrated by Jane Feuer), the animated film is better equipped to bring about distanciation, the effect "whereby the spectator is lifted out of her transparent identification with the story and forced to concentrate instead on the artifice through which the play or film has been made". The animated film can make visible its own invisible frame and plasticity as well as its artistic conventions. Jane Feuer, "The Self-Reflective Musical and the Myth of Entertainment", *Quarterly Review of Film Studies*. (Aug. 1977): 313–326.

7. Paul Ricoeur, quoted in Dudley Andrew, *Concepts in Film Theory* (New York: Oxford UP, 1984), 181–182.

8. C.S. Lewis, *Experiment in Criticism* (Cambridge: Cambridge UP, 1960), 139.

9. Polan, 662.

10. Schneider, Steve. *That s All Folks: The Art of Warner Bros. Animation,* (New York: Henry Holt, 1988), 30.

11. Steve Seidman, *Comedian Comedy* (Ann Arbor, MI: UMI Research, 1981).

12. Lewis, 85.

13. Andre Bazin, *What is Cinema?* Vol. I (Berkeley: U California P, 1967), trans. Hugh Gray, 79.

14. Leonard Maltin, *Of Mice and Magic* (New York: New American Library, 1980), 259.

15. Maltin, 258.

16. Richard Corliss, "Warnervana", *Film Comment* 21:6 (November – December 1985), 18.

17. Roland Barthes, "The Death of the Author", *Image-Music-Text*, trans. Stephen Heath (New York: Hill and Wang, 1977), 148.

18. G.K. Chesterton, *As I Was Saying*, ed. Robert Knille (Grand Rapids: Eerdmans, 1985), 264.

19. J.R. Tolkien, "On Fairy Stories", *Essays Presented to Charles Williams*, ed. C.S. Lewis (New York: Oxford UP, 1947), 67.

20. Woody Allen, "The Kugelmass Episode", *Side Effects* (New York: Ballantine, 1980), 67.

21. Donald Crafton, *Before Mickey: The Animated Film, 1898–1928* (Cambridge, MA: MIT, 1982), 11.

22. Crafton, *Before Mickey*, 338.

23. Crafton, *Emile Cohl, Caricature, and Film* (Princeton: Princeton UP, 1990).

24. Crafton. *Before Mickey*, 187.

25. John Canemaker, "Animation for Adults", *Take One* (November 1978), 37, 40–41.

26. Marie-Helene Davies, *Laughter in a Genevan Gown* (Grand Rapids: Eerdmans, 1983), 133.

27. Gerald Peary and Danny Peary, eds., *The Animated Cartoon: A Critical Anthology* (New York: EP Dutton, 1980). See also Chuck Jones's *Chuck Amuck* (New York: Farrar Straus Giroux, 1989) and Jones's address at the Illusion of Life Conference, "What's Up, Down Under?", *The Illusion of Life: Essays on Animation*, ed. Alan Cholodenko (Sydney: Power, 1991): 37–66.

28. Robert Russett and Cecile Starr, *Experimental Animation* (New York: Van Nostrand Reinhold, 1976), 14.

29. Russett and Starr, 38.

30. Jean Baudrillard, *The Evil Demon of Images* (Sydney: Power, 1984), 13. As cartoon characters are the quintessential simulacra of an image industry, their texts are ontologically related to themselves and to their evolved oeuvre. As their identities become encrusted and reified, they are realized in shopping malls, on tee-shirts, coffee mugs, and a plethora of trivial consumer objects.

31. Siegfried Kracauer, *Theory of Film* (New York: Oxford UP, 1960), 31.

32. Donald Crafton, *Before Mickey: The Animated Film 1898–1928 (*1982. Cambridge, MA: MIT, 1987), 343.

33. Stanley Cavell, *The World Viewed* (Cambridge, MA: Harvard UP, 1979), 122.

Lindvall, Terry and Matthew Melton. "Toward a Postmodern Animated Discourse: Bakhtin, Intertexuality and the Cartoon Carnival", *Animation Journal* 3:1 (Fall 1994), 44–64. ©1994 Terry Lindvall and Matthew Melton

9

Innocent Play or the Copycat Effect? Computer Game Research and Classification

Jørgen Stensland [2001]

n Norway, film censors have had the same status as customs officers or parking attendants. This has to do with a long tradition of film classification dating back to 1913. We are less concerned with our popularity than our main task: the protection of youth and children.[1] This is contrary to what many Norwegian citizens think, namely that we enjoy prohibiting films, in general, and more specifically, limiting peoples' personal freedom.

In the old days, film censorship agencies around the world kept society relatively 'tidy' by censoring films. All that changed with the coming of television and, in Norway especially, the liberalization of broadcasting laws and the technological evolution that brought us videos and satellite dishes during the 1980s. Electronic video and computer games followed a short time later. The introduction of each new technology has created its own media panic. The latest was brought on by the Internet, what some would call 'the medium of

pornography, child abusers, cyberstalkers, and Nazis'.

Many believe that the next evolution of the media will be its convergence.[2] The Norwegian Commission regarding Convergence in the Media has concluded that we need to bring together the laws of different media, since it seems they all will glide into one entity in the future. In other words, you can surf the Internet on television or on your cell phone, watch television on your computer, or read a book on your personal communicator/cell phone. We are also seeing cinema films becoming digitized and transmitted to theaters via satellites. This convergence and digitalization of the media will present media classification agencies all over the world with a huge challenge.[3] We must ask how are we to fulfill our main objective, the protection of kids, when technological and maybe judicial developments make our ways of protection obsolete. I see two ways to do this in the future, and only one of them is plausible in a democracy.

The first method is to regulate the media as it is done in countries like Iran or Singapore. The media regulation in these countries achieves what everyone claims to be impossible: full censorship of the Internet. I will not get into the technical specifications of their work, but I will provide a general example. In Singapore, censorship is based on an all-inclusive penalizing of the people, institutions and companies involved in the use of illegal material. For example, if a teenage boy in Singapore downloads sexually-explicit photos, not only will he be punished, but so will the telephone company that owns the wires the images were sent through and the people who run the servers that supply the material to him. In other words, everyone who has something to do with the action will be put before the magistrate and sentenced. As you can imagine, this is very preventive, particularly when you consider the length of sentencing in Singapore.[4] This example shows that, contrary to many beliefs, you can control almost anything – but not without costs to democratic ideals.

That leaves us with the other alternative I propose: using public relations, information management, relationship building and research. We cannot control the flow of moving images or hypertext on the Internet, mainly because most of the consumption of these images is conducted within private homes. That leaves us with the strategy of educating the users themselves: teach children not to give out personal information on the Internet, educate kids and adults about the dangers out there, and to try to stop people from having irrational fears. Most importantly, we must try to bridge the gap between the children's increasing knowledge of technology and the parents' relatively small understanding of the Internet and other new media products.

Classification Systems in Various Countries

As an example of the new challenges we are facing, I will discuss the development of classification systems regarding computer games. The public panic created by computer games illustrates the dynamics that come into play when a new medium enters private spheres and public discussions. Computer games also provide a good example of the industry and the government working together to give parents a classification system that helps them choose appropriate games for their kids.[5] In this paper, I will first talk about regulation of computer games both in Norway and abroad. Then, briefly, I will provide an overview of research, development theory related to children, general media influence theory, and finally research on computer games.

Norway does not have any specific public regulation of computer games. However, at the request of the Department of Culture, the Norwegian Board of Film Classification did some research on the matter. This research resulted in a report about regulation of computer games, which was published in 1998.[6] In that report, we concluded a few things:

- Computer games shall be covered under the law about film and videos, but shall have their own status under the paragraphs of that law.
- All computer games should be tagged with an age limit before they are sold to a customer.
- The computer game industry itself shall administer this arrangement.
- The Norwegian Board of Film Classification will have the right to

check certain computer games that we think may create public havoc or that we suspect contain sexual or violent matter, and the authority to second or change the age limit put there by the distributors.

The ability of the government to sanction and control is connected with an active and conscious audience, a responsible industry, and the Norwegian Board of Film Classification, which actively monitors the development of computer games. This control competence is built on the voluntary submission of computer games, as well as references to games in the press and other media, including the Internet and computer game magazines. It also relies on reactions and messages from 'ordinary people' who contact us on a daily basis. This type of regulation is very similar to the way that video is regulated in Norway. All video films must be registered; distribution companies send in films for evaluation and the Board monitors those containing a lot of sex and/or violence.

A lot has happened in this area since in 1998, when the report on computer games was made, especially regarding the role of authorities. In recent years, the media panic regarding video and computer games has died in Norway and other countries have developed so-called 'soft-line regulation' solutions, in which the industry is included in the creation of classification agencies to a certain degree. In Norway, as of early 2003, we are participating in the Pan European Games Information (PEGI) advisory system regarding computer games, which I will discuss later in this paper, after I present an overview of the situation in some other countries.

Sweden is also a member of PEGI. In the past, it did not practice any form of governmental control of computer games.

In 1999, the Swedish parliament changed the words in the law regarding video to something that can be translated to "technical recordings" to include computer games. The Swedish Board of Film Classification (Statens Biografbyrå) has had some advances from the Swedish computer game industry, which has sought advice regarding classification of content in violent computer games. However, these incidents are very rare. The Swedish Council on Media Violence (Våldskildringsrådet) has an advisory role regarding computer games and publishes texts directed towards both schools and the general public.

Denmark does not have any adult censorship of film but the Media Council for Youth and Children (Medierådet for Børn og Unge) determines age limits for films and videos targeted to viewers under 15 years of age. There is no governmental regulation of computer games in Denmark, though information about computer games can be distributed as a part of public relations work from the Media Council for Young People and Children. However, they have come up with their own ratings for Danish-produced computer games, having worked very closely with the industry in Denmark. Because most of the games produced by Danish manufacturers are targeted to the youngest children, and thereby are not of a violent nature, they have decided to tag the games with as much information about suitability as possible. Most systems do the opposite, emphasizing harmful aspects rather than suitability. By 2003, Denmark was a member of PEGI.

We find a more traditional way of classification in Finland with their new film law, which includes computer games. All games must be registered and marked with age limits, and those deemed too violent can be banned. They have the right to check computer games regarding harmful content, but as of May 2001 only had checked two games. If the games are marked by PEGI, they will accept the age limits automatically. The Finnish regulation of computer games was instrumental in the industry's move for a common European regulation system. Since the profits on most games are quite minimal, the costs of production must be low.

Otherwise, one can risk a situation like in New Zealand, where strict rules on computer games ensure that most software producers do not bother selling their games there. New Zealand has a rigorous system maintained by the office of Film and Literature Classification, in which computer games are treated under the 'Publications' act.[7] A number of offices and official bodies submit computer games to the Board. Submissions will usually contain text or images that deal with matters such as sex, crime, horror, cruelty or violence. Computer games (and film and videos) are tagged with colors. Green means that anyone can use the game. Yellow means that anyone can use it, but descriptive notes should be checked. It indicates that parental guidance is recommended for younger viewers and that the game is suitable for mature audiences over 16. Red means that the publication is restricted. The computer game "Manhunt" was banned in December 2003 in New Zealand. They stated that "the freedom of expression is outweighed by likelihood of injury to the public good that could result from this game's availability". A result of this is that possession of the game is liable to a fine of 2000 NZ Dollars (1234 USD). If you play

it with under aged kids you may have to pay a fine of 20,000 NZ Dollars (US$12,340).

In Australia, the Commonwealth Classification Board (located in the Office of Film and Literature Classification in Sydney) is responsible for the classification of computer games. The definition of computer games includes single and compilation games on disk, CD-ROM, cartridges, add-ons, playstations and arcade machines. The classifications used are: all ages, 8 years and over, 15 years and over (suitability), restricted to 15 years and over (harmfulness), and, finally, refused classification (material that can not legally be sold, purchased, advertised or exhibited). It is an offense to sell unclassified computer games.

South Africa has a relatively new classification regime, established in 1996. They operate with four categories for interactive computer games: A, 13, 16 and 18. The classifications are not based upon suitability, but harmfulness. One interesting element with the South African classification is that, in addition to the regular categories, they also have 'prejudice' as a judicial element: computer games (or films, for that matter) shall not contain bias or negative stereotyping in regard to race, ethnicity, gender or religion. Except for this criterion, age limits are defined by language, drugs, nudity, sex and violence. Computer games classified as XX are considered illegal to sell or rent in South Africa.

British Columbia provides an interesting example because it has moved from an industry-run regulation system to one run at the province level as a part of their "turn off violence" strategy. In April 2001, legislation made B.C. the first jurisdiction in North America to implement a state-run classification and regulatory system. All games are classified using regulations for computer games established by an industry-level organization in the United States, the Entertainment Software Rating Board (ESRB), with some modification to reflect community standards. However, the age limits used are the same as those employed for film classification in B.C.: all audiences, PG, 14, 18 and restricted. This judicial development came as a result of a public outcry and debate, following the release of the game "Soldiers of Fortune". The rest of Canada relies upon the ESRB rating system.[8]

France has no special law governing computer games. However, a 1998 'minor protection law' created an administrative body that can prohibit both their sale to minors and the advertising of games including harmful content to minors. An industry trade organization, Sell, developed a voluntary system that exists mainly to limit publishers' liability in case of complaints. The ratings are examined every quarter.

The Portuguese board of film classification decides on computer game age classification. The age level of a game's suitability is given with regard to its degree of complexity but also the harmfulness is considered. The decisions of the board may be appealed.

In contrast, Great Britain is the European Union country that has moved furthest in the direction of organized governmental regulation of computer games. It practices relatively strict computer game classification on the same level as its video classification. The quasi-governmental British Board of Film Classification (BBFC) that evaluates movies and videos also classifies the content of computer games, attaching age

limits to them. The classification is regulated by the Video Recordings Act of 1984 and the Criminal Justice and Public Order Act of 1994. It only applies to computer games containing:

- Human sexual activity or acts of violence connected to such activity.

- Mutilation or torture or other explicit acts of violence towards humans or animals.

- Human sexual organs, scat [excrement] or urine.

- Techniques that can be used in unlawful activities.

Only computer games employing physical-storage technologies are evaluated (for example, CD-ROMs and cassettes, as opposed to the Internet). The BBFC banned the computer game "Carmageddon" in 1997, when it was evaluated as containing immoral content. However, the distributors altered the game's content to some extent and, eventually, "Carmageddon" was allowed by the courts with an age limit of 18 years.

The Irish system is similar to the British one. Computer games are covered by the Irish Video recording act, but are generally exempt from classification unless the content is particularly controversial.

Industry Self-Censorship

The Pan European Games Information (PEGI) age rating system is a new, pan-European age rating system for interactive games. Designed to ensure that minors are not exposed to games that are unsuitable for their particular age group, the system is supported by the major console manufacturers, including PlayStation, Xbox and Nintendo, as well as by publishers and developers of interactive games throughout Europe. The age rating system has been developed by the Interactive Software Federation of Europe (ISFE) and has the enthusiastic support of the European Commission, who considers the new system to be a model of European harmonisation in the field of protection of children.

Starting in the early spring of 2003, PEGI replaced existing national age rating systems with a single system that is identical throughout most of Europe. The game rating appears on the front and back cover of interactive games, and retailers provide information on the new system. The age rating system comprises two separate but complementary elements. The first is an age rating, similar to some existing rating systems. The PEGI age bands are 3+, 7+, 12+, 16+, 18+. The second element of the new system is a number of game descriptors. These are icons, displayed on the back of the game box that describes the type of content to be found in the game. Depending on the type of game, there may be up to six such descriptors. The intensity of the content is appropriate to the age rating of the game. The combination of age rating and game descriptors allows parents and those purchasing games for children to ensure that the game they purchase is appropriate to the age of the intended player.

PEGI applies to products distributed in the following countries: Austria, Belgium, Denmark, Finland, France, Greece, Ireland, Italy, Luxembourg, Netherlands, Norway, Portugal, Spain, Sweden, Switzerland and the UK.

In the United States, content control of computer games is voluntary. Industry members send in games (at their own discretion) to the Entertainment Software Rating Board (ESRB), which evaluates a game's content and suitability for children and youth. The ESRB was established in 1994 after massive criticism from the general public and Congress. The ESRB demands that its members follow age limits; it can refuse to tag games and give members fines if they abuse the system. The games contain so-called 'content descriptors' also found on videos in North America, such as 'animated violence', 'realistic blood', and 'mature sexual themes'.

Germany provides voluntary control of computer games through a nongovernmental institution, The Entertainment Software Self-regulation body (Unterhaltungssoftware Selbstkontrolle), which operates for the protection of children and youth. It evaluates the suitability of games and the legality of their content. About 95 per cent of all computer games in Germany are delivered to USK, so apparently it is perceived to be an attractive service for the industry. USK puts age limit recommendations on the games and these tags are thought to give the distributor and their goods a greater credibility on the market, as well as a clearer relationship to German penal law.

The Netherlands began a new system of classification in 2001. The Dutch Institute for Classification of Audiovisual Media (NICAM) was created at the initiative of the government, industry and various bodies to set a uniform system of voluntary classifications for all audiovisual media. Publishers classify their products under the NICAM standard classification system, using labels that provide age recommendations. Publishers can get help from NICAM if they are in doubt of the classification. The NICAM system was used as a basis for the Pan European PEGI system.

Spain employs a voluntary system developed by ADESE, the Spanish organization for leisure software producers. This is a voluntary code of conduct with regard to age classification. The publishers and distributors set an age rating for their products on the basis of a standardized assessment form.[9]

For various reasons, judicial standards concerning content control of computer games are only now being formulated. Most important is the fact that advanced technical and graphical development and huge sales have occurred within the last ten years, which means that the issues they present are relatively new. Many European countries with a tradition of regulating violent content in motion pictures are now in a position of deciding whether the same standards should be applied to computer games. There are divided attitudes about governmental regulation of this area and the preferred arrangement seems to be self-censorship organizations. This does not mean less regulation than if governments where involved, only different regulation. It also does not suggest that rating standards will be lower: for instance, the American industry-run film censorship board, MPAA, is much stricter than its European governmental counterparts regarding sexuality, nudity and coarse language.

Harmful Content?

In classification terminology, we very often speak about 'harmful content'. This brings us to another important consideration outside of the laws built on the politicians' attitudes: the research! Are computer games really that harmful to kids? Are kids today more sophisticated than we were as children? Can they understand the irony of the content, so they are not really scared by it? Development theories provide greater understanding of what 'childhood' entails.[10]

Our traditional understanding, based on developmental psychology, is that we must apply different cognitive levels to various age groups: all ages are different and determine the degree to which a young viewer understands history and structure in the narratives.[11] However, one criticism of 'level thinking' results from the fact that it is difficult to segment children into distinct groups. There are different identities that affect how children perceive things; for example, gender, race, and social status. In the United States, recent studies have found that ethnicity is a very important factor when it comes to children's appreciation of their world and their cognitive horizon.[12] Nonetheless, a developmental prospective provides a useful way to begin thinking about child viewers.

Children ages 2–11 have some common traits:

- Discovery: making known the unknown.
- Individualization: moving from being tightly bound to the parents to being more and more independent.
- Long-term gratification: understanding the difference between short- term and long-term payoffs (is it better to have one candy bar today or two candy bars tomorrow?).

Other traits are seen within specific age groups:

- 1–2 years: They understand that they are individuals with an environment around themselves. Mainly physical and emotive development.
- 2–5 years: They have a concrete and immediate understanding of the world.
- 5–9 years: A huge cognitive development.

• 9–11 years: A huge emotive development. They start to put appreciation from friends and peers as high as that of adults and parents. This is often called the '10 year-old leap'.

In development theory, some have claimed that there has been compression and that kids are making this leap earlier than before, from the age of 8 or 9 – that children are getting older when they are younger, moving faster through their development. They think more abstractly, form groups of friends at an earlier age and place more importance in social meaning. However, a study by Michael Cohen suggests that this conclusion can be refined. He divided child development into three traits: emotive, physical and cognitive. He found that kids got older faster when it came to the cognitive and the physical parts, but not the emotive. In other words, he found that there has not been emotional compression; they know a little more, but they are just as likely to get frightened as before.[13]

Research on Media Violence

Research about media violence is unevenly distributed in the world. Mainly it has been done in North America and Western Europe, especially in Scandinavia. Australia and Japan also have produced studies on the topic. It is imperative to remember that huge cultural differences impact an understanding of not only the images of the media but also the narratives. For instance, animation and other narratives produced within Japan are inclined to show the suffering of the victims, while in Western narratives the protagonist (or antagonist, for that matter) tends to simply move on. In any case, most research focuses on the way in which children act out the violence they have seen; not so much has been done on

other aspects of the issue, such as fear or angst, for instance.[14]

Traditionally, there have been two competing perspectives. Catharsis theory, which is not well-regarded by scholars today, contends that watching violence has a sort of cleansing effect. More persuasive is learning theory, which is based on the argument that children's actions and thoughts are affected by their environment and that media is similar to other impulses a child receives. It further explains that children learn by imitation; such learning can include an understanding of situations where violence is acceptable – for example, as a conflict-solver. Some learning theory states that kids can be stimulated by violence in the media to the extent that they then are compelled to act out the violence. Another theory talks about 'immunization': how kids become tolerant of violence in the real world by watching it on television. To a certain degree, these theories are in opposition to each other.

So what can we really say about kids and violence? When I give lectures to the Norwegian public, I usually say that, regarding this question, I have bad news and good news. The bad news is that there appears to be a positive relationship between violence in the media and violence in real life. The good news is it only affects the behavior of less than one per cent of the population. Media provide only one type of influence and most studies show that, when it conflicts with influence on a personal level, the personal is dominant; individuals with relatively stable backgrounds are in no danger. On the other hand, some research shows that media violence is more likely to emotionally arouse kids who have been mistreated, abused or neglected. There are also gender differences. Though we are still talking in generalizations, boys get more violent, while girls tend to be scared. It also seems that already aggressive children seek out aggressive material. However, in our work in film classification, we are bound by law to take the perceived 'average viewer' into consideration, so when we evaluate for age limits, we do not make special considerations for 'high-risk kids'.

So, to conclude, media violence can have damaging effects and can be a catalyst for latent aggressiveness. But, fortunately, this only applies to a tiny part of the population.

Research on Computer Games

The research discussed so far focuses mainly on live-action media, such as feature films and television. Can the same findings be applied to computer games? Certainly, there are differences between computer games and other media on several levels, with two being especially interesting: interactivity and the social character of games. Here are some facts about the use of computer games:[15]

- Boys are more frequent users than girls.
- Young people are more frequent users than older people.
- The use of computer games is increasing.
- Computer games are mainly a social activity.

The last point is perhaps the most important one. A lot of public anxiety has been focused on the idea that young boys playing computer games are sitting alone, shooting or driving people down (as in the game Carmageddon). The fact is that computer games for young people function mainly as a social event. They sit together, laugh and fight, like in a normal play situation. And play is very central to this argument. Carsten Jessen, a Danish researcher, has claimed that problem-solving is at the heart of the medium. The children are playing computer games rather than watching them and this interactive standpoint creates a distance between the user and the medium. It is not based upon identification, like we find in films, but more on problem-solving play situations you find in board games and similar types of entertainment.

The first research about computer games, conducted in the mid-1980s, focused on differences between film, television, video and computer games. Silvern and Williamson compared the effect of cartoons and computer games to find out if the latter, with their interactive nature, would make kids more violent.[16] Their research showed no difference in the level of aggressive behavior between kids who had played computer games or watched cartoons.[17] A number of these studies were conducted and none could prove that kids got more violent or aggressive with computer games, compared to other media. Most of this research was done when computer games were not very technically advanced, but new research on games with better graphics has not changed in outcome.

Children's use of computer games is a complex field of research and traditional 'effect' approaches may be a bit simple. They have been criticized for using laboratory research situations and for being conducted over too short a time span. The hardest criticism has been toward the lack of definition of what constitutes 'violent behavior' and 'aggression' concerning children.

Researchers have been increasingly sensitive to the concept that even if kids appear to act violently while playing video games, there is a difference between aggression during play and games and regular aggression. The threshold for applying aggression is much lower in the game scenario.

Research has moved away from the effects tradition; more and more, it is an investigation of what kids do with the media, not the other way around. This reflects a general development in social sciences during this period. A lot of work in reception theory has been done in the last twenty years, with varied findings.[18] For example, it has been suggested that teenagers use violent or horror movies as part of a rite of passage, instead of using violence as mean in itself.[19] The research that connects violence in the media with the children's game culture conclude that there is a big difference between 'play' violence and 'real' violence: children always have had violent games, but now they are moved from the backyard into the living rooms, so that parents can see it. There have been few studies of computer games concerned with this subject, but those that have been done all underline children's understanding of the game as play and the social aspects of playing computer games.

Should We Regulate Computer Games by Law?

For the time being, there seems to be little reason to regulate computer games by law. Research tells us that the interactivity and the social nature of computer games actually creates less identification than, for example, a film. Problem solving is in the center of it. However, some critics (more politicians and religious groups than researchers) are worried about the tactile effects of 'shoot 'em up' games. For instance, after the Columbine High School murders in Colorado, this theme returned to public debate. But it does seem like the moral panic about computer games has subsided. Politicians do not appear to be very concerned with computer games and classification agencies around the world do not seem to find them interesting either. With a few exceptions, all classification concerning computer games are being conducted by quasi-governmental or private classification agencies. However, the classification agency in British Columbia has moved in the other direction and maybe other provinces, states or countries will follow. Whether the classification systems are public or started by the industry, I think these categories can be a useful tool for parents in choosing which games are suited for their children. 🍎

Notes

1. Jørgen Stensland, "Teksteori i praksis: Om filmtilsynets filmavgjørelser", *Norsk Medietidskrift* Skogerbø and Muhleisen, ed. (Bergen,1999).

2. Thomas Baldwin, D. McVoy, and Charles Steinfeld, *Convergence. Integrating Media, Information and Communication* (London: Sage, 1996).

3. Nicholas Negroponte, *Leve Digitalt* (Oslo: Tiden, 1995).

4. Elisabeth Staksrud, "Ideology of Survival. Freedom of Expression, Internet Regulation and Polical Legitimization in Singapore", thesis, Cand. Polit., University of Oslo, 1999.

5. Dag Asbjoernsen, "Regulering av dataspill", Statens filmtilsyn (The Norwegian Board of Film Classification), 1998. Jan Christofferson, *Monstermassakern* (Stockholm: Våldskildringsrådet, 1999)

6. Dag Asbjoernsen "Regulering av dataspill".

7. 'Publications' is defined widely to include films, videos, magazines, computer discs, video games,

CD-ROMS, printed clothing, posters, sound recordings and playing cards. However, non-filmic publications are not required to be submitted for classification and, therefore, are not automatically labeled.

8. The Provinces of Yukon and Saskatchewan follow B.C.'s film and video ratings, but to my knowledge they do not include computer games.

9. Austria, Belgium, Greece, Italy, Iceland, Luxembourg, have no system of regulation and, as far as I know, there are no other countries with governmental or voluntary content regulation of computer games. If you know about other systems, please write to me at Jorgen@kino.no

10. A variety of studies might be consulted for more information. See, for example, Andreas Demetriou, ed., "The Neo-Piagetian Theories of Cognitive Development: Toward an Integeration", *International Journal of Psychology* 22 (1987); David Henry Feldman, *Beyond Universals in Cognitive Development* (Norwood, New Jersey: Ablex,1994); Jerome Kagan,ed., *A Cross-cultural Study of Cognitive Development* (Chicago, 1979); Geoffrey B. Saxe, *Culture and Cognitive Development: Studies in Mathematical Understanding* (Hillsdale, NJ: Erlbaum, 1991); Irving Sigel and Rodney Cocking, *Cognitive Development from Childhood to Adolescence: A Constructivist Perspective* (New York: Holt, Rinehart and Winston, 1977); Peter Valletutti and Leonie Dummet, *Cognitive Development: A Functional Approach* (San Diego: Singular, 1992); Valerie Walkerdine, *The Mastery of Reason: Cognitive Development and the Production of Rationality* (London: Routledge, 1988).

11. Jean Piaget, *The Place of The Sciences of Man in the System of Sciences* (New York: Harper & Row, 1974); Jean Piaget and B. Inhelder, *The Growth of Logical Thinking from Childhood to Adolescence: An Essay on the Construction on Formal Operational Structures* (New York: Basic Books, 1958). This view has been criticized by some; see, for example, Lev Vygotsky, *Thought and Language* (Cambridge: MIT, 1962).

12. Michael Cohen, "Child Development" lecture, Summit 2000 Conference, Toronto, Canada, 13–17 May 2000; Martha Bernal and George P. Knight, ed., *Ethnic Identity: Formation and Transmission among Hispanics and Other Minorities* (Albany, NY: State University of New York Press, 1993); Jean Phinney and Mary Jane Rotherham, ed., *Children s Ethnic Socialization: Pluralism and Development* (California: Sage, 1987).

13. Cohen, "Child Development" lecture.

14. Ulla Carlsson and Cecilia von Feilitzen, ed., *Children in the New Media Landscape* (Gothenburg: Nordicom, 2000); Kevin Durkin and Low Jason, Current Research in Australia and New Zealand", *Children and Media Violence*, Ulla Carlsson and Cecilia von Feilitzen, ed. (Gothenburg: Nordicom, 1998); Olga Linnè, "What Do We Know about European Research on Violence in the Media", *Children and Media Violence*, Ulla Carlsson and Cecilia von Feilitzen, ed. (Gothenburg: Nordicom, 1998); Sachiko Imazumi Kodaira, "A Review of Research on Media Violence in Japan", *Children and Media Violence*, Ulla Carlsson and Cecilia von Feilitzen, ed. (Gothenburg: Nordicom, 1998); Elise Seip-Tønnesen, "Understanding a Story. A Social Semiotic Approach to the Development of Interpretation, Cultural Cognition, *New Perspectives in Audience Theory*, Birgitta Høijer and Anita Werner (Gothenburg: Nordicom, 1998).

15. Eirik Befring, "Dataspill forklart for akademikere, "Cand. Philol. thesis, University of Oslo, 1995; Jan Christofferson, Monstermassakern; Mark Griffiths, "Video Game Violence and Aggression", *Children in the New Media Landscape*, Ulla Carlsson and Cecilia von Feilitzen, ed. (Gothenburg: Nordicom, 2000); Carsten Jessen and Birgitte Holm Sørensen, "Det er bare noe der er lavet ...", Statens Information, Copenhagen, 1999; Faltin Karlsen, "Dataspill og vold", Statens filmtilsyn (The Norwegian Board of Film Classification), 2001.

16. S. Silvern and P. Williamson, "The Effects on Videogame Play on Young Children's Aggression, Fancy and Prosocial Behaviour", *Journal of Applied Developmental Psychology* 8 (1987).

17. Jessen and Holm Sørensen, "Det er bare noe der er lavet ...".

18. Gunter Barrie, *Poor Reception* (Hillsdale: Lawrence Erlbaum, 1987); Sonia M.Livingstone, *Making Sense of Television: The Psychology of Audience Interpretation* (London: Comedia, 1990); David Morley, *Television Audiences & Cultural Studies* (London: Routledge, 1992).

19. Tove Arendt Rassmussen, "Actionfilm og killkultur", *Spelrum. Om lek, stil och flyt I*, Dahlèn, Rønnberg, Rasmussen, ed. Ungdomskulturen (Stockholm: Brutus Østlings bokforlag, 1990).

Stensland, Jørgen. "Innocent Play or the Copycat Effect? Computer Game Research and Classification". *Animation Journal* 9 (2001). 20–35. Revised. ©2001 Jørgen Stensland

Animation in
America

10

Winsor McCay

John Canemaker [1980]

Winsor McCay (1867–1934), one of the most innovative early masters of the American comic strip, was also a pioneer experimenter and master of the animated film. Long before the debut of his first film *Little Nemo* in 1911, McCay was an "animator" per se in the print medium. His reportorial illustrations for Midwestern newspapers (1898–1903), editorial cartoons (c. 1899) for humor periodicals (such as *Life* magazine), and ground-breaking comic strips "Dream of the Rarebit Fiend" (1904) and "Little Nemo in Slumberland" (1905) celebrate movement and burst with kinetic energy.

McCay's Leonardo-like eye captures subtle phases of motion in extraordinary and assured draftsmanship. In his epic dream strip "Little Nemo in Slumberland" (a child's version of the mythic theme of "the quest"), there are continuous sequential changes of characters, settings and patterns within the borders of its imaginatively flexible panels.

In McCay's ten known animated films, he patiently experimented with motion, timing, color, and, most importantly, characterization. In fact, "personality animation" – investing characters with a unique individuality basically through the way they move – is

an indigenously American contribution to the art form that has its roots in two of McCay's earliest films, *How a Mosquito Operates* (1912) and *Gertie the Dinosaur* (1914).

His animation style – realistic designs full of detail; smooth natural movements; the illusion of weight in the characters as well as distinctive personalities – predates by more than two decades the Disney studio's mature period that began in 1934. (Ironically, the year of McCay's death.)

Commenting on McCay's uncannily advanced techniques, Chuck Jones, the celebrated Warner Bros. cartoon director, once said: "It is as though the first creature to emerge from the primeval slime was Albert Einstein; and the second was an amoeba, because after McCay's animation, it took his followers nearly twenty years to find out how he did it. The two most important people in animation are Winsor McCay and Walt Disney, and I'm not sure which should go first." New York Times DVD reviewer David Kehr recently wondered "what more, apart from greater technical sophistication, was really left for Disney to add".

Roaring through McCay's work in print and film is a 20th century American energy, restlessness and love of motion. In his comic strips, he often depicted a high-tech world of space travel (predating wild futurist fantasies) which spilled onto the movie screen, i.e. *The Flying House* (c. 1921). His films celebrate physical movement; be it the magical appearances and antics of the cast of *Little Nemo*, the increasingly difficult flight of the stinging protagonist in *How a Mosquito Operates*, Gertie's ungainly "dance", or the slow, agonizing demise of the luxury liner in *The Sinking of the Lusitania* (1918).

McCay created his films by himself (with one or two assistants), and for himself. He never established a formal studio or explored commercial possibilities in mass-produced animated series. In this respect, he has much in common with modern independent animation filmmakers.

They also share a monk-like discipline and all-consuming love of the medium and its often tedious processes. Although animation never brought him the fame or the financial rewards that he garnered as a comic-strip artist, McCay claimed shortly before he died: "The part of my life of which I am proudest is the fact that I was one of the first men in the world to make animated cartoons".

Beginnings

Winsor McCay entered animation early in the art form's history, but late in his own. At age 44 (when he completed his first film) he had already enjoyed a classic turn-of-the-century success story in publishing and performance art (he appeared in his own vaudeville "chalk talk" act). Census records indicate he was born on September 26, 1867 in Woodstock, Canada, the birthplace of his parents.

Raised in the woodlands of Spring Lake, Michigan, his drawing ability and effortless visual memory for intricate details revealed itself early. However, his pragmatic father, a real estate agent for lumber firms, insisted his son study at the Cleary Business College in Ypsilanti in southeastern Michigan. McCay never attended classes, preferring to play hooky in Detroit, drawing and selling his caricatures at a "dime museum" called Wonderland. Such establishments combined aspects of vaudeville, funhouses, and circus freak shows under one roof. They influenced McCay's lifelong fascination with the grotesque and circus imagery. Distortion mirrors, monsters, giants, wild animals, and eccentric staircases, etc. are leitmotifs in much of his art.

He was briefly a student at Ypsilanti Normal School where he received his only instruction in art. McCay studied perspective under Professor John Goodison, a teacher of solid geometry. However, McCay was basically self-taught and learned on-the-job and through the exigencies of the commercial marketplace.

Then, in the great American tradition of artist-adventurers, he took to the open road. In 1889, the footloose young man was employed as an apprentice at the National printing and Engraving Company in Chicago, helping turn out garish colored woodcuts for circus and advertising posters. In the process, he gained an intimate knowledge of mass production printing techniques.

McCay may have traveled as a sign painter with one of the traveling carnivals, for he arrived in Cincinnati around 1891and became "a poster and scenic artist" for a resident freak show – Kohl and Middleton's Vine Street Dime Museum. He lived in a room on the top floor of the museum and turned out a seemingly inexhaustible series of colorful

freak art. This contact with "bearded
women, sword-swallowers, fire-eaters,
and similar attractions" fueled McCay's
taste for the fantastic, the exotic, clowns,
distortion mirrors, and carnival/circus
motifs that would enriched and enliven
his comic strips and animation art.

During his years in the "Queen City
of the Midwest", he married Maude
Dufour, with whom he had two children
(Robert and Marion), and he contributed
illustrations to the *Cincinnati Commercial
Tribune*. From January 11 to November 9,
1903 for the *Cincinnati Enquirer*'s Sunday
supplement, he devised a proto-comic
strip titled Tales of the Jungle Imps by
Felix Fiddle.

A spoof of Rudyard Kipling's "Just
So Stories for Children", Jungle Imps was
McCay's first attempt in an extended
series format to bring together his eclectic
talents into a cohesive graphic style:
exquisite draftsmanship, dynamic staging,
caricature, mastery of perspective, feeling
for motion, and his version of the
decorative art nouveau style.

The success of the Imps series
attracted the attention of James Gordon
Bennett, publisher of the *New York Herald*
and the *New York Evening Telegram*, and he
wooed McCay to New York in 1903 to
work as a staff illustrator on his papers
covering crimes, trials, and social events.
For Bennett's newspapers, McCay created
his early comic strips. These include Little
Sammy Sneeze (1904) and Hungry
Henrietta (1905), two child-strips that
were sustained efforts that consciously
tested principles of animation through
subtle sequential changes in the characters
movements. His adult-oriented strips
include Pilgrim's Progress (1905) and
Dream of the Rarebit Fiend, one of
McCay's longest running strips
(1904–1911, revived in 1913), which

featured nightmares, alternative worlds
with emphasis on accelerated changes in
size and age, as well as metamorphosis.

Little Nemo in Slumberland,
McCay's masterpiece, began in the New
York Herald on October 15, 1905. It is
simply the most beautiful comic strip ever
drawn; a supreme work of fantasy
illustration, drama, and compelling
characterizations of developing
personalities (chief among them the
boy-dreamer Nemo, modeled on McCay's
son, Robert). It represents a major creative
leap far grander in scope, imagination,
color, design, and motion experimentation
than any previous McCay comic strip and
certainly those of his peers.

Little Nemo ran in the Herald until
McCay joined the Hearst papers in
mid-July 1911, where it appeared under
another title until 1914, and was revived
in 1924 for two years. The strip made
McCay world famous. Nemo and friends
appeared in product advertisements for
toys and clothing (i.e., Little Nemo's
Barefoot Sandal). In 1908, a three-act,
twelve-scene "musical extravaganza"
version of the strip with music by Victor
Herbert (and employing almost 200 actors
and stagehands) played on Broadway for
123 performances and subsequently toured
American cities through 1910.

The strip was translated into several
languages and McCay's newfound fame,
plus his drive and flair for the theatrical,
enabled him to devise and star in his own
vaudeville act, in which he toured
successfully for eleven years. In his
twenty-minute act, which opened at Keith
and Proctor's 23rd Street Theatre in
Manhattan in June 1906, McCay first
drew members of the audience at random.
The pit orchestra played a two-step by
Fred Day titled "The Dream of the
Rarebit Fiend", a tune "full of queer,

unexpected musical phrases of an amusing nature".

The major section of McCay's act was "The Seven Ages of Man", a series of forty chalk drawings, drawn and erased one every thirty seconds, depicting facing profiles of a man and a woman getting progressively older as the orchestra played "Ah, Sweet Mystery of Life".

John A. Fitzsimmons, a teen-aged neighbor of the McCay family in Sheepshead Bay, New York, often watched the master artist at work at home and on the stage. "I never ceased to be amazed", Fitzsimmons said when he was in his eighties. "The directness with which he could finish a complicated piece of art work was simply fantastic... . [D]uring the blackboard segment of his act with chalk and eraser he altered with lightning strokes the features of first one and then the other of two facing infant heads he had sketched ... With deftly placed strokes and erasures here and there, he carried the boy-girl theme of this fascinating demonstration through all the periods of romance and love from infancy to extreme old age."

The August 31, 1906, *New York Telegraph* detailed McCay's hectic professional schedule:

> In addition to playing twice a day at Hammerstein's for the past four weeks, Mr. McCay in that period drew four full-pages of Little Nemo, four one-half pages of Rarebit Dreams, four three column Rarebit Dreams, four three column Dull Cares, drew a twenty four sheet design, an eight sheet design, and a three sheet design for the Klaw and Erlanger production of Little Nemo; also designed a scene for that big spectacle, and in his odd moments while going to and from meals dashed off a souvenir cover and a programme cover for a theatre.

Discovering Animation

McCay once wrote about how he became interested in making animated films: "Winsor, Jr., as a small boy, picked up several flippers of 'magic pictures' and brought them home to me. From this germ I established the modern cartoon movies in 1909 ... ".

John Fitzsimmons describes these "magic flippers" in more detail:

> The New York American had a Sunday supplement, a half page of the comic section, a little heavier than the news stock. Whoever made it drew a series of pictures you could cut out and put together with a rubber band and flick through your fingers. We were talking about that one day. That must have been the start because they were a novelty, they had advertising, some drug company. It got to be a fad for kids. Get these things, cut them out. I know he was talking about it.

In 1906 newspaper cartoonist J. S. Blackton's short animated film *Humorous Phases of Funny Faces* delighted movie audiences, and two years later the imported shorts of French animator Emile Cohl proved popular. Both Blackton's and Cohl's techniques were as simple as their elementary drawing styles, i.e., circle faces and stick figures.

McCay borrowed from both of these pioneer animators in his first film *Little Nemo*. From Blackton, he adapted the iconographic motif of a god-like live artist drawing characters that come to life; from Cohl, he used free-flowing abstractions of pencil lines forming into recognizable characters. Where McCay differed from his peers was in his ability to animate his drawings with no sacrifice in linear detail. This, plus fluid motion, naturalistic timing, a feeling of weight, and, eventually, the injection of personality traits into his characters are qualities

McCay first brought to the animation medium.

Fitzsimmons remembers that McCay finally made his first film as the result of a friendly bet with cartoonist-cronies George (*Bringing up Father*) McManus (who from 1912 to 1914 worked on animated films with Emile Cohl during the Frenchman's brief stay in America), Thomas "Tad" Dorgan, and Tom Powers:

> [T]he three or four of them were down in a saloon near the old American building at William and Duane Streets right under the Brooklyn Bridge ... I think McManus kidded McCay because he was such a fast worker ... Jokingly, McManus suggested that McCay make several thousand drawings, photograph them onto film and show the result in theatres ... McCay claimed he would produce enough line drawings to sustain a four or five minute animated cartoon showing his Little Nemo characters and would use the film as a special feature of his already popular vaudeville act.

McCay had no precedents to study for his kind of animation techniques; he was pioneering all the way. Silent movies flashed sixteen frames per second onto the screen and, according to Fitzsimmons, McCay "timed everything with split-second watches. That's how he got nice smooth action. For every second that was on the screen McCay would draw sixteen pictures ... He had nothing to follow, he had to work out everything for himself."

McCay's first three animated films were animated on six-inch by eight-inch sheets of translucent rice paper, the drawings were lightly penciled in first, then details were added in Higgins black ink with Gilliot #290 pens in holders. Fitzsimmons recalls, "After each drawing was completed, and a serial number assigned to it, marks [crosses] for keeping

it in register with the other drawings were placed on the upper right and left corners".

As each scene progressed to the "mounting" stage, the animation was checked for "smoothness of action" on a device McCay built based on a penny-arcade viewing machine. It was a box, twenty-four inches by twelve inches wide and twenty inches high, open at the top with a shaft running through it onto which a hub containing slits held the drawings. A crank revolved the hub and the drawings while a brass rod running across the top caught the cards momentarily, thus creating the interruption of vision provided by the shutter of a projector.

The Films

Little Nemo (1911)

Scores of drawings (allegedly 4,000) were drawn for this film by McCay alone. They were photographed onto one reel at the Vitagraph Studios in Brooklyn by Walter Austin, with a live-action prologue directed by James Stuart Blackton. The prologue featured McCay, George McManus, various Vitagraph executives, and John Bunny, the screen's first "star" comedian. Completed in early January 1911, the film was shown on 12 April as part of McCay's vaudeville act at New York's Colonial Theatre on Broadway near 63rd Street.

In the *New York Dramatic Mirror* of 29 March 1911, Vitagraph announced it was releasing the film on April 8 ("Winsor McCay, Famous Cartoonist of *The New York Herald* with his unique moving picture comics. A distinct novelty. Approximate length, 647 feet.").

An odd review appeared in the New York *Telegraph*; it fully described *Little*

Nemo's live prologue but not the animation:

> Something new in the line of novelty entertainment was provided by the sketch artist, Winsor McCay. "Moving pictures that move" is the way the offering is described on the programme and the idea is being presented for the first time on any stage. On a screen the Vitagraph shows pictures of Mr. McCay in company with several friends at a club.
>
> He is telling them of his new idea. The idea is made a subject of ridicule. They consider such an invention impossible. The artist, undismayed by this discouragement, signs a contract, agreeing to turn out 4,000 pictures in one month's time for a moving picture concern.

A slide is then thrown on the screen showing the artist at work in his studio. He makes good his threat and at the end of the month has fulfilled his contract. Congratulations from his friends now pour in on him and he produces his new discovery at the club, where the friends had scoffed at the idea. The fun derived from this invention in the moving picture field was thoroughly enjoyed. The *Telegraph* reporter, Robert Speare, went on to describe McCay's in-person chalk-talk act and never told what took place on the screen in Little Nemo's animation. It is quite probable that the reviewer was confused by the quality of the animation – its smooth timing and realistic drawings – and didn't know what to make of it since nothing of its like had ever been seen before.

McCay once admitted, "The first picture I made for stage use was Little Nemo and Flip, the Princess, Doctor Pill and the Imp, moving in a picture drama. It was pronounced very life-like, but my audience declared it was not a drawing but that the pictures were photographs of real children." This mistaken notion was reinforced in the vaudeville print of the film, for McCay painstakingly hand-colored each character in every frame of the 35mm film in primary colors.

In the film, after the live-action prologue, McCay's hand, holding drawing 1 (a profile of Flip with a cigar in his mouth) inserts it into a wooden slot in front of the horizontal camera. We (the camera's point of view) move in past the register marks of the drawing to a screen-filling close-up of Flip. The words "Watch me move" appear over his head, disappear, and his cigar tips jauntily up and down. He blows a sensuous Art Nouveau stream of smoke at us and majestically waves it away as he starts to bound in a dreamlike floating way into the distance. There are no backgrounds, just a limitless limbo. Perspective is indicated by the enlargement and reduction of the figure sizes. There is no plot and the characters appear magically as abstract lines that metamorphose into Impy, Nemo, and the Princess.

There is continual movement in the film: Nemo is formed by lines resembling steel filings attracted to a magnet (he is resplendent in a red cape and hat with red and yellow plumes); the Imp and Flip contort their forms as if they were fun-house mirrors; Nemo sketches the form of the Princess, she comes to life, and a rose grows just in time to be picked for her by Nemo. As a grand finale, a magnificent, three-dimensionally drawn and animated green dragon-chariot carries off the two children to Slumberland. Flip and Impy return in a jalopy that explodes and they land on Dr. Pill. The last drawing holds its position as the camera pulls back, revealing the wooden slot contraption that held the drawings in register.

American architect and author Claude Bragdon wrote of *Little Nemo*, "... it excited me greatly and no wonder! I had witnessed the birth of a new art".

How a Mosquito Operates (a.k.a. The Story of a Mosquito) (1912)

This film provides the first example of "personality" animation, in which an animated character appears to think and exhibits an individualism through its actions. This type of animation reached its zenith a quarter-century later in Walt Disney's *Snow White and the Seven Dwarfs* (1937).

McCay wrote of his second film, "I drew a great ridiculous mosquito, pursuing a sleeping man, peeking through a key hole and pouncing on him over the transom. My audiences were pleased, but declared the mosquito was operated by wires to get the effect before the cameras." The 600-foot film was completed in December 1911 and was sold to Carl Laemmle with the stipulation that it would not be shown in the United States while it was being screened in McCay's vaudeville act. He had competed with himself with Little Nemo and wished to limit the availability of his future films. (His animation was widely circulated in Europe and perhaps this explains why he is better known as an animator there.)

It was at this time that McCay began to tout the novelty called animated cartoons as a new art form. He declared in interviews that in the future people would not be satisfied with going to an art gallery to view "still" paintings:

> Take, for instance, that wonderful painting which everyone is familiar with, entitled The Angelus. There will be a time when people will gaze at it and ask why the objects remain rigid and stiff. They will demand action. And

to meet this demand the artists of that time will look to the motion picture people for help and the artist, working hand in hand with science, will evolve a new school of art that will revolutionize the entire field.

Gertie the Dinosaur (1914)

On 2 April 1912, McCay told the Rochester Post, "I myself have already been approached by The American Historical Society' to draw pictures of prehistoric animals, the present evidences of which are limited to their skeletons, which would represent some connected incident in their lives ... they could be shown on screens all over the world".

McCay considered his first two films "experiments", but he felt that with Gertie he had finally achieved "real success": "At last I had people convinced that they were looking at a picture drawn by hand, in which an animal was made to look like a living, breathing creature".

The initial performances of Gertie the Dinosaur took place at the Palace Theatre in Chicago in March 1914 and the following week at Hammerstein's in New York City. McCay lectured in front of the screen on which film of the cartoon dinosaur was projected. "Gertie was made to come out of a cave at my command and go through her stunts", he once explained:

> When the great Dinosaur first came into the picture, the audience said it was a papier-mache animal with men inside of it and with a scenic background. As the production progressed they noticed that the leaves on the trees were blowing in the breeze, and that there were rippling waves on the surface of the water, and when the elephant was thrown into the lake the water was seen to splash ... I made her eat boulders and pull up trees by the roots and throw an elephant into the sea. Gertie was made

to lie down and roll over and obey commands which I emphasized by a cracking whip ... This convinced them that they were seeing something new – that the presentation was actually from a set of drawings.

McCay asked his young Brooklyn neighbor, John Fitzsimmons, to assist him by retracing the stationary background of the rocks, trees, and water that appear behind Gertie in over 5,000 drawings. "He had a master drawing of the background and he would make the drawing featuring the animal. I would lay that over the master background and trace in pen and ink", said Fitzsimmons. Fitzsimmons's tracings are remarkably consistent and the background objects vibrate mildly but do not distract from Gertie's foreground antics. The trees do seem alive and windblown, the earth warm, the water sparkling; McCay once noted that he preferred to "animate even the 'still' figures, which some movie cartoonists don't do ... Unless all the live figures vibrate, the picture really isn't animated ... ".

McCay continued to experiment and improve upon his animation techniques with Gertie:

> When she was lying on her side I wanted her to breathe and I tried my watch, and also stop watch, to judge how long she was inhaling and how long it took her to exhale. I could come to no exact time until one day I happened to be working where a large clock with a big second dial accurately marked the intervals of time. I stood in front of this clock and inhaled and exhaled and found that, imitating the great Dinosaur, I inhaled in four seconds and exhaled in two. The result was that when the picture was run, instead of the Dinosaur panting as you would expect, she was breathing very easily. The breathing was shown by the sides of the monster expanding and contracting like a bellows.

McCay also discovered the labor-saving value in reusing drawings for a repeated "cycle" action. "When I drew Gertie breathing", he said, "I only drew her once, but I photographed that set of drawings over fifteen times". In the corner of the drawings, McCay would make notations for the cameraman; for example, "46 after 41", "45 back to 41", indicating the drawings to be reused.

McCay had, by this film, devised a technique he called the split system, which "greatly simplifies the process of timing and placing, which is intricate enough at best". Instead of animating an action "straight-ahead" from, say, drawing 1 to 33, McCay would "split" the action and draw first pose 1. He would then place another sheet of paper over the first drawing and make pose 33. On a third sheet of paper he would find the halfway pose, drawing 17 and continue to split the distance between drawings for the entire action. Most of the animators in the studios that began to spring up starting in 1913 preferred to animate straight-ahead. A few discovered their own split-system shortcuts, but it wasn't until the advent of sound cartoons in 1928 that Walt Disney insisted on the "pose (or extreme) drawings and in-between drawings" method, a refined version of McCay's split system.

Premiered in McCay's vaudeville act as a multi-media performance – McCay in person cracked a whip while commanding his cartoon dinosaur on the screen to obey him – *Gertie the Dinosaur* is a triumph of personality animation. The film inspired a generation to enter the movie cartoon field, including Paul Terry, Walter Lantz, Otto Messmer, and numerous future Disney animators, i.e. Vladimir Tytla, Richard Huemer, among others.

The Sinking of the Lusitania (1918)

On Friday, 7 May 1915, the English Cunard liner Lusitania, homeward bound from New York to Liverpool, was torpedoed without warning by a German submarine off the coast of Ireland. The ship sank in eighteen minutes, killing 1,198 people, including 124 Americans. The public's emotional response to this tragedy was a major factor in bringing the United States into World War I. "McCay was especially incensed at such wanton brutality", recalls John Fitzsimmons. "He proposed to make an animated cartoon graphically depicting the horrible tragedy."

This film, the only one McCay based on an actual historical event, is the first film in which he utilized celluloid instead of rice paper for the action drawings, thus allowing a stationary background to be used that didn't have to be drawn over again for each frame. Fitzsimmons, again assisting McCay, came up with the idea of using loose-leaf "binding posts ... attached to drawing boards and the sheets of celluloid were punched to fit snugly to them, thus the annoying problem of movement or shifting of drawings while being traced was reduced to a minimum ... [It] also facilitated the photographing of the drawings immeasurably and proved well-worth all additional expense."

Apthorp (Ap) Adams, "a very amusing friend" of McCay's from his Cincinnati newspaper days, who "liked to hit it up every once in a while" (have a drink), visited New York and McCay "shanghaied him" to work on the film for two years. Ap was responsible for one of the bigger technical errors that plagued the picture: a principal scene showed the Lusitania sailing along a horizon of gently rolling waves in the moonlight. McCay devised a series of sixteen drawings of waves that would be redrawn in sequence

on each drawing of the ship. When McCay had completed the 750 animation drawings of the ship, it was Ap Adams's chore to indicate by number which of the sixteen waves young Fitzsimmons was to draw on each celluloid. After several weeks when all the drawings had been completed for the scene, McCay placed a large segment of them into the testing machine. "The result was a catastrophe!" wrote Fitzsimmons. "Instead of the waves flowing smoothly as designed, the foreground resembled nothing so much as a drunken sea with ink lines shooting every which way. All 750 drawings had to be cleaned off and the series started all over from scratch. I had not been fed the wave numbers in proper sequence."

The Sinking of the Lusitania, containing approximately 25,000 drawings on cels, took twenty-two months to complete and was copyrighted on 19 July 1918, and released the next day by Universal-Jewel Productions. "The picture attracted attention at this time by virtue of its length and because it was a propaganda picture for the war", wrote Earl Theisen, Honorary Curator of the Motion Picture Division of the Los Angeles County Museum of Art in 1933.

The film resembles an editorial illustration in motion. The somber mood of the film, the animation's realistic timing, and detailed draftsmanship make it appear, in certain scenes, less a cartoon and more of a live-action documentary. Events are slowly presented in real time, making the film even more real despite stylized, serpentine smoke patterns emerging from the ship's funnels. A full spectrum of gray tones was used in the billowing smoke from the explosions within the ship's hull. This is one of the greatest animated films ever made; a

profoundly moving masterpiece of
propaganda that is truly ahead of its time.

The Centaurs (c. 1918–1921)

Three minutes and five seconds are all
that remain of this fantasy cartoon.
McCay was using celluloids for his
characters and more detailed wash
backgrounds. In the film a woman, nude
to the waist, strolls through a forest of
white birch trees, and soon we see her
torso is that of a calico horse. A
handsome centaur throws a rock and
knocks a vulture out of the sky. He
approaches the female and together they
walk slowly toward a pair of elderly male
and female centaurs. A baby centaur
(literally a child's head and torso attached
to a pony's trunk and legs) bounds into
the middle of the group, shows off with
back kicks, and the film abruptly ends.
McCay chose mythological beasts again
to prove to his critics that he worked
independently of photographs and
models. The centaurs and "centaurettes"
in Walt Disney's *Fantasia* two decades
later may have been inspired by McCay's
character designs in this film. Many older
Disney storymen were from New York
and might have seen McCay's films when
they were first released; for example,
Richard Huemer re-created McCay's
Gertie vaudeville routine, word for word
from memory, for a 1955 Disneyland
television show.

Flip's Circus (c. 1918–1921)

Another fragmented film that lasts only
five and a half minutes in its present
condition. Flip, the rascal from the Nemo
strip, returns to the screen as a trainer of a
Gertie-like creature. Flip juggles, does
balancing tricks, and beats the sluggish
dinosaur-thing as it eats his automobile.

Gertie on Tour (c. 1918–1921)

The shortest (1 min., 5 sec.) and strangest
of the fragmented remains of McCay's
films. Gertie, now inked and painted on
celluloid acetate – one cel level for her
body, another for her head and tail –
walks near a railroad or trolley track the
New York skyline in the distance. Cut to
Gertie dancing on a rock surrounded by
several "still" dinosaurs. In another brief
scene she halts a trolley car.

Dreams of the Rarebit Fiend: The Pet (c. 1921)

The film reminds one of Tex Avery's 1947
MGM-short *King-Size Canary*. Both deal
with house pets who drink a potion that
increases their small sizes to gargantuan
proportions. In McCay's film there is an
impressive panorama camera move
depicting the ten-story-high monster-pet
roaming *a la* Kong among the skyscrapers
while being buzz-bombed by a fleet of
dirigible airplanes.

Dreams of the Rarebit Fiend: Bug Vaudeville (c. 1921)

A hobo dreams he is attending a theatrical
performance by a troupe of talented
insects. He applauds heartily juggling
grasshoppers, a trick-cyclist roach, boxing
beetles, an eccentric-dancing daddy
longlegs spider, and a corps de ballet of
lovely white butterflies. The spectator's
delight ends when a giant black spider
attacks him.

This is film critic Andrew Sarris's
favorite McCay cartoon: "Only a man
who knew showbiz to his bone marrow
could conceive of the two bugs who pass
back and forth a handkerchief with which
to dry their sweaty palms before doing
their hand-flips. Fellini would be honored

by such insight into the ritual of performance."

Dreams of the Rarebit Fiend: The Flying House (c. 1921)

"Drawn by Robert Winsor McCay using the Winsor McCay process of animated drawing", reads a title card at the film's head. But this was most probably a collaborative effort by McCay and his son.

A husband and wife attempt to evade their creditors by equipping their house with wings and a motorized propeller. They succeed so well that they fly into outer space, encounter a giant on the moon, and are finally blasted by rocket. "This is not the wild but innocuous plunge that is the staple of cartooning", wrote Richard Eder in 1975. "It is a real nightmare fall by real desperate people."

They fall toward earth and wake up in their bed. It had only been a dream brought on by a supper of troublesome rarebit. The animation of the human characters is rather stiff, but the special effects of the tiny house flying through the galaxies are spectacular.

Conclusion

Winsor McCay stopped making animated films around 1921 or 1922, for reasons that can only be guessed at. He was in his early fifties when *The Flying House* was completed; perhaps the workload of his newspaper duties, plus the effort of creating his particular brand of complicated animation films without the aid of a staff finally began to wear down his phenomenal energy and drive.

Perhaps he felt out of step with the times. He always insisted he had "invented" the animated film, but by the mid-1920s most people had forgotten McCay's animated efforts. Felix the Cat

was then an international cartoon star; by the end of the decade, a mouse named Mickey would lead Walt Disney to total domination of the field.

"For a time McCay had the field to himself", wrote Claude Bragdon (in a 1934 *Scribner s* magazine article that ironically was published the same month as his death – McCay died on 26 July at his home in Sheepshead Bay of a massive cerebral hemorrhage):

> [He] carried on single-handed the enormous labor of making thousands of drawings for a few brief moments of entertainment ... it seems a pity that McCay, with his delightful fancy, should not have continued in this field which he had made his own. Walt Disney has so far eclipsed him that McCay's animated cartoons are remembered only by old-timers like myself.

Perhaps the real reason McCay stopped creating animated films was his deep disappointment that, as far as he could see, his beautiful dream of animation as an art had not become a reality. His distress over this fact is illustrated in an anecdote recalled by veteran animator I. Klein in the magazine *Cartoonist Profiles*.

Klein tells of a dinner held in the fall of 1927, "a gathering of the animators of New York" (about thirty existed at that time) to honor "the originator and founder of animation – Winsor McCay". Both McCay and his son attended and after dinner and "a considerable amount of bootleg liquor" had been consumed by everyone, Max Fleischer, who was presiding, announced, "McCay created the miracle of animation and another miracle was getting all the animators into one big friendly gathering".

McCay was introduced, and his speech was brief. "[H]e gave some technical suggestions which I don't think his professional audience took much stock in", said Klein. "He wound up with a statement that has remained in my mind ... 'Animation should be an art, that is how I had conceived it ... but as I see what you fellows have done with it is making it into a trade ... not an art, but a trade ... bad luck.' He sat down. There was some scattered applause." 🐛

Canemaker, John. "Winsor McCay". *The American Animated Cartoon*. Ed. Donald Peary and Gerald Peary. New York: E.P. Dutton, 1980. 12–23. Revised.
©2004 John Canemaker

11

The Live Wire: Margaret J. Winkler and Animation History

J.B. Kaufman [2004]

People unfamiliar with the American silent-film era are sometimes surprised to learn that women wielded more real power in Hollywood during the silent period than they would again for decades afterward, if ever. Mary Pickford, Lois Weber, Frances Marion, Alice Guy-Blaché, Dorothy Arzner, June Mathis ... the list is a long and distinguished one. And although the animated-cartoon business was still considered a poor stepchild of the film industry at large during the 1920s, it was not without its own stereotype-buster: the film distributor Margaret Winkler.

A native of Hungary, Margaret Winkler (1895–1990) immigrated to the United States with her family at the age of nine and attended public school, then secretarial school.[1] In 1914, at the age of nineteen, she went to work at Warner Bros., as private secretary to Harry Warner. During her seven years as Warner's secretary, Margaret cut her teeth in the film business in a decisive way, for the real power in the film business has always been in distribution, and she learned film distribution from the ground up. In addition to her work in Warner Bros.'s New York office, she traveled around the country, attending exhibitors' conventions and visiting the West Coast production centers. By 1921, she had amassed a wealth of practical experience and, equally important, a nationwide network of contacts. Armed with these advantages – and with the blessing of Harry Warner, who had been favorably impressed with her talent and business acumen – Margaret left the employ of the Warners and went into business for herself. By the end of the year Margaret had become M.J. Winkler, film distributor.

What makes Winkler's accomplishment worthy of note is not simply the fact that she was a woman, but that she established an extraordinary track record. During her short term at the helm of her own company, Margaret Winkler played a pivotal role in American animation history. Between 1921 and 1924 she recruited and distributed, arguably, the three most important animated-cartoon series of the silent era: Max Fleischer's "Out of the Inkwell", Pat Sullivan's "Felix the Cat", and Walt

Disney's "Alice Comedies". Each of these series owed some of its success to Winkler's savvy, energetic promotional work; Otto Messmer described her admiringly as a "great, live-wire saleslady".[2]

Fleischer's "Out of the Inkwell" had previously been one of the short segments in the *Goldwyn-Bray Pictograph*, a "screen magazine" produced by film pioneer J.R. Bray. Each *Pictograph* offered audiences a variety of general-interest features, including a smattering of animation by Fleischer and others. By 1921 "Out of the Inkwell" had outgrown its original status as a brief novelty. Retaining the series' original premise – a cartoon clown (christened KoKo in later years) who comes to life on the drawing board and mischievously defies his creator – Max and Dave Fleischer expanded the clown's adventures to fill a full single-reel subject. Breaking away from the Bray organization, the Fleischers established their own independent studio. Winkler distributed their films by the *states rights* method: she contracted with the Fleischers to pay them a set fee for each title, then sold the exhibition rights for individual states or territories to secondary distributors. The Warner brothers, her former employers, demonstrated their support for her new venture by buying the rights to "Out of the Inkwell" for California, greater New York, and northern New Jersey.

Similarly, "Felix the Cat" began as one of several alternating segments in the *Paramount Magazine*, sharing screen time with Earl Hurd's "Bobby Bumps", Frank Moser's "Bud and Susie", and Paul Terry's "Farmer Al Falfa". From humble beginnings, Sullivan's black cat – actually animated by Otto Messmer, who was uncredited at the time but has since

become famous as the real artistic force behind Felix – quickly gained popularity with audiences and soon was prepared to headline his own series of one-reel cartoons. Winkler contracted with Sullivan in December 1921 to distribute the Felix series, and soon her energetic promotion had launched Felix into a new and fabulously successful phase of his career.

What makes Winkler's accomplishment all the more significant is that she not only had an eye for incipient animation talent, but, once these soon-to-be-legendary artists were signed, she seemed to bring out the best in them. The "Out of the Inkwell" cartoons had been ingeniously conceived and executed from the start, but during the Fleischers' tenure with Winkler the series really blossomed. The rocky screen relationship between the live-action artist, Max Fleischer, and the rebellious little cartoon clown who sprang from his pen, reached new heights of delightful, inventive visual fantasy in the new forum that Winkler provided. In *Invisible Ink* (1921) the clown defies Max's attempts to erase him, continually reappearing on the paper, and later jumps directly into Max's mouth; in *Jumping Beans* (1922) he reproduces himself ad infinitum, forming an army of clowns who attack Max and tie him up; in *Bedtime* (1923) he grows to monstrous proportions and, Kong-like, stalks Max through the city streets. These uninhibited flights of fancy represent the first full flowering of the Fleischers' genius, as well as a harbinger of things to come.

Felix the Cat, too, moved into a new league under Winkler's aegis. Felix's early appearances in the *Paramount Magazine* had been amusing and entertaining, but John Canemaker has found evidence suggesting that Winkler demanded a higher artistic and filmmaking standard of Pat Sullivan and Otto Messmer before committing herself to the Felix series. Messmer later recalled that, at the end of the Paramount contract, he had put extra care into *Felix Saves the Day* (1922), sparing no effort to make the film an impressive "pilot". In *Felix Saves the Day* the Cat joins forces with a boys' baseball team, the Nifty Nine, and attempts to help them beat the Tar Heels in a big game. (Despairing of beating the opposing team, Felix solves the problem by batting a pop fly high into the clouds. The ball beans "Jupiter Pluvius" on the head, prompting a retaliatory storm that rains out the game.) Messmer invests the slight story with an extra measure of production values; most noticeably, there's an element of live action – a standard part of the "Out of the Inkwell" formula, but relatively quite rare in the "Felix" series. Felix scampers around in a cityscape which is, sometimes, the real thing; he hails a real taxi for his ride to the ballpark; and the climactic game between two neighborhood boys' teams is attended by thousands of fans in a real stadium! Through hindsight, it's not hard to imagine Messmer deliberately adopting an element of the Fleischers' technique in an effort to impress their distributor.

Once Felix had come under Winkler's management, Messmer abandoned this live-action tactic. The Cat's subsequent adventures evolved more along the lines of witty, resourceful ideas like his manufactured rainstorm. Such clever gags, combined with a spunky personality and Messmer's engaging animation, created a character that connected immediately with audiences. Seizing on this appeal, Winkler aggressively promoted the Cat and his films. Within a few months of her distributorship of the series, Felix had attained a level of popularity previously unheard of for an animated-cartoon character. Comparisons with Mickey Mouse's later success story are inevitable and, indeed, Felix was easily the most popular animated-cartoon star in the world until the rise of Mickey. The popularity of the Felix films inspired a Felix newspaper comic strip (reversing the route of earlier characters like Mutt and Jeff), and he set a new standard for the merchandise licensing of a cartoon character: Felix stuffed toys, Felix wooden dolls, Felix dishes, and a Felix crystal radio quickly appeared on the market. After Winkler negotiated a European distribution contract with Pathé, Felix's popularity became international, and a song inspired by the character's trademark pacing action, "Felix Kept On Walking", became a hit in England.

Such success came at a price. Winkler's tough, no-nonsense style achieved a notable level of success for the short subjects she distributed, but her working relationships with both the Fleischers and Pat Sullivan were often strained. The Fleischers, after distributing two "Out of the Inkwell" series through her offices, parted company with her in mid-1923 and contracted with Earle W. Hammons' Educational Films instead. A similarly volatile relationship existed with Pat Sullivan. In his book on Felix the Cat, John Canemaker has traced the stormy history of Winkler's dealings with Sullivan.[3] After several contract disputes, Sullivan ended his agreement with Winkler in 1925 and, like the Fleischers, took his business to Educational.

Meanwhile, Winkler had taken on the distribution of another series by an up-and-coming young producer with ambitious ideas: Walt Disney. Once again, the new series featured the combination of animated cartoons with live action. These were the "Alice Comedies", in which a little girl named Alice entered a cartoon world and interacted with cartoon characters. Disney's fledgling Kansas City production company, Laugh-O-gram Films, had failed in 1923, and its last production had been *Alice's Wonderland*, produced by Disney as a sample to sell a possible "Alice" series. Once again Winkler knew a winner when she saw one, and the "Alice Comedies" were added to her stable of short subjects.

The correspondence between Winkler and the young Walt Disney has survived, and provides a revealing insight. Disney first contacted Winkler in May 1923, before the completion of *Alice's Wonderland*, as part of a last-ditch effort to find a national distributor for Laugh-O-grams' cartoons. After the little Kansas City company's demise and Disney's relocation to California, he continued to court her attention assiduously. Although Winkler had preceded Disney into the national arena by only a couple of years, she was already a seasoned veteran, and his early letters to her make it clear that he was eager to defer to her wishes. Her letters, on the other hand, take the same hard line that she had previously taken with the Fleischers and Sullivan. In September 1923, unaware that Disney was scrambling to form a new studio with his brother Roy, she wrote to him: "We have been corresponding with each other since your first letter to me of May 14th. It seems that this is about all it has amounted to."[4]

The Disney brothers did, of course, establish their new studio, and their production of "Alice Comedies" for

Winkler's distribution became a reality. At this point the Disney-Winkler correspondence becomes even more remarkable; Winkler not only asserts herself with regard to contract terms and release schedules, but takes an active role in determining the *content* of the films. Capitalizing on Disney's use of a black cat in *Alice's Spooky Adventure* (1924), she writes to him: "I might suggest that in your cartoon stuff you use a cat wherever possible and don't be afraid to let him do ridiculous things".[5] The message is clear: in the spring of 1924 Winkler was in the midst of an ugly contract squabble with Pat Sullivan, and undoubtedly saw a separate cartoon series featuring a black cat as a desirable insurance policy to help keep Sullivan in line. Enter Disney's recurring black cat, ultimately christened Julius, who would appear throughout the rest of the Alice series and, in fact, would come to dominate the films.

And Winkler's influence over Disney's films didn't end there. For the first few "Alice Comedies" in 1924, Disney was instructed to ship not only the completed negatives, but *all* the raw footage so that Winkler could exercise creative control, recutting the films in New York. Upon seeing the outtakes from *Alice's Wild West Show*, she wrote: "I don't know why you eliminated from your original reel the barroom sequence. We had that printed up and found that it fitted very well into the picture."[6] The barroom sequence stayed in the picture, and can still be seen in modern prints. More significantly, Winkler repeatedly stressed the importance of adding as many gags as possible. After commenting on technical improvements in *Alice Hunting in Africa*, she added: "The comedy situations, however, are still lacking and I wish you would do your utmost to see that this end of the series be improved ... . The only hitch up to now in the selling of this series to the various territories has been the lack of humor".[7] Disney took these words to heart and focused on gag content in his films, and this became one of his central principles in story construction. Throughout the rest of the 1920s and into the golden age of Mickey Mouse and Silly Symphonies, his films would be distinguished by an endless variety of fresh, ingenious comedy situations. We can infer that Winkler had been just as free with comments and suggestions in her dealings with the Fleischers and Sullivan. And, considering the dominant role that Disney came to play in animation history, Margaret Winkler's place among his early influences becomes especially important.

For all her success, Winkler's moment of glory was relatively brief. In November 1923, before even the first of the "Alice Comedies" began to appear on theater screens, Margaret J. Winkler married Charles B. Mintz, whom she had met at Warner Bros. Although the company retained the name Winkler Pictures Inc., Mintz gradually assumed control of the business, and by 1926 Winkler herself had retired from show business to raise their children. Again the company's correspondence with Disney provides a barometer of the situation: within a year of the Mintz-Winkler wedding Disney found himself corresponding with Mintz. It must have been a sobering experience. Mintz continued his wife's policy of active criticism (and her demand for a high volume of gags), but whereas Winkler had occasionally tempered her criticism with praise, Mintz rarely did so. Disney, for his part, was quickly maturing from a cooperative young newcomer to an experienced professional with faith in his

own ideas, and he soon realized that Mintz' harangues and criticisms were, quite often, simply wrong.

Mintz' influence transformed Winkler Pictures in other ways. In addition to the works of Messrs. Fleischer, Sullivan and Disney, the company took on the distribution of other series which are little remembered today: "Memories", a series built around popular songs; "Just Folks", based on the works of Edgar Guest; and the travelogues of Burton Holmes. Margaret Winkler had originally intended to produce films as well as distributing them, and in 1923 she had announced a new series titled "You Said It, Marceline", to be produced in collaboration with the syndicated columnist Marceline d'Alroy. The "Marceline" series never materialized, but after their marriage Winkler and Mintz did attempt production of a live-action series called "Reg'lar Kids", one of the many current imitations of Hal Roach's enormously popular "Our Gang" comedies. Mintz apparently was more interested in live action than in animation, and had formed a separate company in his own name in 1922 to produce several series of live-action shorts. Needless to say, nothing much came of any of these alternate ventures.

Perhaps it's unfair to place all the blame for the downhill slide of Winkler Pictures on Mintz. We'll never know what road the company might have taken if Margaret Winkler had remained in power. The facts of Mintz' administration are fairly straightforward. After losing Sullivan's "Felix the Cat" in 1925, Mintz launched yet another entry in the cartoon cat sweepstakes, "Krazy Kat". (It's interesting to note that George Herriman's "Krazy Kat", one of the classic newspaper comic strips of all time, *never* enjoyed a worthy screen adaptation – perhaps not surprising, since Herriman's surreal, cerebral humor was difficult to adapt to animated cartoons.) It was on Mintz' watch that Disney's second major cartoon series, "Oswald the Lucky Rabbit", was started in 1927, and it was Mintz who engineered the infamous coup against Disney in 1928, stealing Oswald and most of Disney's staff from him. This move soon backfired on Mintz when he, in turn, lost Oswald to Universal in 1929. By the 1930s he was producing a sound-film version of "Krazy Kat", and other lackluster cartoon series, for Columbia. It was a sad irony: the man who had assumed a dictatorial control over Disney ten years earlier was now desperately, and vainly, striving to catch up with him.

The record of Margaret Winkler's professional career – regardless of what *might* have happened – is equally clear. During a period of roughly three years, she brought to the screen the three foremost cartoon studios of her time. Despite some difficult business relationships, she not only promoted and distributed the films of those studios but exercised some influence over their content. In doing so, she earned an indelible place in American animation history. 🦋

Notes

1. Along with other sources, this essay draws heavily on unpublished lecture notes by Ron Magliozzi, to whom grateful acknowledgement is hereby made. Special thanks, too, to Fleischer scholar Mark Langer, who contributed invaluable information during the writing of this essay.

2. Otto Messmer, quoted in Ron Magliozzi's lecture notes.

3. John Canemaker, *Felix: The Twisted Tale of the World s Most Famous Cat* (New York: Pantheon, 1991). See especially pp. 66, 71, 80–84, and 89–95.

4. Letter, Winkler to Disney, 7 September 1923, collection of the author. Winkler's correspondence can be found in the Museum of Modern Art and the Walt Disney Archive.

5. Letter, Winkler to Disney, 7 April 1924, collection of the author.

6. Ibid.

7. Letter, Winkler to Disney, 31 January 1924, collection of the author.

Kaufman, J.B. "The Live Wire: Margaret J. Winkler and Animation History". Unpublished essay. 2004. ©2004 J.B. Kaufman

12

Disney and the Art World: The Early Years

Bill Mikulak [1996]

The animated films of the Disney studio have long generated arguments about their status as art. Despite the attention paid to the critical discourse surrounding them, one aspect of artistic recognition has been relatively overlooked: museum and art gallery exhibits of drawings, paintings, and other fine art created for the films' production. The exhibits of Disney art during the 1930s and early 1940s offered critics a glimpse behind the scenes of a production process that defies categorization as either "lowbrow" popular culture or "highbrow" elite culture. While the exhibitors presented Disney within an elite art context, they could not contain animation within that context's traditional boundaries. By displaying the hybrid nature of Disney's art, these exhibits offered a means for some critics to question the applicability of our inherited cultural categories to modern society.

The traditional cultural hierarchy that values highbrow over lowbrow imposes class biases on what is assigned to each category. Elite culture is assumed to be more complex, more innovative, and more individualistic than middle and lower class popular culture. In this view,

elite art is the unique product of a single artist's vision, created for the few whose distinguished taste allows them to appreciate it. According to this hierarchy, a descent into the middle and lower classes yields culture that is increasingly simplistic, formulaic, and collectively based. These classes are thought to eventually assimilate innovations of the upper class into their cultural products, but are not expected to exert any influence in the other direction.

However, this scheme of culture is socially constructed and historically bound. Historian Lawrence W. Levine argues that the hierarchy emerged slowly during the nineteenth century in the United States.[1] Early in that century, heterogeneous audiences enjoyed heterogeneous culture, in which a single night's entertainment might include scenes from Shakespeare, novelty acts, farces, operatic arias, parlor tunes, and acrobatics. Gradually, the upper class restricted access to their cultural activities by segregating them into discrete organizations, such as symphonies, legitimate theaters, and museums, whose boundaries they could guard. Middle and lower classes gravitated toward such cultural venues as musical theater, vaudeville, sporting events, dance halls, parades, and fairs.

This history contradicts the assumption of essential differences between the cultures of different classes. In fact, sociologist Diana Crane rejects the dichotomy between elite art and popular culture as conceptually outmoded in the face of our society's varied cultural production and reception. She finds that mass media (e.g., films, books, magazines, television) reach audiences that are much larger and more heterogeneous than any reached by nineteenth century culture. Instead of distinguishing among audience members by class, these media increasingly target people on the basis of lifestyle choices.[2]

Crane counters the hierarchy's assumptions by demonstrating that avant-gardes, which she considers to be innovations that attract relatively small audiences, exist in all forms of culture and not merely in those labeled high art. Nor does complexity necessarily correspond to the class origin of any particular cultural offering. Consequently, my subsequent mentions of the traditional class-based cultural hierarchy will refer to the ideological construct I described above, not an actually existing relationship between people and their culture. Crane finds the only milieu in which culture is differentiated along class lines is the urban center, and even there, age, race, and gender divide people into subcultural groupings. The urban art galleries and museums I examine in this paper are upper class in origin and leadership and are part of the elite art worlds within their respective cities.

Mass media draw from all strata of today's urban cultures, just as they drew from all of the above-mentioned nineteenth-century cultural genres. When they mix cultural categories and audiences, the legitimacy of the traditional class-based cultural hierarchy is undermined. It is precisely this subversion of ruling class culture's authority that Marxist aesthetician Walter Benjamin champions regarding mass media's capacity for infinite mechanical reproduction. He claims that the multiple copies of art works distributed via mass media have "exhibition value" in their availability for all to critique and enjoy. He finds this superior to the "cult value" of unique, authentic art works, which stems from the aura of mystery that religion and capitalism invest in them. Thus, his oft-quoted dictum: "That which withers in the age of mechanical reproduction is the aura of the work of art".[3]

People with an investment in the cultural hierarchy counter this assertion by preserving that aura as a distinguishing characteristic of elite art. The fine art world disproportionately rewards those few artists whose reputations can command high prices for each original work of art they produce. In comparison, members of this art world equate the commercialism, industrial mode of production, and ubiquity of mass media with the inferiority of middle and lower class culture. Indeed, cultural observers regularly forecast society's imminent collapse under the sheer volume of material issuing from our burgeoning mass media outlets.

Given how mass media have undermined the traditional class-based cultural hierarchy, museum and gallery exhibits of Disney art offer fertile ground for research. This paper will examine how they positioned themselves within the shifting cultural landscape and, likewise, how exhibit reviewers staked their own claims as tastemakers. Before examining three emblematic exhibits, I would first like to consider which strategies tend to reinforce the hierarchy and which depart from it, and the vested interests served by each.

The strongest partisans of the cultural hierarchy would reject Disney as a debased popular culture having no place in the rarefied halls of an art museum. During the 1930s, it was hardly a common practice for art museums or art galleries to display production artifacts from commercial animation studios. Disney had little company from other animation producers in the halls of elite cultural institutions.[4] When museums have displayed Disney art, they have had to address the concerns of conflicting constituencies. On the one hand, museums must respond to their elite core patrons and trustees, who wish to selectively preserve only the most valuable of society's culture; on the other, museums are often chartered to educate the public about that culture.

A museum favoring the former may justify Disney's artistic worthiness in the same terms it uses to venerate fine art, by emphasizing the cult value of the unique, handcrafted production artifacts and by assigning authorship of the films to Walt Disney alone. These tactics follow the fine art world's tradition of locating value in individual artistic genius. Sociologist Howard Becker argues that even in art worlds that are collaborative (e.g., music, theater, dance), much effort goes into defining the "core activities" that distinguish the honored artist from the support personnel.[5] Those core activities need not involve actual manipulation of artistic materials, but may be limited to producing the instructions that craftspeople follow, or, as in the case of

Disney, guiding and reviewing the work of subordinates during every step in the production process.

Pierre Bourdieu argues that with these strategies, museums act as institutionalized sites for cultural sanctification that can make "entirely prestigious cultural assets" of what others might dismiss as banal. Disney art takes on connotations of fine art by its contiguity to other art the museum displays because "the very meaning and value of a cultural object varies according to the system of objects in which it is placed".[6]

In its role as cultural pedagogue, a museum can instead focus on presenting the complex process of creating animation, using various production artifacts for illustration. This approach accents the artifacts' exhibition value as carriers of information rather than as objects to be coveted as autonomous works of art. The museum may signal its acceptance of Disney films as commercial art by stressing the cartoons' broad appeal and collective mode of production, and by emphasizing their debt to such earlier examples of mass media art as caricatures, comic strips, and illustrations in newspapers, magazines, and books.

Regarding critical responses that early Disney exhibits garnered, this paper will show that nearly all exhibit reviewers considered Disney films as art in some respect, but they were far from uniform in how they categorized that art. Several accepted the final films as art, but not the production artifacts; some restricted Disney to one of the traditional categories; some juxtaposed popular and elite aspects of Disney art; and some acknowledged that the technological and economic milieus of Disney production have no counterpart in the old hierarchy.

Critics who were dependent on the urban elite art world for recognition of their taste served the interests of that world by adhering to its categorizations of culture. Those oriented to the broader readership of the newspapers and journals for which they wrote were more likely to reject the old hierarchy. In condoning mass media-based art exhibits, they displayed their critical foresight in appreciating that which the conservative elites still considered of dubious value.

Documentation is particularly extensive for three of the exhibits of Disney art during the 1930s and early 1940s.[7] They are the Philadelphia Art Alliance exhibit, "Walt Disney, Creator of Mickey Mouse", in 1932; the Los Angeles County Museum (LACM) "Retrospective Exhibition of the Walt Disney Medium", in 1940; and the Museum of Modern Art (MoMA) exhibit, "Walt Disney's *Bambi*: The Making of an Animated Sound Picture", in 1942. The bulk of this paper will examine them in detail before discussing as a group the art gallery shows from 1938 to 1943, which were all part of the Disney company's marketing program coordinated by the Guthrie Courvoisier Gallery in San Francisco.

The Philadelphia Art Alliance Exhibit

Credited as the first arts organization to exhibit Disney production artifacts, the Philadelphia Art Alliance gave critics an opportunity to appreciate Disney's appealing graphic designs in comparison with those by other artists. In so doing, it moved Disney from the realm of mass media to that of the urban high art world. The verbal descriptions the Alliance provided with the exhibit also emphasized the complexity of the animation process, encouraging the displayed items to be

considered as more than a collection of pretty pictures.

The Philadelphia Art Alliance was a relatively young seventeen year-old organization when it hosted the exhibition, "Walt Disney, Creator of Mickey Mouse", but already it had established itself in Philadelphia social circles. Founder Christine Wetherill Stevenson saw the Art Alliance as an instrument to "create our own standards, not in imitation of those of Europe, but chiseled boldly out of our different experiences, traditions, and ideals".[8] Its early exhibitions presented arts and crafts, drama, engravings, oil paintings, watercolors, sculpture, and music in an attempt to provide a space in the heart of Philadelphia for both visual and performing arts. While modernist painters such as Wassily Kandinsky were exhibited by 1937, earlier exhibits centered on more traditionally representational works by the likes of Winslow Homer, Rockwell Kent, and N. C. Wyeth. Therefore, Disney's representational art was in good company there. The Alliance concentrated on animation drawings, background paintings, and paintings of characters and foregrounds on clear plastic cels that overlay the backgrounds. It also presented original illustrations created for "Mickey Mouse" books.

The Disney exhibit ran for two weeks in fall 1932 and its opening was marked by an evening of screenings and lectures, including one titled "The Art of Disney", by art critic and Art Alliance board member Dorothy Grafly. She and other critics covered the event in the local newspapers' sections devoted to "society" and "women", whose readership participated in fine art openings among other high society functions. More than merely convincing general readers of

Disney's achievements, these critics justified the entry of the studio's products into elite art circles.

The Art Alliance's *Bulletin* carries a page-and-a-half announcement of the exhibit that opens with an aesthetic claim for the work: "From two points of view the exhibition is exhilarating, the excellence of the 'stills' *per se* and their unique character as adapted for moving pictures, for they are, possibly, the outstanding achievement in the world of an artist in the relatively new medium of motion – and as such, point to possibilities as yet undreamed of in motion pictures".[9] After praising Disney's leap into synchronized sound with Mickey Mouse, the remainder focuses on the mechanics of producing Disney cartoons.

This announcement accomplishes a number of things. On one hand, it isolates drawings and paintings that provide continuity with familiar art forms the Alliance already exhibited. On the other, it claims foresight in recognizing Disney as a harbinger of what was to come in a new artistic medium. In discussing the mechanics of cartoon production, the announcement conveys the labor involved with numbers: each cartoon short required eight weeks and between 8,000 and 10,000 drawings done by Disney's 25 or 30 associates. It also calls attention to Disney's "wholly new idea of synchronizing [cartoons] to music". This presents a picture of technical innovation and collaborative labor that is elided in critical appraisals modeled on romantic auteurist visions of Walt Disney.

Reviewers put this information to use in their commendations of the exhibit. An unsigned column in the *Philadelphia Inquirer* states, "Those who know Disney only through the movies are here enabled to see how the camera trick is turned and

how indefatigable must be the creator and his 25 to 30 assistants in making the many drawings for the resultant film". Therefore, the columnist suggests, "it's a privilege to be able to examine the Disney work closely and to realize how much beauty of design and line there is in his pictures".[10] An unsigned review in the Philadelphia *Public Ledger* likens Disney to a mural artist who develops a "school" of painters around him, acknowledging the input of Disney's artists by saying "the animated cartoon is a co-operative and collaborative problem, often enriched by the interplay of several minds".[11] It is clear both reviewers acknowledge the work of his employees, but they accord Walt Disney alone the pre-eminent status of artist. They both convey their understanding of how the items on the walls contribute to the "completed canvas" of the motion pictures themselves.

Dorothy Grafly's appreciation of Walt Disney in the *Public Ledger* echoes Christine Wetherill Stevenson in promoting animation as an American art that is not beholden to European aesthetics. In fact, she sees Disney as a restorative for the diseased modern painting that Europe had generated: "The reason why art has suffered a steady popular alienation may be found in its gradual and sometimes precipitate retreat from life, and its wandering on the borderlands of the psychopathic. The art of the animated cartoon is as healthy as that of so many of our modernists is sickly."[12]

Grafly does not cast aside all of European art in her claims for Disney; instead, she situates him within a long history of storytelling through pictures, from ancient Egyptian temples and cathedral bas reliefs to Cézanne and others who tried to capture motion in painting. She values the communicative goals of this tradition, which she feels modern painting has largely abandoned. Her view is shared by aesthetic communication scholar Larry Gross, who sees grave costs in the elite art world's continual pressure on artists to distinguish themselves from predecessors and competitors. He claims, "The resulting pattern of constant innovation in the arts undermines their ability to embody the common experiences and meanings of the society, to serve the central communicative functions of socialization and integration – roles now assigned to the domain of the popular arts and the mass media".[13]

Grafly advocates Disney as a means to restore the arts to their central social role. She asserts that through the "Silly Symphonies", "the great mass of the people may yet be brought back to impulsive delight in the work of art, not because they are taught art in the schools, but because they share the delight of an art experience, and that delight is as natural to the human being, when art is capable of providing it, as pleasure in fields, sunshine and the sound of water". Thus, popularity, far from signaling an artform's baseness or commercialism, is instead a sign of successful communication.

As for those who would not deign to venture beyond the museum and gallery for aesthetic experiences, "such minds are still circumscribed by the four sides of a canvas and lack the very imagination that makes of a Walt Disney creation a new experience". The threat of such snobbery is very real to Grafly and the other *Public Ledger* reviewer. Grafly bemoans that, although "we have witnessed the birth of an American art" in animated cartoons, "there are many among us who not only

repudiate this rare gift but who would deny it any place in the art field". The unsigned review suggests that "even the high and mighty student of the painted canvas who, perhaps, will turn up his nose at a popularized art" could learn from Walt Disney "the good old lesson of composition, in which all rhythms are inherent".

Grafly also uses the exhibit to occasion a critical ranking of the "Silly Symphonies" over "Mickey Mouse" films. Grafly claims, "less popular than the Mickey Mouse [films], the Silly Symphonies are more definitely an art form". She calls the "Mickey" films "contemporary folk art" while she elevates the "Symphonies" to "where Monet and the Impressionists stood some decades ago". It is interesting that Grafly cites Impressionists rather than nineteenth-century illustrative artists Wilhelm Busch, Gustave Doré, and Honoré Daumier, whose visual motifs and themes were direct inspirations for early Disney cartoons, according to art historian Robin Allan.[14] Instead, she links Disney to prestigious fine artists whose experimentation ceased to shock all but the most old-fashioned. The elite art world still has value to her, if only it would open its gates to Disney and those who still create communicative art.

To sum up the Philadelphia Art Alliance exhibit, this venue was actually well-suited to introduce Disney to elite art circles because Philadelphia was a city whose tastes were conservative with respect to the latest trends in modern painting and sculpture. Its fine art world participants only needed to be shown that individual Disney studio drawings and paintings matched those tastes to a large extent, even if they served the lowly art of cartoon entertainment. Dorothy Grafly's attacks on the uncommunicative and alienating canvases emerging from Europe suited the sensibilities of Philadelphia's social register and paved the way for acceptance of Disney's more conventionally attractive designs. It also served a sense of national pride to credit Disney with creating an art form indigenous to America.

Disney as an American Anti-artist

Grafly is only one of many critics who touted animation as Disney's own art form, American to the core. While the Disney studio incontestably made immense contributions to the cartoon, to claim it produced the entire medium is to ignore the many other practitioners in the field. Neither Disney nor American animation in general monopolized the innovation of imbuing stories and images with life. By 1932, animated films had been produced in many European countries, the Soviet Union, Japan, and even Argentina,[15] yet Disney became a homegrown real-life Horatio Alger hero, who fathered in Mickey Mouse not only a national mascot but an art as well.

Much critical writing about Walt Disney through the 1930s praised, analyzed, and mythologized him in this light.[16] As he accumulated medals, Academy Awards, and honorary degrees from universities spanning the globe, he became a symbol of the entrepreneurial American entertainment industry that had swept into international theatrical markets with films of seemingly universal appeal. Disney had by that point developed a homespun wariness of pretension in his responses to various interviewers who sought his opinion on art whenever he received some form of recognition.[17]

For example, when interviewed for the *New York Times* in 1938, after receiving honorary degrees from Harvard and Yale, Disney responded to the question "What is art?" by asking "How should I know? ... Why should anybody be interested in what I think about art?"[18] To another interviewer the following year he answered, "Art? You birds write about it, maybe you can tell me. I looked up the definition once, but I've forgotten what it is. I'm no art lover!"[19]

Yet Disney was willing to express definite preferences for utilitarian craftsmanship: "I think someone who makes a bed with good lines, in which you can sleep comfortably, is more of an artist than the one who paints a picture which gives you a nightmare".[20] And he valued representational styles that could convey emotions through caricature, praising these abilities in da Vinci, van Gogh, and Delacroix. In addition, one writer found that Disney's artists studied Degas, Rouault, Cézanne, Renoir, and Sèurat for inspiration.[21] However, Disney often returned to the fact that his studio's work "is accomplished not alone by means of drawing and sound but with the assistance of a thousand and one technical tricks". Thus, he said, "we are not artists but only moving-picture producers trying to offer entertainment".[22] While creating art that defied the cultural hierarchy, Walt Disney believed in its categories enough to disqualify animation as art on the basis of "technical tricks".

In contrast, a few academic critics highlighted those technical tricks to proclaim Disney animation a triumph of mechanized art. In some cases their insights into the Disney studios came from actual on-site research and observation of the production process, which offered an even greater context for assessing Disney art than did museum exhibits. At the

Disney plant, the exhibition value of the films themselves dominated over the cult value of any particular production artifact.

Whether through access to the studio or not, critic Jean Charlot displays a knowledge of the process and an antipathy to the cult value the art market cultivates. Charlot's 1939 article in *American Scholar* magazine argues that Disney cartoons were able to solve problems depicting motion over time that such artists as Dürer, Duchamp, Giotto, and Picasso had long attempted to address. After invoking this fine art pedigree, Charlot claims animation succeeded where Cubists failed in creating an impersonal art that "could be multiplied by mechanical means" so that "the world might rid itself of the idolatry of the 'original'" and "resuscitate ancient collective traditions, Gothic and Egyptian". The problem the Cubists faced was that "neither dealers nor collectors wished to endorse an art that was not for the few".

However, Charlot claims, "In [the animated] cartoon the impersonality of a work of art has been captured, the cult of the 'original' has been smashed. The drawings are manipulated by so many hands from the birth of the plot to the inking of the line that they are propulsed into being more by the communal machinery that grinds them out than by any single human being." Charlot also notes that early animation roughs are "worthy of a Museum" for going "further into the alchemy of transmuting form into motion than did many of the Masters" but are "still not sufficiently purified for the severe standards of the cartoon. Personality is squeezed out through multiple tracings until the diagram, its human flavor lost, becomes an exact cog within the clockwork".[23]

For Charlot, this transformation is a triumph of artistic purification beyond that required for museum display. In the process, animation is made available to everyone as an "art-for-all". Charlot takes impersonalization as an aesthetic virtue that can only be produced through a technical and mechanized process. Accordingly, Disney's artists were successful to the extent that they eliminated idiosyncratic flourishes, the better to cohere into a unit that could precisely synchronize sound and images. Charlot argues that, after centuries of striving to accomplish through painting what Disney now accomplishes, we should elevate animation from its status as "a nondescript bastard medium into which art critics will not dip".[24]

Another person seeking respectability for Disney was art historian Robert Feild, who was on-site at the Disney studio from June 1939 through May 1940. He emerged to rail against the academy's narrow elevation of art from the past and its condemnation of the machine as the enemy of art. In his thorough examination of the studio's organizational structure, Feild gathers evidence that Disney "breaks down forever the barriers between the old bugaboo of the 'all-done-by-hand' and the machine as an instrument of artistic purpose".[25] Feild notes a transformation similar to that described by Charlot, in which "the artist's individuality" in rough animation drawings "have to be absorbed into the [motion] picture as a whole", resulting in the exchange of aesthetic appeal for a precision and consistency of line in cleaned up animation drawings.[26] Thus, he suggests that if the cleaned up drawings are studied "without the prejudice resulting from a too-long familiarity with 'still' drawings, a different sort of subtlety will be discovered and a technical proficiency that commands respect".[27]

The Los Angeles County Museum Exhibit

The Los Angeles County Museum's retrospective exhibit of Walt Disney's career occasioned by *Fantasia* combined many of the above perspectives. The catalog essayist balanced paeans to the Disney studio's artistry with healthy doses of Walt's skepticism regarding the acclaim. The exhibit featured not only production art, but also such technical items as a cut-away model of a multiplane camera. Animators from the Disney studio were even on hand at times to demonstrate the skills involved in their jobs. However, only one name from the studio merited mention in the exhibit materials: that of Walt Disney, himself. Even Feild's book took pains to keep all but Walt and Roy Disney anonymous in recounting the staff's many and varied contributions to the films.

"A Retrospective Exhibition of the Walt Disney Medium", originated in the Los Angeles County Museum before traveling to museums in seven other U.S. cities.[28] For the exhibition, the LACM issued an elaborately illustrated catalog, which deserves consideration for its presentation of Disney to museum patrons and Los Angeles's elite fine art world.[29] Museum director Roland J. McKinney was responsible for the exhibit, which the *Los Angeles Times* applauded as a well-attended critical triumph.[30]

The unsigned exhibit catalog essay begins by claiming, "In twelve years Walt Disney has elevated animated pictures from a crude form of entertainment to the dignity of a true art", but then counters, "Disney prefers to ignore that his craft has become an art. He will discuss it only in

terms of entertainment." Finally, Disney's approbation is secondary to his achievements: "... whether or not Disney disdains the tribute, he remains a master artist by every definition". It is obvious that Disney accepted the tribute enough to fund the exhibit and copyright the catalog essay under Walt Disney Productions.

To shape this representation of Disney as an artist, the catalog selectively retells the Disney story. Although purporting to span Disney's entire career, the exhibit included no art from his cartoons prior to Mickey's inception. The catalog essayist mentions that period briefly, only to claim Disney "had discovered unrealized possibilities in his medium" even though he had not yet attained them. Thus, the essayist makes Disney into a visionary in the retrospective glow of his subsequent achievements.

This claim entailed some historical revisionism. In 1928, a bitter contractual dispute with his distributor, Charles Mintz, stripped Disney of his star character, Oswald, and several key staff members. The essay transforms this event into "the Declaration of Independence of Disney and the animated cartoon", in which Disney had quit Mintz because "his artistic integrity and self-respect demanded that he be able to give the best that was in him to his job".

The essay also asserts *Three Little Pigs* gave the studio a prestige that drew artists to Disney's employ, which omits Disney's aggressive recruitment of talent from other animation studios and art schools. And the essayist cites artistic freedom rather than economic returns for Disney's entry into feature production: "The feature-length field offered an inexhaustible source of fresh story material" compared to the "galling ...

limitation" of the shorts. All of these steps necessarily led to *Fantasia*, "the brilliant summation of twelve years of continuous growth".

The catalog's selectivity in presenting Disney's career yields a story linking one artistic triumph to the next. Disney's eight years laboring during the silent era constituted little more than an apprenticeship; the inception of Mickey Mouse at the dawn of the talkies was already the defining moment that lifted Disney out of obscurity and into the pantheon of Hollywood legends. Even when other contemporary writers, such as Paul Hollister, discussed the pre-Mickey years, including those of Disney's youth, it was primarily to convey Disney's rags-to-riches saga rather than to extol the virtues of the silent era films.[31]

The Los Angeles County Museum exhibit contextualized the production art on display by developing a narrative of two parallel paths of evolution: that of Disney's career and that of the multistep process of producing an animated film. Panels alternated between illustrating, for example, the "Layout and Background Relationship" and the "Development of Mickey Mouse". By the end of the exhibit, two stories intertwine: the ascent from early inspirational sketches to camera-ready art informs the transformation from rudimentary cartooning to breathtakingly innovative animation. This effectively creates a teleological portrait of the studio's ascent to perfection modeled on the pre-planned succession of refinements that produce a finished animated film. The narrative smooths over the deadends Disney pursued and the reversals the company endured on the road to *Fantasia*.

The view behind the scenes extended beyond art works to pieces of technology.

A cutaway model of a multiplane camera allowed visitors to adjust the distance of cels from the camera and see how Disney created three-dimensional effects. Visitors during the weekends were treated to such Disney artists as Fred Moore and Wolfgang Reitherman demonstrating in person how animation drawings were made. Classical music from *Fantasia* played throughout the exhibition space and excerpts of various Disney animated films also were screened regularly. To show the primitive beginnings of animation before cinema, flipbooks and optical toys from the nineteenth century were included.[32] While the exhibit highlighted the art's contribution to the final films, it also played up the quality of individual pieces as free-standing art, especially in the case of the three-dimensional models of characters that, according to one reviewer, were "displayed on velvet thrones like little queens in the galleries".[33] Overall, pedagogy triumphed over fine art elitism in this exhibit, even if the lesson was somewhat hagiographic toward Walt Disney.

The newspaper and news magazine art critics at each stop of the tour were generally enthusiastic about the exhibit, although it heartened *Time* magazine to see more than the production art itself, because "considered simply as drawings and paintings, most Disney stills rate only a notch higher than Christmas cards". However, in terms of animation, *Time* claims "Walt Disney Productions, Ltd. is revolutionizing art faster than all the long-hairs of Greenwich Village".[34]

In contrast, the Cincinnati *Enquirer* art critic Mary L. Alexander argues, "In many instances the drawings in black and white and color are truly as much works of art as Mickey Mouse, Dopey or the

Three Little Pigs are personages of moment to children and even grown-ups".[35] Alexander also highlights those drawings that contain Walt's written comments because, "if one follows the drawings through, the Disney notations constitute a valuable criticism, for he actually visualizes every form and movement and is decisive in every little detail".[36]

Other critics shared Alexander's interest in animation production methods. To John K. Sherman, art critic of the *Minneapolis Star Journal*, the exhibit provided "a clear and fascinating picture of how science, art and incredible attention to detail produce such delightful things as the Silly Symphonies and Pinocchio".[37] According to the *Los Angeles Times* reviewer, "The show is a tribute to Walt's own genius and his singular gift of drawing out the best in his large group of associated artists and technicians producing their collective product", which, not incidentally, "stepped up the art level of this region ... by giving good artists employment".[38] These critics were not bound by the cultural hierarchy's categories, but accepted Disney animation on its own terms, as an art that is both mass-produced and handcrafted.

The Museum of Modern Art

Long before its 1942 Disney "Bambi" exhibit, the Museum of Modern Art also had begun to include hybrid industrial/handcrafted art. However, its interest in this art was guided by the underlying assumptions of the traditional cultural hierarchy. To a much greater extent than the Philadelphia Art Alliance or the Los Angeles County Museum, MoMA was committed to novelty as a defining characteristic of elite art and it

sought that novelty primarily in Europe, as far as fine art was concerned. However, when MoMA established its film collection, it found much to admire in Hollywood films in general and Disney cartoons in particular. It also followed a mandate to educate the public about modern art and its "Bambi" exhibit employed a format similar to that of the LACM, which illustrated the production process. MoMA's longstanding interest in Disney also helped counter accusations during World War II that it had a Eurocentric bias.

Before I discuss Disney in particular, I would like to note how MoMA generally placed mass-produced art beside fine art. Under founding director, Alfred H. Barr, Jr., the museum displayed commercial arts like film, industrial design, photography, and architecture by demonstrating the modernist formal qualities they shared with modern painting, sculpture, drawings, and prints. For example, Barr curated two landmark exhibits in 1936, "Cubism and Abstract Art" and "Fantastic Art, Dada and Surrealism", which linked examples of photography, furniture, typography, posters, theater, film, painting, and sculpture into a genealogy of artistic movements.[39] Barr tracked successions of innovative visionaries, whose work he decontextualized from their original environments in order to highlight their relevance to modernist aesthetics. His artistic lineages emanated from European paintings and sculpture, but often included American practitioners of such commercial art as film and architecture.[40]

Upon receiving trustee approval and funding in 1935, Barr hired the Museum's librarian, Iris Barry, to be curator of a new department called the Film Library. Barry applied Barr's genealogical orientation to films by tracing the evolution of various branches of motion pictures, which she divided into international developments in comedy, drama, avant-garde film, documentary, and animation. An early statement on the Film Library's mission promises to screen "films of the past thirty years which are worth reviving because of their artistic quality or because of their importance in the development of the art. Gradually it is hoped to accumulate a collection of films of historic and artistic value."[41]

The Film Library's concern for history as well as art aided its justification for collecting Hollywood films in addition to foreign and experimental films that were more self-consciously artistic statements. Through methods similar to Barr's, the Film Library linked artistic crosscurrents between Hollywood and Europe.[42] An additional impetus to seek out Hollywood films came from Film Library president John Hay Whitney's financial investments and personal connections in the industry. His letter of introduction and funds made possible a late summer dinner party that Mary Pickford threw in 1935 to let Iris Barry and her husband lobby for donations to start the Film Library. Walt Disney was among the attendees whom they solicited. He immediately accommodated their requests for prints of a number of his films as well as production art showing the animation process.[43]

By 1936, the Museum included the early "Mickey Mouse" cartoons *Plane Crazy* (1928) and *Steamboat Willie* (1928) in their circulating film programs devoted to American silent film and the birth of the talkies, respectively. Thus, Mickey Mouse is accorded a privileged position at the juncture of film's momentous transition to sound amidst such other

landmark films as Alan Crosland's *Jazz Singer* (1927), Lewis Milestone's *All Quiet on the Western Front* (1930), and Josef von Sternberg's *Last Command* (1928). In addition, Disney's *The Skeleton Dance* (1929) ended a program tracing the history of American film comedy.

However, it was on their circulating program, "A Short History of Animation", that Disney took center stage. After five silent animated films by different individuals and studios, the program's last four shorts were all Disney films: "Newman Laugh-O-Grams" (1921), *Steamboat Willie* (1928), *Flowers and Trees* (1932) and *Les Trois Petit Cochons*, the French-language version of *Three Little Pigs* (1933). Iris Barry's program notes give a wide-ranging account of animation's forerunners, influences, and developments, which culminated in the Disney studio's aesthetic exploitation of the new possibilities of technological advances in synchronized sound and color.[44]

While MoMA was establishing animation as part of its film collection, it also was beginning to include animation in its other exhibitions. The Museum may have first displayed Disney animation art in Alfred Barr's "Fantastic Art, Dada and Surrealism" exhibit, which included a cel from Disney's *Three Little Wolves* (1936) featuring the Wolf being trapped by the Practical Pig's "Wolf Pacifier".[45] Disney appeared in the company of American satirists Rube Goldberg and James Thurber, but the overwhelming majority of displayed artists were Europeans, ranging from Hieronymus Bosch to Marcel Duchamp and Salvador Dali.

MoMA's 1938 exhibit in Paris at the Musée du Jeu de Paume, "Trois siècles d'art aux États-Unis" ("Three Centuries of American Art"), included stills of films by

Disney and others (these may have been photographic prints rather than original production art). Back home that year, an exhibit, "Walt Disney – Original Drawings", was listed as being in preparation, but I have seen no documentation that it came to fruition.[46]

MoMA's largest exhibit of Disney animation production art during these early years came in the summer of 1942. "Walt Disney's *Bambi*: The Making of an Animated Sound Picture" was designed to coincide with the film's release. While the Museum did place the *Bambi* exhibit in its Young People's Gallery, the press release does not dwell on Disney's specific suitability for children. Instead, it quotes Iris Barry as saying, "Nothing more joyous or more genuinely American than the Disney cartoons has ever reached the screen ... Their simplicity, their tremendous gusto and defiant disrespectfulness at once caught the public fancy and have steadily maintained it, despite some few flights into artiness and sentimentality in the longer experimental features."[47] Barry lauds the Disney studio's achievements and berates its failures in the context of films in general. Its triumphs and excesses were measurable beyond the circumscribed bounds of what was good for children.

Barry's exultation at Disney's Americanism was infused with more than the national pride of Dorothy Grafly (especially since Barry was British). It is important to understand that, in the early 1940s, MoMA was in the midst of aesthetic and political cross-pressures that pitted elite tastes in European modernist painting styles against nativist American populism. While the Museum had a longstanding interest in Disney, in the midst of World War II, the studio provided MoMA with an art that helped

counter accusations that its Eurocentrism was un-American.[48]

The Museum's *Bambi* exhibit of 1942 included a detailed narrative of the technical process of producing feature-length animation the Disney way. In addition to drawings, cels, and background paintings, on display were "photographs of the Disney staff at work, exposure sheets, production schedules, the instruments and gadgets with which they produce sound effects, and even a three-dimensional block of the huge Disney studio in Burbank, California".[49]

The *Bambi* exhibit suggests a shift in MoMA's presentation of Disney. Barry's 1940 program notes for "A Short History of Animation" refer to Walt Disney alone in discussing his films (for example, she explains "from the moment Disney added sound to his drawings, the whole medium gained new scope and vitality"). In contrast, when the press release for the 1942 *Bambi* exhibit describes the step-by-step process of production, it mentions Walt Disney as participating with his "idea-men" only in the first step, "Visualizing the Story". In the subsequent steps, it instead discusses the work of artists, actors, musicians, background and layout men, animators, and the "200 girls" in the inking and painting department. In addition, the release described the Disney studio as being "built very much like a modern factory".[50]

This open view of Disney's employees went beyond that of the Los Angeles County Museum's exhibit. A number of factors may have influenced the decision to increase that emphasis. In late spring of 1941, a portion of Disney's employees staged a strike that lasted most of the summer before government conciliation settled it. This forcefully brought Disney's employees into public consciousness. More generally, preparations for war increased industrial production across the country and strengthened public support for organized labor; thus, artistic laborers gained recognition as well.

MoMA provided an in-depth view of the degree to which the Disney studio had segmented its production process into sequential, specialized tasks within separate departments. One critic, Emily Genauer, questioned the aesthetic value of this look behind the scenes. She argues, "I don't think the exhibition ... can properly be considered an art event... . It has no more significance as art than would an exhibition which showed you how canvas is woven, pigments are ground and camels hunted for the hair which makes an artist's brush".[51]

In contrast, an *Art Digest* editorial from 1942 cites the Museum's exhibit materials to bolster the claim that *Bambi* "should be placed in the column of films that support the contention of critics who evaluate the Disney art, not only as great, but as a democratic, group-created art which, in its use of both machines and personal talent, best symbolizes the twentieth century".[52] This editorial welcomes the Museum's evidence of "the backstage evolution of Disney films" as a means of categorizing the animated film as neither popular culture nor high art, but modern, twentieth-century art.

While the Philadelphia Art Alliance exhibit began to break down the old divisions between high and low art, and the Los Angeles County Museum showed machinery alongside production art, the Museum of Modern Art offered even more details of how factories could produce art. MoMA already had displayed architectural models and industrially designed objects whose

artistry was in no way compromised by the collaborative and technical processes of their production. While individual artists in Disney's factory remained anonymous in each exhibit, their importance to the process was increasingly emphasized.

This would not be the case when Disney marketed its own art under Walt's name alone. Galleries presented each framed piece of Disney production art as complete and valuable in itself. The Disney company participated in transforming these works from by-products of filming into art objects by selling cels of various characters with specially prepared presentation backgrounds. Thus, in the gallery context the cels no longer represent a step in the filmmaking process; they become individual portraits of characters.

Gallery Exhibits of Disney Art

In 1939, the *New York Times* reported that Walt Disney began the art marketing program with the Courvoisier Gallery to maintain staff levels: "He began making his composite drawings for the galleries so he wouldn't have to lay off any of his employees during the slack season. Instead of cutting his staff, he made work – assigned people to cut up the celluloid drawings, mount them on backgrounds and wrap them with cellophane."[53] Most of these composites utilized hand-prepared backgrounds to highlight the cels. Only a few of them matched cels with their original background paintings as seen in the films.

The inspiration for this make-work came from exhibits such as those held by the Philadelphia Art Alliance and other arts organizations. The Disney announcement for the first series of specially-mounted art from *Snow White* states that the studio began to offer the art "because of the overwhelming demand for the celluloids not only from the general public but from museums and art collectors as well".[54] Thus, the early exhibits at the Philadelphia Art Alliance, the Art Institute of Chicago, and the New York Public Library created a new purpose for Disney's industrial by-products. They also provided a model for Disney's own attempt to market animation cels – not in department stores beside the "Mickey Mouse" merchandise, but in bona fide art galleries.[55] Other museums, such as New York's Metropolitan Museum of Art, the Albright-Knox Art Gallery in Buffalo, and the San Francisco Museum of Modern Art all responded to the marketing program by purchasing cels.[56]

In contrast to the museums, the Disney marketing program stressed the art's cult value as collectibles over their exhibition value as components of Disney films. Disney had co-opted techniques employed in the elite urban fine art galleries that prized art "for the few", in Jean Charlot's parlance. This meant altering the art so it was more easily displayable as portraiture and creating scarcity out of ubiquity. Disney's announcement makes clear that, "although 475,000 paintings were photographed during the making of *Snow White*, only about 7,000 of the most suitable will be marketed. All others ... have been destroyed."[57]

The Julien Levy Gallery was the first New York gallery to offer the Disney originals. The invitation to the exhibit's opening in September 1938 accentuates both the scarcity of the art and the aesthetic legitimacy already accorded it: "Museums, art connoisseurs and collectors are acquiring these celluloids as

fast as they can before the limited selection is exhausted". To elevate the paintings into their own sphere apart from the films, the invitation quotes Dorothy Grafly:

> The artistry of Walt Disney's *Snow White and the Seven Dwarfs* does not lie in its story-telling, but, like all great art, in its picture-making. Divorced from their context such pictures are pure abstractions; for the abstraction on a gallery wall is little more than a thought or emotion severed from the continuity of experience. That Disney's abstractions are recognized as such only by the most discerning is a tribute to his fuller and deeper appreciation for life.[58]

Typical of the enthusiastic responses to this initial exhibit is Melville Upton's relief that the Disney art offering overcame the "danger that the boundless popularity of his creations in their animated film form might tend to overshadow their claims to consideration as really exquisite works of art as well".[59] Some, like *Harper s Bazaar*, incorrectly attribute that artistry to Disney's own hand but presciently predicted, "they'll undoubtedly grow more valuable with the years".[60]

Peyton Boswell echoes this sentiment when he suggests about a later gallery showing of *Fantasia* art, "It's a good bet to predict the growth of a cult of Disney collectors, possibly along the lines of the Currier & Ives lovers, who today think nothing of trading the price of an automobile for a colored lithograph that once sold for 20 cents".[61] These prognostications did not begin to come true until the 1980s. America's entry into World War II interrupted both the Courvoisier marketing program and Disney's critical ascent. However, for over a decade prior to that, critics who saw exhibited production art of the Disney studio gained better insight into Disney's aesthetic achievements.

Conclusions

I have attempted to show that, although the Disney studio produced animation within the realm of mass culture, urban elite fine art organizations singled it out for appreciation. During the 1930s and early 1940s, museum exhibits increasingly demonstrated how Disney animation defied the simplistic hierarchy of high art and low art despite their investment in aspects of the traditional cultural hierarchy. They showed that Disney films were at once communicative and innovative because they experimentally adapted narrative and representational conventions to motion pictures. Museums revealed how animation joined the handicraft of unique fine art objects to sophisticated technologies and organizational hierarchies in order to create art on the theater screen. In response, critics increasingly expressed their enthusiasm for Disney art without feeling the need to make it fit into outmoded concepts of elite art.

As Disney diversified into live-action filmmaking, television, and theme parks, museum exhibits dwindled and production cels became souvenirs. Only in the 1970s did museum exhibits recur. In that decade, too, the animation art market began a slow growth that turned into a boom in the 1980s.[62] My ongoing research analyzes how these trends have intersected with critical assessments of Disney, especially in light of the rapid expansion and diversification of the Disney corporation.

This essay is a tentative step toward understanding a larger process by which artistic reputation is forged across cultural boundaries. It offers some perspectives on animation's reception to complement the growing body of research on its production. Much work lies ahead to determine what influence, if any, critical modes of reception have on the ways animation is produced and circulated. For example, animation festivals deserve sustained investigation as sites for animators seeking aesthetic responses to their work.[63] Similarly, industry awards, such as the Oscars, and arts grants might be examined systematically for the effects they have on recipients and nominees as well as on those omitted from consideration. The impact that animation scholarship has on the stature of animation is another avenue of exploration, as are some of the more marginalized forms of appreciation practiced by animation fans. Such research would help situate animation in the variety of cultural arenas where contesting groups stake claims for the legitimacy of their tastes, desires, and identities. 🐾

Notes

1. Lawrence W. Levine, *Highbrow/Lowbrow: The Emergence of Cultural Hierarchy in America* (Cambridge: Harvard UP, 1988).

2. Diana Crane, *The Production of Culture: Media and the Urban Arts* (Newbury Park, CA: Sage, 1992).

3. Walter Benjamin, "The Work of Art in the Age of Mechanical Reproduction", *Film Theory and Criticism*, ed. Gerald Mast and Marshal Cohen (1936; reprint, New York: Oxford UP, 1979), 852. Also, see Miriam Hansen, "Of Mice and Ducks: Benjamin and Adorno on Disney", *South Atlantic Quarterly* 92: 1 (Winter 1993): 29–30, on the differing versions of this article extant.

4. Examples of contemporaneous exhibitions of animation art include the following. The Museum of Modern Art (MoMA) collected and periodically displayed paintings used in the abstract animation of

Léopold Survage (created in 1912–14, but never filmed), Douglass Crockwell, Mary Ellen Bute, and others. On 4 April 1934, the Society of Illustrators in New York hosted Winsor McCay's final public appearance and a notice in the *New York American* stated: "NEMO AGAIN! – Little Nemo, delight of millions of children, will come back to life, with Flip and the others, when Winsor McCay shows the originals of his animated pictures at the Illustrator's show". The *New York American* notice was reproduced in John Canemaker, *Winsor McCay: His Life and Art* (New York: Abbeville, 1987), 201. However, the notice does not make clear whether this was only a film screening or if production art was on display as well. As for art from other cartoon studios, according to Joe Adamson, the Leon Schlesinger Corporation was set up in 1937 to license commercial tie-ins for the Warner Bros. cartoon characters, which included production cels with Schlesinger's signature on them. The sale of these cels did not last long and I found no record of museums or galleries purchasing or exhibiting them. Joe Adamson, *Bugs Bunny: Fifty Years and Only One Grey Hare* (New York: Henry Holt, 1990), 66.

5. Howard Becker, *Art Worlds* (Berkeley: U California P, 1982), 16–17.

6. Pierre Bourdieu, *Distinction: A Social Critique of the Judgement of Taste* (Cambridge: Harvard UP, 1984), 88.

7. Documentation of the exhibits I have chosen not to cover in-depth are as follows. The Philadelphia Art Alliance exhibit subsequently traveled to the Milwaukee Art Institute and the Toledo Museum of Art, according to Martin Krause and Linda Witkowski, *Walt Disney s Snow White and the Seven Dwarfs* (New York: Hyperion, 1994), 9. The Associated Press reported that "Mickey Mouse Is 'Art' to Chicago's Institute" (*New York Herald-Tribune*, 15 December 1933), where 100 original pieces of Disney production art were displayed. The Leicester Galleries of London held a Disney exhibit, according to "Mickey Mouse on Exhibition", *Listener*, 20 February 1935. In the Walt Disney Archives, Burbank, is an invitation to another exhibit: "Walt Disney and His Animated Cartoons; Exhibition of His Original Working Drawings, 20 May to 15 June 1935" at the Harris Museum and Art Gallery in Preston, England. Also, Walt Disney Productions Press Release 9860 announced "Original Mickey Mouse and Silly Symphony Drawings on Exhibition at New York Public Library" on 6 August 1936 (Walt Disney Archives, Burbank). There may have been other exhibits during the 1930s and early 1940s of which I am unaware.

8. Quoted in Theo B. White, *The Philadelphia Art Alliance: Fifty Years 1915–1965* (Philadelphia: U Pennsylvania P, 1965), 28.

9. "Exhibitions of the Month", *(Philadelphia Art Alliance) Bulletin* (Oct 1932): 3–4, Philadelphia Art Alliance Records, Special Collections, University of Pennsylvania Library, Philadelphia.

10. "In Gallery and Studio", *Philadelphia Inquirer*, 23 October 1932, Society section.

11. "Disney Has Debut in Art Circles", *(Philadelphia) Public Ledger*, 23 October 1932, Women's section.

12. Dorothy Grafly, "Animated Cartoon Gives the World an American Art", *(Philadelphia) Public Ledger*, 23 October 1932, Women's section.

13. Larry Gross, "Art", in *International Encyclopedia of Communication*, vol. 1, ed. Tobiah Worth (New York: Oxford UP, 1989), 113.

14. Robin Allan, "European Influences on Early Disney", Paper presented at Society for Animation Studies Conference, Los Angeles, CA, October 1989.

15. Giannalberto Bendazzi, *Cartoons: One Hundred Years of Cinema Animation* (England: John Libbey; and Bloomington: Indiana UP, 1994): 25–52, 101–105.

16. For a survey of this critical literature from the 1930s and early 1940s, see Gregory A. Waller, "Mickey, Walt, and Film Criticism from Steamboat Willie to Bambi", *The American Animated Cartoon*, ed. Danny and Gerald Peary (New York: E.P. Dutton, 1980), 48–57. More recent citations as well items from that era are provided in Kathy Merlock Jackson, *Walt Disney: A Bio-Bibliography* (Westport, CT: Greenwood, 1993).

17. In *Walt Disney: A Bio-Bibliography*, Jackson offers numerous examples of Disney's self assessment as an uneducated entertainer rather than an artist. Among the many other sources of such statements from Disney in the late 1930s are: Douglas W. Churchill, "Disney's Philosophy" *New York Times Magazine*, 6 March 1938, 9+; "Disney Puzzled by College Honors", *New York Journal-American*, 20 June 1938; "Disney Honored, Wishes He Had Gone to College", *New York Herald-Tribune*, 24 June 1938.

18. S.J. Woolf, "Walt Disney Tells Us What Makes Him Happy", *New York Times Magazine*, 10 July 1938, 5.

19. Frank S. Nugent, "Disney Is Now Art But He Wonders", *New York Times Magazine*, 26 February 1939, 4.

20. Woolf, 5.

21. Nugent, 4–5.

22. Woolf, 5.

23. Jean Charlot, "But Is It Art?" *American Scholar* 8: 3 (Summer 1939): 269–270.

24. Charlot, 262.

25. Robert D. Feild, *The Art of Walt Disney* (New York: MacMillan, 1942; London: Collins, 1947): 87.

26. Feild, 254.

27. Feild, 259.

28. The University Gallery in Minneapolis was the first stop of the touring exhibit, followed by the Cincinnati Art Museum, the St. Louis City Art Museum, the Art Institute of Chicago, the Detroit Institute of Arts, the Cleveland Museum of Art, and the Worchester Art Museum.

29. "A Retrospective Exhibition of the Walt Disney Medium", LACM exhibit catalog, with introduction by Roland J. McKinney, director-in-charge, 1940, Walt Disney Archives, Burbank.

30. "Mickey Mouse Exhibition at Museum to Open Tonight", *Los Angeles Times*, 29 November 1940, part 2; "Disney Show Climax in Museum Director's Work" *Los Angeles Times*, 8 December 1940, part 3.

31. Paul Hollister, "Walt Disney: Genius at Work", *Atlantic Monthly*, December 1940, 689–701. Hollister also was given access to the Disney plant, but he related the inner workings less to aesthetic concerns than to the films' success as entertainment. See Waller and Jackson for other contemporary accounts of Disney's early years.

32. "Mickey Mouse on Parade", *Time*, 6 January 1941, 32; mention of Moore and Reitherman in Edwin Schallert, "Lloyd Nolan Probably Bedtime Story Lead", *Los Angeles Times*, 6 December 1940, part 2. "A Retrospective Exhibition" discussed Joseph Plateau's phenakistoscope, an example of which may have been exhibited. "Disney Show Climax" described a "merry-go-round type of animated picture" at the exhibit, which may have been a zoetrope.

33. Frances Greenman, Frances Greenman Says, "Walt Disney Is Just Folks", *Minneapolis Times-Tribune*, 9 March 1941, sec. 15.

34. "Mickey Mouse on Parade", 32.

35. Mary L. Alexander, "The Week in Art Circles", *(Cincinnati) Enquirer*, 6 April 1941, sec. 3. Some of Alexander's comments were exact duplicates of those made in "Disney Has Debut in Art Circles", which raises the possibility that either clippings of that review of the 1932 exhibit were included in press kits for the 1940 exhibit or that Alexander obtained or even wrote the original unsigned review herself. I did not find use of these comments in other articles on the exhibit, which suggests that Alexander alone may have had access to the original review.

36. Mary L. Alexander, The Week in Art Circles, *(Cincinnati) Enquirer*, 13 April 1941, sec. 2.

37. John K. Sherman, "Le Seuer Dance Themes, Disney Art Exhibited", *Minneapolis Star Journal*, 9 March 1941, sec. 1.

38. "Disney Show Climax".

39. Annette Cox, "Making America Modern: Alfred H. Barr, Jr. and the Popularization of Modern Art", *Journal of American Culture* 7 (Fall 1984): 21; Alice Goldfarb Marquis, Alfred H. Barr, Jr.: *Missionary for the Modern* (New York: Contemporary Books, 1989): 149–150.

40. See Cox, 23–25, and Marquis, 79, 141–144, for discussions of Barr's Eurocentric outlook on modern art that did not change until after the emergence of the New York Abstract Expressionists in the 1940s.

41. "Films and the Museum", *Bulletin of the Museum of Modern Art* 1: 6 (1 February 1934; reprint, New York: Arno, 1967): 3.

42. "The Founding of the Film Library". *Bulletin of the Museum of Modern Art* 3 (November 1935; reprint, New York: Arno, 1967): 1–6.

43. A letter from Walt Disney Productions, Ltd., to the MoMA Film Library, 27 August 1935, MoMA Film Study Center, New York, listed all of the materials to be donated. Each phase of Disney's career was documented: Disney's first animated film ("Newman Laugh-O-Grams", 1921); one example of each of the "Fairy Tale" series (1921–22), the "Alice" comedies (1923–27), and the "Oswald the Lucky Rabbit" series (1927–28); the first "Mickey Mouse" (*Plane Crazy*, 1928); the first sound "Mickey" (*Steamboat Willie*, 1928); the first "Silly Symphony" (*Skeleton Dance*, 1929); and the first Technicolor "Silly Symphony" (*Flowers and Trees*, 1932) and "Mickey" (*The Band Concert*, 1935). Donated production material included not only art, but scenario suggestions, exposure sheets, and music sheets.

44. Iris Barry, "A Short History of Animation", program notes, 1940, Museum of Modern Art Film Study Center, New York. The program led off with the filmed lantern slides of Skladanowsky (ca. 1879), followed by Emile Cohl's *Drame chez les Fantoches* (1908); Winsor McCay's *Gertie the Dinosaur* (1914); an Associated Animators "Mutt and Jeff" film, *The Big Swim* (1926); and the Pat Sullivan studio's *Felix Gets the Can* (1924). An alternate program for 16mm projectors instead of 35mm replaced *Flowers and Trees* and *Les Trois Petit Cochons* with Lotte Reiniger's *Carmen* (1933) and Disney's *Mad Dog* (1932). This

latter program is currently available from the Museum of Modern Art, according to the *Circulating Film Library Catalog* (New York: MoMA, 1984): 29.

45. "Modern Museum a Psychopathic Ward as Surrealism Has Its Day", *Art Digest* 11: 6 (15 December 1936): 5–6.

46. "Program for 1938", *Bulletin of the Museum of Modern Art* 5 (January 1938; reprint, New York: Arno, 1967): 2.

47. "Museum of Modern Art Shows Original Material from *Bambi* and other Disney Films in Exhibition of Animated Film Making", *Museum of Modern Art Press Release* #42713–47, 13 July 1942, MoMA Library, New York.

48. Barry acknowledged these accusations in "The Film Library", *Bulletin of the Museum of Modern Art* 8 (June/July 1941; reprint, New York: Arno, 1967): 10, when she wrote: "Recent events have led to a wide recognition of the use and value of studying propaganda material. But ... the acquisition of foreign material of this kind gave rise to a whispering campaign (originating, it seemed, among small groups of film enthusiasts with axes to grind) that the Film Library or the Museum as a whole, or perhaps even the Board of Trustees (!) was infiltrated with Nazi principles (this was in 1937 and 1938) or with Communist principles (this was in 1940) or at best with some 'un-American' spirit". This followed on the heels of the November 1940 *Bulletin*, which was entirely devoted to defending the Museum's promotion of American art.

49. "How Walt Disney Works Told in Exhibit at Modern Museum of Art", *Bridgeport Post*, 27 July 1942.

50. "Museum of Modern Art Shows Original Material".

51. Emily Genauer, "Disney Techniques Exhibited as Art", *New York World-Telegram*, 18 July 1942.

52. "Disney's *Bambi* Rated as Democratic Art", *Art Digest* 16: 19 (1 August 1942): 15.

53. Nugent, 5. According to Tom Tumbusch, *Tomart s Illustrated Disneyana Catalog and Price Guide*, (Radnor, PA: Wallace-Homestead, 1989), 60, preparing art at the Disney studio was costing more than the money the cel set-ups generated. After the studio prepared art for *Pinocchio*, Courvoisier took over the preparation of set-ups using artists from local San Francisco schools.

54. "Dopey, Grumpy & Co.", *Art Digest* 12: 20 (1 September 1938): 14.

55. In his article "The Art of Animation", Leonard Maltin states that Disney's merchandising representative, Kay Kamen, had already experimented with sales in a St. Louis department store before Courvoisier wrote a letter to the studio saying, "I feel that there is a better opportunity to sell these celluloids through the channels provided by the fine art market than in a commercial way, such as through department stores... . Mr. Disney's reputation as an artist of great importance will at the same time be maintained. The position he now holds in this respect is outstanding." Leonard Maltin, "The Art of Animation", *Museum* (July/August 1982): 56–59.

56. Maltin, 57.

57. "Dopey, Grumpy & Co."

58. "First National Showing and Sale of the Original Watercolors from Walt Disney's *Snow White and the Seven Dwarfs*, 15 September to 4 October." Julien Levy Gallery invitation to exhibit opening, 15 September 1938, MoMA Film Study Center, New York.

59. Melville Upton, "First in Art Season Field", *New York Sun*, 17 September 1938.

60. "Walt Disney Originals", *Harper s Bazaar*, 15 September 1938, 31.

61. Peyton Boswell, "The Wonder of Fantasia", *Art Digest* 15: 5 (1 December 1940): 3.

62. For a study of the animation art market's growth in the 1980s and early 1990s, see William Mikulak, "Animation Art: the Fine Art of Selling Collectibles", *On the Margins of Art Worlds*, ed. Larry Gross (Boulder: Westview, 1995), 249–264.

63. Some work in this area includes: David Ehrlich, "Experimental Animation as Formal Narrative and Its Proper Role within the Traditional Animation Festival", Paper presented at Society for Animation Studies Conference, Ottawa, Canada, October 1990; Maureen Furniss, "Rituals of Celebration: Community and Communitas at the Ottawa International Animation Festival", Paper presented at the Society for Animation Studies Conference, San Francisco, October 1994.

Mikulak, Bill. "Disney and the Art World: The Early Years". *Animation Journal* 4: 2 (Spring 1996). 18–42. ©1996 Bill Mikulak

13

The Art of Chuck Jones: John Lewell Interviews the Veteran Hollywood Animator

Interview by John Lewell [1982]

dolised, now, by the New Wave of the American cinema, he has entertained every one of us for nearly half a century. Successive generations all over the world continue to enjoy his films, among which are some all-time cartoon classics. He has been nominated for fourteen Academy Awards, and has won three. His lifetime spans almost the entire history of Hollywood, a place that he might describe as being his "natural environment". His name is Chuck Jones.

Born in 1912, in Spokane, Washington, Charles M. Jones moved to Hollywood at the age of six months. It was a very sensible move. For now, 500 films later, and still creating, Jones has become a legend in his own lifetime. Says Peter Bogdanovich, writing in Esquire: "His stuff remains, like all good fables and only the best art, both timeless and universal". Praise, indeed, and typical of the affection with which Jones is regarded.

The characters, of course, are much more famous than their prime mover. There is Bugs Bunny, the world s smartest rabbit, and Daffy the egocentric Duck. There is Pepe le Pew, the amorous skunk who pursues every female cat that has a white stripe. And then there is Wile

E. Coyote who consistently fails to catch the Roadrunner, that high-speed bird of perpetual motion.

They are the stars of the Jones s galaxy. But there are many others, too. Let us not forget Porky the Pig – or Michigan J., the mysterious singing frog from One Froggy Evening. Perhaps Jones would rather we did forget the Minah Bird, and we rarely see Gabby Goat these days. Yet the unmistakable Jones s versions of Sylvester the Cat, and Tom, of Tom and Jerry, were infinitely more personable than any of the best-selling cats of the Eighties.

In moving all these characters, Chuck Jones has made about fifty million drawings. Although Warner Bros. destroyed many originals, there are enough remaining to make the animator s personal archive in Costa Mesa bulge at the seams. As if to spite the ghost of Jack Warner, drawings and cels are now being sold as individual works of art by mail order in the United States.

Chuck Jones began directing animated films when he was twenty-five. His first film was called The Nightwatchman, made in 1938. Until then, he had trained in all aspects of the craft, first at Chouinard Art Institute, and then in a commercial art studio where he was discovered by Ub Iwerks, one of the pioneers of early animation. In his brief autobiographical notes, Jones says that for Iwerks he "washed Flip the Frogs with distinction and alacrity". Later, he joined the Leon Schlesinger studio and, by the time it was sold to Warner Bros., Jones was directing – "the first time a cel-washer had accomplished this without detection". Assigned with Bob Clampett to the Tex Avery unit in some run-down buildings nicknamed "Termite Terrace" he began work on Porky the Pig and the "beginnings of the wildly insane version of Daffy Duck".

It was not until after the Second World War that the golden period really began. In these years, Jones developed a long association with writer Mike Maltese, animators Ken Harris, Phil Monroe, Abe Levitow and Dick Thompson, and with Maurice Noble and Phil DeGuard (layout and background). Hundreds of Merry Melodies and Looney Tunes were produced – all of them beautifully crafted, brilliantly timed, and quite devoid of the sentimentality for which Disney has often been criticised. In 1950, Jones was rewarded by his peers with two Oscars, one for Pepe le Pew and For Scenti-Mental Reasons, and another for So Much For So Little, the first cartoon to win in the documentary category.

For a few weeks, in 1958, the Warner Bros. cartoon studio closed down. Eventually, Warner realised his mistake, and Jones and the others were re-hired. The whole farcical episode was, unfortunately, typical of the brusqueness with which animators were once treated by the big studios. Had the studio bosses known that cartoons were destined to earn some $30 million on the new medium of television, perhaps they would have behaved differently. As it was, they regarded their greatest artists as menial employees – yes, as termites! – who could be conveniently forgotten so long as the work kept flowing.

On several occasions, Jones has had his revenge. When speaking of those people he admires, such as Tex Avery or Friz Freleng, his generosity is unbounded. But when he talks about "the bosses" he is devastating. "I built a house above Jack Warner in Hollywood so I could spit on him when he drove to work". And as for Eddie Selzer, the producer: "He was a fox gnawing at my innards for twelve years".

When the Warner cartoon studio finally closed in 1963, Chuck Jones took a brief holiday from animation and returned to painting. The walls of his offices are hung with some striking art from this period. It was not long, however, before MGM asked him to make some Tom and Jerry cartoons, for which Jones assembled his old crew from Warners. Together again, they made The Dot and the Line that promptly won yet another Academy Award. And while still with MGM, Jones co-wrote and co-directed The Phantom Tollbooth, a full-length feature that emerges sometimes at film festivals, described by its author as "a critical success, a box-office question-mark".

Now Chuck Jones has his own company, making TV specials for the big American networks. For ABC, he made the Singing Cricket Trilogy, including The Cricket in Times Square. For CBS, three Jungle Book stories have been produced: Rikki-Tikki-Tavi, The White Seal and Mowgli's Brothers. Each one is a half-hour show, made to the same high standards as the earlier Warner cartoons, and a world away from the cheap Saturday-morning "illustrated radio" that most Hollywood animators are now producing.

Nor is this the final chapter in an epic career. "Please let there be new Bugs Bunnies, Roadrunners, Pepe le Pews", said Peter Bogdanovich in an open letter to Warners. "If you knew that for a few thousand bucks you could bring back Bogart, Tracy, Lombard. Gable, Monroe – wouldn t you do it? Well, Bugs and the other boys are stars too."

And lo! In 1980 there were new Warners

shorts. Bugs Bunny's Bustin' Out All Over *contained the first of them. Their titles are more sophisticated than before.* Portrait of the Artist as a Young Rabbit *has a youthful Bugs confronting an infant Elmer Fudd.* Soup and Sonic *is a new Roadrunner in which the Coyote actually catches the bird. And in* Duck Dodgers in the Return of the 24th Century *we have a sequel to the 1953 short so beloved by Spielberg and Lucas.*

On American television, the art of Chuck Jones is seen nearly every day of the week. The CBS *Bugs Bunny-Roadrunner Show has played on Saturdays for nearly thirty years, while from Monday to Friday syndicated packages have been shown on other channels. Sunday is the only bad day – you have to get up at 6.00am to see them.*

Indeed, a remarkable amount of prime-time television is devoted to animation in the United States. Jones s work is especially popular at Christmas-time, and for the last fifteen years the Dr. Seuss fable How the Grinch Stole Christmas *has been aired at peak period. Can there be anyone in the entire country who has not seen a Chuck Jones picture? I doubt it.*

In person, Jones is a soft-spoken and genial man, both alert and remote at the same time. I cannot better Tom Shale s description of him in The Washington Post *as being "a mildly distracted combination of Thomas Alva Edison and Andy Warhol". To my mind, he is greater than either. He is an American humorist in the tradition of Mark Twain.*

John Lewell: You once said that "animation in itself is an art-form". Do you agree that there are different ways of watching cartoon films? You can watch them, as a child does, and enjoy the action and the gags. But you can also watch them solely for their aesthetics.

Chuck Jones: Oh, yes. Certainly the message itself can be enjoyed. One of the best examples of that was when we finished a picture at Warner Bros. We would always run it as a pencil test to see if it worked without sound, music, colour, or anything else. Then you could see the beauty of the movement.

JL: In fact, animation is a logical development of Western Art, adding the element of movement to the artist's vocabulary.

CJ: That's true. But animation – and films in general – probably have more to do with music than with other forms of graphic art. This is because animation is a series of visual impacts. Music is a series of auditory impacts. You hear notes in relation to other notes, and the same is true of film. It has a time factor. If you didn't retain the visual image, the accents wouldn't work.

JL: There are many techniques used in animation. How do you select from them?

CJ: There are many film graphics. But the term "character animation", which was what the Disney group was all about, was where it all started. We started with *Three Little Pigs.* While we had three characters who *looked* more or less the same, they *acted* differently. And that was the first time it happened.

Very few writers have ever noticed that this style of animation – that is, character animation – is unique to the United States. I'm not saying this jingoistically – but it's like jazz! And it's mostly come from Southern California. No other country has come up with any sort of cartoon character that can safely cross borders. There is no such thing as a French international character, or a

British international character. And yet, although we didn't plan it that way, all of ours are international. It's very curious. In Japan, Bugs Bunny and Tom and Jerry are recognised. And recently we got a tiny royalty payment from one of those little republics that Nixon was always buttering up! I forgot which one it was, but their $18 dollar cheque must have been the equivalent of an $18 million cheque from the United States.

JL: Let's try and think why this is so. Did the star system in Hollywood, in the Twenties and Thirties, help to create a climate where cartoon characters could become stars?

CJ: Yes, there's no question about it. One of the reasons why other countries didn't develop a star system is that they didn't make enough pictures. People like Chaplin and Keaton had the advantage of doing series, of doing thirty or forty or even a hundred pictures. And during that time they could develop their character. God knows, when Chaplin started out with Lonesome Luke – that was hardly "Chaplin"! It was just by happenchance that Chaplin picked up the uniform he wore from that time on. And later, Laurel and Hardy wore the same uniform: Derby hat, tight collars, shoes too big, and so on. The "look" of the great comedians had nothing to do with the way they moved. But the series did.

All of our stuff was "block-booked". This was an enormous advantage because the pictures were sold before they went out. We had the chance to experiment with different characters, and over a period of time I directed close to two hundred Bugs Bunnies and maybe twenty-five or thirty Roadrunners. It was an enormous advantage – and it developed stars.

JL: A cartoon character, of course, does not have a life off-screen for the gossip columnists to write about!

CJ: I think it would be better if live action actors didn't! Chaplin was often in trouble for his politics. Yet his greatest political comments were in *City Lights* and *Modern Times,* both of which were made as comedies. I don't think he thought about politics any more than Laurel and Hardy did.

JL: Were people like Chaplin and Laurel and Hardy a bigger influence on you than were other animators?

CJ: Oh, yes. Other animators had very little influence, beyond the fact that the climate was created by the Disney studios. It was like Harold Ross at *The New Yorker* saying that he was creating an atmosphere where the artist could flourish. Ross did it deliberately, whereas Walt did it without being able to put it into words. But, after all, he gave those people a chance to make *Fantasia.* He was doing it – and he inadvertently did it for us too! That was the reason animation flourished.

From that point on we began to grow characters that were notable for the way they moved. That's true of any actor or of any great comedian. It's not what the actor *looks* like. A comedian is not a person who opens a funny door – he's the person who opens a door funny.

JL: So you could learn the secrets of timing from the great comedians …

CJ: Certainly. We took note of all those things. I tried Bugs Bunny, once, using a Groucho Marx walk – and it worked fine. But I didn't use it again because I learned what the lesson was. You learn ways for the character to move by doing it once – for instance, as

Groucho – then I knew that Bugs would have his own style.

JL: I was going to ask you about that! Someone said that Bugs was "modelled on Groucho". That would be an exaggeration?

CJ: Yes. Bugs learned from Groucho. And Groucho himself learned from Buster Keaton. As Jacques Tati pointed out, Keaton had to do everything with his feet! Since he couldn't move his face he would take little steps forwards and little steps backwards. From his movements you could tell just what he was thinking. Indecision was sideways. Fear was backwards. He even had one like the Knight's move in chess!

Bugs Bunny came along after Max Hare, the Disney character, but he had almost nothing in common with him. But again, Max Hare inspired it, just as he probably inspired me to do Roadrunner because that was the first time that blinding speed was used.

JL: It was proved that there was room for lots of characters of the same species!

CJ: Oh yes. And all of them represent something in yourself. If you're a dissolute person, you do not find that dissolution in another person, you find it in yourself. Everyone has some dissolute parts! I think that's why people like *How the Grinch Stole Christmas,* because here's a guy who hates Christmas! Well, it doesn't take much effort on our part to realise that *we* hate Christmas, too, but maybe we try to keep it to ourselves. But when someone comes along who hates Christmas completely and openly – we love it! It's like W.C. Fields: anybody who hates dogs and babies can't be all bad. That phrase was attributed to Fields, but it was really

what he was all about. It reminds me of a friend of mine who said "I've only met *one* man I didn't like – and that was Will Rogers!!" Isn't that great?

JL: Shameless! Of course, in animation you can construct the personality to fit the part.

CJ: That's right. But it also means digging into yourself. When you're doing Daffy Duck, who's a conniving, self-serving person, you realise that – sure, I'm selfish, too. Hopefully I must keep most of it under control. But Daffy doesn't do that. He's selfish, then he explains. He builds a rationale for it. When he betrayed Bugs one time, in a film we made called *The Abominable Snow Rabbit,* Daffy said to the audience: "I know it's a terrible thing to do, but it's better it should happen to him than to me. I'm not like other people – pain hurts me!" Right? That's rational! We do naughty things, then we explain it to ourselves.

JL: How did it come about that Daffy and Bugs started to try to kill each other, in films like *Rabbit Fire* and *Rabbit Seasoning*?

CJ: Well, no they were just transferring the aggression to each other. There again, you don't have to go very deep inside yourself to realise that's true. In a more solemn way, one of the greatest guilt feelings during the war was when your buddy was killed and you found you were happy about it.

JL: Because it didn't happen to you ...

CJ: Exactly. All we're saying is: if you're happy afterwards, you might as well say it beforehand. But looking back, Bugs outwitted Daffy. It wouldn't have worked if Daffy hadn't started it.

JL: He was the provocateur?

CJ: That's precisely what he was. Bugs, in all of his pictures, was a counter-revolutionary – not a revolutionary. He did not go out, like Woody Woodpecker, and just bedevil people for the fun of it. Bugs was always minding his own business at the beginning of the picture. He was always in a natural rabbit environment. Then someone would come along and try to remove his foot or his body, or his soul – and he would fight back. Like Groucho, he had to say: "You know this means war". That was the line of Groucho's I could not refrain from stealing. It was so natural for Bugs to say that.

JL: Bugs was a laid-back rabbit hero.

CJ: Yes. Unlike most comic characters, Bugs was a comic hero. There aren't many of them around. It's hard to think of any. Nearly all comedians are losers – Keaton, Chaplin, Harold Lloyd, Woody Allen. Even Diane Keaton! All of them, as comic characters, are losers.

JL: It's the idea that humour is an antidote to disaster?

CJ: Yes. Our lives are made up of errors and mistakes. I mean, we can't even get a spoonful of food into our mouths without making fifteen or twenty corrections to our arm movements. I think that's why, when a baby has proved he can do it, he loses interest for a while. What's going on beyond the spoon is suddenly more interesting. When we learn that we can hit our mouth without looking at the spoon – that's one of the most startling discoveries.

Feedback is an amazing sense. How do we know where our arm is, without seeing it? All this information comes to the brain, till the brain can say: "Oh, *that's*

where you are!"

JL: We create a kind of "map" in the brain which tells us where everything is. For instance, if someone loses an arm, he can still "feel" it.

CJ: But it's a combination of so many senses besides the pictorial one. We always think everything is pictorial, don't we? We say "I see" meaning "I understand".

JL: Animators gain insights into human character because they observe. In order to portray movement you have to watch people very closely. And, if you watch people, you can see what they do, and you have a better understanding of them.

CJ: Precisely. It's like leading with eyesight. I once saw a slow motion film of someone dropping a cat, and as the cat fell, the head turned before the body did. Apparently, the whole body adjusts to what the head sees. The cat doesn't think it out. The legs just came around to relate to the head. And it happens so damn fast!

When we were doing *Rikki-Tikki-Tavi,* we had to study some film of a cobra striking so that we could be accurate in showing a fight between a mongoose and a cobra. In one clip the cobra actually struck the camera. They're pit-vipers, you know. They like the warmth. Like a Sarn missile. Now, apparently this cobra was eight feet away when he struck the camera – and yet there was only one frame between the two positions! He traveled eight feet in a twenty-fourth of a second. That's pretty fast. Yet when a mongoose and a cobra are fighting, the mongoose gets up to within a few inches and *dares* it to strike. When it finally does strike it all happens at such an enormous speed that maybe the cobra draws back a tiny bit – perhaps in a thousandth of a second – but it's enough to warn the mongoose to pull away. This is the case where animation cannot exaggerate the action because, when you have only one frame to work with, the only way you could show it would be with strobe lights at a thousand frames a second.

JL: Returning to more lovable animals, do you have a personal favourite among all the characters you've worked with?

CJ: Well, as I say, each one represents something different. But Pepe le Pew – the little skunk – and Bugs are naturally characters I'd like to be. They have the appeal of absolute certainty. They're able to handle a situation, and I wish I could always do that. But I also recognise the Coyote because, like him, I have an absolute failure with tools. I can understand his problem. The Roadrunner never does anything to him, except say: "Beep, beep". And so all the failures are his own. Then Daffy represents something in me that I keep inside – but that he lets out. So all of them represent something. A character I really didn't understand – but I love him – is the singing frog in *One Froggy Evening*. But he's not a favourite, as such.

JL: You didn't get along with the Minah Bird!

CJ: Well, I didn't understand it! I directed the thing – and Disney saw one of them, and he loved it. So he called the guys together and they all tried to find out what I was doing – but they couldn't understand it either! I made them only because the exhibitors demanded them.

You see, to me the essence of all fantasy is logic. You've got to believe it. And you have to remember that we're not starting out with drawings. As Norman McLaren said, animation is not a bunch of drawings that move – it's a bunch of

drawings *of* movement, movement that already exists in the director's mind. There's a big difference there.

JL: Moviegoers today are more aware of the different job functions in a cartoon production. They can distinguish between a writer and a director and an animator and a layout man. Would you describe yourself as a director and designer rather than as an animator?

CJ: No. It didn't work that way, not at Warner's. At Warner's it was different from Disney's and different from MGM. At MGM, Bill and Joe (Hanna and Barbera) worked together on Tom and Jerry. Joe would do the drawing and Bill would do the timing. But at Warner Bros., the animation director had always been an animator – because you don't know how to time a picture unless you've animated it. There's no way – except when there's dialogue, because then you can time to the dialogue. So we had to lay the pictures out completely, and I had to do all the key drawings – about three hundred of them. That's not the animation, mind you, but those key drawings have to be related to the animation. They're not just still drawings. When you have a layout man who's not an animator he tends to make a drawing that has nothing to do with animation.

What I tried to do was to keep the expressions – so that when the Coyote falls off a cliff he appears not to be worried about being hurt, but he *is* worried about being humiliated. So when he crosses his arms as he's falling through the air, and looks at the audience, angrily, it's because he doesn't want them to see him. So, yes, I'd design the characters, but I'd also time the entire picture before it went to animation – something that would drive live action directors mad even to think about it! We didn't edit at all, afterwards. Maybe a few frames. If a picture was 540 feet, six minutes, we would never overshoot and never edit.

The director was actually a producerdirector, and he had absolute authority. The entire picture was his problem. But, of course, we still need good actors, just as a live action director does. In our case, the animator is the actor. Very few animators are humorous – so they don't contribute much in that way – but they do contribute brilliant animation. An exception was Ken Harris, who died recently. He was a brilliant comic animator, very unusual. His stuff would always be funnier than what I had described to him. He was a very kind and gentle person, but he did broad animation. Richard Williams used him a lot, too.

JL: You've also worked with Richard Williams, on *A Christmas Carol*. What did you think of Williams's approach to animation?

CJ: I think Dick Williams has a problem because he can't make up his mind what he wants to be – whether he wants to be a director, an animator or a clean-up man. Yes, he even cleans up drawings! But I admire him tremendously.

JL: He's very dedicated, isn't he, and he goes into every aspect of the craft.

CJ: Truly dedicated! But I think he should clarify his relationship to his projects. He should clearly be the director, and not try to animate or to clean up people's drawings. Rather, he should try and provide whatever they need to allow them to clean up their own drawings. I think it's very unusual to find someone who can both direct and act.

TJL: There have been some great actor/directors – Chaplin for example.

CJ: Of course. But there's not very many of them. Dick's probably capable of it, but I don't know how long he can push that one feature along.[1]

JL: I understand that he sees the feature as being the only way to get people into the cinema and to make a big impact. Was that not Disney's secret – and isn't that why there's a great Disney empire today? Disney insisted on full-length animation.

CJ: Yes, but that's not what made it. The first feature was possible because the shorts were so successful. If they hadn't been made, people wouldn't have gone to the features. Disney and animation became synonymous. Features are fine, but they're not the sole reason for Disney's success.

I've never made anything for an audience. When I make a special, I make it because it interests me. The commercial aspect of it doesn't enter into it at all. The point is: if you know how to make yourself laugh, you'll make other people laugh. I'm puzzled by Dick Williams, not by what he does. He's certainly the Disney of commercials. At Filmex last year we had a showing of all the things he'd done with commercials. They were incredible. I mean: some of the best things *ever* done in animation. It was a goddamn textbook of animation! And then Dick got up and said: "You haven't seen anything yet. That stuff's junk!" Well, that's absurd. It *isn t* junk. He shouldn't even think that way.

JL: He told me that he just contributes skill to his clients.

CJ: Maybe. But I've never known an artist go to the point of talking about the meaning of his work. It usually means he's lost track of what he's doing. I've been talking about my work – but only retrospectively. At the time of doing it, I can't think that way.

JL: Do you agree with the critics – like Richard Thompson – who have analysed your work so thoroughly?

CJ: Oh, I don't mind what they say, however much culture they pile on. I like it! It hasn't much to do with what I do. And I don't agree with it – no – because I don't agree with anything. The only reason I have is this: a blank sheet of paper. It's what *you* have. You're a writer, so you know that. All I know is that when I finish a film – boom! There's that damn blank thing staring at me again! And it's not a screen. It's paper. Our tools are a flurry of drawings and a pencil. The rest is just additional stuff – ink, paint, backgrounds – all of that. They contribute to the film, but they're not what *makes* the film.

JL: People make films! Going back, for a moment, to some of the people you've known and worked with ... can you tell us: what exactly was Jack Warner like, as an employer?

CJ: Well, what he was like was nothing! We had nothing to do with Jack Warner. After fifteen years of direction (and the other person present, Friz Freleng, had directed longer than that) we were finally invited by him to have lunch in the executive dining room. This was reserved for executives and favourite directors. Jack Warner was there. And Harry Warner was there. Jack didn't say very much to us. He was talking to other people about other things. But Harry Warner said: "The only thing I know about our cartoon department is that we

make Mickey Mouse". Well, that was a little startling. It was the early 1950s, for God's sake! And so when we left, I said: "Don't worry, Mr Warner, we'll continue to make good Mickey Mouses!" And he patted me on the back.

As far as Jack Warner was concerned, he didn't even know the difference between Friz and me. When he went into television, we met him, and he couldn't remember our names. So he called us Mutt and Jeff. That was after we'd worked for Warners for twenty-five years. He didn't even know where the department was!

JL: That's the most extraordinary thing. I mean, you'd made a huge fortune for the studio – and you'd won several Academy Awards!

CJ: Friz had won five Oscars. I won three. But the main thing was the films made an enormous amount of money. The TV show has been on now for twenty-five years – since 1957. It's probably the longest-running show on the network. Personally, we got no money from it. We were just employees. But I would guess it's earned twenty or thirty million dollars. And that's after the movies were paid for by theatrical release.

Full animation is commercially a very sound investment. *How the Grinch Stole Christmas* – which we made independently in 1967 – has run on prime-time television each Christmas for fifteen years, for a minimum of $150,000 per run. So you're getting around $2 million for something that cost $350,000, and was paid for by the network.

JL: And they don't date!

CJ: Most of our cartoons never dated. We simply ignored anything that was happening temporally. I don't know why.

JL: Do you object to animation being used for propaganda purposes? In wartime, for instance?

CJ: Well, it's certainly one of the best teaching techniques. The *Snafu* series we did was not aggressive. It was all to do with the protection of our lives. "Keep away from mosquitoes", and so on. Up till then they had been making pictures using actors as soldiers, or using soldiers as actors. Neither method worked too well. But when you made a cartoon film, no one could object to it, and every soldier related to it. We had to know the mental attitude of the audience. These guys were usually very tired, and often in overheated barracks, when they saw these films. So we used some pretty salty language to get their attention.

JL: Disney was very successful with his wartime films.

CJ: Oh yes. We also made a few of those Bell Telephone science films, *Gateways to the Mind.* Disney made one called *Our Friend the Atom,* which was one of the most remarkable things I've ever seen. It explained how atomic energy works. They took a table, about twenty feet long and ten feet wide, with mousetraps and ping-pong balls all over it. Then they threw one ping-pong ball into the middle of the table, and that triggered off another two ping-pong balls into the air. Almost faster than you could think, the whole air was full of ping-pong balls. Can you imagine setting it all up without accidentally setting off a mousetrap?

JL: We're back full circle to the thousand-and-one techniques of animation.

CJ: I prefer to use the term "animation" – which in the dictionary means "to evoke life" – as being restricted to full character animation. Many of the others do *not* invoke life. They invoke movement. Many people, like Bob Kurtz and his friends, are really dealing more with film graphics. You do not believe in the personality of the character.

So coming back to the idea of a clown: a clown is someone who's funny to look at. Everything a clown has to say to you, you get in a few seconds. I'm not talking about people like Emmett Kelly, because they're not funny to look at – they're sad. Emmett Kelly is a comedian, even though he dresses as a clown. He's funny only when he starts to move. Now, a lot of animation is like the other kind of clowning. It's funny to look at, but not because of the way it moves. Those things that Kurtz does – all those dinosaurs – they're funny to look at, but you can't tell one dinosaur from another. They all move the same.

JL: When you say that "animator" is a "giftword" – how many animators, in that sense, are there today?

CJ: Maybe ten, including the Disney guys.

JL: Which are they, and who are they?

CJ: The people at Disney probably represent most of them. But there are guys like Phil Monroe, Ben Washam, people who worked with us at Warner Bros., all these people are around. We had maybe fifteen. Originally, all told, there may have been a hundred – so I'm just talking about those who are still practising. There are a few overseas. Dick Williams is one. You see, there are not very many. If you tried to name actors of the same quality as Laurence Olivier or Alec Guinness – how many would there be? You couldn't include Gary Cooper or John Wayne who were stars because of their individual personalities. But nobody knows what Guinness is – as a personality. And how many actors can do that? A hundred?

JL: Students often wonder how to get started in animation. What do you recommend?

CJ: They should get a copy of the big Disney book. It's great not only because of its historical importance, but if students would first learn how to draw the human figure, and then did all the exercises in the book, they'd be animators. It's all there. It's a great book.

I'd also recommend that they get Kimon Nikolaides's book *The Natural Way to Draw*. By the time they finish that one they'll be able to draw the human figure – or anything else – and then they should start on the Disney book. It would take them a year to go through Nikolaides, and probably two years more to go through the Disney book. Maybe three. But by yourself you can have a university education on how to animate.

JL: There have been several rebellions against the idea that animation has to be based on little men or little animals. Animators in England, for instance, have been experimenting in other areas, for instance by recording live soundtracks in public places and then re-creating the characters. Sometimes it works well. Do you think animation can develop in many other ways than we've already seen?

CJ: Sure. Any experiment is fine. One thing I do wish people would do, though, is to explore a discipline once they've discovered it, and not jump from discipline to discipline. We stuck to what we did, and so did John Hubley, to some extent. But very often these guys will do

one style, then they'll go leaping into another before they've found out what it's all about and how it works.

When you come right down to it, isn't it true that one artist is identifiable by what he contributes to other artists, and not at all by what the public thinks of him? Every artist of any importance, and that includes writers and musicians, is a person from whom other artists can glean something to use in following generations. If Beethoven had written a symphony, then turned around and tried to do jazz, we should never have understood anything about him. People should stay with what they do, and then it would be useful to all of us.

JL: Perhaps people are not certain whether they've tapped a rich enough vein!

CJ: Well, then they don't believe very much in what they're doing, do they? They're saying: "This is an exercise". But eventually, you've got to stop exercising. You've got to stop doing calisthenics and start to use the muscle you've developed.

In art school, it's vital for a student to make his own film, by himself. A student should do the inking, and the painting – everything – because you learn that way. I started as a cel washer, and did inking and painting and ran the camera, and eventually had to do all my own pasting up. It's a fantastic field to be in – and the entire history of animation has taken place within my lifetime. I was born in 1912. So even the full animators are Cro-Magnons – if we're lucky, since Cro-Magnons were so darned good! Their paintings covered four-fifths of the entire history of art, so they were hardly primitive.

Now we keep coming back to the idea that people don't want to do fuzzy little animals! Is *Fantasia* fuzzy little animals? Is *The Old Mill?* Some people are always talking of "fuzzy little animals" as though that were all we, or Disney, ever did. None of our characters was fuzzy! Indeed, until Xerox came along you couldn't even make a fuzzy animal! It's ridiculous.

JL: Perhaps there's an over-emphasis today on originality. Surely, no work of art can be totally original. If it were, no one could understand it.

CJ: True. Then you're standing on top of a pyramid. So what can you do? Make the pyramid a little taller? You have to look at what's supporting it. The idea of being different for its own sake is like standing in front of those distortion mirrors in an amusement park. People come up, and look in those mirrors – and they're distorted. But everyone is distorted in the same way. So that's not "editorial opinion", and it's not caricature.

All art is caricature, and all art is editorial – in the sense that you're exaggerating something to prove what we all think about it. We exaggerate, or we understate. Take Jimmy Durante – when you caricature him you make his eyes smaller in order to make his nose look bigger. That makes it work. One of the best descriptions I've ever heard is a verbal caricature: "Durante is the only man I know who can take a shower and smoke a cigar at the same time". Isn't that great? That's better than I could draw! It forces you to think.

JL: Yes. It creates participation in the art. On this subject, do you think that when Disney made everything 3-D in Disneyland that it was all too explicit, that it took something away from our imaginative perception in the characters?

CJ: Yes. I think that's true. But it's probably a product of our times. Nearly all children's toys now are so explicit. There's very little room left for children to explore for themselves.

When I first went to Disney, he told me that when he was a kid and used to go to amusement parks he was disappointed because everything was papier-mache. The log cabin wasn't made of real logs. The guns were not real guns. And Disney said he wanted something that would be believable – always believable. That's what he was driving at. And personally, I love Disneyland – as does Ray Bradbury. One time Bradbury asked Disney to run for Mayor of Los Angeles, and Disney's reply was: "Why should I run for Mayor when I'm already King?"

You see, that's why Richard Schickel was so wrong in his book. If there was one thing Disney was not, it was practical. The day he died, the stock went up twelve points! He just had the world's biggest toy.

JL: Did Disney push perfection to the point where it was totally uncommercial?

CJ: That did happen. When Disney was alive the animators reached a point where their work was never right first time. Now, spontaneity is very important in animation – so they fought back by doing the work, putting it in a drawer, and then re-animating another way. After a number of corrections, they'd pull out the originals and submit it as the finished piece! That's a very dumb way to run a railroad! Anyway, that's what they told me, and I believe it.

JL: Your characters became more developed, and polished, over the years. You took them further from their animal origins. Daffy, for instance, became more elongated when you took him over.

CJ: Yes. Except for Sylvester. I always used him on four legs but Friz always used him standing up. All four-legged animals work differently. Grim Natwick said that a journeyman animator should have a thousand tools. One of these tools would be a horse trotting. Just one tool! And that includes fat horses, thin horses, lame horses. Then you still have 999 other tools to master. Grim Natwick is one who has all of these.

JL: Do you think it's a shame that animators are not as well-known as their talent would justify? After all, there's a lot of mediocre modern art – even in the Museum of Modern Art – but the public knows the names of the artists. Yet relatively few people have heard of Grim Natwick – and his is a name one doesn't easily forget!

CJ: People are getting more understanding now. Some of our animators are better known in Europe than they are here. Unfortunately, even when they were given credits, it was still hard to tell who did what. You can usually tell Bill Tytla's work, though. It was a tragedy that he went out during the Disney strike in 1941. I was one of the leaders of that strike, but Bill should never have gone. He would have been one of the Nine Old Men.

JL: What was Mel Blanc like to work with?

CJ: Very good. But again, Mel implies that he originated characters. Yet he never wrote any dialogue. We would decide on the character and write the dialogue – then ask Mel to come up with a voice. He was a lot of fun. It was his versatility that made him great. Mind you, he's the only one who ever got residuals, although we originated the characters.

JL: A lot of people now lay claim to each character!

CJ: Each character came out of a unit. A director can probably take credit for characters that came from his own unit. I did all the Roadrunners and Coyotes and all the Pepe le Pews. Tex Avery breathed the fire into Bugs, although there were two or three pictures made about the rabbit beforehand. Tex deserves the credit, if credit is to be given. And Friz [Freleng] directed the Yosemite Sams.

But all of us did Bugs Bunny. Bugs was an unusual rabbit. He had several fathers, rather than a multitude of children. And at Warner's, we worked parallel to each other. We helped each other, but we had no control over each other. At that time, I don't think that anyone in animation was consciously in competition with anyone else. You can't compete with someone unless you're in the same area.

JL: You actually worked at Disney's for a very short time. What happened?

CJ: I worked at Disney for about four months when Jack Warner closed the studio because 3-D had come along. We made one 3-D cartoon, *Lumberjack Rabbit.* But Warner was going to turn everything into 3-D. Perhaps he thought that every baby would be born with one green and one red eye. A few months later, he opened up again, and had to pay a lot more for the same people. "I returned to Warner's because after I got to Disney's, in 1956, I noticed that nothing moved unless Walt moved it. At the time, they were working on *Sleeping Beauty,* and when they finished a sequence they had to wait for Walt. It could take six weeks – and what do you do in that time? I was used to working under pressure. Walt asked me why I was leaving, and I said: "There's only one job around here worth having – and that's yours!" And he replied: "You're absolutely right. Unfortunately, it's full".

JL: When Warner's finally closed down the cartoon studios in 1962, how did you make out?

CJ: I didn't have much choice. My trade was making full animation. I looked around to see what was available, and it turned out that TV specials have the money necessary to do this kind of work. I've tried to do two half-hours a year. I've not done quite that many – but enough.

JL: Is the budget really sufficient?

CJ: Oh yes. It wouldn't be enough for Disney, but I can work within it. There's the same quality of animation on *The Cricket in Times Square* and *Rikki-Tikki-Tavi* as there was at Warner Bros. Our animators would do twenty-five feet a week, whereas at Hanna-Barbera they do two hundred feet.

JL: Do you approve of the cheap animation?

CJ: Well, I don't call it animation. I call it "illustrated radio". They do a minimum number of drawings to a pre-recorded soundtrack. You can turn the picture off and still tell what's happening.

JL: Does the existence of this technique make it more difficult for people to distinguish the full character animation?

CJ: I don't think so. The Bugs Bunny shows have been running for twenty-five years, and new generations see them and like them. But I think it's criminal to go back to the basic necessity of the 1920s, when no one knew how to animate fully, and to merely show the good guys and the bad guys by their appearance. We're back to that now. If people are big and ugly – they're bad. If they're pretty and cute – they're good.

But it shouldn't matter what a character looks like. A good comedian can be identified by the fact that he can be imitated. You can imitate Chaplin, or Keaton, or Bugs Bunny, or Donald Duck. And where would Rich Little be if he had to look like all the characters he imitates? He doesn't. It's the physical way he moves. It's Jack Benny folding his arms, putting three fingers on his chin. He said three fingers were funny, four fingers aren't. That's true – but why? Nobody seems to know. People are wrong to complain about violence in cartoons while overlooking a much more sinister thing – educating children to think that people are what they look like rather than how they act.

JL: You can "smile and smile, and be a villain", as Shakespeare said.

CJ: Absolutely. ☙

Note

1. See interview by John Lewell, "Richard Williams: Making His Own Legend", in April 1982 *Films and Filming*, about *The Thief*.

Lewell, John. "The Art of Chuck Jones". In *Films and Filming* 336 (September 1982), 12–20. Reprinted with permission of the author. ©1982 John Lewell

14

The Disney Studio at War

Charles Solomon [1998]

"Creative personnel accustomed to racking their brains for a new switch on some problem near and dear to Donald Duck s personality found themselves commissioned to explain to men at Navy bases all aspects of the functioning and maintenance of the gyroscope, and its relation to the overall functioning of an aerial torpedo."
Carl Nater, "Walt Disney Studio – A War Plant", *Journal of the Society of Motion Picture Engineers*, March 1944.

The outbreak of World War II profoundly affected the Disney studio. The war in Europe cut off the foreign markets that supplied nearly 40 per cent of the studio's income, exacerbating Disney's financial problems when *Pinocchio* and *Fantasia*, both released in 1940, failed to duplicate the box office success of *Snow White*. Within hours of the attack on Pearl Harbor in 1941, the US Army was billeting troops and storing ammunition in Disney studio buildings for the defense of California. Military security was introduced and everyone, including Walt, had to wear an identification badge.

"The main changes at the studio were that a lot of the men went into the service and we were not doing the regular freewheeling entertainment that we did before and after the war", recalls Marc Davis, one of the key group of studio animators Disney called "The Nine Old Men". "In an effort to keep his organization together, Walt really made a military reserve of the place. We all had to be thumb-printed and cleared by the FBI and so on to work there."

The animated training film, pioneered by Max Fleischer during WWI, would play a key part in preparing troops and support personnel throughout the war. Tests revealed that trainees learned faster and had better retention when material was presented in animation, rather than in live action or illustrated lectures. Walt Disney seems to have anticipated the importance of animation to the war effort: in early 1941, he produced *Four Methods of Flush Riveting*, an instructional film in limited animation for Lockheed, on his own initiative and at his own expense. John Grierson, who organized the National Film Board of Canada, bought the Canadian rights to *Four Methods* and commissioned Disney to produce a training film for a new anti-tank rifle, as well as four shorts urging viewers to buy war bonds.

"I think for a man who was totally involved in the fantasy world we lived in, this stuff brought him to a sudden stop", says Joe Grant, who headed the Model Department, which served as Disney's think tank during the late 1930s and 1940s. "But once he understood what was necessary, he threw himself into it completely. It was typical of him to be confronted with an entirely new atmosphere and play his role."

By the time the Canadian bond-buying shorts were completed in 1942, the Disney studio had become an essential industry, operating under the rules of the War Manpower Commission and turning out scores of films for the US military. Prior to the outbreak of the war, the largest annual output of the studio had been 37,000 feet of film; during fiscal year 1942–43 alone, Disney turned out more than five times that amount – 204,000 feet of film, 95 per cent of it for government contracts. This unprecedented increase was achieved although nearly one-third of the studio personnel had joined the military.

"Many of the films were fully animated, although some were diagrammatic", says Davis. "They had one series they called 'The Rules of the Nautical Road', thousands and thousands of feet that they turned out, done very simply, on what various lights meant and so on. But we really animated many of those things: I did some animation as well as story work on them. We used top flight people where they were available."

A 26-part, 207-minute introduction to naval signals and regulations, "Rules of the Nautical Road" (1942) was longer than *Snow White* and *Pinocchio* combined. "Rules" was dwarfed by a six-hour filmic maintenance and repair manual for Beechcraft airplanes completed in 1943. Many of the films were in the 5–30 minute range, but nearly a dozen projects ran an hour or longer. These films had to be produced quickly and cheaply, often on budgets of $15,000 or less; Disney had

spent more on a seven-minute short a decade earlier.

"We made a lot of things for Lockheed", says Ward Kimball another of the Nine Old Men. "I made one that Elmer Plummer designed about using the torque wrench: Up until the time it was invented, you went by the way the wrench felt when you were tightening a bolt. Well, with aluminum parts, people were tightening nuts to the point that they'd crack with the first vibration. We'd work on these things in between other projects; that was the crazy thing about them. I'd dash out the animation, maybe spend a week on it. I don't who the characters were, sometimes they were those dull-looking Mr. and Mrs.-type things."

It's difficult to establish how involved Walt Disney was in the production of the military film, as the notes and artwork were considered sensitive to national security and removed from the studio by government agents when the films were completed. Given the sheer volume of material produced during the war, it seems unlikely that Disney could have supervised them as closely as he did the cartoons shorts and features. Studio artists recall that he grew tired of having "professors and authorities and high military officers running his operation", and was glad to return to purely entertainment projects after the war.

Disney was not the only studio working to satisfy the seemingly endless demand for animated training films: Warner Bros., MGM, Walter Lantz and independent contractors were also busy with government commissions. Some of the top artists from Disney, MGM and Warner Bros. served in the 18th Air Force Base Unit (First Motion Picture Unit or FMPU) at "Fort Roach", the old Hal Roach studio in Culver City. Under the command of Major Rudy Ising, FMPU turned out more animated footage than any of the Hollywood studios. Other animators used their talents for special assignments:

"Dick Kelsey, who was a flamboyant, exuberant guy became a captain in the South Pacific", recounts Davis with a chuckle. "He made this model of the island they were about to attack – he could do models so fast and so well, you couldn't believe it – and General MacArthur came in with several of his officers, and was enormously impressed with it. MacArthur said, 'Captain, may I ask what you did before the War?' He was expecting to hear he was from MIT or someplace in geology, and Kelsey said, 'I worked for Walt Disney'. MacArthur looked at him and said, 'Oh' and walked off."

Disney artists designed more than 1400 logos and insignias for military and civil organizations, many of which featured the studio's famous characters. Mickey Mouse donned a hard hat in posters for the Aircraft Warning Service Volunteer Observers, and Pluto steered an aerial bomb on badges for the Sikorsky Aircraft Experimental Service Department. Donald's cocky attitude and feisty temper made him the most-requested character; the Duck appeared on more than 200 insignias. Although these logos cost the studio about $25 apiece, Disney supplied them free, as he felt he owed something to the men and women serving America who had grown up watching Mickey cartoons.

In addition, the Disney staff did volunteer projects for service organization. Studio artists painted a mural Mary Blair designed for the Hollywood Canteen. Marc Davis and Milt Kahl did a cartoon map of

Hollywood for the Hollywood USO center, and also did drawings of Disney characters for returning servicemen at a center in Santa Monica.

Not all of the studio's commissioned films were done for the military. Beginning with *South of the Border with Disney* (1942) and *The Winged Scourge* (1943), Disney produced a dozen and a half health films for Nelson Rockefeller, the Coordinator of Inter-American Affairs (CIAA), and the head of the film division, John Hay "Jock" Whitney. Aimed at a largely illiterate Latin American audience, the films explained principles of hygiene, nutrition, sanitation and infant care.

But CIAA officials were worried that German and Italian immigrants might be fomenting pro-Axis sentiment in South America. In 1941, Whitney asked Disney to make a goodwill tour of the region, where his characters enjoyed widespread popularity. Disney initially declined; his studio was in the middle of a bitterly fought strike, and he owed the Bank of America a daunting $3.4 million. Whitney countered by offering to underwrite $70,000 in expenses and advance up to $50,000 for each of five cartoons based on material from the tour. In August, 1941, Disney, his wife and fifteen of his artists, an entourage they called "El Groupo", visited Brazil, Argentina, Chile and Bolivia.

Rather than release them individually, Disney combined the South American-themed shorts into two package films. *Saludos Amigos* (1943) consists of four cartoons loosely joined by 16mm footage of El Groupo: "Pedro" is the story of a little mail plane in the Andes; in "Lake Titicaca", a recalcitrant llama gets the better of Donald Duck. The Goof charges across the Pampas with his customary enthusiasm and ineptitude in

"El Gaucho Goofy"; "Aquarela do Brasil" ("Watercolor of Brazil") introduces the ebullient parrot, José Carioca, who teaches Donald the Samba. Although the film was well received in both North and South America, it was overshadowed by its wilder and more polished successor.

Originally entitled "Surprise Package", *The Three Caballeros* (1945) begins with Donald Duck receiving a projector and three films about "strange birds": Pablo, a morose little penguin who hates the icy Antarctic; the Aracuan, an obnoxious clown; and a flying burro, the companion of a little Gauchito from Uruguay. José Carioca appears to take Donald on a stylized journey to Baia, Brazil, followed by a series of wild live action-animation sequences. When Aurora Miranda (Carmen's sister) sings "Os Quindins de Yaya" ("The Cookies of Yaya"), Donald immediately falls for her. Panchito, a Mexican cowboy rooster, emerges from a shattered piñata and leads Donald and José on a tour of his homeland. Donald frolics with a bevy of bathing beauties in Acapulco, flirts with Dora Luz, who sings "You Belong to My Heart", and dances with Carmen Molina. Molina also dances with a group of somewhat phallic animated cacti. The film ends with an explosive performance of the title song by Donald, José and Panchito.

Critics praised *Caballeros* for its energy, but were taken aback by Donald's flirtations with live actresses. *The New Yorker* noted that Molina's dance with the saguaro cacti "would probably be considered suggestive in a less innocent medium." The Disney artists developed enough material to make at least one more South American feature, but neither *Saludos Amigos* nor *The Three Caballeros* did

well enough at the box office to warrant a third installment.

In addition, the Disney artists somehow managed to turn out as many as 19 theatrical cartoons each year. Four of the shorts released in 1943, *Der Fuehrer s Face*, *Education for Death*, *Reason and Emotion* and *Chicken Little* combined propaganda with entertainment. *Der Fuehrer s Face* won an Oscar for Best Cartoon Short and introduced Oliver Wallace's title song, which became a hit when Spike Jones recorded it. The film is a surreal nightmare, with Donald Duck as an unwilling Nazi factory worker, laboring at an accelerating conveyor belt. Awakening from his dream, Donald embraces a model of the Statue of Liberty and declares, "Am I glad to be a citizen of the United States of America!"

Based on the book by Gregory Ziemer, *Education for Death* juxtaposes scenes of German schoolchildren being brainwashed with a hilarious, pseudo-operatic duet between a blowzy, obese Germania and her knight in shining armor, a scrawny caricature of Hitler. *Chicken Little* warns of the dangers of believing rumors. When Foxey Loxey convinces the gullible Chicken Little that the sky is falling, he creates a panic in the poultry yard. The dimwitted chickens flea to a nearby cave, where Foxey devours them.

Reason and Emotion depicts the conflicts within one John Doakes and a pretty young woman. Inside Doakes' head, Reason is personified as a prissy caricature of artist Martin Provenson; the simple-minded caveman Emotion is a caricature of Ward Kimball. Their counterparts inside the unnamed woman's head are cartoonier than other female Disney characters of the 1940s. The narrator contrasts the need for a sane balance between these extremes with the irrational fears and hatreds expounded in Nazi propaganda.

"Walt was always trying to take these dull subjects, and goose 'em with a little comedy", says Kimball. "Proportioning the characters in *Reason and Emotion* with big heads and small bodies was part of that: you'd have a built-in laugh. If we'd had characters who were the regular eight heads high, the stuff wouldn't have been funny. Also, the more exaggerated our characters were, the more exaggerated our animation could be. We could deviate from normal movements to exaggerate them, stretch them, make them more imaginative."

"It was a problem not to make things *too* entertaining, but to be sure the message was clear", cautions Grant.

Mixing entertainment and propaganda was not unique to Disney. All the Hollywood cartoon studios caricatured the Axis leaders and spoofed civilian shortages: Bugs Bunny sold war bonds; Superman fought Japanese saboteurs; Andy Panda and Barney Bear planted Victory Gardens. At the end of Tex Avery's *What s Buzzin Buzzard?* (MGM, 1943), a photograph of a T-bone steak reappears on the screen – by popular request. When *Der Fuehrer s Face* won the Oscar, the nominees included Paul Terry's *All Out for V*, *The Blitz Wolf* (MGM) and George Pal's *Tulips Shall Grow*, in which a peaceful country is invaded by the Screwball Army. As Kimball notes, "That seemed to be the important thing, to make fun of Hitler."

US Secretary of the Treasury Henry Morgenthau apparently played an active role in the creation of the entertainment/propaganda films. Grant recalls traveling to Washington, DC, with Disney to go over material:

Dick [Huemer] and I were working on one of the propaganda shorts, and we'd already pitched it back and forth to each other, but Walt hadn't been involved in it at this particular phase. Morgenthau sat in his office in his bedroom slippers, with a Great Dane – alive – on either side of his desk. He looked like some great nobleman. When we got there, Walt went in and talked to him, then came out and said, 'Mr. Morgenthau would like to have you tell the story'. But as Dick and I were going in to pitch it to him, Morgenthau came out and said, 'Oh no, no, just Walt'. They went in and closed the door: Walt had to ad lib the whole damn thing!

Morgenthau also oversaw what would become Disney's most controversial wartime film, *The New Spirit* (1942). Recently passed laws would require 15 million Americans to pay federal income tax for the first time. Morgenthau wanted a film that would explain why these payments were necessary – and he wanted it in theaters in six weeks.

The Disney artists hastily prepared a scenario in which Donald Duck's radio asks, "Are you a patriotic American, eager to do your part?" Donald replies that he is – even if it means doing an unglamorous job that won't earn him a medal. Following the radio's instructions, he fills out his return. Repeating the slogan, "Taxes to beat the Axis!" Donald races across America to deliver a check for the $13 he owes to Washington. An estimated 60 million people saw "The New Spirit" in 1,100 theaters and a Gallup poll revealed that 37 per cent of taxpayers were more willing to pay after seeing it.

But the Treasury Department had to request a special allocation of $80,000 to pay for "The New Spirit" ($40,000 in production costs, and an additional $40,000 for 1,000 prints). The request triggered a storm of criticism from Republican Congressmen looking for examples of Democratic overspending, and Disney was unfairly accused of profiteering. He actually lost money on the film; it had cost $47,000 to produce and his studio had lost at least $40,000 when theater owners showed "The New Spirit" (which the government supplied gratis), instead of paying for a new Disney cartoon.

Disney's oddest wartime project was an animated/live action feature based on Major Alexander de Seversky's controversial book, *Victory Through Airpower* (1943), in which he argued for the creation of an air force as an independent branch of the armed service, built around long-range bombers.

"Seversky got Walt interested in that project", explains Grant. "The idea had been floating around the Pentagon for some time, but Seversky was a very persuasive man, and when he got out to the studio, he described it all to Walt. Walt's imagination carried the thing to oversized planes and all that stuff. *Victory Through Air Power* sounded like an extraordinarily good idea, because you didn't get your hands dirty and you could bomb the whole area. He charmed Walt no end."

The 65-minute film includes a comic history of aerial warfare, limited animation of air raids and live action footage of Seversky at a desk, expounding his philosophy and criticizing his opponents. In the dramatic finale, a malign, globe-circling octopus representing the Japanese Empire is attacked and killed by the soaring eagle of American air power. *Victory Through Air Power* lost almost $500,000 at the box office and, as Marc Davis observes, "By the time the film was finished, air power was more than a reality".

Disney also considered making a feature based on an unpublished story, "Gremlin Lore", by Royal Air Force flight lieutenant (and future novelist) Roald Dahl. Gremlins were "imps of bad luck" who were blamed for otherwise inexplicable mechanical problems RAF pilots encountered during the Battle of Britain. As no one had ever seen a Gremlin, the Disney artists had to create their appearance, settling on bulbous-nosed elves with small horns. Extensive storyboards were prepared, and production costs passed $50,000. But in late 1943, Disney wrote to Dahl that he was abandoning the project. Although the film was never produced, the Disney Gremlins appeared on more than two dozen military and civilian logos, and a book based on Dahl's story "with illustrations from the Walt Disney production" was published by Random House in 1943. Around the same time, Grant and Huemer began developing "The Square World", a graphically sophisticated satire on the enforced conformity of the Fascist regimes. Like "Gremlins", it was never completed but subsequently appeared in print, as part of a storybook, *Walt Disney s Surprise Package*.

"When you look over the amount of film we produced then, it *is* amazing", Grant reflects. "How did we do all of that? With the impetus of the war, everybody seemed to come awake; it was a Rip Van Winkle sort of thing, because it had been easy before that. The drive was there." ❧

Solomon, Charles. "The Disney Studio at War" in *Walt Disney: An Intimate History of the Man and His Magic* (1998). ©Walt Disney Family Foundation

15

UPA

Jules Engel [1984]

was visiting an artist-friend once, and she said, "Oh, that's an old drawing of mine".

I told her, "Wait a minute. Would you talk about an *old* Rembrandt or an *old* Picasso: Art – *good* Art – doesn't get old. It gets finer with age, and being *early* is a matter of pride."

She smiled, and said, "You're right. It is an early drawing of mine."

The same principle applies to animation films. Only a cartoon that was bad in the first place – and there were lots of them – ages and becomes old or dated. True works of Art, milestones, always seem as though they were done yesterday. Take Disney's *Clock Cleaners*: it's 50 years old now, but it is so vital. There's no feeling of its being antiquated, any more than a good painting. It's a fresh, *early* masterpiece of animated cinema.

This strikes me about UPA, too. How *many* of the fine films we made at UPA are still fresh and vital and astonishing. After 30, 35 years, they have become early masterpieces, too. We had a pretty good batting average. The great success of UPA stems from several factors, but most important, perhaps, is that the cartoons were made by artists, and they were meant to be art works in the first place.

When people talk about European

animation, they mean the independent, often experimental, artistic work. When they discuss Hollywood, they usually mean the industry, and there is a lot of false nostalgia about the "Golden Age" of the cartoon. But for every brilliant work of Tex Avery or Bob Clampett or Chuck Jones, there are also a dozen tedious, imitative cartoons with very little artistic aspiration. When you consider the tremendous richness of the European and Canadian traditions, and the potential of the young animators breaking new ground, you realize that the Golden Age of Animation lies in the future. What happened in the 30s and 40s may have sparkled, but wasn't gold. It was bronze. It shined, but it was Bronze Age of Animation.

This is not a digression. UPA was a unique combination of industry and independent artists. UPA started with Zack Schwartz and Dave Hilbermen, who were artists and layout men, and the studio was small enough that they could even paint their own cels. Then they were joined by John Hubley and Bill Hurtz, who was also an artist and layout man. Herb Klynn and I joined UPA as color consultants. Herb is one of the best graphic artists, and a first class colorist. Zack Schwartz knew my work at Disney, where I colorkeyed sequences in *Fantasia* and *Bambi*, and I was hired at first to design and choreograph colors. All of us were active in art. And we intended to make our films as artistic as possible, which was really something new for industry animation. The other studios were run by animators who were really craftsman and not artists. Most of live-action comedies and their gags were repeated and copied so much that a lot of people got up and went out for popcorn when cartoons came on – that's the "Bronze Age" as it really was! We were fortunate at UPA to have good, imaginative animators like Pete Burness, who did all the Magoos, but above all, we had Bobe Cannon, whom I consider one of the great geniuses of animation as an art. Bobe was a perfect craftsman of animation – he could do anything you wanted – but he was also an artist of animation, because he wasn't interested in just imitating live-action footage. He knew that animation is a separate world, a drawn world that does not necessarily obey the laws of everyday reality. So Bobe regularly invented movement, invented styles of action, calligraphies of gesture that were appropriate to the style of the graphics and the mood of the story. I'll come back to Bobe in a moment, because he was one of the most important figures at UPA. First I want to go on and clarify some of the goals of UPA.

I don't mean to denigrate any other animators or studios, and it is very important to understand that UPA did not either. It's foolish to downgrade your competition, and it's foolish to try to do exactly what they do. Do you hear sportsmen saying that the other team is lousy, or using their opponent's exact plays and strategies? No. The UPA was not anti-Disney. Most of the key people had come from Disney, and we had left

during times of strike and business difficulties. We were not interested in destroying anything, but rather creating something new. We wanted to add to and enrich the artistic possibilities of animation. With painting, you have a Velasquez and a Vermeer and a Goya, but then comes along a Cezanne and a Kandinsky, and they don't destroy nor cancel out each other. They add new insights and styles, start new traditions. A museum shows a Titian and a Van Gogh and a Monet and a Mondrian and a Pollock all at the same time. And the Guggenheim and the Museum of Modern Art and the Metropolitan all have exhibits, different or the same, and they are not in competition with one another. Animation should be like that – many styles, many possibilities.

UPA looked for new avenues. We used many devices of modern art in the graphic design and color, and we very soon were dubbed "The Layout and Background Studio". But people who saw UPA cartoons in the theatres said over and over, "I liked what I saw. Maybe I don't understand it, but it was good to look at."

UPA also paid attention to content. Not only were the cartoons pleasant to the eye, but they were also about something. We turned to people like Poe and Thurber and Bemelmans for good stories, so we had an interesting content.

And we involved people from all the arts. Musicians like Ernest Gold and Boris Kremenliev and Shorty Rogers, who might never have done music for a cartoon, were hired by UPA. Dory Previn wrote rhyming scripts for the *Twirliger Twins*. Filmmakers from the avant-garde, like John Whitney and Sidney Peterson, were also hired. And we tried to get several people that never agreed to work for us, like Oskar Fischinger. Herb Klynn and Oskar and I had a three-man painting show at the American Contemporary Gallery in Hollywood around 1946, and I had worked with Oskar at Disney on *Fantasia*, so we were goods friends. We asked Oskar to join us at UPA, but his experience at Disney was so traumatic that he had vowed never to work at a studio again. He used to come to our screenings and the annual art shows we had, though.

The UPA studios were also democratic. Everyone was respected as an artist in his own field, and we all had the same presence. Everyone – even the Ink & Paint, which is usually the bottom of the heap – everyone was invited to the story conferences. We were all on the same level – no second class. Even though Pete Burness worked almost exclusively on Magoo, he was never left out of the conferences on other projects. I think this was the first time in the industry that someone tried a system with no hierarchy, and no lowerarchy. Steve Bosustow owned UPA, but each person had a voice!

We also crossed over into each other's areas sometimes, which was good because we could experience what somebody else's job was like. I proposed the stories for *Madeline* and *Jaywalker*, for example. I found *Jaywalker* in a book somewhere, and it was appropriate in the UPA ambience for me just to take it in to the writers and say, "Here, I think this is a good idea for a film. We ought to buy it." I think it cost about $300, as a matter of fact.

Many people, even people working at the studio, didn't really believe in us until the great success of *Gerald McBoing-Boing*. Then they started saying, "You've got something here". Columbia never really believed in us. They loved the Magoos,

because they were like traditional series cartoons, but they were always suspicious of the 'specials'. We had an exhibition of our animation artwork – cels and backgrounds – at the Museum of Modern Art in New York, in June 1955. That was one of the first times a major art museum showed animation work. Originally the exhibit was only scheduled for three weeks, but it was so successful that it was extended to about three months. We made three films for the Museum of Modern Art, too: three films for children, about artists – Raoul Dufy, Henri Rousseau, and the famous 18th-century Japanese wood-block print designer Sharaku. They were good films, cast in an appealing fable mode that kids or anyone could enjoy. When *The Moustache Of Raoul Dufy* was premiered at the Museum of Modern Art, it was written up very favorably in newspapers and magazines. But Columbia wouldn't distribute it. All three artist films were finally shown on the "Gerald McBoing-Boing Show" on TV, but Columbia wouldn't buy them. They only wanted Magoos. I think *Jaywalker* (1956) was the last 'special' they took.

The influence of UPA was enormous. To the general public, regardless of what Columbia thought, UPA was a mark of quality and delight. People came to us all the time. James Mason came to the studio to visit, and volunteered, right on the spot, to do the narration for *Tell-Tale Heart*. Because of the union rules, we had to pay him scale, but that was just a fraction of the salary he could have commanded. Herb Klynn and I used to arrange annual shows of the studio artwork, but people started coming in from out of state, and it just got too crowded, so we had to give it up.

The style of UPA influenced the entire industry. Herb Klynn did animated sequences for the Stanley Kramer feature, *The Fourposter* (1952), and it revolutionized the concept of movie titles. Those titles and transitions you see in *Fourposter*, that's Herb's talent. It was a big hit, with Rex Harrison and Lilli Palmer, so it was seen all over the world, so the modern UPA graphics swept Zagreb and the other production houses over there. We also hired Alvin Lustig to design titles, and he was the top graphic designer in the country then.

Naturally, with so much talent seething all in the same place, it was also explosive, and after a while, one by one, we all left. Then the UPA style and some of the UPA ambience seeded out through the whole animation world. Gene Deitch went to Czechoslovakia. Bill Hurtz went to Jay Ward to do the "Bullwinkles". Bob Dranko and Alan Zaslove went to Hanna-Barbera. Herb Klynn and I made our own company, Format Films, and so did Ernie Pintoff and Fred Crippen and many others. Bill Melendez, too. So the UPA talent was influential everywhere.

One other "influence" that we were sometimes accused of is the so-called 'limited" animation. What a misunderstanding of Bobe Cannon's art! There is no such thing as limited animation, only limited talent. Live-action documents reality, and too many animators try to copy that, and think they have to prove they can animate by having something moving everywhere all the time. Or maybe they try to distract from their bad drawing with motion. Bobe Cannon was a fine draftsman, and he had a fine sense of movement – and he knew the two had to mesh. Each style of graphic and each kind of gesture has its own requirements for motion. Bobe would invent appropriate movements to suit the context, the way dancers invent new

movements that people don't do in everyday life – except breakdancing, maybe, which is quite inventive. And when no movement is called for by the story, why not have a moment of stillness?

In layout, too, Bobe knew that sometimes you can just imply a room with a rug or a picture on a non-existent wall. But other times you may need full detailed furnishings for some psychological reason. We took our cue from modern art. If there is no need for perspective, why bother? But when, for example, Magoo got lost in an eerie amusement park, sharp perspectives, like DeChirico, dwarf him.

When you look at any of the films Bobe did, you see how inventive he was. In *Gerald McBoing-Boing*, when the doctor comes to examine Gerald, you have a tableau like a stage set: Father, Mother, Doctor and Gerald all together, so they are not all four moving all the time. If this scene were shot with live actors, you would break it up into close-ups and two-shots. But here it's like a stage play, where simple gestures are telling, because you can see everyone continuously and you have their stillness to compare with the tiniest gesture. Or when Gerald brings home a letter for his mother, she stands still while reading, quite appropriately. And Gerald sits still for a moment while he waits. Then he gets up to snitch a cookie, and when he makes a noise, Mother "realistically" glances back at him quickly – a simple touch that builds character. No wasted action. But no short cuts or reductions for the sake of thrift, either. Only what's called for, what's suitable and proper.

Bobe conceived a lot of those nice touches, which were never in the story script nor storyboard. When the Doctor absent-mindedly drops his hat on the Father's foot, or when Gerald goes off to school, he forgets his lunch and comes back for it: those are Bobe's touches that he just made up as he was animating. There's clear example of Bobe's invented movement: when Gerald goes off to school happy, there's a little skip in the walk once every third or fourth step, a little hop – not a realistic movement, but an abstraction perfectly expressive of his excitement and happiness – and syncopated, so that it adds a kind of musical rhythm to the overall design. Any other animator would have just had Gerald walk off in regular "Muybridge" steps.

Yes, Bobe was a real talent, and he was a very good person. But he was very sensitive and shy. He created instinctively, on a gut level, with no words. After *Gerald McBoing-Boing* won the Oscar, Bobe became a kind of celebrity in demand. All the papers wanted to interview him, and I had to talk and talk, sternly, too, to get him to agree to an interview. But when the press people arrived at the studio, Bobe was nowhere to be seen. I knew exactly where he was – running down the street away from the studio. I mean running! It was all I could do to catch him. But it was no use. When faced with people he didn't know, he just sat quietly. Regardless of what the reporters asked, he would only say, "yes" or "nope" – the briefest possible utterance.

Only a couple of times did his shyness get in the way of his work. When we were doing *Jaywalker*, after several weeks on the project, when the animation was maybe half done, one day Bobe came out in the hall and said to me, "I can't do it".

I was very surprised, needless to say. I asked him why, but he just kept repeating, "I can't do it". After a while, he gave in and went back to work. And the finished film was one of his best. I didn't understand at the time why he was so upset about the film but much later it occurred to me that maybe, he was a Christian Scientist, and he didn't want to do anything that might be harmful to others, and perhaps he was afraid some would take the Jaywalker seriously, rather than as a parody, and really jump out in front of a car. Maybe that's why.

One other time he refused to do a scene. We were working on Bemelmans' *Madeline*. At first Bill Scott was the writer, and he created a whole subplot that has to do with a cat, so all the storyboard sketches had a cat in them that wasn't in the original story at all. I went out and bought two copies of the book, and cut them apart and pinned up Bemelmans' own pictures, so we would stay as close to the original as possible. In Bemelmans' drawings, when Madeline is first introduced, she is shown with a seamstress measuring her for a new dress. Bill Scott said, "Look, there's nothing about this in the text, and it doesn't have anything to do with the story. How can we use it?" But then I had an idea for a gag, which would really have been funny, but also tasteful, I thought. Madeline is being measured for a dress. The seamstress takes her tape measure and holds it to her height, the length of her arm, and then puts it around Madeline's chest and walks around back behind her to get the chest measurement. While the seamstress is going behind her, Madeline innocently grabs the tape measure and pulls it out so she can see it. When the seamstress takes the measurement from behind, she is astonished, makes one of those French expressions and says, "Ooh-la-la!" softly. It would all have passed quickly, and been a subtle joke for the grownups. But Bobe absolutely refused to animate it. I guess he really felt it would have been smutty.

By the way, Bobe's animation artistry did influence animators. Jan Lenica, for example, uses a style of motion in *A* that perfectly matches the graphic style – and a type of animation that would never do for a Disney storybook fable, but it's just right for *A*.

Bobe died fairly young, and they say it was from a broken heart. After UPA folded, he went to Hanna-Barbera and hoped to revolutionize their style with a set of bold designs, but they were rejected and he just couldn't take it. Yet he was a perfectly capable administrator – he directed the "Gerald McBoing-Boing" TV show and managed to juggle all the people and projects that were put together in each half-hour show. Each animator is a unique human being, and we must learn to accept and use and appreciate their special talents. There's room for all kinds! Just like an art museum, we should be able to see a Disney and a Fleischer and a UPA and a Lenica and an Engel and a Dennis Pies or a Margaret Craig or a Caroline Leaf side by side. Variety is the spice of life. 🍏

Engel, Jules. Untitled essay in "The United Productions of America: Reminiscing Thirty Years Later". Edited by William Moritz. *ASIFA Canada* (December 1984). 15–17.

16

Blacklisted Animators

Karl Cohen [1997]

The labor history of Hollywood is a complex and fascinating study that unfortunately includes the censuring of people in the animation industry. Several talented individuals were fired or forced to quit and then were refused work elsewhere in the industry because political beliefs they had once held had since become unpopular. The first part of this essay focuses on the firing of people for union activities. (It did not matter that federal law made it illegal to fire someone for being pro-union.) The second part discusses the blacklisting of people for political reasons.

The censure of a person can be far more damaging than the censorship of a film. When a film is cut, the public loses something that might have occupied the screen for only a few seconds. When a talented person is denied work in his or her chosen field, the public may lose the achievements of a whole career. Some people suffered great hardships from being forbidden to work in animation, while others were able to turn their work in new directions that might not have developed if they had continued working for their old employers. For example, if there had not been a strike at Disney, Walt Kelly might not have created the comic strip "Pogo", Bill Scott might not have written and produced the delightful "Rocky and Bullwinkle" television series, John Hubley might not have gone on to win four Oscars with his creative talents, and Phil (P.O.) Eastman might not have written his wonderful children's books.

The Rise of Unions in the Animation Industry

People rarely think of an animation studio as an industrial plant with a series of production departments. When Walt Disney showed his animators busy at work in his films, on his television show and at Disneyworld, the public saw happy artists creating wonderful images. No one bothered to explain that many of the jobs in the facility were non-creative, labor-intensive positions that were menial, repetitive, boring, low paying and gender-biased.

A letter to a woman who asked about employment opportunities at a large animation studio in 1939 sums up the division of labor that existed then. The letter, from a secretary in the ink and paint department, explains:

> Women do not do any of the creative work in connection with preparing the cartoons for the screen, as that work is performed entirely by young men. For this reason girls are not considered for the training school. To qualify for the only work open to women one must be well grounded in the use of pen and ink and also of watercolor. The work to be done consists of tracing the characters on clear celluloid sheets with India ink

and filling in the tracings on the reverse side with paint according to directions.[1]

When it came to salaries, animators were considered highly skilled artists and were paid impressive wages. Art Babbitt, a top Disney animator, lived in a luxurious house with a view, employed servants, drove fine cars, and made about $300 a week. On the other hand, women in the ink and paint departments at Fleischer and Terrytoons in New York and Disney, MGM, Lantz and other studios in Hollywood were hired at $12 to $18 a week.

It was not always easy for a union to organize staff at the studios. Most owners and top administrators hired lawyers and fought the union. They knew that meeting the demands of people who were organizing for better pay and working conditions would cost the company money.

Employers had many tactics for fighting off a union trying to organize a company. They might improve working conditions and pay so employees would not feel a need for a union; fire the people trying to organize the company from within; intimidate employees; or create a company union. Some of these tactics became illegal when the Supreme Court upheld the Wagner Act of 1935 on 12 April 1937. The act gave employees the right to organize, established the National Labor Relations Board (NLRB), established the workers' rights to protect themselves from unfair labor practices, and prohibited companies from discharging or discriminating against an employee who reported violations of the act to the NLRB.

With the approval of the Wagner Act, the nation's animation studios began to organize. Strikes, a painful way of addressing the problems of studio labor, were held at the Fleischer Studios in New York City in 1937, Schlesinger (Warner Bros.) and Disney in 1941, and Terrytoons in 1947. The Fleischer strike lasted more than five months, the Disney strike more than three months and the Terrytoon strike about eight months. MGM and several other Hollywood animation studios signed with the Screen Cartoonists Guild and avoided strikes. Schlesinger signed after a six-day lockout that ended the day the Disney strike began. Paul Terry signed a one-year contract with the union in 1944 after considerable pressure from the NLRB, but he refused to extend the contract.

The Disney Strike

The labor unrest at Disney had many causes, including low starting pay for the women in ink and paint (about $18 a week), no overtime pay, a long work week, and odd rules at the new studio that kept the women in a building some distance from the rest of the production staff. Another rule was that assistant animators and in-betweeners were allowed only on the ground floor of the animation building unless they had a special reason to go upstairs.[2]

Job security was a serious issue for many of the Disney employees. Before the strike, the studio had begun to cut back the size of its staff. Rather than follow the rule of laying off the last people to be hired, the studio laid off animators and other experienced artists who were better paid. Another issue that bothered many of the artists was the lack of screen credit for the work they did. Disney believed that the public did not really need to know who did what, so he kept the number of names in the credits to a minimum.

Equitable wage scales were another issue. Animator Art Babbitt complained that while he was very well paid, Bill Hurtz, his assistant, made only about one-sixth of his salary (about $50 a week).[3]

Like Max Fleischer, Walt Disney thought of his staff as an extended family and had a difficult time accepting the idea that some of them wanted to communicate with him through a union. He felt his company could not afford many of the changes his staff requested because the coming war in Europe meant several countries could no longer exhibit Disney films, which would mean a loss of income for the studio. While *Snow White* had made money, *Pinocchio* and *Fantasia* (both 1940) were not yet profitable. Shares of Disney stock were not selling well in 1941 and were undervalued. Another problem was that Disney had increased the company's overhead by moving from his Hyperion Avenue studio to a new state-of-the-art facility in Burbank.

Early in 1941, Disney gave his staff an emotional speech warning them against joining the Screen Cartoonists Guild, a union affiliated with the Brotherhood of Painters, Decorators and Paper Hangers. To avoid a labor union coming into the studio, Disney established a company-controlled union. Art Babbitt was appointed one of the officers of that union. He took his job seriously and began to study the issues. Instead of working to prevent the Screen Cartoonists Guild from organizing the studio, he joined that union and began to tell Disney employees that they needed the Screen Cartoonists Guild, not a company organization. No doubt feeling betrayed, Disney fired Babbitt and several other people for union activities in May 1941. The strike began the next day, partly to protest the firing of Babbitt.

Three weeks after the strike began, Walt Disney told the FBI his version of how it started. An FBI report in Disney's file dated 21 July 1941 says the Bureau interviewed him as part of an investigation concerning "the possible criminal violation on the part of [name blacked out] or others in which an effort might have been made to extort monies from the Disney Studio in settlement of the strike". Disney denied that anyone ever demanded or received a payoff.[4] Regarding the strike Disney again stated:

> due to the curtailment of the showing of his pictures abroad, it was necessary for him to cut down on his staff of employees at the studio. As a result of this, he stated, he laid off approximately nineteen men, some of whom had been in his employ less than one year ... . Mr. Disney stated that as a result of this layoff, these nineteen men, and [name blacked out], went around to the various other employees at the studio and stated that approximately two hundred were to be laid off by Mr. Disney. As a result of this "whispering campaign", a general strike was called at this studio. A picket line was maintained at the gates of the studio, and a "goon squad" of about 15 men was organized to prevent any trucks from entering the plant. Mr. Disney stated that the men who instigated the strike, and [name blacked out] were making exorbitant demands upon him in settlement of the strike to the extent that all men were to be re-hired, and that no men were to be fired in the future.

Disney told the FBI that the strike had begun on 28 May 1941; that 40 men had returned to work in the first two weeks of the strike; and that 297 were still on strike. He said the strikers were trying to get union projectionists to refuse to show Disney features in their theaters. He also described the latest demands of the strikers and stated that negotiations were completely broken down.

In 1947, Disney gave a different account of the strike in his testimony before the House Un-American Activities Committee (HUAC). He claimed the strike was organized by members of the Communist Party. He was not only insistent on this, he also clearly contradicted his 1941 statement when he boasted, "I have never had labor trouble, and I think that would be backed up by anybody in Hollywood".[5]

An FBI memo from Los Angeles dated 17 November 1947, about the film industry's reaction to the hearings, said the Screen Cartoonists Guild ran an ad in *The Hollywood Reporter* (30 October 1947) that disagreed with Disney's statement that the strike was not a labor issue. According to the memo,

> Bill Melendez, President of the Screen Cartoonists Guild stated that the strike was caused by (1) the company's unwillingness to recognize the union and to bargain and negotiate a contract; (2) the firing of one of our members for union activities. It was also pointed out that the National Labor Relations Board later reinstated this discharged member with full pay for the time he was out.

The man Disney refused to rehire was Art Babbitt. Disney had a legal obligation to rehire him with back pay, so he did that and then fired Babbitt again. The union filed charges against Disney over Babbitt's second dismissal. While the case was pending, Babbitt enlisted in the Marines. Babbitt believed his enlistment was delayed due to negative statements about him by Walt Disney in his personnel file.[6]

Art Babbitt was rehired by the Disney studio after the war, but it took a court order to get him back in. Once rehired, he was assigned to projects that Disney did

not intend to complete, and Walt Disney did his best to avoid speaking with him. Babbitt – the man who animated the dancing mushrooms in *Fantasia* and the Queen in *Snow White* – must have felt his alienation strongly during the last two years he remained at the studio, but eventually he moved on to become one of the top animators at UPA. His later career included numerous television commercials for Hanna-Barbera and other companies, and in the 1970s he worked on Richard Williams' *Raggedy Ann and Andy* (1977). He was also active teaching animation classes at Richard Williams' studio in London, where he trained a generation of British animators in the work methods he learned at Disney. His classes were considered so important that Williams invited artists from other studios in London to attend.

A disquieting aspect of the strike is that Disney was willing to bring in Willie Bioff, the corrupt head of IATSE, as a strike negotiator. Bioff ran IATSE like a dictator, while the Guild was a democratically run union. During the strike Disney tried to reorganize his company union and affiliate it with IATSE. Apparently Disney decided that if a union was inevitable, he preferred Bioff's organization over the Guild, probably because Disney hated Herb Sorrell, the Guild's business agent. An often-told story about the strike is that Sorrell had tried to intimidate Disney with his power as a labor leader. The attempt enraged Disney, who apparently told people that Sorrell had threatened to "make a dustbowl" out of the studio if he did not sign with the union.[7]

At the time of the strike, Bioff was well known as a gangster. During the strike, *Daily Variety* ran a headline reading, "Bioff Blocks Strike Washup,

SCG walks out as Hoodlum Walks In". The 2 July 1941 article reported that the SCG walked out of labor negotiations when they learned that "Willie Bioff, Chicago labor hoodlum, was in contract with company executives and was attempting to dictate the peace terms". Bioff was eventually indicted for extortion, for taking money from Hollywood producers in exchange for promises to keep labor costs down and to avoid strikes.[8]

The Disney strike was a union victory. The base pay for inkers went from $18 a week to $35. Animators started at $85 instead of $35 a week. The company agreed to numerous benefits including screen credit on shorts as well as on features.[9] However, Maurice Noble – best known for his background designs and layouts for Warner Bros. classics directed by Chuck Jones (for example, *Duck Amuck, What s Opera Doc?,* and the Roadrunner cartoons) – says that although they won their long and difficult battle with the studio, when he went back to work things had changed. None of the people who had remained loyal to the company would talk with him. His new office was a former broom closet. He had to stand on a chair to reach the window if he wanted to open it. The studio did not give him any work to do, so when he reported to work each day he read while waiting to get an assignment. Two or three weeks later, he was laid off for lack of work.

Noble says he still has mixed feelings about running into people who did not go on strike at Disney. He is not bitter, just realistic. They benefited from what he and the others fought for. All that most of the strikers got for their efforts was severance pay.[10]

Probably the most unfortunate result of the strike is that many other talented strikers left the studio after it was settled. Disney lost several outstanding artists, including Walt Kelly, who later did the "Pogo" comic strip, the cartoonist Virgil Partch, and Bill Tytla, who returned to New York to work at Terrytoons and later on television commercials. John Hubley left and worked for several studios, including UPA. By the late 1950s, he had his own studio and was one of the hottest television commercial animators in New York. The list also includes cartoonist Sam Cobean, as well as Steve Bosustow, David Hilberman and Zachary Schwartz, who opened the studio that became UPA.

For Walt Disney, the strike must have been a personal tragedy. He lost the battle, and he lost talented people who were alienated by the strike. The rise in the cost of labor and the loss of markets in Europe resulted in the company's output being reduced. In November 1941, he began massive layoffs. Ward Kimball said that at one point in the late 1930s the studio had about 1,500 or 1,600 employees. The staff was reduced to about 300 people in the early 1940s.[11]

The Investigation and Blacklisting of Alleged Communists in the Animation Industry

> The committee has no preconceived views of what the truth is respecting the subject matter of this inquiry. Its sole purpose is to discover the truth and report it as it is ... with such recommendations, if any, as to legislation on these subjects as the situation may require and as the duty of Congress to the American people may demand.
>
> In investigating un-American activities, it must be borne in mind that because we do not agree with opinions or philosophies of others, does not make

such opinions or philosophies un-American. The most common practice engaged in by some people is to brand their opponents with names when they are unable to refute their arguments with facts and logic. Therefore, we find a few people of conservative thought who are inclined to brand every Liberal's viewpoint as communistic. Likewise, we find some so-called Liberals who stigmatize every conservative idea Fascistic. The utmost care therefore must be observed to distinguish clearly between what is obviously un-American and what is more or less an honest difference of opinion with respect to some economic, political or social question.

So said Martin Dies, chairman of the first House Un-American Activities Committee (HUAC), on 12 August 1938.[12]

When the Iron Curtain fell across Europe after World War II, some Americans became concerned about protecting the country from a perceived communist threat. In Hollywood, Roy Brewer was saying, "The communists were determined to get control of the movies". Brewer had become head of IATSE, the largest union in the film industry, around the end of the war.[13]

Several people working in the animation industry were identified by HUAC as having once been communists. They were not said to have done anything subversive; they were simply accused of having anti-American beliefs. Calling somebody a communist was enough to get that person fired and blacklisted. The label ruined careers, put one animation house out of business and resulted in the substantial purge of employees at another.

The committee often looked at events that were 10 or 15 years old to determine if somebody was a communist. It did not matter that the person might no longer be a member. The committee also seemed to overlook the fact that the Communist Party was a legal political entity. During the 1930s and 1940s, the Communist Party ran people for office and was the chief group fighting for the rights of the poor in the United States. Its members fought for improvements in social security, welfare benefits and unemployment benefits. They were also anti-Fascist. One party member from this time said, "There was a depression on. I wasn't into International Stalinism as much as basic issues that were worth fighting for."

Few people spoke out against HUAC's persecution of people in animation and other industries, or its vicious abuse of power in its treatment of suspected communists. The committee was not a court of law, but a government body with its own set of rules. Members were not required to show a witness the evidence against him, or to prove that their accusations were grounded in fact. The period of HUAC activity is often called the McCarthy Era, after the Senator who fueled much the investigation into the Army and other organizations: Joe McCarthy. The hearings concerning the film industry took place in the House of Representatives.

People who were subpoenaed by HUAC could not defend themselves or explain their beliefs and past actions unless they fed the committee names of friends and other people who would in time become victims of HUAC themselves. A person who discussed his or her political past and then refused to name names could be sent to jail for being in contempt of Congress. As a result, many individuals chose to say nothing except their name, education and occupation under the rights provided in the first and fifth amendments of the Constitution. Those who exercised these rights remained blacklisted, and the press gave the public the impression that they might be hiding incriminating evidence.

The Testimony of Walt Disney

The House committee's investigation of communist infiltration in the movie industry began in 1947. First, the committee interviewed a series of friendly witnesses including Walt Disney. Disney was an ideal celebrity to call upon. His product was well loved by the public, and he was well known as an anti-communist.

Disney testified that the strike at his studio in 1941 was the result of communist agitation. He blamed labor leader Herbert Sorrell for the strike and said, "If he isn't a communist, he sure should be one". He claimed that David Hilberman, one of his animators, "was the real brains of this and I believe he is a communist". Disney said he based his opinion on an employment application indicating that Hilberman had no religion and that he had studied theater arts in Moscow for six months while he was a teenager. Later, Disney said William Pomerance, a former business manager of the Screen Cartoonists Guild, was also, in his opinion, a communist.

On 25 October 1947, a page-one headline of *The New York Times* read, "Critics of Film Inquiry Assailed; Disney Denounces Communists". The reporter briefly described what was said and then went on to note that Disney, the principal witness of the day, failed to fill the hall with spectators as Ronald Reagan had the previous day. This is an odd observation unless one subscribes to the theory that HUAC was investigating Hollywood so its members could make headline news with their diligent pursuit of communists.

Disney first asserted his belief that the communists were behind the strike in an ad that he ran in *Variety* on July 2, 1941. In the ad he said, "I am positively convinced that communistic agitation, leadership and activities have brought about this strike".[14] The validity of Disney's statements is questionable. Pomerance was hired by the union after the strike and had nothing to do with it. Herbert Sorrell was certainly hated by Disney, but there is no reason to believe he was a communist. The only communist officer of the Screen Cartoonists Guild mentioned during the hearings was Charlotte Darling, who was elected to the position of secretary in 1936. Her term ended in 1937. She was a friendly witness who identified several people as communists, and she was in a position to say if Sorrell was one. She did not identify him as a communist. She testified on 2 June 1953.[15]

David Hilberman denies that he was one of the brains behind the strike. Before the strike Babbitt was in charge of the Disney Unit of the SCG and Hilberman was second in charge. He said his role in the strike was to study labor law at a library to find out how one forms a union, and to hold one meeting at his house. At the meeting people were asked if they wanted to sign cards saying they wanted the SCU to represent them at Disney. Hilberman was one of several people who gathered the cards. When a committee of workers told Disney they had over 300 signed cards and asked him to call a vote under the labor laws established by the Wagner Act, he refused. Hilberman was just one of several hundred people who went on strike. As for Hilberman's trip to Russia, he worked with a theater company and was lonely and homesick, as he met only one person who spoke English.

Hilberman has pointed out that when he joined the Disney studio the publicity department considered his training in Russia an artistic plus.[16]

People who knew Disney say he rarely talked about politics, but the newspaper ad from 1941 suggests how he felt about communists. In a 1980 interview, Ward Kimball said Disney called the strike organizers "commie sons-of-bitches, but that was Walt's overkill". He said that at the time of the strike people called anybody a commie who was slightly to the left or pro-union. Calling somebody a commie was "a buzz word". It was an easy way of discrediting somebody. Kimball thought the real villain of the strike was Gunther Lessing, the head of the studio's legal department, who gave a lot of advice to Walt about unions.[17]

In 1944, Disney became a founder and vice-president of the Motion Picture Alliance for the Preservation of American Ideals (MPA). An FBI memo dated 22 March 1944 states, "The MPA originally was organized to combat 'a rising tide of communism, fascism, and kindred beliefs that seek by subversive means to undermine and change this way of life'. Specifically, however, the organization was concerned with combating communism." An article in *Variety* (15 March 1944) questioned the need for the MPA but quoted the organization as saying that had there been no communist threats, Walt Disney and two other men would not have found it "necessary to organize the decent, patriotic element of the industry to combat them for the welfare and safety of the American people".

In 1947, the MPA published a guide for producers that listed some of the "subtle communistic touches" to avoid in motion picture scripts.[18] Among its recommendations:

1. Don't take politics lightly ... . If you have no time or inclination to study political ideas, then do not hire Reds to work in your pictures ... . The Reds are trained propaganda experts ...

2. Don't smear the free-enterprise system ... . Don't attack individual rights, individual freedom, private action, private initiative and private property.

3. Don't smear industrialists ... . You, as a motion-picture producer, are an industrialist... . All too often industrialists, bankers and businessmen are presented on the screen as villains, crooks, chiselers or exploiters ...

4. Don't smear wealth ... . It is the proper wish of every decent American to stand on his own feet, earn his own living, and be as good at it as he can – that is get as rich as he can by honest exchange.

5. Don't smear the profit motive. If you denounce the profit motive, what is it you wish men to do? Work without reward, like slaves for the benefit of the state? ...

6. Don't smear success ... . Personal achievement and success are each man's proper and moral goal. America is the land of the self-made man. Say so on the screen.

7. Don't glorify failure ... . Don't present all the poor as good and all the rich as evil... . In judging a man's character, poverty is no disgrace, but it is no virtue either ...

8. Don't glorify depravity ... . Go easy on stories about murderers, perverts and all the rest of that sordid stuff.

9. Don't deify "the common man". The common man is one of the worst slogans of communism and too many of us have fallen for it without thinking. Don't ever use any line about "the common man" or "the little people". It's not the American idea to be either "common" or "little".

10. Don't glorify the collective ... . Don't preach that everybody should be

and act alike ... that all mass action is good and all individual action is evil.

The Purge at UPA

United Productions of America (UPA) was formed by David Hilberman, Zachary Schwartz, and Steve Bosustow near the end of World War II. UPA's political problems stemmed from work the company did for the United Auto Workers. For the UAW, they produced *Hell Bent for Election* (1944), which supported Roosevelt in his run for a fourth term, and then *The Brotherhood of Man* (1946), an educational short on racial equality. The latter was made to help the union overcome racial prejudice when the auto manufacturers opened integrated plants in the South. By the time *Brotherhood* was in production, Hilberman and Schwartz had sold their two-thirds interest in UPA to Bosustow and had left for New York.

The California Senate's 1948 report on "un-American" activities in California stated that *The Brotherhood of Man* was based on a pamphlet by Ruth Benedict and Gene Weltfish that had been banned by the War Department, and that both authors had affiliations with communist front organizations. The report explained that the film's script had been written by Ring Lardner, Jr., John Hubley, and Phil Eastman, all of whom were subpoenaed by HUAC (Ring Lardner, Jr., was one of the infamous Hollywood Ten, who served jail time). It also noted, "One of the agencies through which *Brotherhood of Man* can be booked is the International Workers Order film division ... cited by Attorney General Francis Biddle (in 1942) as 'one of the strongest communists organizations'." The film was attacked not because of its content, but because of the people associated with it. At no time

during the hearings did anyone ask about communist propaganda being included in animated work, nor was an example ever cited.[19]

The purge of UPA occurred after HUAC returned to Hollywood in 1951. By that time the company was making theatrical cartoons for Columbia, and was about to win an Oscar for *Gerald McBoing Boing.* In an unpublished interview with animation historian Paul Etcheverry, former UPA writer Bill Scott explained how the events unfolded. He says the changes began when the employees' union, the Screen Cartoonists Guild, was in negotiations with UPA. Scott says:

> UPA had never belonged to the Producers' Association, which had a contract with the IA [IATSE]. We were in the middle of negotiations, and the first thing we knew about anything was that it was announced one day that the studio had joined the Producers' Association and therefore our union was disenfranchised because all studios belonging to the Producers' Association had to deal with the IA.[20]

Faith Hubley and Harvey Deneroff have pointed out that Scott's account of the UPA workers becoming IATSE members is oversimplified. Deneroff said that the Screen Cartoonists Guild left both the Conference of Studio Unions (CSU) and the paperhangers' union when Ronald Reagan, HUAC, and others began to attack the CSU. That move left the Guild as a small organization that provided the members with few benefits. Members of the Cartoonists Guild held a vote in 1951 on whether to stay with their own union or join the IA. Guild members at Disney, Warner, Lantz and MGM voted to join the IA, but UPA members voted to stay out. The agreement was for all studio employees to go with the majority, but workers at UPA refused to join the IA and became renegades. Karen Morley sums up the breakup of the CSU: "The right wing rolled over us like a tank over wildflowers".[21]

Scott said the studio was handed over "to a union they despised, not only for its being a crooked union, with ties to gangsters and extortion and God knows what all, but for its long-term red baiting activities. It was really a savage, savage blow. And then, the next thing we knew, there were a number of people slated to be fired." He says some of the people who were fired became terrified when they learned they would be called before HUAC for questioning. Scott believes Bosustow was afraid of losing the studio by being identified as a former communist, so he joined the Producers' Association to show he was anti-communist.

Scott mentioned a rumor that bribes of four or five thousand dollars could be paid to keep a file 'at the bottom of the stack', thus delaying (perhaps indefinitely) one's appearance before the Committee. Scott also said that Bill Melendez, the employee representative on the UPA board of directors, discovered a financial statement that $40,000 had been charged to "petty cash". Nobody knows for sure how it was used, or by whom, but many believe it was used for a payoff or bribe. People have also speculated that the money went to pay legal expenses for UPA employees who cooperated with HUAC, or that some of the money was given to those who helped clear UPA's name. Bill Melendez confirms that $40,000 or $50,000 was taken from petty cash. He says that the studio made some form of settlement to get the employees back to work. Solomon's *The History of Animation* mentioned this rumor as well, but questioned the truth of it.[22]

Once it became the studio's union, IATSE went over a payroll list of the employees to determine who should be terminated. The list was then given to Columbia, which threatened to stop distributing UPA's product if the people were not fired or forced to resign. Melendez said he was surprised that relatively few people were fired, as he thought they would let go anybody who opposed the union. IATSE leaders had once threatened to ruin the careers of anybody that had opposed them or their anti-communist crusade.

A labor lawyer for Columbia Pictures suggested to Melendez that he pay $1,000 to clear his name. He believed the lawyer would donate the money to several anti-communist groups including the American Legion and IATSE. Nobody ever told him they paid a bribe and kept their job, but he believes it happened. "I, of course, was on the IATSE blacklist", says Melendez. "They stated to Columbia Pictures and the American Legion that I was 'pathologically unfit to work in the motion picture industry!' I told Roy Brewer that if they (IATSE) could take my job away from me, it wasn't worth having."

The exact number of people purged from UPA is unknown, but the list includes Bill Scott, John Hubley, Phil Eastman, Charles Dagget, John McGrew, Bill Melendez and others. Hubley, Eastman and Earl Robinson, who did music for *Hell Bent for Election* and other UPA projects, refused to name names or answer key questions when they appeared before HUAC. Zachary Schwartz, who left the company in 1946, and David Raksin, who composed some music for UPA and now teaches at UCLA, were friendly witnesses. Melendez, Scott and McGrew never had to address HUAC.[23]

The economic and social problems of being blacklisted must have been too hard for some people to take. Charles Dagget, who did public relations work for UPA until the week before he testified, refused to name names on September 17, 1951, but on January 21, 1952, he was back and cooperated fully. As a friendly witness he talked about people in the press and public relations business.[24]

Only a few people who remained with UPA offered the purged employees their support. Melendez said one of them was Art Babbitt. He called Babbitt "more conservative than the people that were fired, but ... Babbitt had a decent good heart."[25]

Melendez joined several blacklisted UPA staff members in a lawsuit against IATSE and Columbia for conspiracy in blacklisting them. They could not prove that there was a conspiracy, so they were "paid off $100 each to get lost". During the investigation Melendez showed the judge his pre-strike Disney contract. The judge, who had a labor background, called the document "the worst yellow-dog contract" he had ever seen.

The Canadian Purge

On 6 September 1945, Igor Gouzenko, a cipher clerk with the Soviet Embassy in Ottawa, defected to Canada. He shocked the country when he revealed a Soviet spy ring was operating in Canada. One of the documents he turned over contained a cryptic message: "Research Council – report on the organization and work. Freda to the professor through Grierson".[26]

Prime Minister Mackenzie King ordered an investigation headed by two judges, Robert Taschereau and R.L. Kellock. They revealed that "Grierson" was John Grierson, the founder of the

National Film Board of Canada (NFB), and "Freda" was Freda Linton, his secretary from May to November of 1944. Apparently the Soviets wanted Freda to get Grierson to recommend her to the man whose office was next to his, Dr. C.J. Mackenzie, president of the National Research Council. The National Research Council was doing work with atomic energy.

When the Taschereau-Kellock Commission hearings were held in 1946, Linton vanished. Her employment records were introduced as exhibits, and they showed Grierson had nothing to do with her coming to his office. She was placed there by a government personnel manager. The Royal Commission also found Grierson never recommended her to Dr. Mackenzie. When she was transferred six months later to another department, the transfer was to a distribution unit. A fellow worker called her "annoyingly inefficient" and "not overly intelligent". She resigned from the government, apparently with the knowledge that she was about to be fired.

Grierson was called to testify two times and was cleared of any connection with the Soviet spy ring. Unfortunately, when he was asked if he was a communist or embraced any communist thoughts, he gave an answer that was unsatisfactory. Instead of saying "yes" or "no" to the questions, he explained that he was a public servant trained by Whitehall, the seat of British government in London, and that he was taught to avoid having any party affiliations.

He did call himself "a dyed-in-the-wool liberal democrat". Other comments he made about his political beliefs suggested that he might embrace or be sympathetic to some Marxist ideas, as he indicated that all political thinkers present some valid ideas. He was asked if there were communist cells within the Film Board masquerading as study groups. He denied the allegation and said the atmosphere there was of progressive thought.[27]

His comments resulted in an FBI investigation into his activities (Grierson had resigned from the NFB in August 1945, a few days after Japan surrendered, and was living in New York City). One of the projects he was developing was The World Today, Inc., based in New York. The film group had a contract to produce newsreels and documentaries for United Artists. His work resulted in travel between England, Canada and the United States. When he left for London on February 15,1947, his visa to re-enter the United States was revoked. To the press, the State Department would say only that the decision was based on confidential advice from the FBI.[28]

The investigation of the Soviet spy ring and Grierson resulted in the Royal Canadian Mounted Police (RCMP) investigating the National Film Board. In December 1949, Ross McLean, Grierson's successor as film commissioner of the NFB, was fired, apparently for being too lax about removing possible security risks from his employment. He had been hired by Grierson as assistant film commissioner in 1939, and both he and Grierson felt that a person's politics were none of their business as long as that person did a good job and did not bother other employees with unwanted political discussions.[29]

In 1950, W. Arthur Irwin, the new head of the NFB, was given a list of 36 employees suspected of having left-wing affiliations. He quietly fired three (some say four) individuals, and the NFB was declared safe from communist infiltration.

The fired employees were never charged with any wrongdoing; they were simply released because they could not prove their trustworthiness. There was no publicity about their being let go, as the NFB felt that would injure their reputation and chances of future employment.[30]

A retired animator from the NFB says the list of names given Irwin by the RCMP consisted of people who had been in "harmless" left-wing social clubs and that the three who were fired were "scapegoats". Had everybody on the list been fired, the NFB would have been in serious trouble, so the board chose to remove people whose talents could be replaced. One was an animator who "bored you to death with his talks about Marx and Lenin ... but he was loyal". The fired man moved to another city and started his own production company. The second person fired worked in film distribution. The animator giving this information no longer remembers who the third person was. He says Commissioner McLean was fired "because he didn't act fast enough" in changing the image of the NFB.

What happened in Canada at the National Film Board is regrettable, but at least the Canadians handled the situation in a humane way, with concern for people's reputations. One rumor is that when Irwin was told to clean up the image of the NFB he was given secret instructions to fire as few people as possible. Considering how people suspected of left-wing pasts were treated in the United States, it is remarkable that the Canadians were willing to be so gracious. In some cases, people in other branches of the government were simply moved from a job that needed security clearance to one that did not deal with classified material.

A surprising comment about the purge came from Don McWilliams, Norman McLaren's biographer and the creator of the feature-length documentary *The Creative Process: Norman McLaren.* He said that if anybody should have been kicked out of the NFB, it was McLaren. He had been active with communists in England in the 1930s, and he worked on an anti-Fascist film used to raise money for the anti-Franco forces in Spain. Grierson told McWilliams that Prime Minister Mackenzie King had once instructed him to protect McLaren from trouble (during World War II), as he suspected McLaren was going to be an important figure someday. McWilliams also said Grierson called McLaren politically naive. It appears Commissioner Irwin valued McLaren's contributions to the NFB, and unlike the witch hunters in the United States, he could overlook McLaren's political past. Had McLaren been forced out, the NFB and Canada would have lost the international recognition and prestige that his films eventually brought to his nation.[31] 🐦

Notes

1. A copy of the letter was provided by Dan McLaughlin.

2. Information about the Disney strike comes from interviews with David Hilberman; from hearing other former strikers talk about it in public lectures; from an interview with Reta Scott, who did not go on strike; from a phone call to Bill Littlejohn in 1996; from hearing talks about the strike by Dr. Harvey Deneroff and other scholars; from seeing a British videotape of Art Babbitt that includes his talking about his role in the strike; from Disney's FBI file available from the FBI under the Freedom of Information Act; and from books including Bob Thomas, *Walt Disney, An American Original* (New York: Pocket, 1976); and Richard Schickel, *The Disney Version* (New York: Touchstone, 1968 and 1985). An interesting but not completely accurate version of the strike appears in Marc Eliot, *Walt Disney, Hollywood s Dark Prince* (New York: Birch Lane, 1993). I also used a handout by Dori Littel-Herrick titled *Haifa Century Ago ...* that was distributed in 1991 at a celebration honoring the fiftieth anniversary of the strike. For what it is worth, animators still cannot go upstairs at the Team Disney Building without an appointment.

3. In "Art Babbitt", an interview by Klaus Strzyz (1980), published in *The Comics Journal*, no. 120 (March 1988), Babbitt says Hurtz was paid $25 a week and he wanted Disney to pay him $27.50 a week. Most accounts of the strike say Hurtz was paid $50 a week.

4. The FBI investigation request came from the FBI office in New York City that was investigating "anti-racketeering".

5. Disney's FBI file includes about 45 pages of material concerning his testimony. There are memos, newspaper articles and the entire text of his testimony. The testimony appears in the *United States Congressional Committee Hearings* (80) H 1169-5, pp. 280–290. This government publication is available at public libraries that are government depositories. The testimony is reprinted in *The American Animated Cartoon: A Critical Anthology,* edited by Danny and Gerald Perry (New York: Dutton, 1980), pp. 92–98.

6. From a telephone conversation with Harvey Deneroff, August 15,1996. A second version of the file story is told by Tom Sito, president of the animators' union. He recalled Babbitt saying he never rose above the rank of a sergeant due to something in his personnel file.

7. Thomas, *Walt Disney,* pp. 167–168; Schickel, *The Disney Version,* p. 257.

8. "Art Babbitt", interview by Klaus Strzyz.

9. "Art Babbitt", interview by Klaus Strzyz.

10. Interview with Maurice Noble, February 1997.

11. "Ward Kimball", interview by Klaus Strzyz, *The Comics Journal*, no. 120 (March 1988).

12. Part of Dies' speech on the opening of the first HUAC hearing in 1938. A longer version is reprinted in Eric Bentley, *Thirty Years of Treason* (New York: Viking, 1971).

13. Nancy Lynn Schwartz, *The Hollywood Writers Wars* (New York: Knopf, 1982), p. 255.

14. The ad has been mentioned in several publications including Larry Ceplair and Steven Englund, *The Inquisition in Hollywood* (Garden City, N.Y.: Anchor, 1980), p. 157.

15. Charlotte Darling (later Adams) testified twice. She spoke briefly on 26 March 1953, (83) H 1428 2-B, pp. 471–477, and at length on 2 June 1953, (83) H 1429-8, pp. 2309–2320. Adams said she left the party

in 1946 because "I got tired of being told what to do". Adams worked as a background artist at Schlesinger under the name Charlotte Darling. Martha Segal remembers that she spent a lot of time smoking cigarettes in the ladies' room. She would try to convert her fellow workers when they went to the bathroom and collect money for causes. Segal says, "I never took her seriously." (Telephone interview, May 1995.) A manuscript that may shed more light on Herb Sorrell's politics is his unpublished autobiography in the UCLA Special Collections Library. The working title is *Sometimes You Can Pick Your Friends*.

16. John Canemaker, "David Hilberman", published in *Cartoonist Profiles*, no. 48 (December 1980). Canemaker wrote that Hilberman said he had been a communist before the war, but "the strike itself was not communist-led." Hilberman talked about his life, including his trip to Russia, at an ASIFA-San Francisco event honoring him on 13 May 1990.

17. "Ward Kimball", interview by Klaus Strzyz. Phone interview, 7 April 1990. Logan later read for errors a version of a conference paper that contained the quote. The paper he read was presented at the Society for Animation Studies Conference at Rochester Institute of Technology in October 1991.

18. The booklet was the subject of an article by Harold Heffernan called "Suggested Don'ts for Film-Makers" and circulated by the North American Newspaper Alliance. It ran in an unidentified San Francisco newspaper dated 6 October 1947, p. 8. The article was reprinted in the December 1990 *Release Print by* Film Arts Foundation in San Francisco. The editor said somebody had sent him the article without telling him where it had come from.

19. *Fourth Report, Un-American Activities in California, 1948, Communist Front Organizations* (Sacramento: California Legislature, 1948), p. 192. Maurice Rapf also worked on the film as a writer, but because he was on contract with Disney his name did not appear in the film's credits and so did not appear in the California Legislature report. He was given credit for his work on the film in the *Hollywood Quarterly*, vol. 1, no. 4 (1946), which ran a feature article on the film. He was also given credit in vol. 2, no. 3 (April 1947), which ran an update on the film's distribution success on p. 305. In a letter to the author dated 1 September 1996, Rapf says, "That script took about six months to prepare. Hubley and Eastman were in uniform and working for the Air Force unit at the Hal Roach studio. We met only once a week – weekends – when Phil and John were free. The project and the teaming of Lardner, Eastman, Hubley and me was arranged by the Hollywood Writers Mobilization which was an offshoot of the Screen Writers' Guild, headed by Robert Rossen, for the purposes of producing a variety of writing projects for agencies of the government seeking to further the causes of the war."

20. Etcheverry's interview of Scott dates from the 1980s. Tom Sito says that in the Special Collections Library at California State University, Northridge, there are documents regarding the animation unions in New York and Los Angeles, including a pamphlet written by Bill Scott on why people should not join IATSE.

21. Schwartz, The Hollywood Writers' Wars, p. 253

22. Bill Melendez was interviewed at the Society for Animation Studies Conference at Cal Arts in Valencia, California, 24 October 1992. Faith Hubley, in a letter to the author dated 23 July 1991, confirmed the rumor, but according to Hubley the rumor mill put the sum at $35,000. Charles Solomon in *The History of Animation* (New York: Knopf, 1989), p. 222, mentioned the rumor.

23. David Raksin testified on September 20, 1951, (82) H 1348-6-B, pp. 1682–1695. He named 11 people. Bill Scott in Paul Etcheverry's interview said, "Several minor figures ... assistant animators and so forth" also left UPA for being "disloyal".

24. Charles Dagget refused to name names on September 17, 1951, (82) H 1348-6-A, pp. 1488–1491, but on January 21, 1952, (82) H 1375-7, pp. 2459–2487, he named names.

25. Telephone conversation, 23 March 1993.

26. The discussion on the purge in Canada is based to a large extent on information found in Forsyth Hardy, *John Grierson* (London: Faber and Faber, 1979), pp. 154–155, and Gary Evans, *John Grierson and the National Film Board of Canada* (Toronto: University of Toronto Press, 1984), pp. 240–258.

27. Hardy, *John Grierson,* p. 156.

28. Hardy, *John Grierson,* pp. 156–163.

29. Evans, *John Grierson,* p. 262.

30. Evans, *John Grierson,* pp. 258–265.

31. Telephone conversation with Don McWilliams, 1 December 1993. He mentions McLaren's connections with communists in *The Creative Process: Norman McLaren*.

Cohen, Karl. "Blacklisted Animators". *Forbidden Animation: Censored Cartoons and Blacklisted Animators in America.* Jefferson, NC: McFarland, 1997. 155–191. Edited. Published with permission of McFarland & Company Inc.

17

Clay Animation and the Early Days of Television: The "Gumby" Series

Michael Frierson [1994]

The advent of television, which began its first period of sustained growth in 1948, is cited as a chief cause of the decline of the Hollywood studio system that began during the 1950s. This drastic upheaval had the unlikely effect of returning clay to the mass audience after decades of relative obscurity.[1]

Film studios, panicked by the threat of competition from television, at first tried to buy their way into the medium. But under scrutiny for antitrust violations, and recently ordered to divest themselves of their exhibition outlets by the Supreme Court decision in *United States v. Paramount, et al.* (1948), the major studios were prevented by the Federal Communications Commission (FCC) from making significant inroads into television ownership. The studios opted for the technological "quick fix" of Cinerama, Cinemascope, Vistavision, and 3-D, as well as an increase in color film production – in an effort to make their product more attractive than that of television.

They also searched frantically for budget-cutting measures to take in their operations. With their relatively high production costs per minute, the cartoon production units of Hollywood studios were targets for reduction throughout the 1950s and 1960s. Warner Bros. cartoon production for 1949–1952 averaged 30 films a year, but one decade later (1959–62) that number had fallen to 20 films a year. Ultimately, the cartoon units were closed down: Columbia/Screen Gems' in 1949, MGM's in 1967, and Warner Bros.' in 1969. The studios also began syndicating their animated product to television as part of a package that included feature films. This move ultimately brought cartoons to any local television station in search of program material to fill the dead spots in the local kiddie hour.

The Growth of Children's Programming

While theatrical exhibition was declining in the 1950s, television was beginning to exhibit a greater sophistication in its programming strategies, including an emerging understanding of how to

program for children. "The Howdy
Doody Show", which ran on NBC from
5:00 pm to 6:00 pm Saturday evenings
from 1947 to 1960, generally is regarded
as the first children's television program;
however, the first children's show to have
a profound impact on networks,
producers, and advertisers was "The
Mickey Mouse Club", an hour-long show
scheduled for 5:00 pm weekdays, that first
aired 10 October 1955.

The show was a remarkably astute
move for all the parties involved. In 1951,
ABC-TV, which had emerged from the
NBC Blue radio network but lacked the
capital to take advantage of the growth of
television, had merged with United
Paramount Theatres, the newly divested
arm of Paramount that was flush with
capital and already worried about the
decline of moviegoing. Disney, searching
for capital and publicity for its new
amusement park, Disneyland, saw
ABC-Paramount Theatres as the solution
on both counts. ABC-Paramount bought
roughly a one-third interest in Disneyland,
and Disney began to produce "The
Mickey Mouse Club" as a break-even
proposition that was little more than a
vehicle for advertising the new park and
the entire Disney product line. ABC
gained a broad family audience through
the high visibility of the Disney characters
and the first television run of Disney
theatrical cartoons.[2]

What was truly remarkable about
"The Mickey Mouse Club", however, was
the way it transformed children's
advertising on television. Cy Schneider,
the account executive for Mattel Toys at
the Carson/Roberts Agency, points out
that "[i]n 1955 there were no recognized
brand names in toys. Household names
such as Mattel, Hasbro, and Fisher-Price
were unknown to the consumer. An adult

buying a toy for a child went into a
conventional toy store and asked for
something appropriate for a six-year-old
girl or a nine-year-old boy or perhaps the
fad product of the particular season, if
there were one. (Imagine doing that today
at a Toys-R-Us.) Since children had
limited exposure to specific toys, even
they hardly knew what to ask for."[3] "The
Mickey Mouse Club" changed all that
because, "[f]rom 5:00 pm to 6:00 pm on
weekdays, the show dominated the
airwaves, and every Wednesday from 5:30
to 5:45 when Mattel played their three
commercials, 90 per cent of the nation's
kids were watching the first toy
commercials ever put on film".[4] The
astounding success of the Mattel "Burp
Gun" during Christmas 1955 – a product
featured in those ads – was testament to
the newfound power of television for
children. With the Burp Gun, Mattel more
than doubled its overall sales volume in
one year, and the symbiotic relationship
between networks, program producers,
and advertisers of children's products was
forged.[5]

As television grew phenomenally in
the 1950s and the recycling of studio
cartoons became absurdly repetitious,
broadcasters looked for new programming
sources to fill the lucrative and expanding
children's market. The search for
cost-efficient program material – cheap
shows that delivered large audiences of
children to advertisers – gave rise in 1957
to Hanna-Barbera's application of the
limited animation techniques that were
rediscovered by the animators of United
Productions of America (UPA), an
unforgivable crime in the eyes of many
animation fans. Television made
household names out of Hanna-Barbera
characters – Yogi Bear, Huckleberry
Hound, Pixie and Dixie, the first cartoon

stars born not in movie theaters but in the broadcast medium.

At the same time that Hanna-Barbera began reshaping cel animation, clay had its first chance in many years to re-establish its audience; television programmers were eager to try out anything on kids as long as the "cost per thousand" (the price advertisers paid to buy 1,000 viewers) was reasonable. In this speculative climate, driven by television's hunger for programming, clay animation brought forth its first television superstar, an offbeat character who represents a convergence of the forces shaping children's television in the mid-1950s: Gumby.

Gumby, Art Clokey, and his Mentors

Art Clokey is the sculptor-filmmaker behind the blue-green clay star of the 127 "Gumby" episodes produced between 1955 and 1971. (Three more films were produced in the series that did not feature Gumby.) "Behind" is an appropriate word here, because Clokey invested a large measure of his personal philosophy and creative energy in each episode. Transferring the bedtime stories he told his children to film, Clokey presented Gumby and his horse and sidekick, Pokey, in creative six-minute episodes that refrained from indulging in the cynicism and violence Clokey disliked in classic Hollywood cartoons.

Television provided Clokey with the opportunity to explore not only a different medium but also a message quite different from that of traditional theatrical cartoons. Gumby embodies a simplistic ethic of fair play and kindness toward his fellow animated creatures. He is forever good-natured, open, caring, and happy. With his tiny mitten hands, bell-bottom legs, and whimsical pompadour (suggested by a high school portrait of Clokey's father with a cowlick), Gumby is almost irritating in his utter cuteness.

Gumby's unwavering sense of goodness is the logical outgrowth of his creator's lifelong interest in religion. Clokey believes that Gumby is a reflection of the underlying innocence and idealism that have permeated his relatively sheltered life. Clokey was born on 12 October 1921 in Detroit, the son of Arthur Wesley Farrington and Mildred Shelters Cairnes. He was raised a Christian Scientist, lived in a foster home with a woman spiritualist, and was adopted by a devout Episcopalian, Joseph W. Clokey, a composer at Pomona College in Oregon. Clokey studied to become an Episcopal priest before attending film school at the University of Southern California (USC) in 1951. In the mid-1960s, along with the Beatles and a large percentage of the population of Southern California, he explored the burgeoning self-awareness movement through a number of groups. "I explored ways to become a better director by getting into all kinds of self-awareness. Encounter groups, psychotherapy, Esalen. You name it, I tried it", he says.[6] Clokey's continuing interest in Eastern philosophy is evident in his 1975 film *Mandala*, a work with spiritual overtones in which a camera takes a seemingly endless journey through a long series of richly detailed, sculpted clay archways. Clokey says, "I attempted in *Mandala* to suggest a time- and mind-expanding experience, the evolution of consciousness, by orchestrating deep cultural symbols from the collective unconscious". Moreover, Clokey believes that part of Gumby's appeal also comes from our collective past: the appeal of clay is universal, the clay itself being "a symbol of the basic nature of life and human beings. As I've toured the country with Gumby, I've realized that kids pick up on that. Their fascination with Gumby is a gut reaction to clay – not the character – just to the clay itself."[7]

In 1979, Clokey and his wife Gloria journeyed to India to visit the avatar Sathya Sai Baba and came away confirmed believers. Clokey claims to have seen the guru materialize objects in his bare hands, and is convinced that he eventually will take control of the world's problems because he has supernatural powers. Sathya Sai Baba is also credited with Gumby's resurgence: "I stood there with Gumby [before Sai Baba], and he did this circular motion with his arms. I could see the sacred ash ... coming out of his hand. He plopped it right on Gumby, and when we came home things started to happen across the nation – college and theater tours. The episodes started appearing on TV again, sales of the Gumby toys began to pick up, and then Eddie Murphy did his Gumby skit on 'Saturday Night Live'."[8] Later incarnations of the Gumby spin-off toys reflected Clokey's deeply held beliefs: some models had the Sanskrit word for "love" emblazoned on the chest.

While religious beliefs have shaped the content of Clokey's work, his visual style has been guided by another guru: Slavko Vorkapich, whom he studied under at USC. A Yugoslavian immigrant and a student of painting, Vorkapich came to Hollywood in 1921. Best known for his collaboration with Robert Florey and Gregg Toland on the experimental film *The Life and Death of 9413 – A Hollywood Extra* (1928), Vorkapich wrote a few articles outlining his filmmaking theories (ca. 1930). In his application of graphic art principles to filmmaking, Vorkapich

parallels Eisenstein's thinking about "conflicts within the shot" (or "montage cell") when he states: "Like lines, colors and sounds, different motions have different emotional values ... . There are many such fundamental expressive motions and their possibilities of combination are unlimited. To mention briefly only a few: Descending motion: heaviness, danger, crushing power (avalanche, waterfall); Pendulum motion: monotony, relentlessness (monotonous walk, prison scenes, caged animals); Cascading motion, as of a bouncing ball: sprightliness, lightness, elasticity, etc. (Douglas Fairbanks)."[9]

Vorkapich's methods of compressing motion and visual energy into a shot earned him a niche in Hollywood as a montage expert, directing special montage sequences for features, including *Crime without Passion* (1934), *The Good Earth* (1937), *The Last Gangster* (1937), and *Shop Worn Angel* (1938). A 1937 *New York Times* article summarized Vorkapich's methods of montage: "Now, a 'montage', it might be wise to explain, is a panoramic effect in which the events covering a period of time are boiled down to a succession of rapidly paced interlocking 'flashes'... . It is a far different thing from simple continuity cutting and Vorkapich refers to it as 'film ideagraphy.'... In preparing a 'montage', the first task is to ascertain exactly what is to be told. He then writes his own script, listing the central idea involved, with suggestions for expressing them [sic] pictorially."[10]

Clokey says with some reverence, "Vorkapich got down to basics. His theory was that motion pictures dealt only with motion and the illusion of three-dimensional objects created by the director's use of shapes, shadows, colors, and motion. He said if you understand how to organize those things through camera angles, camera movement, pace, and so forth, you could make any film more interesting. And it happened to me. I got my first job doing commercials for Coca-Cola and Budweiser because people were fascinated with how I could make the screen come alive in ways that other people couldn't."[11] Clokey continued to study under Vorkapich after leaving USC through private seminars that Vorkapich held in his home.

Vorkapich's reliance on fundamental graphic shapes and his concentration of imagery into a kind of visual shorthand is evident in Clokey's abstract animation, particularly in an early work called *Gumbasia* (1955). Clokey notes: "In *Gumbasia*, I filmed geometric and amorphous shapes made from modeling clay of many colors. These shapes moved and transformed to the background rhythm of jazz. I wanted to avoid as much as possible the distraction of recognizable forms in *Gumbasia.* It was an experiment in pure movement, where the whole plane moved out in different shapes this way and that. *Gumbasia* was filled with movements that, when put together, created a feeling."[12]

Vorkapich's tenets, integrated over many years of filmmaking into Clokey's work, are deeply embedded in the "Gumby" series. First, and perhaps most evident, Clokey purposely drew the character designs of Gumby and Pokey from basic geometric shapes, combining simple forms like cylinders, triangles, and circles. This style of character has several advantages for the clay animator. It reduces the time needed to construct a character and simplifies the animation of movements suggested by the narrative. Visually, it offers a cleaner, simplified form for character action and dialogue,

regardless of the setting. Moreover, in a medium in which the restraints of simple stories and short running times often require a character's external design to directly objectify its inner state, Vorkapich's "ideagraphy" – making ideas visually concrete and easily identifiable – is clearly useful. For instance, the character designs of Prickle – an erect dinosaur with triangular spines – and Goo – a rounded water droplet with soft locks of hair – visually express what Clokey regards as the two fundamental types of people in the world: "The prickly are the rigid and uptight, and the gooey are easygoing and flowing".[13]

Second, Vorkapich's theories of montage are also evident throughout Clokey's work. In many shots in the "Gumby" series, there is careful attention to screen vectors – the angle and direction that a character moves through filmic space. The careful and creative use of these vectors from shot to shot gives the episodes a seamless, flowing style. For example, in the title – theme song sequence that opens most episodes, there are four shots in which Gumby (or his body rolled up into a ball) moves screen left to right along a vector line; the cuts guide the viewer's eye, using very precise matches in screen direction and screen position. In one shot of this sequence, Gumby glides along the established vector line, standing on one foot. The camera tracks along with him effortlessly. In the background, a series of artfully arranged objects break up the screen space, creating a contrasting, syncopated rhythm and providing a visual counterpoint to the flow of Gumby and the camera. At the end of the shot, Gumby collides with an object and appears to tumble into the next shot – a different location – simply through carefully crafted editing. While maintaining continuity of screen vectors is commonplace in film editing, the careful construction of these cuts in "Gumby", reflecting Vorkapich's influence, often approaches true artistry.

Jim Danforth (*When Dinosaurs Ruled the Earth* [1965], *Flesh Gordon* [1975], *Caveman* [1982]), a stop-motion animator who began his career in the Clokey studio after he graduated from high school in 1958, feels that Vorkapich's influence broadened Clokey's filmmaking talents more than it focused his skills as an animator:

> I guess [Clokey] was, and still is, basically a good filmmaker rather than specifically an animator or special-effects person. With his background in film aesthetics and editing, he taught me a lot about editing – much more about editing, in fact, than about animation. Art introduced me to this kinetic, arabesque style of cutting that he'd picked up from Vorkapich.

> But once he'd taught me all these wonderful things about editing, the paradox was that, if I started applying them, he'd get real upset. I remember one scene where 1 had a character fall backwards into the camera lens, block the image completely, then roll away from the camera and stand up in the next shot. I remember Art got annoyed at that – it smacked of some kind of editing, and we were supposed to be animators. Art would still rather be making art films. So he'd toss in some of Vorkapich's philosophy into these little puppet films when he could, but somehow it wasn't okay for us to do it.[14]

After leaving USC and Vorkapich's tutelage, Clokey struggled to find work wherever he could. At a prep school in Studio City, California, Clokey taught everything from art to chemistry and tutored a child whose father happened to be Sam Engel, the powerful producer from Twentieth Century-Fox and head of

the Motion Picture Producers' Association. "Sam was fascinated with *Gumbasia,* the art film I'd made under Vorkapich", Clokey recalls. "He said it was the most exciting he had ever seen and suggested I animate clay characters in films for children. He financed the first *Gumby* pilot film, so he's sort of the Godfather of Gumby."[15]

"Gumby" went into production in 1955 and aired on NBC in the summer of 1956. The first five episodes were aired in rotation on "The Howdy Doody Show", beginning 16 June 1956 and continuing through 20 October 1956. Five new episodes premiered between 3 November 1956 and 2 February 1957.[16] Gumby soon got his own network show, which ran Saturday mornings from 10:30 to 11:00 on NBC from 23 March to 16 November 1957.[17] The show was set in Mr. McKee's Fun Shop, with Bob Nicholson, formerly of "Howdy Doody", hosting as Scotty McKee. Clokey's production budget for the clay-animated segments was $650 per minute, roughly half what Hanna-Barbera was spending at the time for a minute of limited cel animation. By contrast, Clokey prided himself on producing full animation – in three dimensions – that capitalized on the inherent advantages of the medium: the movement in space of objects that create their own shadows and perspective; a high level of surface detail, found naturally in clay and in the children's toys used for props and set pieces; and the screen "presence" a three-dimensional character has when photographed at eye level.

Though NBC gave Clokey complete artistic freedom in his animations, the technical simplicity of many episodes reflects the limited budgets and short production schedules under which he worked. Colored gobo patterns thrown on cycloramas were frequently the only backdrop for an obvious tabletop set. Mistakes were often not re-photographed. Flying objects whose wires are visible, objects that lose registration, and clay that sags over a number of frames were commonly left in the final cut. The pacing of the action is much slower than in the classic Hollywood cartoon. Clokey's rejection of the studio aesthetic of gags, takes, and violence and his reliance on slower pacing did, however, provide one benefit: longer screen time for any given shot. Special effects were usually simple and occasionally obvious to the point of shattering illusions. In *The Small Planets*, the filmmaker resorts to the most basic low-tech special effects: scratching the emulsion off the film to suggest retrorockets firing, and using cotton to suggest smoke. Throughout Clokey's mise-en-scene, miniature objects, dollhouse furniture, small plastic plants, and children's trains, trucks, tractors, and spaceships are prominent. These objects provided simple solutions to the problem of set design.

But, more importantly, the toys and miniatures reflect Clokey's fascination with creating narratives set in a "pretend world", a childlike approach that has obvious appeal for children. For adults and older children, the inclusion of real objects prompts a continuous decoding of the image, a constant comparison of scales and surface features to determine the nature of each object, a search of the frame for identifiable objects. An unconscious set of questions runs through a "Gumby" episode: Is this object clay or not? What material is it made of? How big is it really? Frequently, a mass-produced object of popular culture, or an object of known size and composition, provides the Rosetta stone to decode these questions:

Gumby stands on a 45rpm record; Gumby gets entangled in a toy gumball machine; Gumby stands near an egg that has smashed a toy car; the Blockheads hide behind real toy building blocks. Compared with the early work of Will Vinton, whose mise-en-scene is richly detailed and almost entirely made of clay or clay-covered objects, this style looks quaint and unsophisticated, a pastiche that serves only as a backdrop for the narrative. Clokey argues, "Using only clay and clay-covered set pieces gives Vinton's work a certain sophisticated appeal to the intellect, to the artist and adults. Vinton's work is good art. But I'd go crazy, I wouldn't have the patience to do the fabulous things he does. Our stuff has a mass appeal, particularly to kids, because we included real toys and used other materials to dress our sets. We used a mix of media simply to get across a narrative."[18]

Gumby ran only one year on the network. When a management dispute prompted the NBC board of directors to fire the network president, Pat Weaver, in 1957, the ax fell on "Gumby", too, since the series was a pet project of Weaver's. Clokey scraped together the money to buy the rights to the episodes NBC had financed and, rather than paying a distributor 40 per cent of the gross, traveled the country himself syndicating the program in major cities. Clokey was struggling now with two full-time jobs: both producing and marketing "Gumby". While he was trying to continue production on new episodes, Lakeside Toy Company of Minneapolis, Minnesota, impressed with the show's performance in major cities, approached Clokey with a licensing agreement to manufacture Gumby toys. Relying on a strategy as old as Felix the Cat, Clokey hoped spin-off merchandise would increase the profitability of the animated series and simultaneously increase the popularity of the show.

Gumby toys were a smashing success. Given the immense new marketing power of television to reach into the American home, it was not surprising to find a set of Mickey Mouse ears, a Davey Crockett coonskin cap, and a Gumby doll in most television homes. Lakeside representatives now roamed the country, buying and bartering local spots for their toy line (including Gumby) and using those purchases as a bargaining chip in syndication deals with local stations for the "Gumby" series. The stations received good children's programming at a reasonable rate, and Lakeside cultivated the profitable symbiosis between broadcasting and toy manufacturers that Mattel's Burp Gun had pioneered. With Lakeside handling most of the syndication chores, Clokey was free to concentrate on production.

After "Gumby" had become successful, Clokey was approached by the Lutheran Church in 1959 to produce a series of puppet films illustrating Christian ethics for children. Using articulated puppets, Clokey created the "Davey and Goliath" series from 1959 until 1972. Each episode ran 15 minutes, over twice the length of "Gumby". With two series in production, Clokey employed almost 20 people in his growing operation: 4 storyboard artists, 6 to 8 animators, a camera technician, and 3 people building sets, as well as a battery of people in the front office. Clokey also produced 6 television half-hour specials for the Lutheran Church using Davey and Goliath: "Christmas Lost and Found" (1965), "Happy Easter" (1967), "New Year Promise" (1967), "School ... Who

Needs It" (1971), "To the Rescue" (1975), and "Halloween Who-Dun-It?" (1977).[19]

Gumby Resurrected

The revival of Gumby in the 1980s had its roots in the growth of filmmaking courses on college campuses nationwide, the heightened awareness of animation created by the rise of independent animators during the 1970s, the 1974 Academy Award for *Closed Mondays,* and a nostalgia for almost any television show from the 1950s. A low-technology medium, clay has for years shown growing popularity with the independent, low-budget student filmmaker. Riding this initial wave of interest in clay, Clokey made some personal appearances around Los Angeles and toured college campuses in the early 1980s. He was astonished at the enthusiastic response that greeted him. College audiences packed auditoriums and sang the "Gumby" theme song that television had etched into their childhood memories over 20 years earlier.

About the same time, Eddie Murphy brought forth on NEC's "Saturday Night Live" his stand-up foam-rubber version of the green clay hero and the now-famous refrain, "I'm Gumby dammit!" Television's power to highlight, to glamorize, hit full force when it returned a fading animated figure to a high place in the nation's consciousness. Clokey's reaction to the ensuing hoopla was typically low-key. He saw Murphy's act as part of the renewed interest in the lost innocence of the 1950s, and characteristically, he viewed that interest in religious terms: "I never minded the whole Eddie Murphy thing. I've got a good sense of humor, and I think it's a reflection of his true response to the series. We're always being put down today. People tell us, 'You're a lousy person.

You're an inferior person.' But now people are responding, saying, as Eddie Murphy says, 'I'm Gumby dammit!' That means, 'I'm what Gumby represents: an innocent, good, pure person'".[20] Spurred by the free network publicity, sales of "Gumby" episodes on videocassettes and of Gumby paraphernalia revived, and have remained steady.

In 1987, with the Gumby revival in full swing, Clokey signed a deal with Lorimar Telepictures to produce a new series of episodes for national syndication. The $8 million budget was to fund the production of 99 new six-minute episodes. These episodes were combined with some of the older existing episodes to make a syndication package of 65 shows, three episodes per show. With Lorimar's backing, Clokey was able to produce animation with "better sets, large crowd scenes, finely crafted soundtracks, complex computer-controlled camera movements, and other luxuries that were not available when the original series was produced some 21 years ago".[21] Thematically, the new shows parallel the old ones by "stressing positive attitudes and values including consideration, cooperation and the ability to resolve problems without resorting to violence".[22] The package was syndicated in 92 markets around the United States, representing 79 per cent of the viewing audience.[23]

From 1989 to 1992, the studio produced a feature-length film called *Gumby 1*. Working independently, Clokey took the profits, existing sets, and many of the animators from the new series to ensure that he retained complete control of his original script. The crew of 18 animators for the series was pared down to 5, and the 87-minute feature took $3.2 million and 30 months to shoot. The story is "authentic Gumby, through and through", according to Clokey, and revolves around the evil Blockhead's attempts to foreclose on Gumby's barn-studio. Gumby organizes a miniature version of Farm-Aid with his new rock band to benefit the locals. Before the film ends, Gumby has journeyed into the Middle Ages, flown into outer space, and made a music video with his girlfriend. The film is expected to open in the fall of 1993.[24]

Art Clokey, the man who revived clay animation by exploiting its potential in the new electronic medium of television, has clearly played a crucial role in the medium's coming of age. A spiritual person, Clokey brought forth a nontraditional character in a nontraditional medium and managed to survive under the economic demands imposed by television. The durability of the "Gumby" series stands as the best evidence that clay animation is viable and appealing filmmaking, and Clokey's perseverance in finding a niche for his series paved the way for the new generation of clay animators. ℰ

Notes

1. John Izod and Douglas Gomery cite a number of other contributing factors. John Izod, *Hollywood and the Box Office, 1895–1986* (New York: Columbia University Press, 1988), 134. Douglas Gomery, *Movie History* (Belmont, Calif.: Wadsworth, 1991), 280.

2. Izod, 163.

3. Cy Schneider, *Children s Television: The Art, The Business, and How It Works* (Chicago: NTC Business Books, 1987), 18.

4. Schneider, 21.

5. Schneider, 22.

6. Interview with Art Clokey, 1982.

7. Interview with Art Clokey, 1982.

8. Interview with Art Clokey, 1982.

9. Slavko Vorkapich, "Cinematics: Some Principles Underlying Effective Cinematography", *Cinematographic Annual*, ed. Hal Hall (Hollywood: ASC Holding Co., 1930), reprinted in *Hollywood Directors 1914–1940*, ed. Richard Koszarski (New York: Oxford University Press, 1971), 257–258.

10. "He Calls It Ideagraphy", *New York Times*, 5 December 1937.

11. Interview with Art Clokey, 1982.

12. Louis Kaplan and Scott Michaelsen, *Gumby: The Authorized Biography of the World s Favorite dayboy* (New York: Harmony, 1986), 1.

13. Kaplan and Michaelsen, 4.

14. Telephone interview with Jim Danforth, 28 October 1982.

15. Interview with Art Clokey, 1982.

16. Personal correspondence with E. Roger Muir (the executive producer of "The Howdy Doody Show"), 6 January 1992. According to Muir, these early episodes included "Moon Trip", "Mirrorland", "Lost and Found", "Gumby on the Moon", and "Trapped on the Moon".

17. Stuart Fischer, *Kid s TV: The First 25 Years* (New York: Facts on File, 1983), 96.

18. Interview with Art Clokey, 1982.

19. See George Woolery, *Animated TV Specials: The Complete Directory to the First Twenty-five Years, 1962–1987* (Mctuchen, N.J.: Scarecrow Press, 1989).

20. Interview with Art Clokey, 1982.

21. Karl Cohen, "Gumby", *Animation Magazine 2* (Summer 1988): 8.

22. Cohen, 8.

23. Telephone interview with Art Clokey, 28 April 1993.

24. Interview with Art Clokey, 1993.

Frierson, Michael. "Clay Animation and the Early Days of Television: The 'Gumby' series". *Clay Animation: American Highlights 1908 to the Present*. New York: Twayne, 1994. 116–131.

18

Commercial Breaks

Bill Hanna & Tom Ito [1996]

The future looked bright to our growing company during the soaring sixties, and we ambitiously decided to share that vision with our television audience. During the crowded months of preparation for the great leap forward into our own studio, Joe and our writers were also busy with the development of a new cartoon series designed to propel viewers into the ultra-modern world of the twenty-first century. Encouraged by the growing popularity of "The Flintstones", it seemed creatively logical to conceive a show calculated to transport our audience from the first frontier of the Stone Age to the final frontier of the Space Age.

Similar in format to "The Flintstones", the new series would focus on the adventures of another typical suburban family – with one major difference. This new cartoon cast would be launched into a futuristic setting where they would literally become stars in their own inter-galactic society.

"The Jetsons" premiered on ABC in September 1962. The new show featured a well-rounded family who were introduced one by one in our main title song:

Meet George Jetson
Jane, his wife
Daughter Judy
His boy Elroy

In addition, the Jetson family unit included a rambunctious family dog named Astro. He was evolved enough in rover intellect to actually communicate in English with his owners, despite an inescapable tendency to begin every word with the letter "r" – "Rots of ruck!" (Astro's impertinent aptitude for speech would later be adapted for use by another cartoon canine with timid instincts and a ravenous appetite named Scooby Doo.) Completing the household was a robot with maternal instincts named Rosie who was the prototype of hired hardware help.

In general theme "The Jetsons" may appear to be the mere flip side of "The Flintstones", but each series had quite a distinct look, tone, and feel of its own. The visual elements employed in "The Flintstones" were to look as solid in suggestion as the name of their hometown of Bedrock. The paints and colors used in the scenes were generally earthy and warm, and the artwork thick-textured and substantial. Boulders, caves, and primitive implements were all drawn in a manner calculated to project a massive and rounded physical impression of the Stone Age.

While "The Flintstones" were vividly earthy in appearance, "The Jetsons" series, by contrast, was distinctly airy in its overall design. The characters and costumes, along with the vehicles, props, and structures of the show, were drawn in a streamlined mode distinctly suggestive of what our artists envisioned as being the look of the distant future.

In addition, the selection of colors used for the series appeared to come from an entirely different palate than those used in "The Flintstones". Earth shades and pastoral hues were distinctly colors of the past. In their place our artists referred to a whole new spectrum of celestial blues, metallic grays, and synthetic pastels in order to impart distinctly modern tones to the computerized and climatized world of "The Jetsons".

The one element in this series that was definitely not alien in principle to "The Flintstones", nor any of our other shows for that matter, was the fine cast of voice talent assembled for the production. The late veteran actor George O'Hanlon provided the voice for George Jetson, and actress Penny Singleton, famed for her many film portrayals as "Blondie", was cast as the fetchingly futuristic wife, Jane. Daughter Judy was voiced by Janet Waldo, Daws Butler provided the pre-adolescent inflections of the Jetsons' son Elroy, and Jean Vander Pyl endowed the metallic Rosie, the Robot, with a transistorized irony all her own.

To our disappointment, however, although we were able to get "The Jetsons" off the launching pad, the series essentially failed to go into orbit in the primetime galaxy. Despite a great cast, the repletion of gags, gimmicks, and what seemed to us to be very clever and funny storylines, the ratings for "The Jetsons" seldom managed to climb as high as their family space vehicle.

In retrospect, there were probably several reasons why the series foundered at the time. Most obviously daunting was the fact that we were placed in a time slot opposite the formidable competition of two other established family shows, "Walt Disney's Wonderful World of Color" and "Dennis the Menace."

Well, you can't win 'em all – right away, that is. Despite a game struggle to hold its own in a primetime slot, "The Jetsons" headed for an untimely splashdown at the end of the season. Joe attributes some of the show's early difficulties to an observation that despite the success of "The Flintstones", adult television viewers may not have yet been ready to receive a greater influx of nighttime animation shows. "Let's face it, Bill", he recently remarked. "'The Flintstones' hung in there for six seasons, but do you remember the bum reviews we got on the show for the first two seasons it was on? We were trying to whet the viewers' appetites for an expanded menu of our product and they weren't ready for the main course yet."

Viewers may have been still munching on the appetizers, but we were going to stay in the kitchen working on the entrees. We knew our programs were appealing entertainment, and we were betting that they would want more – during the dinner hour and beyond. "The Jetsons"'s saga was not concluded. The series was rerun in syndication on Saturday mornings the following season and were a great success among young viewers. Over the years, despite numerous network shifts, the series continued to build a huge following, and by 1987 we eventually produced fifty-one new episodes of "The Jetsons" that were added to the original shows in syndication.

Although the initial lackluster ratings of "The Jetsons" following its premier were disappointing, we were still proud of the quantum leap the series creatively symbolized at the time. Joe still claims the show was ahead of its time and I'm inclined to agree. Many of the futuristic elements devised for the series were remarkably clever and imaginative. Some of the concepts, in fact, have proved to be downright visionary. In viewing some of the original episodes from that first season, I marvel at how Elroy's television wristwatch and George's household treadmill that seemed so fantastic back in 1962 have become increasingly commonplace items today.

Beyond the gimmickry and gadgetry, however, "The Jetsons" possessed much of the warmth, wit, and humor of our other cartoon shows. The characters were likable, they were funny, and you could tell that they cared about each other. In many ways the human condition never really changes. I think every age will face its dilemmas of apprehension, anticipation, frustration, and confusion, and just enough encouraging success to keep us going. The funhouse reflection of these daily challenges provide the basis for what are basically timeless qualities in family entertainment. Our viewers, I would like to believe, have found these elements consistent in our shows from Stone Age to Space Age, and it is their response that ultimately proved to make "The Jetsons" a perennial favorite show of new generations.

In all frankness, I must confess that hindsight and luck has a lot to do with how I characterize a lot of those old shows today. People kindly term them "classics" now, but in those years any endeavor to "immortalize" these cartoons never entered our minds. By the mid-1960s Joe had built his staff of writers into a solid creative corps capable of developing a profusion of appealing and varied concepts for cartoon pilots.

The majority of those storylines seemed to me at the time wonderfully refreshing in nature. We tackled the production of every new show that sold with as fervent a commitment to cooperative craftsmanship as we had exerted on the last.

Production was a prayerful word to me, for it in essence defined in three syllables my professional motivation and the very reason for my existence in this business. In my mind it actually made no real difference as to what show we were working on in production, for the work itself was always enjoyable regardless of whether it was for Augie Doggie or Baba Looey. A Hanna-Barbera product was a Hanna-Barbera product, and as long as it bore our company name it merited its own measure of professional devotion.

The basic rudiments of limited animation production devised by my partner and me had laid the foundation for our company's industry. Foundations, however, are meant to be built upon, and the dynamics of our increased production compelled continual refinements in production technique and methods.

Over the years, Joe and I have taken our share of heat from critics who have referred to us as purveyors of "cookie cutter" cartoons because of the limited animation system we advanced. Our shows have sometimes been criticized as lacking the artistic appeal of the traditional full animation theatrical shorts, and our characters described as moving in a wooden or mechanical manner.

These are in great part, I believe, analytical observations often made from the standpoint of reviewers enchanted by the sweep in motion picture cartoons. Such pictures, including I might add those of our own Tom and Jerry, were indeed visually wonderful and marvelous examples of what can be achieved in production nourished by lavish budgets.

Joe and I loved these cartoons as much as anyone else. We loved watching them and we loved making them. But I don't believe that spectacle in animation was ever meant to provide the sole element of a cartoon's entertainment appeal. If that had been the case, then animation as an industry might well have entered an indefinite eclipse with the termination of those original motion picture cartoon studios.

Like so many things in life, nature, and culture, the motion picture cartoons and the industry that fostered them once found themselves endangered species faced with the prospect of adapting or dying.

It had been my good luck to watch the animation industry grow up. From 1930 to the mid 1950s, I had seen cartoon entertainment develop from the primitive black-and-white talkie shorts to the rich color productions in Cinemascope. These changes issued from the continual refinement and sophistication of production techniques and methods. The budgets, schedules, and general creative and mechanical scope of cartoon making, however, remained constant in the sense that they were all geared to accommodate the production needs of the motion picture medium. The profession radically changed, however, when television entered the picture. Suddenly, the challenge confronting us was not one of the mere continuation of technical advancement, but the grim necessity of surviving as an industry.

What could we do? Well, we could have elected to go out in a blaze of glory with a swan-song, big-screen cartoon that saluted the demise of the animation business. One final Tom and Jerry picture

for the road and then maybe a career in real estate. Forget it. That was never a serious option for either Joe Barbera or me.

The very circumstances that compelled us to look to television as a recourse, also provided many of the reasons why it was necessary for animation to embrace a new form. Dispossessed by the silver screen, cartoonmaking either had to conform to the test patterns of the embryonic television medium or disappear altogether.

Anyone who remembers those early, hazy, black-and-white, six-inch images on diminutive screens may smile along with me in recalling how marvelous a phenomenon we thought TV was at the time. Never mind the reduction in size, scope, and spectacle from big-screen movies. This was an intimate medium with a potential for colossal growth that by 1957 had already become dramatically apparent by the flourishing variety of programs.

The scale of production involved in turning out such a consistent flow of weekly entertainment imposed revolutionary challenges for those of us in Hollywood who were essentially direct transplants from the motion picture industry. A myriad of creative, mechanical, and technical adjustments confronted us if we wanted to carve out our niche in TV. They all essentially funneled down to two distinct concerns: time and money. Gone forever were the deep pockets and lenient deadlines that allocated dollars and indulgent production schedules to us with such golden profusion. In their place appeared initial shoestring budgets of daunting severity and that implacable television specter known as the air date.

Like radio, television from its virtual

inception adopted as a trademark concept the series format as a means of cultivating an intimacy with its audience. Weekly one-hour and half-hour programs were the staple fare for a viewing market that consumed on a nightly basis an infinitely greater volume of entertainment than the public's occasional visits to the movies ever did.

The differing complexions of the two markets were vividly evident. Television had become a daily and nightly viewing habit, while motion picture attendance became relegated to a periodic family "event". Personally speaking, going to the movies had always been an enjoyable occasion for my wife and kids and me. But the accessibility of television as a kind of personal theatre with free admission significantly diluted the mystique of film entertainment when adventure, romance, the news, and laughs could be had as items all included in the price of our monthly electric bill.

It was at times a little unnerving for some of us who had allied ourselves with television production in those early days – to see in our own homes the undeniable magnetic influence that that glass-and-metal box commanded over our families and household. It was spellbinding. Hour after hour after hour of constant broadcast entertainment were absorbed by mesmerized viewers including ourselves and our own families. Television viewing was definitely a personal matter and our kids, neighbors, and friends were the very representatives of the ravenous market that demanded from us an unceasing flow of intimate and immediate entertainment that would a few minutes later become yesterday's reruns.

This was a form of enchantment entirely different than the ritualistic occasional reward of "going out" and splurging on tickets that purchased the velvet seats of a film palace every weekend. America was beginning to stay at home more and more, and to reaffirm – over Jiffy Pop and Dr. Pepper – viewer loyalties that were growing from repeated exposure to television series stars and their ongoing adventures.

Television air dates provided the axis upon which the entire industry relentlessly turned. These were broadcast deadlines that ruled producers with an iron hand. Production schedules were high-stakes regimens upon whose efficiency or inaptitude we would either prosper or perish.

As cartoon producers, we generally had thirteen weeks to deliver thirteen half-hour shows for a cartoon series at a rate of one show a week. This actual production schedule was preceded by an intense period of promotional and development activity. A proposal for a new show, consisting of a sample script and prototype artwork displaying characters and settings, was initially presented to network or agency executives. This was the "pitch", and its presentation was entirely in Joe's province. In short order, my partner had developed into a formidable salesman for our company with a proficiency in closing these deals that often astonished and occasionally in later years dismayed me. In those early years we were, of course, grateful for every minute of airtime secured. But as the popularity of our shows increased, the momentum of supply and demand shifted dramatically, and I eventually found our units surfeited with production work resulting from a growing volume of sales.

If the show sold, we would receive an order from either the network or series sponsor to deliver the standard quota of thirteen half-hour shows to be delivered on time for the debut of the fall season. The months between January and September, when the first show aired, were committed to a season of relentless production activity in which we were required to deliver a show at a rate of one a week. The entire production process was geared to meet this weekly deadline. We were required to deliver what was known as an answer print, in essence the entire show on film that included all the music, dialogue, and effects synchronized to the picture. The answer print became the master print from which copies were made.

The creative demands of such an endeavor were intense. All of the elements – from conceptualizing the story, developing models for any new or additional characters in the show, refining the artwork, and casting and directing the voice talent to the final dubbing session – had to be completed within that thirteen-week period.

Such stringent production demands would have been virtually impossible to meet if we had been making these cartoons in full animation. The stern curtailment of time and money was the unrelenting onus of television. The limited animation techniques we'd devised, I believe, were entirely in scale with the visual dimensions and production boundaries of television. In addition to achieving the necessary adaptation to the small screen with this method, Joe and I were both convinced that this style of animation had distinct and vivid entertainment merits of its own.

By the strategic filming and artful timing of selected images, this new animation conveyed a convincing illusion of action that was enhanced by clever and descriptive dialogue. The characters may have moved in a limited form, but they walked, ran, flew, and most critically, talked, joked, or sang in a way that made them appear alive and real to our viewers.

A lot of the criticism that belittled TV cartoons, I feel, issued from the same attitudes that rebuked television itself. Animation production for the small screen pretty much grew up with television. Like the development of any art form or industry, television had to undergo its primitive age along with the horseless carriage, the telephone, and even motion pictures themselves.

Every one of them in their time faced their share of derision and were dismissed as mere novelties impertinently attempting to supplant the revered traditional forms that preceded them. Such lessons of history might be better employed if critics, reviewers, and analysts were encouraged more frequently to employ hindsight of past progress as a means of embracing a more appreciative vision of those things that augur the future.

Joe and I believed in television. We were both moved by the exciting commercial and creative potential it implied in those early years. If we had not envisioned, for example, the eventuality of color television, we would never have ventured to produce our first cartoons with full color artwork while the shows were still being broadcast in black and white.

In all frankness, we felt that we had no choice *but* to believe in its destiny if we were to have any professional future in the business we loved. Changing times had brought us a commercial break, and some compelling challenges in having a hand both in building a business and developing an aspect of a new medium.

Despite our optimism, however,

neither of us ever imagined the amazing technological and artistic advancements that ultimately transformed television entertainment into such a nonpareil art of its own. What we were lucky enough to maintain a hands-on relationship with, however, was the dynamic refinement and growth of our own cartoon industry. Limited animation production has come a long way from the first vintage "Ruff and Reddy" and "Huckleberry Hound" cartoons. Over the years the pictures have grown more fully dimensional and the special effects increasingly stunning, and the foundation crafts of writing, animating, and editing have acquired a high gloss of stunning excellence.

It is said that what *evolves* must first be *involved*. Neither Joe Barbera nor I really felt that there would ever be any lasting limits to limited animation. But once upon a time, we could see that if cartoons were to survive to grow up, they would first need a new beginning. ❧

Hanna, Bill and Tom Ito. "Commercial Breaks". *A Cast of Friends*. Dallas: Taylor, 1996. 131–139.

19

"Cartoon, Anti-Cartoon"

George Griffin [1980]

Introduction

The following essay, written 25 years ago, was meant to describe my contradictory, almost dialectical relationship with animated cartoons. It ended up being more of a personal manifesto than the reasoned, analytical essay suggested by its title. If I cringe a bit today at the shrill rhetoric ("appalling lack of imagination"; "shocking lack of personal vision") or the shortsighted prediction that independent animation would be the wave of the future, replacing the "dead-end realm of the studio system", at least I can claim that youthful idealism played no small part.

"Cartoon" and its negation were important to me because I felt alienated from both the crass world of popular entertainment and the elite world of high art, still in the sway of an abstract vanguard. This was a time when "cartoony" was a pejorative; my generation wanted to change that.

Unlike most independents I had worked in cartoon studios and valued the apprenticeship experience and my rebellion against it – my discovery of another way of animating. In the late 60's, studios in New York were devoted to commercials or tepid "limited animation"

Saturday morning fare. Feature production ("Yellow Submarine" not withstanding) was in eclipse and the short film was an orphaned genre, at least in the U.S.

The 1970s changed all that. Independent filmmakers (primarily documentarians and animators) emerged as a creative elite, forming associations, getting grants, expanding their audience base. There was a parallel rejuvenation of experimental (formerly known as "underground") filmmaking and artists began pouring out of schools after studying painting, dance or film. My original article addressed a community of like-minded artists who felt they were on the verge of a great discovery.

To promote our vision independent animators held meetings in downtown lofts arguing about what "independent animation" meant; published a book of drawings and statements; organized special screenings and collaborated on numerous gallery shows. The New York ASIFA chapter, bewildered by this new form of "non-sponsored" animation during the early 1970s, became wholly won over by it by the 1980s.

Now, a quarter century later, the animation landscape has undergone a tectonic shift. The industry has rebounded from its doldrums with a huge increase in production in an almost textbook case of bifurcated globalism, routinely outsourcing 2D animation work to overseas cartoon factories, while keeping 3D feature work at home where, presumably, it will benefit from technological innovations.

Television has experienced an explosion of creativity, first with MTV graphics (often based on experimental techniques), then with more sophisticated series largely due to clever, satirical writing and edgy, self-conscious design (e.g. "The Simpsons", "Ren & Stimpy", "South Park").

Film school curricula have absorbed our generation's paradigm of independent animation production, and digital tools make the process easier. But if my own teaching experience is an accurate barometer, students have become more conventional in their work and more conservative in their aspirations, focusing on their portfolios to get a studio job which (in the U.S.) may be nonexistent.

Another ironic twist began with the fall of Communism. Many of us had been influenced by the graphic audacity, deep lyricism and caustic wit of Soviet and Eastern Bloc animation. This work had thrived because of a need for a kind of private language; messages were implied amidst startling visual experimentation. Now those artists too are cast into a free market jungle where brands and folkloric classics are more important than contemporary ideas.

Is there a future for the independent animator? While short films still aren't economically viable in themselves, they do act as crucial laboratories of technical and artistic innovation; they offer artists a form for personal expression, a chance to deal with marginal, risky subjects. And

today it is more common for animators to work on personal and commercial projects simultaneously.

It may be too soon to assess fully the effect of computers on experimentation in animation, but I would distinguish between production practice and presentation. The former includes grafting the computer onto an existing cartoon, collage and graphic workflow, as well as using the computer as the exclusive tool, as in 3D CGI. The latter includes peripheral developments which in turn fold back to influence what independent artists produce and who sees it. New media such as the DVD have become a cheap, universal vehicle of distribution to mass and niche markets; the Internet makes delivery of animation both free and global; PCs can drive digital projectors in a wide variety of venues, from a multiplex cinema to a storefront gallery or billboard.

When I migrated from film to computer technology to stitch together drawings and graphics, I found that certain intriguing distinctions vanished: photography and drawing melded into one kind of data file; the static image and the movie image lost their paradoxical relationship and became part of the same temporal map; the materiality of the artwork, which often added its own contradiction to film recording, slipped into virtuality. The technology obliterated the visual noise I had become accustomed to. It lurked behind several scrims (software, operating systems, hardware with its own sets of burned-in codes), essentially inaccessible to self-referential art-making practice, yet requiring constant maintenance.

Another problem lay with the unchallenged, unexamined predominance of photo-realism within the computational esthetic. This is evident in both design (in ever more complex rendering of texture, fur, skin and light) and animation (with motion capture naturalism threatening to supplant animation's choreographic invention). Perhaps "lifelike" has become the revanchist cry of all those who hated "cartoony" animation.

For most of us the computer holds enormous promise: cheap software like Flash, intuitive graphic tablets, digital delivery systems for a variety of sites – all converge to enhance production and presentation. Design and animation can be easily synthesized by a single author and distributed on the Web; it can be interactive or in your face.

My generation took an ecumenical view toward experimentation, embracing cartooning, abstraction, puppetry, altered live action and the various direct techniques. This heterodoxy has become even more robust with the digital revolution. And when I fear that technology may inhibit experimentation

in favor of the production bottom line, along comes "Waking Life", Bob Sabiston's startling cartoonization of live action, or Chris Hinton's scribble-scrabble "Flux". There is even a healthy anti-digital backlash, a return to roots, as in the work of William Kentridge who makes personal narratives by drawing and erasing charcoal.

I cannot help but be optimistic about the future when I regularly encounter animated installations in galleries, or when 11 mostly younger independent animators band together cooperatively to produce a DVD collection of our work called "Avoid Eye Contact". Sold on our Web site, it took only 3 months to show a profit (which will finance a second selection of animators). All this with a minimum of organization, meetings, and no manifesto.

– George Griffin, NYC 8/2004

★ ★ ★ ★ ★ ★ ★

George Griffin is the prototype of the "new" animator. Without ever abandoning the revered methods of traditional cartoon animators, Griffin is striving for liberated and original forms for his works. As he explains, "I came from a self-taught background in drawing, still photography, and poster design. A one-year apprenticeship in a New York cartoon studio and subsequent free-lance work served as an introduction to character animation. I am attempting to reconcile this experience in a popular art form with the medium s potential for experimentation and self-expression. My work has moved from cartoons with obliquely narrative structures to anti-cartoons: films that explore the illusionistic process of animation."

In the most important sense, Griffin s

essay should be taken as a representative statement by one animator for a generation of experimentalists in cartoon animation. But Griffin is a truly important young animator, whose thrilling homage to the early cartoon, Viewmaster *(1976), is a certified animation masterpiece.*

The studio production system of making cartoons is inextricably bound up with one technique – cel animation – and therein lies its insurmountable handicap. Central to the technique is an assembly-line compartmentalization of labor, beginning with the separation of two basic functions – "design" (the look of a single frame) and "animation" (the spatial displacement that occurs *between* the frames), and percolating down through other stages: backgrounds, inking, opaqueing, camera, editing. There is no crossover among these functions, no integrated attitude toward the final film, and no personal involvement with the materials and process of creation. The ultimate result is artistic alienation: the separation of worker and product.

For the modern studio cartoon, the designer is usually an illustrator who may or may not develop a storyboard, may or may not oversee or execute the background, may or may not pick the color schemes, but never does s/he make the sequence drawings necessary for animation. The animator, on the other hand, must be content to move a predetermined character within a scene that is already carefully prescribed by someone else's layouts and track. The animator's creativity is thus confined to touches, flourishes, and fine points of timing. In most cases, the animator's duties focus only on creating rough extremes, poses in the character's action, and filling out the exposure sheet (the sequence plan for shooting the drawings). The task of drawing all the intermediate poses is then left to a Byzantine hierarchy of assistants: clean-up people, assistant animators, in-betweeners. Their responsibilities, of course, are even more restricted, by the character-model sheet and the animator's spatial notations. As for their "artistry", it is measured in footage for the animator and actual number of drawings per day for the lowly in-betweeners. Those who produce the final stage of the artwork, the inked and opaqued acetate cel, are usually accorded the same honor as any factory worker: the time-clock punch.

The collation of all these artwork

production stages occurs in the animation camera. Because traditionally thought to be a forbidding, mysterious process where all the magic takes place, photography is left to a "professional", which means someone who can follow the animator's instructions, control dirt while changing the cels, and expose the film correctly. This is accomplished on the animation stand, an imposing mechanical apparatus designed to shoot frame-by-frame and move the artwork by slight increments. The operator mustn't deviate, even by a frame, from the exposure sheet "script", or the delicate chain of illusion will be broken. Although the animator must know the stand's capabilities, s/he is never allowed to operate it.

Within this process directorial control is exercised at each stage, but with primary emphasis on the earliest stages: character design, storyboard, recording, layout, and animation extremes. However, once creative decisions are made and the studio organism is set in motion, deviation, or creative initiative, cannot be tolerated.

Historically, the issue of initiative is tied to subjective role designation. The early pioneers Emile Cohl and Winsor McCay worked as artist/entrepreneurs, solely responsible for the story, design, and animation. Because they were inventing a grammar of synthetic figurative movement practically from scratch, the production process was, by necessity, slow paced and experimental. As the cel animation production-line process was perfected, roles became more differentiated, yet the relationship between character design and animation remained dynamic. One thinks of Otto Messmer's Felix the Cat, drawn with Deco comic-strip boldness, possessing an indomitable spirit of ingenuity, possible only with animation's capacity for transformation – the prototypical animator's character. During the Golden Age of the Hollywood cartoon, background, story, and character design increasingly became the domain of specialists, although animators still retained "authorship" by their use of a highly developed vocabulary of personality. "Squash and stretch" cannot begin to describe the kinetic inventiveness of Donald Duck, Popeye, or Bugs Bunny. But ironically it was the isolating of character animation as a craft at the expense of other formal and narrative elements that led to today's studio animators acting chiefly as interpreters of pre-sold comic-strip characters (the Peanuts gang, Fritz the Cat, Raggedy Ann). Character animation has thus changed from an experimental interplay of form and sequence to a formulaic technique harnessed to an approved design vehicle. The end product is invariably a television commercial or program material designed to deliver a target audience (usually children) to an advertising sponsor. Is it any wonder that the term *screen cartoonist* now has a hollow ring?

Compare the 1930s–1940s work of the Disney, Fleischer, and Warner Bros. organizations with that of today's children's television series, specials, and occasional features to see that dynamic, rubbery characters have become stiff, mechanical, pedestrian; that florid, airbrushed rendering has been replaced by a Xerox edge; that delicate gouache storybook backgrounds have turned to color-aid monotone; that everywhere there is an appalling lack of imagination.

Outside the dead-end realm of the studio system is a vigorous, expanding art form, which relies so much less on budgetary and marketing considerations and so much more on a personal exercise of the medium in the spirit of the early cartoon pioneers, as well as those whose work has made the very term *cartoon* inappropriate: Hans Richter, Norman McLaren, and Robert Breer. In many cases independent animators began working with dance, photography, painting, or drawing before turning to animation. They have also come from art schools and universities where courses in animation and film production in general developed dramatically during the early 1970s. Including a seemingly equal number of men and women, in sharp contrast to the sexist studio division of male animators and female opaquers, they often perform all the tasks necessary for productions themselves: design, animation, coloring, shooting, even animation-stand building. Because all responsibilities are assumed by the filmmakers, each stage can become an area for experimentation and discovery in itself. And no time clock.

A discussion of all the tendencies within the spectrum of independent animation must be left to a future study. By examining some of my own work as a representative of this movement, I hope to suggest the range of concerns the new animation embraces. My first film, *Rapid Transit* (3 min., 1969), was made at night, after work as a studio assistant animator. Instead of cel animation, or even sequence drawings, I chose to manipulate silhouettes on a simple animation stand that I had set up in my apartment. Upon a sheet of back-lit white Plexiglas were placed hundreds of dried black beans to form mandala-like patterns that I shot on black-and-white high-contrast film. Compared to the tedium of the daily studio procedures, this technique was immediately satisfying. It broke all the rules of specialization by allowing design and animation decisions to be made simultaneously, recorded on film, then instantly altered according to creative whim or preconceived plan before shooting the next frame(s). After a weekend of shooting I was left with a pound of beans, a three-minute record of their movement, and a vivid illustration of Norman McLaren's suggestion that animation is not moving drawings but the act of drawing movement. For me, the process of animation and the film's eventual shape were discovered in manipulating the material itself, not by imposing a technique from above. The result was a kind of reductive shorthand, not unlike calligraphy, a direct transfer from my hand to the film plane/screen. The process forced me to step completely outside the figurative complexity of my previous concerns and deal with the problem of drawing in time.

In *Rapid Transit* the design as well as the animation tended to be both abstract *and* highly personalized. Besides circular and square patterns shifting and bouncing off one another, associative elements were included: silhouettes of a film reel, a hand, and a bean-patterned self-portrait that vibrates briefly before being whisked away unceremoniously. I had originally planned to use only circles and lines to discipline and "purify" the design, but as references to both the film process and my own presence kept creeping in, I decided to allow these impulsive flights to remain, contending with the anonymity of the abstract forms. The film owes a debt, more in spirit than in style, to Robert Breer, whose work fuses both abstract and representational ideas into unified, pulsating exercises of perception and form. Technically it is similar to the direct

approach of Eli Noyes, whose *Sandman* (3 min., 1973) is a whimsical, kinetic poem executed with textured and silhouetted grains of sand.

Besides blurring the distinction between abstraction and representation, the new animator can also operate within the pictorial cartoon tradition. As above, this new cartoon may bear only a passing resemblance to the entertainment short of the past and it may even actively parody its style and intent. One way it often differs is in the treatment of themes once considered taboo – like sex. In the Golden Age, cartoon sexuality was either sublimated (for example, Betty Boop as the cutesy vamp and Disney's infantile barnyard humor, later sanitized for family consumption) or expressed overtly as in *Everready Harton* (c. 1928), the anonymous stag film classic dealing with the trials of outrageous proportions.

Seeking to extend *Everready s* genitalian hyperbole and yet create a cartoon statement on sexual discrimination and male bonding, I made *The Club* (4 min., 1975). Here "members" loll about in stuffy Edwardian decadence, sipping sherry, reading *The Wall Street Journal,* watching TV, or working out in the gym. Inspiration for the characters came from the phallic satires of Japanese Shunga scrolls, but the sensibility is also heavily indebted to *The New Yorker* magazine's businessman's club cartoon genre. The only womanly presence is a painting, dimly lit in the background, depicting a frontal close-up of hips and pubic hair. Most of the art on the walls depicts a variety of manly heroism (war, sports). Rather than rely on a narrative structure, the film adopts a voyeuristic point of view, roaming from room to room observing the members in their habitat. There are a few sight gags (like penis push-ups in the gym) engineered mainly for punctuation in what is otherwise a one-line joke. Once the visual incongruity of giant penises behaving like men is accepted, we can reflect on a society in which only men (white) are admitted to the hallowed halls of privilege and power. There is little else to call *The Club* except *cartoon,* a word sorely in need of resuscitation after years of referring only to kiddie films – as though children are the only audience suited for humor and satire.

The Club shares with other new animation both a direct technique of manipulating cutout drawings and a focus on personal and cultural secrets. Victor Faccinto's cartoons *(The Secret of Life* [1971], *Fillet of Soul* [1972], *Shameless* [1974])* use highly stylized, almost mythical characters, set in an elaborately patterned fetishistic world, mercilessly to expose the depths of his subconscious. Suzan Pitt Kraning's *Crocus* (7 min., 1971) is a painterly, surreal "family film" depicting young parents' sexual pleasure and fantasy in the face of their baby's own selfish needs.

In 1973 I began to question formally, through my films, the proposition that animation is, in fact, "cinema". If "bringing to life through the illusion of movement" qualifies as its definition, then animation is well possible without the technology of cinematography, sequence photography, and projection. In fact, animation had its origins in the pre-cinematic phasic constructions that made their way into nineteenth-century parlors in the guise of toys like phenakistoscopes, zoetropes and flipbooks.

Sequence photography from Muybridge and Marey to the Mutoscope, which depended on the individual viewer to turn a crank to read the spool of photographs, worked brilliantly without a projection system. Likewise I began printing and producing flipbooks to keep my film's images in their original medium. As a cheap, disposable art, flipbook animation depends on viewer initiative and expertise. Page/frames can be read forward, backward, upside down, and at any speed – like the Mutoscope but in contrast to the projector's uniform direction and speed for "movies".

A further evidence of animation's independence from the material and theoretical demands of cinema is the non-insistence on photography. Images can be drawn directly on the film base and brought to life when projected. As developed by McLaren, Len Lye, and Harry Smith, here is perhaps the most perfect form of reflexive animation, in that it continually reaffirms the actual size and properties of the medium.

This ability to bypass either projection (via flipbook) or camera (drawing on film) suggests a potential unity of intention, method, and effect comparable to painting, but with the added dimension of time. To illustrate this unity I made a film of a flipbook, *Trikfilm 3* (3 1/2 min., 1973), in which I intercut between two scenes: the first a normal view of animated line drawings in which there is the typical illusion of movement; the other a wider view showing the physical environment in which this illusion is created. *Trikfilm 3* is one of a series of flipbook films set to sections of Bach's *Well-Tempered Clavier,* in which I explore variations in shooting small-scale sequences drawn on dime-store memo pads. The title, referring to the German word for animated film, contains an appropriate connotation of magic. The imagery is of a metamorphic fantasy involving Mayan architecture, water, and sex between two New York City skyscrapers. But the real subject of *Trikfilm 3* is the unmasking of illusion. The wide frame shows the artist's coffee cup, dinner plate, drawing pad, and speeding hands as the drawings unfold. It is an anti-illusionist documentary that suggests that the very mechanism of fantasy is of greater interest than its symbolic content.

Winsor McCay's *Gertie the Dinosaur* (1914) was introduced by an elaborate live-action narrative using sets and actors to dramatize the artist's motivation (a wager that he couldn't do it) and his methods (huge barrels of ink and cartons of paper are delivered to the studio). The opening shot *of Little Nemo* (1911) shows the animation stand and identifying numbers on the animating drawings before moving closer into the drawing field. This preoccupation no doubt derived from McCay's career as a quick-sketch artist in a burlesque act (also a setting for his early film presentations). He was already involved with revealing process. Similarly, when we see Max Fleischer drawing Koko the Clown or Betty Boop, or inadvertently allowing them to pop out of the inkwell, he is accentuating the tension between three-dimensional "reality" and flat drawing/film space as well as reaffirming a parental symbiosis between the creator and the created.

Live photography or reference to process was used in this early animation as a framing device. Today it is a key to understanding self-referential animation. *Head* (10 1/2 min., 1975) continues the examination begun with *Trikfilm 3*. It is different in that it relies heavily on structural editing rather than on the linear development of a single concept. I had haphazardly executed a great number of

flipbooks, photomat mug shots, and footage of their animation without a clear idea of whether they belonged to the same film. Then, using the camera, both for single-frame self-portraiture and recording masklike sequence drawings (sometimes simultaneously), I constructed a symmetrical scheme that contrasted photography's reality to drawing's fantasy. Where *Trikfilm 3* reveals only the animator's hands at work, *Head reveals* his face as well, setting up a system of mirrored self-images. A sync-sound, live head shot of the animator at the film's beginning, explaining that his drawings have become simpler in style as his face has aged into complex "character", is contrasted to an animated self-caricature who delivers the same monologue at the film's end.

Head then is self-referential in its double focus on the mediating process of art and the image of the artist. Both gain meaning most when seen in relation to one another. This impulse toward self-discovery in process is also found in the work of Kathy Rose, particularly *The Doodlers* (5 min., 1976). Using an expressionistic linear and color sense close to that of Saul Steinberg, she constructs a bizarre kindergarten of jabbering artists who frantically paint, draw, criticize, until brought under control by their creator, Miss Nose, a realistically drawn character resembling the animator.

My most recent films have dealt with visual and sequential circularity. The most accessible is *Viewmaster* (3 min., 1976) in which a host of running characters (stick figures, cartoon bugs, mechanical men, a happy blob) are slowly revealed by an oddly curved tracking shot. Just as the first character reappears and a sense of dejá vu occurs, a cut to a long shot reveals all the characters jogging in place around a circle. The animation was created by eight drawings, each containing all the characters. By executing a slow circular pan at a very tight field, I scanned the artwork much like a microfiche. Through this process the drawings lose much of their reference to film frames and assume an affinity with a book's pages. In the clearest sense *Viewmaster* reveals animation's power to shape static art by framing, in both time and space. It is a cartoon homage to Eadweard Muybridge, the original sequence photographer of the "wheel of life".

The new animation ranges from cartoon to anti-cartoon, "naive" fantasy to self-conscious examination of form and process. It has grown from both popular entertainment and fine art traditions and now addresses a totally new, expanding audience in museums, galleries, festivals, and noncommercial theatres. But if the new animators gain something in personal expression through their direct control of the medium, they must acknowledge certain fundamental handicaps. Working alone, for instance, can severely limit the artist's output. A five-minute film can easily take a year to complete, and anything approaching feature length (at present the only commercially viable format) is out of the question. But even more problematic is the psychological myopia that occurs without the benefit of feedback from collaborators. Having overcome alienation from the process, today's independent animators might easily become alienated from each other. Many with a few short films under their belts have begun to talk enthusiastically of producing a longer, personal film without reverting to the hierarchic studio system and cel animation. One alternative would be a project involving a group of animators who pool their talents without

giving up their individual approach to the medium. This might take the form of a Canterbury Tales-type of narrative collection, each told in a different style and technique: ten diverse animated shorts that add up to a unified whole. Another approach could be the use of music. *Yellow Submarine* (1968) used only the Beatles and, except for George Dunning's brilliantly rotoscoped "Lucy in the Sky" sequence, Heinz Edelman's graphics. Imagine a feature incorporating the variety of, say, jazz (classical, big band, bop, free form, avant-garde) as a thematic underpinning, allowing the graphics to range from abstract to figurative to restructured photographic animation – a contemporary *Fantasia* that would acknowledge the dynamics of variation.

The Golden Age cartoon is dead. As mass entertainment it thrived in a naively optimistic cultural climate when the guys and the gals at the studios were a swell gang; and their innocent art still delights even the most hard-nosed realist. But it is a serious error to resort to the same production apparatus for contemporary animation. As an independent animator I deplore the spectacle of a $4 million production like *Raggedy Ann and Andy* (1977), in which fine animators, a competent director (Richard Williams), and composer (Joe Raposo) could not get close enough to their material and their personal sense of fantasy to make a satisfying film. Nearly every scene and musical number is designed for aesthetic overkill, and although there are flashes of individual animator's genius, the film as a whole is impoverished by a shocking lack of personal vision. *Raggedy Ann and Andy* operates as a merchandising gimmick on the part of an anonymous media concern: a pre-sold product, not a work of art.

It is the task of the new animation,

whether it addresses a limited art audience or a more general entertainment audience, to stretch and redefine its form through experimentation while realizing the medium's potential for expressing a personal vision. 🍎

Griffin, George. "Cartoon, Anti-Cartoon". *The American Animated Cartoon*. Ed. Donald Peary and Gerald Peary. New York: E.P. Dutton, 1980. 261–268. Revised.

20

Computers, New Technology and Animation

James Lindner, Tina Price, Carl Rosendahl, and John Lasseter [1988]

A panel at the Second Annual Walter Lantz Conference on Animation, on 11 June 1988

James Lindner (Fantastic Animation Machine): Computer animation isn't new any more, but if you look at what was going on in early filmmaking for the first ten years, and compare it to what's gone on in computer animation the first ten years, I think there are some interesting parallels. Early filmmaking concentrated on the fact that you could point a camera, move some acetate through it, develop it and project it, and you could get a picture. It took a while before people figured out that you could actually take different pieces of film and stick them together and you had a wonderful thing called editing. A little while later, when cameras got smaller, they said, "Look at that, we can edit, and we can also move the camera around". And during that entire transition – and this is not a short transition – people learned the medium's potential, what worked and what didn't. Computer animation is at that juncture: it's a technology that now works, that's not new anymore, and that many people have access to. Now is the time to consider

computer animation as a filmmaking tool, and to look at storytelling using computer animation.

At the beginning the people doing computer animation were software people. The people who are doing computer animation today are graphic designers and artists. Maybe the people who should be doing computer animation are filmmakers. Look at who is making computer animation. For the most part, they're people who are not trained in film language. They're people who don't understand screen direction and concepts like close-up, point of view, concepts that are assumed by filmmakers, by people who go to film school. When I went to film school I took a course called "Sight and Sound". They handed me a camera and said, "Make a two-minute film of someone going to a grocery store. Tell a simple story." That doesn't happen in computer animation. We have people doing computer animation who are not trained in animation language, either. The language of squash-and-stretch, the dynamics and timing of animation, all the things that separate good animation from stagnant movement. Most of the people haven't been trained in comedy, don't have any experience in scripting, and aren't writers. There are very few people trained in editing. Computer animators tend to work with very long shots, moving the camera or moving the object. The majority of computer animation contains no cuts. There isn't any editing going on whatsoever.

In the first stage, we had computer science people who had access to the equipment, knew how to write software and therefore could do it. The second stage is intermixed; graphic designers started to get involved, and that's the stage we're at. Now all the things we've learned as filmmakers have to be applied to computer animation.

A lot of work in computer animation has been creating images that look real. Maybe that's the wrong direction, in the sense that less is more. Perhaps our images look so real that it's difficult for an audience to transcend reality, to look at those pictures as characters they can empathize with. When you look at computer animation as a medium, you realize that it isn't just another lens. It isn't another filtering system, or a modification in our lighting system. We've invented a new way of making pictures, and it takes you a while to figure out what works and what doesn't. Artificial set construction, synthetic environments – getting away from physics and being able to do things that would be virtually impossible with a real set – is one area of interest.

The benefactors of computer animation, to a very large extent, have been advertising agencies who have a large amount of money per screen second to support computer animation, to allow computer animation to grow, to support the companies that do computer animation. While that's important, we need to look in a longer-term perspective. If we're going to be making longer pieces in computer animation, pieces that tell stories more than thirty seconds long in a live-action spot, then we have to have people willing to underwrite and pay for it. That's one of the really big problems today in computer animation.

In summary, I think that people involved in computer animation have to start learning the language of cinema. We have to continue to have technology that is accessible, easier to use, less expensive to produce, and in an overall sense, better. Better does not necessarily mean that it has six million types of shading, but that it has to be able to produce a quality image. We don't have to have images that look real to tell a real story. And we have to have clients. Computer animation has to have people who are willing to say, "Here's some money, make a movie", because there are people who want to see it.

Storytelling in animation is not something computer animators usually talk about. In the panel here we're lucky to have what I consider to be the foremost people producing the best computer animation that does tell a story, that does buck the trend of spinning metallic logos. People who look at a potential tool for creativity, and look at the world a little differently through the use of a different technology.

Tina Price (Walt Disney Animation): What I want to talk about is how we at Disney have incorporated 3-D computer animation into our existing traditional animation process today. I say today because this is a relatively new tool for us, and it's advancing at such a rate that the way we used it two years ago is different from the way we use it today, and we will probably approach it differently a year from now. But today our production graphics team consists of a combination of programmers and animators. It's basically driven by the story, or project we're currently working on, and to use the computer as a tool, to enhance existing story points, in combination with hand-drawn character animation. We're just beginning to explore the advantages a 3-D computer can offer us to better express our stories. In *The Black Cauldron* (1985) we used it for small props and special effects. In *The Great Mouse Detective* (1986) we had three minutes inside Big Ben, and in *Oliver and Company*, our current feature to be released this Christmas, we have 12 minutes of computer animation.

Historically, computer graphics have evolved as a product of technology rather than art. But as more artists, animators and filmmakers get interested in using this tool, I think you'll see more computer animation taking on the kind of quality we're acquainted with in hand-done art. Since this tool has evolved from technology, it seems to be coming at us in two different directions. We've got the computer animation simulation research being done, where they actually program into the computer physical dynamics of gravity and weight, and get the character to react to the laws of nature. Or we have an animator sitting down and using it as a tool, and just animating it, as he would if he were just doing it by hand. Either way, we still have to know who that character is, why he's there, is he old, is he fat, is he having a bad day, and that's what creates the illusion of life that makes our animation believable, and the expression of that life tells our stories. Done by hand or on a computer, or in combination, good storytelling is what we're after.

As an animator, I approach computer animation with the same rules of design, motion and entertainment that I used when I was using a pencil. It handles differently, and there's a lot more variables at my fingertips, but the same basic rules apply. The combination of this kind of science with animation has given us both an artistic and a production tool. We can animate much of the time-consuming, tedious work – props, or what have you – which relieves the character animator and the effects animator, and gives them more time to be creative. Or it can really enhance a story point or emotion by putting the audience right in the environment, whichever is the best way to get across the business that we're trying to express. These are only improvements in what we as animators, artists and filmmakers are going to have at our disposal to express our art and create better and better imagery.

Carl Rosendahl: Pacific Data Images is located in Sunnyvale, California, and is an eight-year-old computer animation firm. Our primary focus is animation for the broadcast and advertising industries, so the majority of our work is in television. Our direction over the years has changed a lot. When we first started the company, the whole idea was to make cool pictures and find someone to pay us to do it. Nowadays it's really changing, as we grow, as the industry grows, as things get newer, better, faster. We really want to tell stories. That's what was burning in the back of our heads the whole time but it just wasn't feasible. You learn in the process that patience is the crucial thing.

When we started we had this idea that we'd tell the computers to do what they were going to do and we'd sit on the beach while they did all the work. I'm sorry to say that's not the case. We have quite a few animators who haven't seen the beach in I don't know how long. Our real direction and push right now is getting into longer form character animation. We're doing that in a few ways – we have a large base for business in the broadcast industry, doing a lot of those flying logos and such. We love it, we do it well and we have a very stable client base in that industry. But we want to expand. About two years ago we hired a very talented person out of Cal Arts to be an artist with the formal training and background, to really help push us and educate us as to what needs to be done. To create not only an external demand from our client, but an internal demand from our animators, for the types of tools and skills and talents that we need. It's had an enormous impact on the company.

We're starting to do quite a bit of work in advertising, oriented in character animation. The reason that we're devoting a lot of effort to getting into the advertising market is to help drive us in our Research & Development efforts and our ability to do animation with some real-world problems and issues that we have to deal with – real budgets, real deadlines. We also, in this effort, are doing quite a bit of in-house work, in order to learn more. So, we decided to give people time in between those projects to experiment, undirected time, the goal being to use the tools and to learn more about them away from the pressures of normal production schedules. That has been enormously successful for us both in the computer animation festivals and in helping to convince clients that we can do good things. The first films, as Jim mentioned, were technologically based – the fact that you could just make those images. Once they decided to start telling stories, it was really an emulation of the stage – putting a camera and film in a

theater and then creating a language of its own for film: cutting, editing, camera moves, all that. Computer animation now is finally starting to tell stories, breaking new ground, but it's still very much in an emulation mode. We're using the film language – cutting, editing – and emulating traditional animation, trying out those techniques, learning how they work. We're emulating reality. One of the big things in the R&D community of computer graphics right now is dynamic simulation, which is basically building physics into your objects, so that they animate themselves to a large degree. But it's still all very much an emulation of things that are already there. What I think's going to happen in the long term is that we'll learn the languages of film and animation and we'll start applying them. We'll experiment with new forms of communication, new ways of using computer graphics, and hopefully not too far down the road, we'll be able to start making films that are not just linear descendants of the types of things that are being done now with other techniques, but a new language of its own and a new way of telling stories.

John Lasseter (Pixar): My background is in traditional animation. I went to Cal Arts, and I worked at Disney as an animator, and of course with both of those backgrounds, the thing that was stressed the most, without question, was the story and the characters. And I'm a disciple of that. I preach that religion as far as I go because I think in any type of medium where you have time as an important element as to the way things look, and the way things are designed, it's very important. I believe you have a responsibility to entertain your audience. It's a tragedy to make someone sit there and watch something and be bored or fall asleep. Because there goes all your hard work, long hours of work down the drain. My history with computer animation actually goes back to Disney, when they were working on *Tron* (1982). Jerry Rees was doing the choreography of some of the computer animation, and he showed me on the Moviola some early footage from MAGI, of the light-cycle sequences. And I had never seen anything like that before in my life. I was so excited. I wasn't excited because of what I was seeing, but I was looking beyond that, excited for the potential for applying character animation to it. After that, I worked with Glen Keane, who's a really talented animator at Disney. We produced a thirty-second test called *The Wild Things Test* [based on Maurice Sendak's *Where the Wild Things Are]*, where we combined hand-drawn character animation and computer-generated backgrounds together. At that time I had separated the role of computer and the role of the animator, and I thought the character should be done by hand and the backgrounds could be done by the computer. I thought that was a good separation. Then the folks at Lucasfilm asked me to work with them on a project to do characters with a computer. I said, "No, you can't do that. That belongs to the animator to be done by hand." They said, "Well, how do you know, has it ever been done before?"

We produced a short film called *The Adventures of Andre and Wally B.* (1985). I'm proud of it – it's moderately successful, producing believable characters and a very short story. The design of Andre and Wally were patterned after early Mickey Mouse, because there were very simple shapes. I was limited to doing things with geometric shapes. But I

was trying to do a cartoon character, and it was fun because it was pushing the medium where it hadn't been before. I learned a lot from that, because I found that the hardest things to do with hand-drawn animation are actually very easy to do with computers, and vice versa. Soft, round shapes at the time were virtually impossible with the computer. So, as one critic said, Andre and Wally looked like characters that were made out of beach balls. It wasn't quite there yet. I was redefining the limitations of what I thought could be done in computer animation. With computer animation you can do anything if you have the time and the money, but, to me, there are some very strong limitations when you're dealing with a character.

Luxo Jr. (1986) came about when I was learning the system, and I modeled this character of a Luxo lamp. It was actually sitting on my desk and I needed some example to model, and so I did it. And so I started moving it around, coming up with ways to give it life. There's one thing you can do in a computer that's very easy: that's take an object and scale it. I took the model of the big lamp, and scaled it down – different parts of it in different ways, and created a baby lamp. I thought, what would a baby lamp look like? Its shade is a little smaller, its springs and arms are the same thickness, but they're a lot shorter, and the light bulb, of course, is the same size, because that's something you buy at a hardware store – it doesn't grow. In animation, you can do any kind of cartoon physics you want, but for a particular film, it's very important to define that and be consistent. So that's why his bulb doesn't grow. I thought of it as a character study. I was at an animation festival in Belgium, and Raoul

Servais, who's a very good Belgian animator, saw the work and was real excited and he said, "Well, what kind of story do you have?" And I said, "Ahhh, I dunno, I just was thinking of it as a character study". Raoul said any animated film, no matter how short, should have a story. I took that to heart, and went back, and I was limited to about a minute and a half. That's all the time we could afford to produce. And so I worked real hard and came up with a story of this parent lamp and a baby lamp.

The success of *Luxo Jr.* was a real surprise to us, to be honest. We really did it initially to show off a new shadow algorithm that helped produce those shadows, and worked with Bill Reeves and Eben Ostby, my partners in crime up at Pixar. When we premiered it at SIGGRAPH, the computer graphics conference, it got a tremendous reaction, and it was scary in a way. Jim Blinn, who's one of the premiere scientists in computer graphics, came running up to me after the screening, and he goes, "John, John, I have a question for you". And I thought, "Oh boy, umm – I don't know much about the technical side of things, not as much as Jim does – he's going to ask about the shadow algorithm or something like that". And he says, "John, was the parent lamp a mother, or a father?" That excited me more than anything else in the world because the film had achieved what I wanted it to: let the story and the characters be the important aspect, not the technology.

At the Canadian festival up in Hamilton, Ontario, I actually had an animator come up and say, "So, what did the computer do? Did it move the lamps around? I don't really understand, what's going on?" But to me, that's exactly where I think computer animation should go. It

is another tool in the artist's toolbox to use for animation. There are rules that govern animation, and they do not differ no matter what technique you use. There is a history of over fifty years of development of traditional animation and now that computer animation is this new art form, it's still moving things around in a frame-by-frame way. There's this wealth of knowledge that has been developed – the principles of animation – that you can't ignore. They govern the way computer objects move around, too. When you see a lot of computer animation, there's a lot of camera movement. And it's because you *can* – you can move the camera wherever you want. But the movement of the camera, as well as the movement of the characters, is defined by the story and by the character's personality. Extraneous movement isn't necessary. There was no camera movement because we couldn't afford to reproduce the background every frame, but that was better because it focused attention on the characters.

We're on a learning curve, you might say, with story and computers, and so we tried to do something more complex with *Red s Dream* (1987), which was produced last year and uses a unicycle as a character. For me, stories and personalities of the characters are by far the most important thing in the work I do.

I want to encourage people working with computer animation, be it from their backgrounds from film, animation, graphic design, or even computers: there's a tremendous history of the development of animation and that definitely should be studied. A lot can be learned from that.

Audience Member: How were the sound effects done?

Lasseter: The sound effects were produced by Gary Rydstrom, up at

Lucasfilm, their Sprockets division. *Luxo Jr.* was nothing special other than taking a Luxo lamp in front of the microphone and going, "eek, eek, eek" in sync with the movie. We actually had a new Luxo lamp for Dad, and then I had this wonderful one that was falling apart and just rattly as all getout and it was used for Junior, to give a difference to the sound.

On *Red s Dream*, it was a synclavier, a digital music computer. We sampled in all of these sounds, and it was really fun because we put them on a keyboard, and you could play the squeaks and rattles of Red, the unicycle. But all the sound effects for *Red s Dream* were edited digitally. For our next film, we have a neat link between the synclavier and our animation system, where the sound effects that are part of the cycle will get the sound from the animation cues within the computer and feed right into the computer so that they will sync up a lot of the sounds.

Audience Member: How much computer time did *Red s Dream* involve?

Lasseter: Both films were about six months' worth of work for a team of about four people. Computer time varies – the dream sequence in *Red s Dream* was produced on a computer that Pixar built, and was roughly about five minutes a frame to render. Some city scenes were still backgrounds and took about four hours a frame to compute. So, there's a range. *Luxo* was about ninety minutes a frame to compute.

Audience Member: When Luxo Jr. is sad, his head bends like a real lamp, but when Red bends, the metal bends. How do you know when to break the rules of the cartoon universe?

Lasseter: It was important in *Red s Dream* not to draw attention to it, but to help give the feeling that he was sad. If we had bending metal sounds, it would have

defeated the purpose. But from the beginning I was making him a little bit flexible, so it wasn't like he was absolutely rigid and stiff, and then at the end he just bent over. It's difficult to see, but in the animation, he's moving around, he's kind of wiggling. In *Luxo*, it was a challenge to use movement that a real Luxo lamp had. I added only a couple movements that they didn't have.

Audience Member: How much did each one of those films cost?

Lasseter: That's for me to know, and you to find out. No, it's very hard to say. They were expensive, of course, but they're done as research, and that's a wonderful way to get out of those questions: say it's for research. There's a lot of time involved in the development. Each one of these films is used to help focus research and development of software and hardware. They say, "John, make a film". So I do, and I don't really think of the cost. For computer animation nowadays the cost is, for the low end, about five thousand a second and the high end is about ten thousand a second for computer animation. I would put these films in roughly the eight- to ten-thousand- dollars-a-second range. So a feature film, imagine – that would cost ... fourteen billion dollars!

Audience Member: From the Disney studio perspective is the long-term goal to replace traditional cel animation with computer animation?

Price: We're doing research and development in the areas of ink and paint, and ways of exploring how to get the imagery out of the computer and on to film. What you saw on screen [a clip from *Oliver and Company*] is still the way we've been doing it for years. Every frame that I generate on the computer is run through a process called "hidden line". We print it out on paper; if there's any character animation involved, the whole scene will go to the character animator. He'll draw right on top of my trike, or car, or whatever it is, and then it's shot under an animation camera stand, just like the rest of the film.

Audience Member: Would you make the analogy to the early film industry to the stage of computer animation today? One of the things that helped advance early film, and early animation, was the standardization of systems, sizes, and equipment.

Lindner: That's hard to answer. All the high-end systems are proprietary in the sense that they've been written by companies who've invested a great deal of money in them. They're willing to share them, but only if you're willing to buy their system. Those are the people who sell hardware, or sell software with hardware. There are certain things that can be exchanged, though – file formats for pictures, for instance. Pixar has come up with a standard for rendering, called Renderman, which is quite good, and I think many people will start conforming to that at some level.

As far as standardization, more important to us is the way that people do animation, with the animators who work with the systems. Although there are many similar things, they're executed differently on different machines. On the positive side, though, some of the people we've hired recently are people who have worked on other systems. They train a whole heck of a lot faster than people who haven't worked on any system. A long time ago, we figured that it would be cheaper for us to hire people and train them our way. And, although we were successful with that, we now find that we hire people who have experience on other systems, because they can understand what we're doing. We're doing the same thing, just in different ways. ❧

Lindner, James (moderator); John Lasseter; Tina Price; and Carl Rosendahl. "Computers, New Technology and Animation". *Storytelling in Animation: The Art of the Animated Image*. Vol 2. Ed. John Canemaker. Los Angeles: American Film Institute, 1988. 59–69. ©1988 American Film Institute

21

The Illusion of "Identity": Gender and Racial Representation in Aladdin

Sean Griffin [1994]

Shape shifting and the like, for either fantastic or comic effect, is common in animating human (or humanized) figures. Such transmogrification is one of the advantages of working in animation rather than in live-action; not being grounded in the actual physicality of a live being, animated figures are capable of transforming at the whim of the animator.[1] In the 1930s, though, another tradition in animation began to develop, which turned away from the transformative and toward rendering the human form in motion in a "realistic" manner. This aesthetic, championed by the Disney studio, presents "believable" humans and animals making "natural" movements. Rather than emphasizing the fantastic transformative dimension of animation, this tradition attempts to give the "illusion of life".

These two tendencies within animation are compelling in the face of much of what has been written in the last few years on the concept of identity. Various theorists have taken a "social constructionist" stance towards the idea of "identity" – that "identity" is created through a social situation rather than through a biological inevitability. Feminist writers began to use this concept in an attempt to free women from societal constraints. Lately, though, many have begun to theorize the construction of masculinity, heterosexuality and racial/ethnic identity to challenge the dominance of the white heterosexual patriarchal system and to destabilize its essentialism.

It is interesting to examine one of Disney's most recent animated features, *Aladdin* (1992), in the light of this discussion. In the film's construction of "appealing", yet "realistic", characters, it draws into question issues of "identity", especially related to masculinity and ethnicity.

Designing Characters with "Appeal"

As Disney animators Frank Thomas and Ollie Johnston describe the "principles of animation" that the studio developed to create the "illusion of life", they discuss the term "appeal". They contend that "your eye is drawn to the figure that has appeal, and, once there, it is held while you appreciate what you are seeing".[2] Although rotoscoping or tracing of actual human figures was employed in the drawing of Snow White and all of her successors – the Blue Fairy, Cinderella, Alice, Wendy, the Princess Aurora, Ariel, Belle, Jasmine – rotoscoping was always "improved" upon to give the character more appeal.[3] These overly-gendered drawings emphasize (*à la* Laura Mulvey) the process of fetishization at work in many instances when the female form is animated in Disney films.[4]

Less successful, however, have been Disney's attempts to create a "realistic" human *male* character who has appeal.[5] In tandem with analyses of the drawing of Snow White in the biographies and filmographies of Disney and his studio are negative assessments of the rendering of Prince Charming. His "woodenness", as Chistopher Finch describes it, or his "jiggling" (which, supposedly, the studio could not refilm in time for the release) speak basically of his lack of appeal, which animators worked on endlessly in creating Snow White.[6] Prince Charming's lack of appeal is further emphasized by his absence from the screen through most of the story. Cinderella's and Aurora's love interests also seem to have never inspired much appeal – although the prince in *Sleeping Beauty* (1959) is at least given more than a minute's worth of screen time. In fact, until *Aladdin*, only *Pinocchio* (1940) and *Peter Pan* (1953) had been successful in presenting male figures that came close to the appeal of Snow White or her counterparts (and it is interesting that both are only ostensibly male – their masculinity is problematized; the appeal of Pinocchio is more in his wooden puppet form than in the human boy he becomes, and the sexual ambiguity of

Peter Pan's persona has been discussed by many).[7]

In the popular press, much writing has appeared on the problems of trying to draw an "appealing" Aladdin. Initially conceived as yet another adolescent boy, Glen Keane modeled the first version of Aladdin on Michael J. Fox. Yet, as he recalls, Princess Jasmine was projecting much more presence than Aladdin; the studio's ability to present Jasmine as spectacle was eclipsing Aladdin as the lead character. Jeffrey Katzenberg, Vice President in Charge of Production at Disney is noted to have said, "I can see what he sees in her, but what I don't see is what she sees in him"[8] – so Aladdin went back to the model sheets. By all accounts, Katzenberg's notion of "appeal" was Tom Cruise; it is reported that Keane kept photos of Cruise pinned to his bulletin board becuase "Jeffrey wanted the hunk side of him present".[9] The final model of Aladdin has a much taller frame with an overemphasized smile and an ever-present (though not overly-muscled) chest exposed. *Aladdin*'s enormous success at the box-office (the first animated feature to take in over $200 million in its initial domestic release) is owed to the appeal of many characters in the film (Jasmine, the Genie, Iago, etc.), yet the appeal of this final model of Aladdin also must be acknowledged.[10]

With its mixture of "appeal" and "realism", Disney's tradition of animated human forms consistently creates performances of gender.[11] These are not men or women but drawings configured and filmed to construct an enactment of a man or woman. A perfect example of such work is Gaston in *Beauty and the Beast*, another character that Katzenberg wanted to take on the "appeal" of Tom Cruise. Gay animator Andreas Deja instead drew

Gaston to look like "these ridiculously vain guys you see in the gym today, always checking themselves in the mirror".[12] Gaston, like the gym rat he is modeled on, continually refers back to the mirror to make relational reference, to make sure the performance of masculinity is convincing.

Aladdin and Jasmine are also constantly performing their engendered identity. As "Prince Ali", Aladdin flexes his biceps, flashes his smile and makes the harem girls sigh, "I absolutely love the way he dresses" (the link between Prince Ali and the spectacle of Valentino's "sheik" persona is very strong). Jasmine, too, is always enacting her gendered role, but twice in the narrative consciously performs femininity – purposely batting her eyes and wiggling her hips as she seduces Aladdin in the palace in one scene and as she distracts the villain Jafar towards the climax of the film. This last instance underlines the effectiveness of her performance: as she kisses Jafar, all the other characters stop what they are doing to gape at her action.

Yet nowhere is the artificiality of identity made as manifest as in the presence of the Genie any time he is on the screen. Although ostensibly male, voiced by Robin Williams, the Genie rapidly shifts into a number of caricatures of famous people (William F. Buckley, Groucho Marx, Ethel Merman, Jack Nicholson and Arsenio Hall amongst others) as well as dressing in drag (a flight attendant, a harem girl, a cheerleader) and even different species (a goat, a bumblebee). The Genie draws on a lot of the traditions of comic transformation in animated cartoons – his continually dressing in feminine garb is quite reminiscent of Bugs Bunny's predilection for drag. Still the manic overabundance of

transformation flaunts performance in the viewer's face, making it clear that the excess of identity associated with the Genie is precisely what gives the character his appeal. He displays "mucho-macho" male heterosexuality one second as Arnold Schwarzenegger, then a caricature of homosexuality in the next second as a swishy tailor measuring Aladdin for his Prince Ali outfit. Everything is overemphasized (the Hirschfeld-inspired drawings, the hyperkinetic voice of Williams) and paced lightning fast. It is all just another costume for the Genie to put on and discard.

Using the shape-shifting advantages of animation, the Genie perfectly embodies Mary Ann Doane's theory of "masquerade" – in which subjects "put on" different personae rather than having one stable subject position.[13] A large portion of recent gay and lesbian studies has been on the culture of drag – subjects enacting female or leather (or whatever) personae – thus becoming both subject and object simultaneously, consciously performing subjectivity, much like the Genie. The notion of "performing" identity is a keystone to Lacanian psychoanalysis – that "identity" is founded relationally, constituted by reference to exterior images, such as the "mirror" which is a fundamental stage in the Lacanian model. Judith Butler describes the gay culture of drag as that which "constitutes the mundane way in which genders are appropriated, theatricalized, worn and done: it implies that all gendering is a kind of impersonation and approximation ... gender is a performance that produces the illusion of an inner sex or essence or psychic gender core".[14] Although the Genie is the most obvious instance of performance, Aladdin and Jasmine re-enact the construction of identity as well: Aladdin pretends to be Prince Ali; Jasmine escapes the palace dressed as a commoner.

Consequently, it may seem that, in some respects, *Aladdin* is an enlightened feature, using traditions in animation to further the decentering of the white heterosexual patriarchy. Yet, in attempting to overthrow the system and deconstruct "identity", many writers have also noticed the pitfalls of "social constructionism", and the loss of a stable subjectivity. For example, Patricia Waugh, writing from a feminist perspective, says, "as male writers lament its demise, women writers have not yet experienced that subjectivity which will give them a sense of personal autonomy, continuous identity, a history and agency in the world".[15] Danae Clark also gives a succinct example of the paradox in discussing sexuality and identity: "if homosexuality were to be classified by the courts as biologically innate, discrimination would be more difficult to justify. By contrast, when a sense of lesbian or gay identity is lost, the straight world finds it easier to ignore social and political issues that directly affect gays and lesbians as a group."[16] Complicating "identity" has not always been seen as a completely progressive development.

If all "identity" is merely "a performance", then all performances of "identity" would seem to be equal – which might seem to justify the inclusion of stereotypical renditions of social groups. Trying to argue the progressive nature of Princess Jasmine and her "too-teensy-for-belly-dancing hips" is difficult.[17] Putting "identity" in quotes, much like I have been doing in this paper, allows for injurious representations to reassert themselves, with the argument

that it is all performance and not a claim to an essential truth.

The problem with placing everything in quotes is in assuming that everyone sees the quotation marks. Carole-Anne Tyler, in her critique of drag's progressive nature, notices this assumption, writing that "parody [of identity] is legible in the drama of gender performance if someone meant to script it, intending it to be there. Any potential in-difference or confusion ... is eliminated by a focus in the theories on production rather than reception or perception. Sometimes, however, ... despite one's best intentions, no one gets the joke."[18] If a viewer isn't aware of the performativity, that viewer may read the performance as true, as revealing an inner essence, rather that revealing the *lack* of same.

Disney's tradition of creating "the illusion of life" perfectly exposes this problem. Although, as previously discussed, the illusion sacrifices attempts at "realness" in favor of "appeal", the end effect doesn't call attention to lack of "real" – in the phrase, "illusion of life", the accent is on "life" rather than "illusion". Whereas the Genie thrusts performativity in the viewer's face, it is often easy to forget the performance of masculinity and femininity in Aladdin and Jasmine, and accept them as "simply" who they "are". And if this is difficult for adult viewers, one can imagine the inability of children to infer performativity onto the proceedings.

Arabian Nightmares

Nowhere are the political ramifications of not reading performance as parody, mimicry or camp more apparent than in the Arab-American reaction to the release of *Aladdin*. Almost immediately upon the release of the film, Arab-Americans began to loudly voice their objections to the portrayal of Arabic culture in the cartoon. Protesting the depiction of Arabs as "cruel, dim-witted sentinels ... thieves and unscrupulous vendors",[19] the American-Arab Anti-Discrimination Committee sought to change portions of the film. One request was to remove a scene which showed "a grotesque Arab, scabbard poised, about to remove Princess Jasmine's hand, simply because she took an apple to feed a starving child".[20] Although this request has gone unheeded, the Disney studio has agreed to another request. In a letter to the Los Angeles Times, Jay Goldsworthy and radio personality Casey Kasem requested a change in the lyrics to "Arabian Nights", the song that opens the feature:

> Oh I come from a land, from a faraway place,
> Where the caravan camels roam,
> Where they cut off your ear if they don't like your face,
> It's barbaric, but hey, it's home.

Goldsworthy and Kasem revealed that lyricist Howard Ashman had written alternate, less offensive, lyrics.[21] After some discussion, the studio agreed to change the lyrics in time for the film's release on video, announcing the new lyrics would appear in any subsequent re-release of the feature.[22]

The original lyrics of this song were part of Ashman's initial vision of *Aladdin*, which composer Alan Menken described as being in keeping with "Hollywood's treatment of Arabian themes";[23] the description seems to posit Ashman's conception of Aladdin's Arabia as an Arabia in quotes – a parody of Hollywood's typical treatment of the "exotic" Orient. Ashman's first draft of the story appears to have overemphasized the racial stereotypes to burlesque the

typical ethnic cliches – including "a big black Genie with an earring", modeled on Fats Waller and Cab Calloway.[24] Disney animation chief Peter Schneider describes the reaction of Disney executives to Ashman's pitch: "We were nervous because his version was much more Arabian".[25] Although the initial song would remain in the final production, as well as jokes about lying on beds of nails, sword swallowing, snake charming and fire eating, the ethnicity of the project was toned down considerably. The color of the Genie would become a non-ethnic-specific blue, Aladdin and Jasmine's skin color was toned down to shades of tan, and there were "a lot of discussions on the arc of the nose".[26]

Behind the interviews for the press by the studio, there seems to be the revelation of a desire to retain "the illusion of life" – an illusion that doesn't overemphasize the performative nature of drawing "Arabic" characters. Unfortunately, hiding the implicit performance of ethnicity that occurs whenever trying to draw an Arab person allows the representations of Arabs to be more easily read as "true". This is not to say that leaving Ashman's original ideas in the film would have kept the American-Arab Anti-Discrimination Committee from raising protests. In fact, judging from the reaction to the lyric that remained in the film, the outcry probably would have been even greater. Having the overemphasis would not have ensured that viewers would see the quotes – that children would realize that it was "only" a cartoon.

Furthermore, to assume that Ashman's intention was to expose racial and ethnic myths through exaggeration is to ignore other possible explanations. A recurrent motif in Euro-American gay culture is the setting of "Morocco" as a sexual playland. For example, the underground film *Flaming Creatures* (1963) by Jack Smith uses the "Maria Montez" school of "Arab-ness" to display a setting of homoeroticism. Yet, although this "camping" of the Orient is used to create a text that challenges received norms about sexuality, it does not necessarily challenge Western received norms about the East. Ella Shohat has argued how colonial discourse speaks even in sexually-progressive texts: "Most texts about the 'Empire' ... are pervaded by White homoeroticism ... Exoticising and eroticising the Third World allowed the imperial imaginary to play out its own fantasies of sexual domination".[27]

Another way of discussing the original concept of *Aladdin* formulated by Howard Ashman, an openly gay artist, is to look at the "camping" of Arabia as a site for speaking about sexuality. One of the main relationships in the film is between the Genie and Aladdin, with the Genie often in drag (or, in one particular moment as a prissy tailor). During one emotional high point in the narrative, the Genie tells Aladdin, "I'm getting kind of fond of you too, kid ... not that I want to go shopping for curtains or anything". The final tearful clinch at the end of the film is not between Aladdin and Jasmine but between Aladdin and the Genie. Ashman, it can be argued, is using the imagery of the Orient as Shohat as described, to imagine a setting capable of allowing a variety of sexual identities, but doing so by replaying the colonial imagery – reinstituting Western domination.

This is not to say that the discourse between colonialism and sexuality is solely for consumption by gay culture. Jack Smith's appropriation of the B-grade exotica of Universal Maria Montez movies displays the popularity of

Arab-setting erotica in mainstream Western heterosexual culture as well. The creation of a literature commonly called "Arabian Nights", from which *Aladdin* is taken is itself a product of colonial discourse, in which the Orient figures as a sexually "Other" place; Rana Kabbani explains that, "emerging from the oral folkloric tradition central to India, Persia, Iraq, Syria and Egypt, ... Frenchman Antoine Galland created a text, ... a circular narrative that portrayed an imaginary space of a thousand and one reveries".[28] The fabrication of Scheherezade in Galland's 1704 publication, *Les mille et une nuits,* portrayed his understanding of Arabic culture as exotic and erotic, in his function as a French emissary in Constantinople. The popularity of this colonial fiction inspired European Romantic writers who fleshed out (so to speak) the sensuality inherent in the tales, in case anyone didn't see the subtleties. English expeditionary Richard Burton's version of *Arabian Nights* spelled out the "sexual customs" in explicit detail. Depicting a land "peopled by nations who were content to achieve in the erotic domain alone", Burton spoke of an Arabia both ripe for and in need of the civilizing hand of Western colonizers.[29]

Western culture, then, often has used the East as a setting to "dress up" and "play out" various sexual identities. This dichotomy of being both liberating and oppressive works in a number of directions though, not just in the above discussion of sexuality versus ethnicity. For if *Aladdin* were to have attempted to display a more historically specific form of Arabic identity, the outcry from feminists at the depiction of a subservient Jasmine would have been heard across the pages of newspapers. In trying to narrate a version of the "Aladdin" legend, the Disney studio found itself in the midst of a number of swirling discussions. Simply hoping that the depictions would be taken "all in good fun" was to ignore the complexity of the issues. To place stereotypes in quotes doesn't keep certain viewers from reading the stereotypes in any different fashion than the stereotypes have always been traditionally read – as *real.*

Attempting to Draw a Conclusion

In this paradox of "identity", it is hard to find a safe place from which to speak or create any sort of representation that is not attacked for being "politically incorrect" in some manner – as Disney has found with *Aladdin*. One possible answer lies in Donna Haraway's suggestion of the notion of "affinity" – speaking "*not* from the power to represent from a distance, *nor* from an ontological natural status, but from a constitutive social relationality", framing the issue in terms of "articulation" instead of "representation".[30] "Affinity" is seen as "precisely *not* identity" – since "affinity" by its definition acknowledges the presence of difference and diffraction that cannot be represented through some totalizing "identity".

The problem comes with working out some way in which the process of "articulation" isn't understood or read as "representation". How this process would work in the filmic medium is a problem that needs to be addressed. Going back to animation's place in this debate, the question posed by Haraway's suggestion then is how a process based on representation can split this hair – to "articulate" an "affinity" rather than "represent" an "identity", how the moral of *Aladdin* can come to mean a call to social interaction rather than self-definition.

The moral? "Be yourself". 🍎

Notes

1. For example, Donald Crafton notices the "polymorphous plasticism" of Emile Cohl's films and of the character Felix the Cat . Donald Crafton, *Before Mickey: The Animated Film, 1898–1928* (Cambridge, MA: MIT, 1982), 66, 329.

2. Frank Thomas and Ollie Johnston, *Disney Animation: The Illusion of Life* (New York: Abbeville, 1984), 36.

3. Grim Natwick, quoted in Leonard Maltin, *Of Mice and Magic: A History of American Animated Cartoons* (New York: McGraw-Hill, 1987), 56.

4. Laura Mulvey describes how classic Hollywood cinema constantly recreates a viewing subject that is engendered male, with the female as a fetishized object, presented with enormous "appeal" to the heterosexual male gaze. Laura Mulvey, "Visual Pleasure and Narrative Cinema", *Film Theory and Criticism*, ed. Gerald Mast and Marshall Cohen (Oxford: Oxford UP, 1985), 803–816.
   Grim Natwick's rendition of Betty Boop for the Fleischers, and later his work at Disney drawing Snow White both lend credence to Mulvey's argument, emphasizing heads larger than the scale of the rest of the bodies and smaller than normal torsos. As Natwick himself admitted, "Snow White was really only about five heads high. [A realistic human form is usually six.] ... She was not actually that real" (brackets in original). Maltin, 56.
   The concern with fetishistic "appeal" at the studio becomes more apparent when one remembers the anecdote in which Walt Disney felt more confident with the decision to make *Snow White* after the success of the character of Jenny Wren in the short *Who Killed Cock Robin?* (1935), a caricature of Mae West.

5. The spectacle of the male body has become a recently noticed phenomenon – but not just recently produced. Sticking to cinema history (the history of the male nude in art would take us back much farther), Miriam Hansen's "Pleasure, Ambivalence, Identification: Valentino and Female Spectatorship", in *Star Texts: Image and Performance in Film and Television*, ed. Jeremy G. Butler (Detroit: Wayne State UP, 1991), 266–297, has analyzed the silent cinema star Rudolph Valentino as an object

"to-be-looked-at", as has Steven Cohen's analysis of the image of William Holden in "Masquerading as the American Male in the Fifties: *Picnic*, William Holden and the Spectacle of Masculinity in Hollywood Film", *Camera Obscura* 25–26 (1991), 43–72. Hansen describes that the presence of a male body as spectacle announces a variety of subject positions, not exclusively engendered heterosexual and patriarchal. Although Mulvey describes female spectatorship as "transvestitism" – taking on masculine subjectivity, the notion of "cross-dressing" in itself complicates the notion of essentializing subject positions.

6. Christopher Finch, *The Art of Walt Disney* (New York: Harry N. Abrams, 1973), 198.

7. For example, Donald Crafton speaks of the "tradition of having him played by a girl or young woman" in stage productions. Donald Crafton, "Walt Disney's *Peter Pan*: Women Trouble on the Island", *Storytelling in Animation: The Art of the Animated Image*, ed. John Canemaker (Los Angeles: American Film Institute, 1988), 125.

8. Mimi Avens, "Aladdin Sane", *Premiere* 6:4 (December 1992), 70.

9. Avens, 70.

10. In June 1993, *Variety* reported that *Aladdin* had made $206,720,775. "Box Office Report", *Variety* (29 June 1993), 6.

11. This is not to intimate that Disney is exclusive in this regard. Most U.S. animation studios that attempt "realistic" animation re-create the same scenario described here.

12. Charles Isherwood, "Cel Division", *The Advocate* 617 (1 December 1992), 85.

13. Mary Ann Doane, "Film and the Masquerade: Theorising the Female Spectator", *Screen* (September/October 1982).

14. Judith Butler, "Imitation and Gender Insubordination", *Inside/Out: Lesbian Theories, Gay Theories*, ed. Diana Fuss (New York: Routledge, 1991), 21, 28.

15. Patricia Waugh, *Feminine Fictions: Revisiting the Postmodern* (New York: Routledge, 1989), 6.

16. Danae Clark, "Commodity Lesbianism", *The Lesbian and Gay Studies Reader*, ed. Henry Abelove, Michele Ann Barale and David M. Halperin (New York: Routledge, 1993), 196.

17. Jasmine's hips are described in this manner in Avens, 111.

18. Carole-Anne Tyler, "Boys Will Be Girls: The Politics of Gay Drag", in *Inside/Out*, 54.

19. Jack G. Sheehan, "Arab Caricatures Deface Disney's *Aladdin*", *Los Angeles Times*, 21 December 1992, F5.

20. Sheehan, F5.

21. Casey Kasem and Jay Goldsworthy, "No Magic in *Aladdin*'s Offensive Lyrics", *Los Angeles Times*, 19 April 1993, F3.

22. The altered lyrics replaced "Where they cut off your ear if they don't like your face" with "Where it's flat and immense and the heat is intense". In this way, the following line, "It's barbaric but hey, it's home" refers to the landscape rather than the culture. David J. Fox, "Disney Will Alter Song in *Aladdin*", *Los Angeles Times*, 10 July 1993, F1.

23. Avens, 67.

24. Avens, 67.

25. Avens, 67.

26. Avens, 70. Aladdin's skin tone is browner than Jasmine's, which could be construed as an indication of their class status (his poverty, her royalty), yet Jasmine's eyes are more slanted or "Orientalized", which might have been done to accent the "exotic" appeal of the Middle Eastern woman in Western society.

27. Ella Shohat, "Gender and Culture of Empire: Toward a Feminist Ethnography of the Cinema", *QRFV* 13: 1–3 (1991), 75, 69.

28. Rana Kabbani, *Europe's Myths of Orient* (Bloomington, IN: Indiana UP, 1986), 23–24.

29. Kabbani, 54.

30. Donna Haraway, "The Promises of Monsters: A Regenerative Politics for Inappropriate/d Others", *Cultural Studies*, ed. Lawrence Grossberg, Cary Nelson and Paula Treichler (New York: Routledge, 1992), 310.

Griffin, Sean. "The Illusion of 'Identity': Gender and Racial Representation in *Aladdin*". *Animation Journal* 3:1 (Fall 1994). 64–73. ©1994 Sean Griffin

22

Selling Bugs Bunny: Warner Bros. and Character Merchandising in the Nineties

Linda Simensky [1998]

Introduction

This essay, which was inspired by the opening of the Warner Bros. Studio Stores, was initially conceived of in 1995, just as the stores were becoming popular. It was written between 1996 and 1997, and was published as part of the book *Reading the Rabbit* in 1998, as the stores became ubiquitous. By 2001, all the Warner Bros. Studios Stores had closed.

I admired the effort and the initial vision of the stores. As a fan of the Looney Tunes cartoons, I was more than happy to purchase on occasion high quality Bugs and Daffy merchandise. But in the course of writing this essay, I found myself transforming from fan to skeptic, and by the end of my research, I was pondering the fate of both the stores and the fate of classic character merchandise. And, of course, there was no way to predict the Time Warner merger with AOL, nor the devastating consequences the merger would have for the company, both economically and creatively.

This essay looks at the licensing and consumer products of Warner Bros. before the merger, at a time when only growth seemed possible.

Merchandising and Animation

The synergy between the corporate and marketing sides of Time Warner in the growth of the Warner Bros. Studio Stores accounts for much of the revitalization of Warner Bros. animation in the nineties. Considered by many to be the smartest effort to market a studio's characters to the widest possible audience, Warner Bros. Studio Stores' retailing of character merchandise, especially cartoon character merchandise, was a substantial share of the $16.7 billion coming from the retail sales of entertainment licensing in the United States and Canada in 1996.[1] The end of 1997 will see the opening of the 179th Warner Bros. Studio Store (146 domestic, 33 international). An examination of the history and development of the Warner Bros. Studio Stores, as well as their philosophy and approach to product development based on the Warner Bros. cartoons, will provide valuable insights to the increasingly important collaboration between film and television production and their merchandising and licensing departments in the nineties.

Merchandising and animation have been linked since the twenties, coinciding with the inception of animated films, the advancement of consumerism, marketing to children, and the development of mass production. Although both animation and merchandising have been written about extensively as separate entities, hardly any scholarly or popular writing exists about cartoon character merchandising. A cursory glance through the majority of books on animation currently available will turn up a great deal of historical information, discussions of technique, reminiscences of artists and creators, and numerous visuals with little mention of merchandising and licensing. When addressed, they are most often depicted through photos of licensed products, with scant information on the merchandising plans or even merchandising philosophies of the studios.

Perhaps the literary absence of merchandising and licensing was a direct result of critical disdain toward the topic. Merchandising was considered part of the "consumerism" of animation; it was neither an "art" form nor an integral part of the business of animation.[2] Nevertheless, a few books have touched on this topic with success. In *Felix: The Twisted Tale of the World s Most Famous Cat*, John Canemaker discusses Felix the Cat through thoughtful analyses of the character's history, art, ownership issues, and filmography, including an excellent discussion of merchandising and licensing.[3] Jim Korkis' and John Cawley's *Cartoon Superstars* acknowledges the importance of cartoon merchandising by singling out which characters had licensing plans, noting the year and type of licensing.[4] And in Eric Smoodin's collection, *Disney Discourse*, Richard deCordova discusses the intertwining of Disney and children in "The Mickey in Macy's Window: Childhood, Consumerism, and Disney Animation".[5] Hence, primarily fan and collectors' magazines such as *Animato* and *In Toon*, as well as industry magazines such as *Animation Magazine* and *Kidscreen* have touched on cartoon character merchandising and licensing. Books on collecting cartoon memorabilia such as Bill Bruegman's *Cartoon Friends of the Baby Boom Era*[6] rarely address much more than the merchandising items in existence and their estimated collectors' values.

Most companies did not take licensing seriously until the merchandising of *Star Wars* in 1977. The film's licensing effort was so successful that other companies began examining their own licensing efforts and re-examining licensing rights, ownership, and back end distribution.[7] The growth of character merchandising and licensing in the late 1970s and 1980s, as well as the resurgence of animation, can be attributed to the change in management of the Federal Communications Commission (FCC), which had carefully regulated children's television until the late 1970s. Mark Fowler, who became chairman in 1981, eliminated many of the existing restrictions that prevented children's programs from becoming advertisements for toys.[8] This new permissiveness permitted the development of shows from existing toys – such as "My Little Pony", "Pound Puppies", "Transformers", "He-Man and the Masters of the Universe" – effectively making children's programming half-hour commercials for toy and licensing lines. People began to despise these programs developed from existing toys because they tended to be of low quality and of dubious benefit to young viewers. The shows were often formulaic and cheaply done; their plotlines and characters sometimes dictated by the toy company. This trend, now avoided by all but the aggressive marketers, has somewhat diminished over the years, but still exists with programming seemingly created to sell toys, such as "Biker Mice from Mars".

The growth of merchandising in the eighties is sometimes given credit for the current boom in animation and the plethora of licensed goods. If merchandised well, a show could not only make back a decent portion (if not all) of the money spent to pay for the production of the show, but the characters could also become internationally known and licensed. Increased profits led to the desire for and production of more "evergreen" characters, animated characters that can appeal to a large number of people over a long period of time, such as Mickey Mouse or Bugs Bunny. By the nineties, a successful merchandising plan was considered crucial and even necessary by business analysts in the launch of a new show or film ("The Real Adventures of Jonny Quest", "Sailor Moon", and *The Lion King*) to help make it a financial success.

The Dawn of Animated Character Merchandising

Entertainment character licensing began with the licensing of comic strip characters in the early 1900s. The first comic strip to be licensed was the Yellow Kid, introduced in 1895 by Richard F. Outcault. The merchandising of animated characters began in the 1920s with Felix

the Cat but expanded to other characters only slightly through the next few decades. Felix's simple black-and-white image could be found on over 200 items of merchandise, including toys, dolls, books, clothing, and sporting goods.[9] The cat's appeal was aimed at adults rather than children.[10] The success of the Felix merchandising proved that a significant sum of money could be earned for a popular character from animated films, leading to a source of revenue somewhat unexpected by filmmakers at that time.

Mickey Mouse, the next animated character to receive a licensing push, would eventually become a cultural icon as well as the best-known of all the licensed and merchandised personalities. Walt and Roy Disney realized that licensing could lead to greater audiences and profits, so they began Disney character licensing and merchandising in-house around 1929. In 1930, concern about "knock-off" merchandise in international markets led the Disneys to contract with the George Borgfeldt Company of New York to merchandise Mickey and Minnie Mouse. Borgfeldt's connections and production plants overseas helped cut down the bootleg merchandise abroad. According to Robert Heide and John Gilman in "Disneyana", Borgfeldt's imported and American products were distributed throughout the United States through the toy trade. Department stores, five-and-dimes, and gifts shops were flooded with porcelain figurines, tea sets, handkerchiefs, and especially toys, mostly made from the cheapest available merchandise, tin and celluloid. As Mickey Mouse cartoons were exported to Europe, international merchandising followed. By 1932, Disney had created a character merchandising division of Walt Disney Productions, to ensure higher-quality merchandise and new alliances with manufacturers, as well as wider distribution. He chose merchandising expert Herman "Kay" Kamen to be the licensing representative in the character merchandising division of Walt Disney Productions.[11]

In the thirties, other studios merchandised their characters: Columbia with Scrappy and Krazy Kat; Fleischer with Betty Boop; Walter Lantz with Oswald the Lucky Rabbit; and Warner Bros. with Porky Pig. These studios would occasionally participate in the merchandising of a character, especially if it was popular, but most of these companies had neither the extensive licensing or merchandising programs nor the organized systems of distribution like Disney. Still, other than Felix the Cat, all early merchandising, including Disney's, was for the most part limited to children's products, such as baby bottles, toys, coloring books, glasses, books, and switchplates. While Disney was making a concentrated effort to create the "Disney lifestyle" through films and products, most companies were more interested in simply making films.[12]

The History of Warner Bros. Character Merchandising

Like Disney, Warner Bros. created now-classic characters that have evolved into cultural icons and have emerged as true entertainment legends enjoyed worldwide by both children and adults. The studio is credited with setting the standard for irreverent, clever humor and inventive quality animation.[13] The list of star characters that came from the studio in the earlier years and went on to become licensing and merchandising successes includes Bugs Bunny, Daffy Duck, Porky Pig, Elmer Fudd, Road Runner, Wile E.

Coyote, Foghorn Leghorn, Sylvester and Tweety, Speedy Gonzalez, Yosemite Sam, and the Tasmanian Devil.

Unlike Disney, Warner Bros. did not have an organized merchandising plan or a merchandising department soon after they began creating cartoons. From the 1930s up to the 1970s, Warner Bros., like the other cartoons studios, did not consider merchandising as part of the filmmaking process or as a major source of revenue. The first Warner Bros. characters to be merchandised were Bosko and his girlfriend, Honey, in the form of stuffed dolls. According to animation historian and cartoonist Mark Newgarden, Warner Bros. became serious about licensing in the mid-thirties with Porky Pig, its first "star". Along with his duo partner, Beans, and a host of other now obscure characters (Egghead, Rosebud Mouse, and Blackie), Porky was merchandised in the form of piggy banks, ceramics, rubber toys and children's books. By 1938, in response to the marketing of Disney cels to the public through the Courvoisier Gallery in San Francisco, Warner Bros. took part in a somewhat unsuccessful cel marketing program along with other studios, selling cels in inexpensive frames at Woolworth's-type chain stores.[14] Producer Leon Schlesinger, who sold the studio to Warner Bros. in 1944, continued overseeing the licensing of the characters until 1948.[15]

Although Porky Pig dominated Warner Bros. licensing in the 1930s, it was Bugs Bunny who headlined the 1940s and 1950s licensing effort. In the early 1940s, Bugs Bunny appeared on stuffed plush toys, ceramics, windup toys, coloring books, rubber dolls, comic strips, watches, and alarm clocks. Other popular Warner Bros. characters also appeared on some merchandise. Even Beaky Buzzard and Sniffles were included on a set of Looney Tunes metal banks. Although Porky remained popular, few Daffy Duck licensees existed until the late forties and fifties when all the popular characters – including Elmer Fudd, Tweety and Sylvester – were licensed. The song "I Tawt I Taw a Puddy Tat" became a big hit, and Mel Blanc recorded children's records based on the Warner Bros. characters.

Although the Warner Bros. studio stopped producing original animation in the late sixties, the cartoons were sold to television and in turn were redirected toward children. At this point, characters began appearing on everything from jelly jar drinking glasses to Halloween costumes. Beginning in 1963, a Warner Bros. division called LCA, or Licensing Corporation of America, handled the licensing of the animated characters. The company was acquired by DC Comics, which was then purchased by Warner Communications. LCA represented a variety of Warner Communications properties, baseball and hockey properties, and some MGM properties. LCA generated a significant amount of revenue for the era, which was small by today's standards. In 1988, LCA was placed under the management of Warner Bros. studios. Warner Bros. President Terry Semel divided LCA into two separate divisions: LCA Sports and LCA Entertainment. LCA Sports remained in New York, eventually becoming Time Warner Sport Merchandising. LCA Entertainment moved its headquarters to the west coast to the Warner Bros. studios in Burbank, and installed Dan Romanelli as president of the division. LCA Entertainment became Warner Bros. Consumer Products in 1992.[16]

By the early eighties, new Warner Bros. character merchandise was sparse. If found, the merchandise was usually off model, inexpensive, and geared toward younger children. Marketing style guides given to the licensees featured off-model designs and model sheets from comic book artists in 1969 and not the model sheets from the original cartoons.[17] A random sampling of Bugs Bunny merchandise available around 1983–1985 included pads of paper (Bugs Bunny on cover), bop (punching) bags, pencil tops, candles, socks, erasers, Pez candy dispensers, puppets, stuffed animals, t-shirts, and children's books. The merchandise was mostly available in five and dime-type stores and toy stores – and to those who had access to the Warner Corner, the Warner Bros. store for employees.

The Warner Bros. studio started a new animation division in 1988 to produce daily and later weekly television series. Its first series, "Steven Spielberg Presents Tiny Toon Adventures", became a syndicated success in 1991, and was followed by "Taz-Mania", "Batman: The Animated Series", "Steven Spielberg Presents Freakazoid!", "Steven Spielberg Presents Animaniacs", and its spinoff "Steven Spielberg Presents Pinky and the Brain". The WB television network first broadcast in 1995 with most of these new shows airing on its youth-targeted block of programming, "Kids WB".

The slight shift in licensing in the later 1980s arose from a wave of appreciation of cartoons by an expanding audience base. Baby boomers, while watching older cartoons with their children, realized that they worked on several levels, renewing their appreciation and enjoyment of them. Cartoons emerged as a group experience at colleges, with students watching them together for comfort and nostalgia reasons. Furthermore, cable channel Nickelodeon and Turner Networks (TBS, TNT, and later, Cartoon Network), aired cartoons during accessible time periods for children and in time blocks traditionally reserved for adults, leading to increased visibility and larger viewing audiences.

The art world and commercial design world's acknowledgment of cartoon characters as recognizable pop iconography also contributed to the rise of animation fandom. The Warner Bros. Looney Tunes characters surfaced in modern and postmodern design: in the feature *Who Framed Roger Rabbit* and on baseball caps to be worn at rave dance parties. The demand grew for Looney Tunes character merchandise in novelty and gift shops. Bootleg t-shirts began appearing in urban areas. Cross-licensing Looney Tunes characters with sports team apparel in all four major league associations further boosted demand for product, converging in a Nike/Hare Jordan commercial (basketball's Michael Jordan and Bugs Bunny) during the 1992 Super Bowl.

The Creation of the Warner Bros. Studio Stores

In the late eighties, capitalizing on the resurgence of catalog shopping, Warner Bros. started merchandising its most popular characters by mail through a well-distributed, glossy catalog called the "Warner Bros. Studio Store Catalog". The earliest catalogs offered a collection of clothing, T-shirts, caps, wristwatches, ties, and other fashion, home and gift products. Visual and editorial tie-ins to Warner Bros. productions – usually feature films released that season – also

were included. Prices were somewhat high, yet the quality of the merchandise was better than typical licensed merchandise. A couple of interesting points became clear: Warner Bros. was targeting adults as well as children, and everyday consumers as well as collectors.

Around the early nineties, Disney (and then Warner Bros.) began marketing directly to an avid public through the pervasive mall culture, although it still continued to license its characters through licensees.[18] The merchandise being offered at The Disney Store (based in part on the design of the company's theme park stores) was mainly targeted toward children, with random exceptions like certain T-shirts, caps, wristwatches, and gift items, including candy in glass jars. The same can be said for the Sesame Street stores, which closed in 1996 after six years of business. Even the short-lived Hanna-Barbera Store (with such characters as Yogi Bear, Scooby Doo, and The Flintstones), which opened in 1990, targeted its merchandise to children, with a small number of limited edition cels to be purchased by adults, most likely for children.[19]

By the time the first Warner Bros. Studio Store opened in September 1991, at the Beverly Center in Los Angeles, California, Disney stores were widespread in malls across the United States. In 1993, Warner Bros. announced the opening of the Warner Bros. Studio Stores chain, beginning with twenty stores and ultimately increasing to over one hundred stores in the United States, eleven in Europe, and a plan for future stores in Hong Kong and Singapore. The Time Warner Inc. 1994 Annual Report noted that the stores were a success, substantially exceeding mall sales averages for retailers.[2]

Most Warner Bros. stores are situated in malls and shopping centers, with some located in airports. They are roughly twice the size of the Disney stores, averaging approximately 7,000 to 9,000 square feet. The flagship stores are even larger. The one in Manhattan,, at Fifth Avenue and Fifty-seventh Street, occupied almost 30,000 square feet when it opened. Other flagship stores, ranging from 14,000 to 28,000 square feet, are in London, Berlin, and Glasgow.[21] For the most part, the stores in every city look similar, with some local flavor added. Thus, tourists visiting the shop in a particular city could purchase licensed items that would double as souvenirs from that city, and, in effect, make the store a tourist destination.

The initiators behind the development of the stores include Peter Starrett, president of Warner Bros. Studio Stores, and Dan Romanelli, president of Warner Bros. Consumer Products. Many employees of the Warner Bros. Studio Stores acknowledge that a key visionary behind the stores during the early years was Linda Postell, senior vice president and general merchandise manager of the Warner Bros. Studio Stores until 1995. With her direction and a team of retail specialists, hundreds of products, including clothing, jewelry, accessories, sporting goods, collectibles, and artwork, were conceived of and developed for exclusive availability through the Warner Bros. stores.

Because the stores are designed to have the feel of contemporary adult apparel and gift stores, children's merchandise is located in the back of average sized stores and upstairs in the flagship stores. Unlike Disney stores, which run videos directed toward younger children, the Warner Bros. stores have immense video walls running continuous feature film trailers, cartoons, and classic movie clips. These videos work fantastically as promotion, since the visuals are not an imposition but part of the store decoration.[22] In a 1993 Warner Bros. press release, Starrett explained the stores' unprecedented appeal: "We've created a unique setting in which to present a complete shopping and entertainment experience. Our interactive displays, presentation areas and multi-media entertainment create an environment that traditional retailers simply cannot duplicate."[23]

The stores' design has a high-tech feel, with a bit of Hollywood fantasy and classic movie theater sensibility thrown in. Yet, it also commands a sense of enormity and importance as one travels on the glass elevator or escalators through a panorama of stylized goods in the New York store.

Also considered as attractions in the Warner Bros. stores are art galleries positioned as a "shop-within-a-shop".[24] The art galleries feature original cels, limited edition cels, collectibles, and designer jewelry related to the Warner Bros. animated characters and DC Comics characters (Batman, Superman). Also featured are contemporary artworks, including pop and modern art by James Rizzi, Melanie Taylor Kent, and Roarke Gourley. Placing an art gallery in a retail store was considered an innovation, as animation art generally was not sold along with other licensed merchandise, but mainly in animation art galleries. While selling original cels from new Warner Bros. cartoons, the galleries often would show the corresponding shorts, generating interest in those cases where the buyers might not be familiar with the films, such as the 1995 release *Another Froggy Evening*.

The merchandise at the Warner Bros. stores celebrates a range of Warner Bros.

personalities with an emphasis on the enduring Looney Tunes cartoon characters, including Bugs Bunny, Daffy Duck, Tweety and Sylvester.[25] As mentioned, the products not only tend to be of greater quality than most licensed material, but also are on model. The merchandise has a sense of humor, similar to the sensibility of the Warner Bros. characters, which are known for their irreverence and sarcasm. According to Postell, the merchandise emphasizes "the classic, but with a twist; the traditional, but with an edge".[26]

The Warner Bros. stores (like the Disney stores) encompass both the toy and gift categories, which historically was not a common retailing approach. The toy category, mainly for children, generally was found in toy stores and wherever toys were sold; the gift category, with products historically for purchase by adult shoppers, was limited to either department stores or gift shops. One can find at the Warner Bros. stores an assortment of adult and children's apparel, fashion and home accessories, miscellaneous gifts and toys, animation art, and contemporary collectibles. The merchandise is based on both classic Warner Bros. characters and series, like Bugs Bunny, and current ones, like Batman and Pinky and the Brain. Prices range from $1.50 for small figurines to over $10,000 for original works of art.

The stores have intriguing dual demographics. Since the classic Warner Bros. characters date back to the late thirties, many adults grew up with the characters and still appreciate them. Thus, the merchandise target audience was broken down so that originally 70 per cent, and now 80 per cent, of the merchandise would be created for adults between the ages of twenty-five and forty-five who were "self-expressive, entertainment-oriented and have an appreciation for nostalgia".[27] The stores' direction was influenced by marketing data showing that adults spent more on discretionary items they bought for themselves than they did for their children. To increase the number of adult shoppers, items such as coffee mugs, caps, and T-shirts, based on Warner Bros. live-action hit movies such as *Batman* and television shows including "Friends" and "E.R.", make up a small percentage of the merchandise in each store.

Because the typical buyers of cartoon character merchandise did turn out to be adults – purchasing gifts for themselves, for other adults, or for children – the success of the Warner Bros. plan to target these buyers proved that the visionaries behind the stores understood their Looney Tunes audience. After all, the original shorts were created for adults.

Warner Bros. continues to license its characters to licensees for inexpensive and standard licensed items sold through separate retail channels, but the merchandise created for the Warner Bros. Studio Stores is exclusive to the chain. Licensing to licensees remains more lucrative for Warner Bros., but the merchandise is of different and often lower quality. Representative from the Warner Bros. stores acknowledge that they benefit from the higher quality merchandise in the stores, for it engenders greater recognition for the company as a brand (and a high-quality brand). According to Karine Jouret, Vice President of Marketing, "Our stores support the brand by giving it a platform where we can display its quality and excitement".[28] Warner Bros. hopes the interest in characters on merchandise will lead to an increased interest in its cartoons. The obvious advantage for consumers wanting the higher-quality Warner Bros. merchandise is that it is now easy to find all in one place.

Exclusivity, obviously, is the way to bring people back to the stores repeatedly. Along the lines of exclusivity, the stores are soon to start a more ambitious program of items that are not only exclusive to the Warner Bros. Studio Stores but available for a limited time. The first of these products is a limited edition set of Space Jam figurines. Other forthcoming merchandise, such as limited-edition videos, compact discs, screensavers, and video games, will no doubt appeal to a crowd different than the buyers of clothing and housewares.

Character Product Development by the Warner Bros. Studio Stores

When Time Warner first made the commitment to establish the Warner Bros. Studio Stores, it began hiring experienced designers and character artists for in-house product development. Ruth Clampett, formerly of Bob Clampett Animation Art, was recruited to Warner Bros. in 1993 as manager of creative design. Working mainly with the art gallery division, Clampett, the daughter of Looney Tunes director Bob Clampett, came with a limitless knowledge of the cartoons and of Warner Bros. history. Eventually, she became director of creative design for the Warner Bros. Studio Stores. Much of the following analysis of the creative process behind character product development is based on discussions with Clampett, as well as with graphic designer Peggy Doody, design manager Cathleen Lampl, and character artist Paul McEvoy.

The direction given to the artists came from the highest levels of management. According to Clampett

(substantiating early remarks in this essay), when Peter Starrett and Linda Postell started the catalogs and then the stores, they made the decision to develop the highest-quality merchandise, which would separate their merchandise from existing licensed Warner Bros. goods.

Developing the products in-house with design teams has many benefits. A larger vision emanates from the top management down to the rest of the staff, helping to guide the creative process and the development of new products. Producing in-house keeps the stores' current themes in mind and creates the necessary and ultimately apparent synergy between the displays in the stores. The approval process remains internal, which has been an advantage because that has allowed greater risk taking and innovation (particularly in the earlier years) on the part of the staff with direct feedback from management with similar goals and direction.

Merchandise initially was designed out of a studio in New York under Postell before the unit was moved to Los Angeles in 1996. According to Doody, teams were set up in New York to include a design director, a senior designer, a designer, and a junior designer, who would then work with the character artists. These individuals had varied backgrounds, although most of the designers had worked at design studios, with many joining Warner Bros. after the Disney stores moved operations to Los Angeles. Clampett finds it is easy to find designers who want to work at Warner Bros. Many character artists and designers do not need much training either, since they are already fans of Looney Tunes and sufficiently know the characters and cartoons.

In the process of designing the

merchandise, each team would be assigned a couple of themes and the design director would determine the direction of each theme, such as the color palette or artistic style. The team would then work together to develop the merchandise concepts, the logo, and the general style of the product. The character artist would further set the tone by creating some key drawings. For reference and inspiration, the designers were supplied with resource materials and cartoons. They were free to research their topics, for example, by using libraries for photo research or by purchasing samples. To keep certain characters uniform, designers followed official style guides developed in the early nineties (although they were still free to work from cartoons instead of a style guide for certain characters, such as Daffy Duck and Bugs Bunny, who have had several designs).

Postell and Starrett saw one major factor that helped determine the success of the Warner Bros. stores: they were creating a store full of characters that people liked. A hurdle, however, was that fans knew the characters so well, they would know when a personality was "out of character". Postell and Starret realized that in the process of developing the merchandise, character consistency must be maintained. Chuck Jones was invited in to talk to the designers about the importance of a character's integrity. During meetings, according to Doody, ideas often sprang from what the character and its personality represented.[29] The personality of the characters was crucial, agrees McEvoy, since people tend to like Warner Bros. animation because they personally relate to specific characters.[30] Since the characters are strong, consistent, and have fully developed personalities, states

Doody, it is easier for a designer to work with them and focus on pushing for quality.[31]

Clampett remarks that a major challenge after the stores' initial success was determining how to reinvent the standard licensed merchandise to maintain sales. One technique is to create new themes; the Warner Bros. store policy is to change the themes and rotate the merchandise every two months, to keep shoppers returning. Concepts such as the Olympics, the beach, baby merchandise, or characters' anniversaries occur fairly frequently now to keep the store's merchandise fresh and current. Meetings are held to watch cartoons, brainstorm ideas, and plan the themes for whatever sales quarter is in development. For example, in May of 1996, the staff already had determined and were working on the themes to be used for the first quarter of 1997. These themes included Daffy Duck's 50th birthday, a Warner Bros. sports shop, golf, soccer, Valentine's Day, garden, DC Comics, and Pinky and the Brain. The stores also would feature a Hanna-Barbera shop, following the merger between Time Warner and Turner, which owned Hanna-Barbera.

Producing practical merchandise was crucial to the success of the Warner Bros. stores. By producing items such as kitchen or gardening equipment, for instance, or by creating clothing that was cutting-edge and fashion conscious, character licensing moved beyond that of past novelty or cheaply made items to useful and constructive merchandise.

Many Looney Tunes fans remark that nearly everyone loves Bugs Bunny or Daffy Duck, but only the true fans know the more obscure characters. In response, Warner Bros. decided to merchandise its secondary characters – such as Pete Puma,

Baby Face Finster, Marvin Martian, and Gossamer – which appeared in only a few Warner Bros. cartoons. By merchandising the more obscure characters (actually, they are probably not so obscure, given the number of times they have aired on television and in theaters), the Warner Bros. stores were able to satisfy the more avid Looney Tunes fans, appealing to their needs as well as those of the general consumer.

The process for determining the sale of animation cels and limited editions also was fan-oriented. Based on fan requests for cels of certain characters and specific scenes, gallery managers would email the head of the gallery division. Subsequently, Clampett flew gallery managers to Los Angeles for meetings to make suggestions, brainstorm, and rate ideas for the merchandising of cels. In fact, cels are the only Warner Bros. store items not exclusive to the Warner Bros. Studio Stores, with 50 outside galleries authorized to sell them as well.[32]

The store's glossy fifty- to sixty-page catalogs, which are mailed to over 200,000 addresses nationwide, often are seasonally themed; for example, the 1996 summer catalog focuses on the Looney Tunes summer Olympic merchandise. Consumers are able to post or phone in orders. Also, the Warner Bros. Studio Stores Internet site features on-line shopping.

Warner Bros. versus Disney

Comparisons to the Disney stores are inevitable and underscore many discussions of the Warner Bros. Studio Stores. The two chains remain successful and profitable, but retail analysts expect some heated competition in the near future. Both Warner Bros. and Disney stores are currently increasing their

number of mall locations. The Disney Stores are now expanding into airports, stadiums, arenas, and train stations with stores smaller than their mall stores. There is incentive for Warner Bros. stores to follow Disney's lead, but Warner Bros. historically has opted for larger stores rather than smaller ones.

Actually, it can be said that Warner Bros., for a change, has one-upped Disney.[33] According to Tom Barreca, a former vice-president of Hanna Barbera Enterprises, the Warner Bros. Studio Stores are more sophisticated; they succeed in terms of using design to their advantage, with unique store style and product displays as well as great gallery spaces. The stores and the merchandise seem as though they were created by fans, for fans. The Disney stores, on the other hand, seem created by marketers, for adults to buy children's gifts. Merchandise, such as simple apparel, toys and plush items, and novelties such as pencils, watches, and theme park gift-type items, supplement a color palette, smaller size, and general product layout geared toward children. This softer, more "Magic Kingdom" type of feel leads ultimately to a more bland and conservative sensibility compared to the Warner Bros. stores' ambience. This distinction underscores the different target audiences of the two companies. Unlike the Warner Bros. Studio Stores, Disney initially did not attempt to appeal to adult consumer base. Only in 1992 did Disney finally realize the need to market to adults in order to continue its relationship with customers from childhood to adulthood.[34]

The differences in development of store merchandise are numerous, remarks Lampl, who worked in the publishing division of Disney in New York before moving over to Warner Bros. From her experience, Disney's material was very story-driven; the products had to make sense with the property. So much corporate control existed that every piece of design artwork was always corrected to be more on model. While the Disney characters had to be portrayed in a more wholesome way, she found the Warner Bros. characters more irreverent and interesting to work with. Since the personality of Bugs Bunny was funnier than Mickey Mouse, she noticed that the designers at Warner Bros. seemed to have more fun and freedom than the Disney designers.[35]

The comparisons between the two stores also give journalists an angle for discussing them. In the *New York Times*, Kirk Johnson wrote that competition between Warner Bros. and Disney doesn't truly exist. Although the target audiences might seem similar, they actually could be quite different. He explains,

> The companies and their starkly different stock of characters, already paired in scores of malls, have a complex relationship that owes more to Edith Wharton drawing-room drama than Buster Keaton pie-in-the-face comedy. They are like two halves of a whole or two sides of the same coin ... . If Disney wants to make you cry, Warner's wants to make you laugh. For their stores, it all makes for a kind of built-in no-compete clause.[36]

Warner Bros.'s Dan Romanelli concurs with Johnson's position on the non-adversarial nature of Warner Bros. and Disney. "Our businesses, we think, complement each other".[37]

But given their similar locations and similar product lines, it is hard to imagine there not being competition, despite claims that each store has its own niche. When a Disney Store opened on Fifth Avenue and Fifty-fifth Street in

Manhattan in early 1996, barely two blocks away from the Warner Bros. flagship store, the battle for a share of the same retail dollar commenced and the comparisons continued. This New York Disney Store, in particular, is aggressively targeting the adult animation market previously dominated by Warner Bros. with the creation of new merchandise such as handbags, jewelry, and the sale of original and newly commissioned cels. With continued competition from Disney, the Warner Bros. Studio Stores have several challenges ahead over the next few years if they wish to maintain their reputation for innovation among studio stores, and challenge the Disney stores for the lead in retail sales.

Creative Barriers and Changes in Direction for the Warner Bros. Studio Stores

Some negatives in working with the Looney Tunes properties have been alluded to earlier in this discussion. The characters are so well known by their fans that sometimes it is difficult to be too creative or innovative with their design. In addition, the spirit the designers must create is not necessarily current enough, sometimes involving a forties and fifties flavor that may feel dated and outworn. While old-fashionedness doesn't bother most of the designers, some wish they had a little more freedom. The newer characters, such as the Animaniacs, do have a more contemporary feel to the designers, but they rarely work with them unless the show is one of the themes for the quarter.

As with many other innovations, shifts have been felt over time. The creatives involved found that although certain design ideas were approved in 1994, similar ones were not accepted in 1996. Some designers feel that the edginess that characterized Warner Bros. animation has been "watered down", with the more unusual ideas not making it into production. Doody attributed the change to Postell's leaving Warner Bros. (she stayed in New Jersey when the company moved to Los Angeles). Postell's firm opinions about the need to be innovative guided the stores through the earliest years. As the company grew larger and more successful internationally, the creative process became more complicated and less innovative in her absence.[38] Instead of just one person approving merchandising ideas, now many people are involved in the approvals process. In-house buyers, not artists like Doody herself, greenlight merchandising ideas for worldwide distribution. Clampett says it is now harder to be innovative and take risks because the stakes are higher; one t-shirt style is a big commitment now.[39] According to Lampl, creativity is blocked by the corporate feeling of "more, bigger, faster" – intense pressure and limited time schedules, with the demand for an incredible amount of work to be finished quickly. She noted that often her team would be in production mode on one theme and when it would have to start the creative concepting phase on another theme.[40]

Also, the process of designing products for the widest possible audience can be difficult when the merchandise must sometimes appeal to the "lowest common denominator". Lampl comments that sometimes the designers would pander to who they "thought" the audience was, rather than creating hipper merchandise. Soon, they would find themselves designing t-shirts for "the beer-drinking guys in the midwest", wondering "Why don't we make merchandise that we would buy?".[41]

Nevertheless, innovative or cautious, Warner Bros. Studio Stores are a success, and Looney Tunes merchandise continues to make money. According to Mark Smyka, editor of *Kidscreen* magazine, the Looney Tunes characters alone ring in $3.5 billion in retail sales around the world each year.[42] An estimated $200 million is through the Warner Bros. stores.[43] And the success of the merchandise has led to unprecedented growth for the division and the stores. In 1995, an International Franchise Operations Division was created to establish more stores through joint ventures with retailers outside of the United States.

In addition, Warner Bros. Studio Stores is currently in the midst of an ambitious expansion and reinvention of its New York City flagship store. According to a March 1996 press release, the store was expanding from its 30,000-square-foot, three-floor space to become a 75,000-square-foot, nine-story shopping and entertainment attraction.[44] The store – located in the heart of one of the world's most expensive, but also most visited and heavily trafficked, retail destinations (Tiffany and Company, FAO Schwarz, Bergdorf Goodman and Bulgari are its neighbors) – has been quite successful.

So what happens when the initial newness of the store concept wears off, and everyone who wants to own cartoon character merchandise already has purchased some? And what if in a few years cartoon character apparel suddenly becomes passé? There is a sense that a saturation of merchandise and a flattening of sales is coming. But many, like Tom

Barreca, feel that since Warner Bros. has been successfully innovative so far, they will most likely continue to find ways to keep their brands fresh and exciting. Barreca credits Warner Bros. for their unfailing ability to shake up the character retail industry by trying new product categories, creating unusual collectibles, and designing unusual store layouts and product displays. He surmises that while Warner Bros. Studio Stores has been mostly about animation, it will most likely begin to branch out more aggressively into live-action properties and television shows – a sort of "retail Darwinism".[45]

The studio will continue to produce new shows, films, and animated shorts that will generate more interest in the stores. Jerry Beck, animation historian and Warner Bros. cartoons expert, has discovered that the animated shorts and television shows are no longer the end product for the studio – the products are. The shorts and shows, in essence, have become "commercials to bring people to the stores".[46] The characters have become "what you can get at the stores", an echo to the toy commercial disguised as children's programming in the eighties.

Space Jam – A Totally Integrated Consumer Product Event and Case Study

As Warner Bros. broadens the scope of Looney Tunes into feature animation, one of the first releases will be the movie *Space Jam*, set to premiere in November 1996. Developed from the successful Hare Jordan ads from Nike, Space Jam will maintain the same mix of animation and live-action as its predecessor. According to *Variety*, Warner Bros. prizes three things from the audience reception of *Space Jam*: a hoped-for $1 billion in merchandise sales; the introduction of several new animated characters to the Warner Bros. pantheon, including Lola Bunny, Swackhammer, and the "Monstars"; and a springboard for future studio forays into feature animation.[47] Thus, Warner Bros. was now taking the Disney approach to feature films: not only did the films have to be international hits in theaters, but they needed to be a consumer products bonanza.

To ensure the attainment of these three goals, Warner Bros. spent approximately $125 million on *Space Jam*. This total included roughly $90 million for production and $35 million on promotion, making *Space Jam* among the most expensive films in Warner Bros. history.[48] What Warner Bros. received was a successful feature film which, as of June 1997, had theatrically grossed over $200 million internationally and sold a million copies of its videocassette on the first day of release.[49]

While the new characters have not necessarily become household names, the sale of *Space Jam* merchandise surpassed expectations, generating approximately $1.2 billion for Warner Bros. At the flagship store in New York, the entire first floor was devoted to merchandise from the film. In some instances, collectors had to visit more than one Warner Bros. store, since merchandise was available at some stores and not others. The merchandise was sold for a brief time, mainly during the film's release. The most successful items, according to Ruth Clampett, were toys and other merchandise for children, figurines, and collectible gift items like cookie jars and gallery cels (especially ones signed by Michael Jordan). Some sold out at the beginning of the film's run.[50] Apparel such as t-shirts and other items considered to be badly designed did not sell quite as well. However, the Warner Bros. Studio Stores, with their completed-long-in-advance schedules, rotating displays, and perhaps savvy planning, had moved out all the Space Jam merchandise within months after receiving it. While the perpetual movement of merchandise makes sense based on store planning, it also makes it difficult to determine a product's longevity on the shelves.

With *Space Jam*, the studio made what seems to be its single biggest push yet in establishing brand loyalty toward its name and characters. In terms of synergy, the Warner Bros. marketing and consumer products divisions began to have a greater say in what films were produced. It has been acknowledged by some, and rightly so, that *Space Jam* was mainly a marketing event. Certain critics have noted that *Space Jam* functioned simply as a "commercial" to drive people to the Warner Bros. stores. This argument was supported by the film's rush to completion. Although the film began production in 1995, many staff members seemed to feel *Space Jam* may have needed a prolonged production schedule. A former producer on the film felt that the film was rushed due to the merchandising and promotion commitments of a November fifteenth release date, and that it should have had at least another year in production.[51]

Space Jam steered Warner Bros. animation in a completely different direction from that of the Looney Tunes and Merrie Melodies shorts. Its look is edgier, and the voices are done by standup comics rather than the late Mel Blanc, who performed many of the voices for the cartoons shown on television. The classic characters come with a set of expectations about how they will sound and act, and some animation industry veterans have expressed concern about their handling. Jerry Beck points out that in the early Looney Tunes cartoons, the characters were from separate universes, and rarely intermingled; in contrast, *Space Jam* has the characters all living together in one world.[52] Many viewers were able to recognize the differences between the classic characters' original and updated looks, from the shading and the airbrushing of the characters' designs to the slight changes in voice characterization. Strangely, some of the irreverent dialogue in *Space Jam* is about merchandising tie-ins, as if to acknowledge the film's purpose as a marketing tool.

Thus far, the Warner Bros. classic characters have been successes based on their original cartoons, and have not had to depend on recent hit movies to sell merchandise. Writers for industry trade publications, animation critics, scholars, and historians have been carefully watching the release of *Space Jam* to determine the full effects resulting from the redefining of the classic characters. If the initiative is ultimately seen as successful for the studio, the public can expect more films along the same lines with similar merchandising efforts. The next feature film release by Warner Bros., *Quest for Camelot* (1998), is based on original characters and will not have the marketing advantages and character recognizability that *Space Jam* had. It will be interesting to assess how the ancillary divisions handle this initiative, and the extent to which their plans correspond to the Disney model. However, because of *Space Jam*, it is safe to suggest that Warner Bros. may try to elevate itself to the Disney level in terms of marketing and licensing for all merchandising efforts in the future.

Warner Bros. Merchandise: Cool or Uncool?

One of the remaining issues regarding the Warner Bros. Studio Stores is the issue of oversaturation and its negative effects on the fan base. The Studio Store concept has helped to widen the general fan base by making everyone a collector; buying cartoon merchandise has become acceptable for adults as well as children and is easy to do. But what impact has the overload of Looney Tunes merchandise had on the long time collector or fan?

Mark Newgarden, who has worked in the cartoon licensing field as well as collected cartoon memorabilia, has found that he remains more interested in the charm of the older, off-model merchandise that is more challenging to find. He has not purchased anything from the Warner Bros. Studio Stores, although he maintains that the merchandise is nicely rendered. While he has found certain items surprisingly clever, such as the Sylvester goldfish bowl or the Mugsy and Rocky vinyl figures, he has not found a need for them. Newgarden believes most long time collectors feel there is too much merchandise to collect. Since most collectors are completists, they find collecting through Warner Bros. stores frustrating because they have no chance of keeping up with the stores' turnover of merchandise. Others collectors have determined that the merchandise is too easy to obtain, or that it is sometimes "dumbed down" as gifts for tourists, and therefore, less special and less collectible.[53]

In an editorial piece entitled "Why Classic Warner Bros. Characters Are No Longer Cool (Nor Classic)" in the animation fanzine *Bea & Eff*, Tim Stocoak

asks if the characters really belong on everything on which they've been plastered. The general public has continued to buy the Warner Bros. store merchandise, he feels, because it functions as nothing more than trendy and "kitschy cartoon conversation pieces". The demand for more cartoons knickknacks has created a situation where the Warner Bros. characters have become over-merchandised, tired and "over". Stocoak mentions another fanzine called *Thrift Store* that contains an article about what will clutter the thrift stores of the future. It names "Warner Bros. cartoon character merchandise, especially anything with the Tasmanian Devil on it".[54] Both Stocoak and Newgarden mention what they considered the worst example of misuse – attempting to make the characters "hip". Examples include depicting the characters dressed in hip-hop/gangsta apparel on oversized clothing[55] or drawn into the logos of sports uniforms. Although such dress may be popular for conformist teenagers, Newgarden finds these appropriations offensive and ugly.[56]

Jerry Beck maintains that merchandising, as it is marketed currently, will not have a negative effect on the older characters with current audiences. Rather the unintended failure of over-merchandised features would more likely impact personal identification between future audiences and classic characters. However, the characters' ability to remain strong for over sixty years proves they can withstand the test of time. The public's emotional connection to Warner Bros. cartoons supports their longevity – characters like Bugs Bunny are "beloved", while Disney characters like Mickey Mouse have lasted simply for being iconic images.[57] Newgarden agrees that other cartoons are often just symbols, while "Bugs Bunny and the Looney Tunes are as close to real characters as cartoon characters can be".[58] Beck suggests Warner Bros. should separate the product lines into classic and new, similar to Disney's remodeling for Mickey and other characters.

The Future in Retailing

Warner Bros. Studio Stores must wrestle with the following questions if they are to adapt to the shifting retail marketplace: How do they keep the merchandise fresh, and the concept of owning it desirable? How much merchandise is too much? If stores and merchandise become oversaturated, will consumers become indifferent and sales flatten out? After the rapid expansion of the stores internationally, what is left in terms of innovation? Will the new stores be even larger, or smaller and more ubiquitous? If more live-action shows are merchandised, will this change the feel of the stores? With what will they fill the nine floors of the store in New York?

The possibility exists for a backlash against limited-edition cels if it ever is determined they have limited investment potential. Such a response could have an effect on the credibility of the Warner Bros. store galleries and the prices of the cels. With actual production cels becoming more rare, the galleries may need to reconsider their focus.

There is the chance, perhaps, that someday the flagship stores may move in the direction of entertainment complexes or high-tech theme parks, which would feature not just merchandise, but other incentives for the public to enter the building – interactive games, films (especially those that are exclusive to the stores and feature amazing special effects),

and rides, for example. The stores then become souvenir shops following the experience. The New York flagship store has already gone in this direction with a new theater in the store showing *Marvin the Martian in the 3rd Dimension*, a 3-D movie.

The challenges ahead for the Warner Bros. Studio Stores are not so insurmountable, as long as Warner Bros. Television continues to create shows (such as "Animaniacs", "Superman", and "Batman") that are both high-quality and marketable. "The challenge", according to Beck, "is simply doing great ideas, concepts, and designs that people will like. Then it doesn't matter if people already have Looney Tunes merchandise."[59]

The issue of competition will no doubt affect many of the decisions made in the future. Disney will no longer be Warner Bros.' only competitor. Other studios are currently creating business plans where the entertainment divisions and production studios of conglomerates will work closely with the studios' licensing divisions to exploit every potential financial opportunity. As companies such as Sony, Time Warner's Cartoon Network, and Viacom's MTV and Nickelodeon develop new and successful characters, the marketplace will either become increasingly competitive or overwhelmingly glutted, with even the most well orchestrated efforts doomed to failure.

According to the *Los Angeles Times*, perhaps a bigger challenge is each chain competing against itself. "Disney, Sesame Street and Warner all receive fees from other retailers who sell their goods through licenses. But with these three companies selling their wares directly, analysts wonder whether department stores will continue to carry those licensed items."[60] Stores such as Too Cute, which specialized in cartoon character clothing from all the animation studios, closed both its Melrose Avenue store in Los Angeles and its Soho store in New York due to flagging sales.

As Time Warner merges with Turner and combines animation libraries, there will be philosophical questions to answer regarding the synergy of the Looney Tunes and Hanna-Barbera characters in the Warner Bros. stores. Management will need to determine how to position Hanna-Barbera's limited animation characters amid the classic Looney Tunes characters. With Warner Bros. stores already adding Hanna-Barbera themes into their rotations, the designers and marketing executives also will need to decide if Hanna-Barbera's classics are "worthy" of being combined on merchandise with Warner Bros. classics. It remains to be seen if the two brands of humor and style will mesh well in the context of the stores.

The Warner Bros. Studio Stores most likely will maintain a clear advantage over its competition for the next few years. The executives in charge of the stores are visionaries, managing to innovate and lead, not follow, in the evolution of the studio store concept. Most importantly, the Warner Bros. cartoon fans are some of the most loyal and energetic fans around (as evidenced by the many sites on the Internet). By producing consistently successful programming with an enduring sense of wit, Warner Bros. should keep viewers and consumers laughing and purchasing for many years to come.

Postscript 2004

By 2001, we had the answer to the question of the Warner Bros. Studio Stores' future in retailing – there would be

no future. The retail environment had become increasingly competitive at a time when the economy in general was suffering. The theme store business had started on a downturn in the late 1990s. Viacom had closed fifteen Nickelodeon stores in 1998, and by 1999, Disney had started closing some stores as well. Discount chain stores such as Wal-Mart and Target began carrying studio-licensed merchandise for the most popular programs and movies, essentially providing the studio stores with additional competition.

Because the decline of the theme stores was industry-wide, there was no reason to blame Warner Bros. alone, but they stood out since their growth had been so aggressive and their demise so quick. The Warner Bros. Studio Stores had proliferated to the point where it seemed that the company had spread itself too thin. "These places were designed to make going there an event. Once they became ubiquitous and were in every shopping mall, there wasn't a compelling reason to go there", said Marty Brochstein, executive editor of The Licensing Letter.[61]

And, of course, the bigger story was the AOL Time Warner merger, which was announced in January 2001. No one completely understood what the far-reaching consequences of the merger would be, but the stores were among the first of the divisions to feel the budget cuts. In the summer of 2001, the company announced numerous job cuts throughout all of AOL Time Warner. At this time, it was announced that all 130 stores would be closed by the end of October 2001. The stores were closed in part because of their inability to show a profit, but mainly it was AOL Time Warner's attempt to streamline the company and shed divisions that were not part of the company's core. Retail would no longer be a focus of the company.

Despite the store closings, the Warner Bros. Consumer Products division still remains a multi-billion dollar business, and is still a force within the Warner Bros. pantheon. The studio still brings in revenue through licensing both Warner Bros. and Cartoon Network shows, as well as live-action movies such as the Harry Potter and Matrix franchises. The merchandise has moved into gift shops, department stores and discount chain stores, so merchandise is still available, although in nowhere near the volume of previous years. In general, the quality of this merchandise is decent, although the intended target audience for the majority of it is children, rather than adults. The merchandise tends to be in the categories of toys, games, clothing and accessories, bedding, school supplies, trading cards and other paper goods, rather than adult collectibles. Yet one can still find the occasional adult-targeted Christmas ornament, golf item, or collectible figurine.

Warner Bros. Consumer Products still tends to limit the number of shows and characters they merchandise, rather than promote all their characters at once. For Fall 2004, the featured characters included Batman, Justice League, Harry Potter, Scooby Doo, the Looney Tunes characters, Catwoman, the Matrix, and the Wizard of Oz.

There is still online shopping (at wbshop.com or shopping.warnerbros.com) which seems to feature the same merchandise available in stores. For the most part, the Consumer Products division retains the power to push shows ahead that will be good for merchandising, and will question the greenlighting of shows that they believe do not have viable merchandising programs.

Looking back at the Studio Stores, it is easy to question the usefulness and even the saleability of much of the merchandise that had been produced for them. Even more than the large number of lifestyle items available featuring the classic characters, there was the question of contemporizing these characters, always a risky proposition when appealing to fans. Much of the merchandise designed to appeal to the youth market was probably too "of the moment" to have any lasting appeal, and too expensive to be purchased casually. I found myself wondering at the time just how many people were going to purchase an expensive multicolored rhinestone Bugs Bunny pendant.

At the time this paper was first written, the frequency of the "repeat" shopper at the stores already was being questioned. The truth was that the stores, with their locations in malls, could achieve a high volume of foot traffic, but the sales did not match the traffic. The stores never quite developed the base of collectors or the constant stream of merchandise to keep both collectors and casual fans coming back. Once the novelty of the stores wore off, the stores' management was never able to come up the new product mix that would reinvigorate the original concept.[62]

The Warner Bros. Studio Stores seemed to overestimate the collectors and the collectibles market, which contributed to the decline of sales in the first place. In a sense, though, the Studio Stores' executives got their wish a few years later. Since the merchandise that was produced during the stores' era is no longer being made, in essence that has made it all somewhat more collectible. A quick scan on the internet shows that many of the

Stores' products that have since been discontinued, such as cookie jars, sets of toys, Christmas ornaments, and certain t-shirts, are now considered collectibles by collectors.

Regardless of the fate of the stores, what is clear is that character merchandising and licensing are a bigger part of the animation industry than ever. Animated shows remain extremely popular among viewers of all ages, and a successful franchise can turn out to be a multi-billion dollar industry for a consumer products division. Because so much money is spent on animation production, but so much can be made back through consumer products, there is no doubt that this sector of the industry will continue to call the shots. It is clear now that no matter how much animation fans love certain characters, to the conglomerates that own them, these characters are mainly important commodities. 🐾

Acknowledgements: I thank the following people for their invaluable assistance in preparing this discussion: Kevin Sandler, who edited the first draft of this essay, Ruth Clampett, Peggy Doody, Mark Newgarden, Liz Gardner, Jerry Beck, Tom Knott, Tom Barreca, Cathleen Lampl, Scott Maiko. Also, I thank Maureen Furniss, who gave me the chance to revisit this essay and achieve some sense of closure.

Notes

1. Jura Koncius, "Getting Reel", *Detroit News*, 19 July 1997.

2. Bill Mikulak, fellow contributor to this volume, has recently written on the canonization of animation as an art form. Please see "Mickey Meets Mondrian: Cartoons Enter the Museum of Modern Art", *Cinema Journal* 35, no. 3 (Spring 1997).

3. John Canemaker, *Felix: The Twisted Tale of the World s Most Famous Cat* (New York: Pantheon, 1991).

4. John Cawley and Jim Korkis, *The Encyclopedia of Cartoon Superstars* (Las Vegas: Pioneer, 1990).

5. Richard deCordova, "The Mickey in Macy's Window: Childhood, Consumerism, and Disney Animation", in *Disney Discourse*, ed. Eric Smoodin (New York: Routledge, 1994).

6. Bill Bruegman, *Cartoon Friends of the Baby Boom Era* (Akron, Ohio: Cap'n Penny Productions, Inc., 1993).

7. Back end distribution is when the creator, producer, writer of other talent takes part in receiving a percentage of earnings form the ancillary activities of a show.

8. James Twitchell, *Preposterous Violence* (New York: Oxford UP, 1989), 265.

9. Canemaker, 4.

10. Ibid., 66.

11. Robert Heide and John Gilman, *Disneyana* (New York: Hyperion, 1995).

12. Jerry Beck, interview with author, Los Angeles, California, 7 September 1996.

13. "Warner Bros. Animation: 65 Years of History", [accessed 24 June 1996], Available from Internet: URL: http://pathfinder.com/@@TLVtSAYAuvWCRWF/KidsWB/history.html

14. Mark Newgarden, interview by author, Atlanta, Georgia, 24 June 1996.

15. Steve Schneider, *That s All Folks!: The Art of Warner Bros. Animation* (New York: Henry Holt and Company, 1988), 88.

16. "Warner Bros. Worldwide Consumer Products", file onesheet faxed by Warner Bros. Consumer Products Press Department to author.

17. A model sheet contains visual interpretations of a character drawn from different angles. It would be used by animators as a reference for the proper design of the character. When artist deviate from these model sheets, the results are considered "off model." That many 1980 licensing artists were using "off model" model sheets underscored the indifference Warner Bros. had toward licensing at this time.

18. Richard Corliss, "What's Hot, Doc? Retail!", *Time*, 9 May 1994, 65–66.

19. Hanna-Barbera experimented with two stores in Los Angeles area malls but closed shortly after they had opened.

20. "Time Warner Inc. 1994 Annual Report", [accessed 24 June 1996. Available from Internet: URL: http://pathfinder.com/@@nzS5eAYA8ests@S3/Corp/official word/ar/arfilm.html

21. Liz Gardner, "Flagship Warner Bros. Studio Stores Fact Sheet" (Burbank, California: Warner Bros. Worldwide Retail Public Relations, 1993), 1.

22. Beck, interview.

23. Liz Gardner, "Warner Bros. Studio Stores Bring Glamour and Excitement of Entertainment Industry to Consumers Nationwide" (Burbank, California: Warner Bros. Worldwide Retail Public Relations, 1993), 1.

24. Liz Gardner, "Warner Bros. Studio Store Galleries Showcase the Art of Animation and the Whimsical World of Looney Tunes in a Unique Blending of Fine Art and High Style" (Burbank, California: Warner Bros. Worldwide Retail Public Relations, 1993), 1.

25. Liz Gardner, "Warner Bros. Studio Store Fact Sheet", (Burbank, California: Warner Bros. Worldwide Retail Public Relations, 1993), 1.

26. Liz Gardner, "Take a Piece of Hollywood Home: Pay a Visit to Warner Bros. Studio Stores" (Burbank, California: Warner Bros. Worldwide Retail Public Relations, 1993), 2.

27. Gardner, "Warner Bros. Studio Store Fact Sheet", 2.

28. Brian McCarthy, "The Entertainer", Index, Warner Bros. Worldwide Retail Public Relations packet, 51.

29. Cathleen Lampl, telephone interview with author, Atlanta, Georgia, 27 June 1996.

30. Paul McEvoy, interview with author, Burbank, California, 2 May 1996.

31. Peggy Doody, phone interview with author, Atlanta, Georgia, 26 June 1996.

32. Ruth Clampett, interview with author, Burbank, California, 2 May 1996.

33. Tom Barreca, phone interview with author, Atlanta, Georgia, 20 June 1996.

34. Lisa Backman, "Store Wars; Disney and Warner Bros. Battle It Out in the Newly Opened Brandon TownCenter", *Tampa Tribune*, 19 February 1995, Business and Finance, 1.

35. Lampl, interview.

36. Kirk Johnson, "What's Up, Bugs? It's Mickey!", *New York Times*, 15 March 1996, 13 (A). The article then proceeds to discuss several prominent New Yorkers in terms of whether they are Warner Bros. or Disney personality types: "New York City's Mayor, Rudolph W. Guiliani, for example is a classic Warner Brothers: high energy, sometimes abrasive, often unpredictable. Former Mayor David N. Dinkins, by contrast, with his deceptively placid demeanor, was Disney all the way."

37. Kirk Johnson, 13 (A).

38. Doody, interview.

39. Clampett, interview.

40. Lampl, interview.

41. Ibid.

42. Mark Smyka, "The Warner Way", *Kidscreen*, July 1996, 56.

43. Kirk Johnson, 13 (A).

44. Peter B. Carzasty and Liz Gardner, "Warner Bros. Studios To More Than Double the Size of Its New York City Flagship Store" (Burbank, California: Warner Bros. Consumer Products Public Relations, 5 March 1996), 1.

45. Barreca, interview.

46. Beck, interview.

47. Ted Johnson, "WB's Toon Targets Ride on 'Space' Case", *Variety*, 26 August – 1 September 1996, 11–12.

48. Kate Meyers, "Court Jester", *Entertainment Weekly*, 22 November 1996, p. 52.

49. According to the *Hollywood Reporter* [online], *Space Jam*, as of 16 June 1997, grossed $90,384,232 domestically in seventeen weeks and three days.

50. Ruth Clampett, phone interview with author, 1 July 1997.

51. Ted Johnson, 11–12.

52. Beck, interview.

53. Mark Newgarden, phone interview with author, Atlanta, Georgia, 21 September 1996.

54. Tim Stocoak, "Why Classic Warner Bros. Characters Are No Longer Cool (Nor Classic)", *Bea & Eff* (fanzine), Summer 1996, 14–15.

55. Ibid.

56. Newgarden, interview.

57. Beck, interview.

58. Newgarden, interview.

59. Beck, interview.

60. Don Lee, "These Characters Mean Business: Disney, Warner Bros. and Sesame Street Retail Stars", *Los Angeles Times*, 1 October 1992, D-1.

61. Doug Desjardins, "Studios to close retail stores – Warner Bros. and Walt Disney Co – Brief Article", 19 February 2001, Available from the internet:
URL: http://articles.findarticles.com/p/articles/mi_m0FNP/is_4_40/ai_71560924

62. "That's All Folks", 9 July 2001, Available from the internet:
URL: http://www.icv2.com/articles/news/528.html

Simensky, Linda. "Selling Bugs Bunny: Warner Bros. and Character Merchandising in the Nineties". *Reading the Rabbit: Explorations in Warner Bros. Animation*. Ed. Kevin S. Sandler. New Brunswick: Rutgers, 1998. 172–192. Revised.

Author biographies

CECILE STARR is a film and animation specialist with a long career as a writer, teacher, lecturer, distributor and occasional filmmaker. Her book, *Experimental Animation: Origins of a New Art*, which she co-authored with Robert Russett, contains chapters on pioneering animation artists whom she knew or worked with over many decades. Her three other books and over 100 published articles have concentrated on her special interest in early film history, documentary films, feature film classics, and women filmmakers.

WILLIAM MORITZ, Ph.D., was an educator, filmmaker, published poet, and playwright. His critical and historical writings in the areas of animation and experimental cinema have been widely published; some of his most notable research focused on the subject of visual music. He taught on the faculty at California Institute of the Arts, where he was an influential mentor to students as well as other researchers.

ESTHER LESLIE, Ph.D, is Professor of Political Aesthetics at Birkbeck, University of London. She is the author of several books, including *Hollywood Flatlands: Animation, Critical Theory and the Avant-garde* (Verso, 2002), co-editor of *Historical Materialism*, and in the editorial collective of Radical Philosophy. Together with Ben Watson she runs the website www.militantesthetix.co.uk.

TERENCE DOBSON, Ph.D., is author of *The Film Work of Norman McLaren* (John Libbey/Indiana University Press). His research areas include the relationship between film, visual art and music, as well as film emanating from the Himalayan region. He teaches animation courses at the University of Canterbury, New Zealand.

PATRICK DRAZEN is author of *Anime Explosion: The What? Why? And Wow! Of Japanese Animation* (Stonebridge Press) and numerous articles on anime for various publications. He has lectured on the topic extensively, and in 2006 he was invited to be Master of Ceremonies at the Smithsonian Institution's Anime Marathon, part of the District of Columbia's Cherry Blossom Festival.

HELEN MCCARTHY has been researching and writing about Japanese animation and popular culture since 1981. She lives in London, and also enjoys studying the history of dress and embroidery.

MARIAN QUIGLEY, Ph.D., is a freelance writer, researcher and editor; an Adjunct Research Fellow at Monash University;

and an animation curator for *australianscreen online*. She is author of *Women Do Animate: Interviews with 10 Australian Animators* (Insight Publications, 2005).

TERRY LINDVALL, Ph.D., occupies the C S Lewis Chair of Communication and Christian Thought at Virginia Wesleyan College and has authored *Sanctuary Cinema* (NYU 2007), *The Silents of God: Selected Issues and Documents in Film and Religion* (Scarecrow, 2001), *The Mother of All Laughter: Sarah and the Genesis of Comedy* (Broadman, 2004), and scores of articles and books. He has executive produced over 50 films, including two Student Academy Award winning films.

MATTHEW MELTON, Ph.D., is Dean of the College of Arts & Sciences at Lee University, where he has taught and conducted research in Media Studies and the Humanities since 1995. He also directs the university's Kairos Scholars Honors Program. He resides in southeast Tennessee with his wife Leslie and son Nicholas.

JORGEN STENSLAND is Director of consultants in the Norwegian Cinema organization FILM&KINO, where he among other things is in charge of the project of digitalization of Norwegian Cinemas. He has formerly worked as the head of public relations in the Norwegian Board of Film Classification and has worked part time as an assistant professor at Hedmark College, teaching courses in cultural studies, film and public relations.

JOHN CANEMAKER has won an Academy Award, an Emmy and a Peabody Award for his animation and is an internationally-renowned animation

historian and teacher. His film, *The Moon and the Son: An Imagined Conversation*, won an Oscar in 2005 for Best Animated Short, as well as an Emmy. Canemaker is also a noted author who has written nine books on animation, as well as numerous essays, articles and monographs for *The New York Times* and *The Wall Street Journal*, among other publications.

JB KAUFMAN is an independent film historian who has published extensively on Disney animation and silent film history. His books include *Walt in Wonderland: The Silent Films of Walt Disney*, which he co-authored with Russell Merritt. He is currently working as a film historian for the Walt Disney Family Foundation.

BILL MIKULAK, Ph.D., is a graduate of University of Pennsylvania's Annenberg School for Communication. His dissertation, "How Cartoons Became Art: Exhibitions and Sales of Animation Art as Communication of Aesthetic Value," contains an expanded version of the essay printed in this anthology.

JOHN LEWELL has authored numerous books and articles on the subjects of photography, digital technology, and Internet related subjects. He has worked as editor and foreign correspondent for several journals, and he is director of his own public relations firm, serving several major clients.

CHARLES SOLOMON is an internationally respected critic and historian of animation, who has written on the subject for *The New York Times*, *TV Guide*, *Newsweek* (Japan), Rolling Stone, the *Los Angeles Times*, and many other publications. He is author of several books, including *Disney Lost and Found* (Disney Press, 2008), and *Enchanted Drawings: The History of Animation* (Knopf, 1989; reprinted, Wings, 1994), which was a *New York Times* Notable Book of the Year and the first film book to be nominated for a National Book Critics' Circle Award.

JULES ENGEL was a filmmaker, painter, sculptor, graphic artist, set designer, and director of live action and animated films, working at Disney, UPA and his own company, Format Films. He founded the Experimental Animation Program at the California Institute of the Arts.

KARL COHEN is president of ASIFA-San Francisco and author of *Forbidden Animation: Censored Cartoons and Blacklisted Animators*, as well as hundreds of articles on animation. He teaches animation history at San Francisco State University, and has presented lectures and programs at festivals and conferences in China, the UK, Spain, Israel, Canada and the US. At the 2008 Ottawa Animation Festival, he received the annual ASIFA Prize for his writing.

MICHAEL FRIERSON, Ph.D., is an Associate Professor in Broadcasting and Cinema at the University of North Carolina at Greensboro. He is the author of *Clay Animation: American Highlights 1908 to the Present* (New York: Twayne, 1994). He has made short films for Nickleodeon, Children's Television Workshop, MSN Video, and AT&T Blueroom, and hour-long documentaries on New Orleans photographer Clarence John Laughlin and the FBI's work to destroy the North Carolina Ku Klux Klan in the 1960s.

WILLIAM HANNA was co-chairman and co-founder of Hanna-Barbera Productions Inc. He had a long career in the animation industry, highlighted by several Oscar awards for his work co-directing "Tom and Jerry" shorts with Barbera at MGM.

TOM ITO is author of several books on a range of historical and contemporary subjects. He assisted William Hanna in writing his autobiography, *A Cast of Friends*.

GEORGE GRIFFIN has produced a varied body of work since he began experimenting with a Bolex in 1969: short cartoons on language, politics and everyday life; reflexive "anti-cartoons" on the arcane process of animation; a professional career producing commercials, industrials and tv programs; interactive "concrete animation" – flipbooks, mutoscopes, installations; intermittent teaching at Harvard, Pratt, Parsons. He lives with his wife, Karen Cooper, in New York City.

JAMES LINDNER is a well-known authority on the preservation of electronic media. He founded Fantastic Animation Machine and Vidipax, and he is President of Media Matters/Samma Systems.

JOHN LASSETER is an Academy Award-winning American animator, and the chief creative officer at Pixar and Walt Disney Animation Studios. He is also the Principal Creative Advisor for Walt Disney Imagineering.

TINA PRICE has over 12 feature film credits in a variety of roles that include Computer Animator in *Aladdin*, Technical Director for *Fantasia 2000*, and Visual Development Artist on *Tarzan*. She also has launched her own companies, Digital or Not, The Creative Talent Network, and Animation Alumni.

CARL ROSENDAHL founded Pacific Data Images and Uth TV. He is currently on the faculty of the Entertainment Technology Center for Carnegie Mellon University.

SEAN GRIFFIN, Ph.D. is on the faculty at Southern Methodist University. He is the author of *Tinker Belles and Evil Queens: The Walt Disney Company from the Inside Out* and *America on Film: Representing Race, Class, Gender and Sexuality at the Movies*.

LINDA SIMENSKY is the Vice President of Kids Programming at PBS in Alexandria, VA, where she oversees development and current series for all of the PBS Kids shows. She also worked at Nickelodeon and Cartoon Network. Simensky has written and lectured extensively on the topic of animation.

MAUREEN FURNISS, Ph.D. is founding editor of *Animation Journal* and author of *Art in Motion: Animation Aesthetics* and *The Animation Bible*. She is on the animation faculty at California Institute of the Arts, and is president of the Society for Animation Studies. She lives in Santa Clarita with her two daughters.